WORKBOOK

to accompany the sixth edition of
An Introduction to Positive Economics

WORKBOOK

to accompany the sixth edition of
An Introduction to Positive Economics

J. A. Stilwell, Richard G. Lipsey
and Rosemary Clarke

WEIDENFELD AND NICOLSON LONDON

First published 1967
Revised edition 1971
Reprinted 1972
Reprinted 1974
Revised edition 1975
Revised edition 1979
Reprinted 1982
Revised edition 1983

Weidenfeld and Nicolson
91 Clapham High St London SW4

ISBN 0 297 78267 3

Text set in 11/13 pt IBM Baskerville, printed
and bound in Great Britain at The Pitman Press,
Bath

Contents

	Instructions for use	vii
1	Introduction	1
2	The tools of theoretical analysis	3
3	The tools of statistical analysis	6
4	The problems of economic theory	11
5	A general view of the price system	15
6	Basic concepts of price theory	18
7	The elementary theory of demand and supply	21
8	The theory of the behaviour of individual competitive markets	33
9	Elasticity of demand and supply	38
10	Applications of price theory: price controls and agriculture	45
11	Applications of price theory: international trade	51
12	(Postscripts and previews – no *Workbook* chapter)	
13	Effects of changes in prices and incomes	55
14	Theories of household demand	60
15	The theory of demand: measurements and tests	71
16	Background to the theory of supply	73
17	The theory of costs	75
18	The equilibrium of a profit-maximizing firm	87
19	The theory of perfect competition	90
20	The theory of monopoly	98
21	Theories of imperfect competition	106
22	Competition, oligopoly and monopoly: some comparative-static predictions	116
23	Competition, oligopoly and monopoly: some predictions about performance	125
24	Criticisms and tests of the theory of supply	131
25	The demand for and supply of factors of production	135
26	The pricing of factors in competitive markets	144
27	The income of labour	148
28	The income of capital	153

29	Criticisms and tests of the theory of distribution	159
30	International trade and protection	161
31	Less developed and developing countries	166
32	The case for and against the free-market system	170
33	Aims and objectives of government policy	171
34	Macroeconomic concepts and variables	173
35	National income in a two-sector model	179
36	National income in more elaborate models	192
37	National income, international trade and the balance of payments	201
38	The money supply	206
39	Monetary equilibrium	211
40	The *IS-LM* model: the determination of national income and the interest rate with a fixed price level	218
41	Closure version 1: aggregate demand and aggregate supply	226
42	Fluctuations and growth	231
43	Demand management 1: fiscal policy	241
44	Demand management 2: monetary policy	252
45	Macro policy in an open economy	264
46	Employment and unemployment	272
47	Closure version 2: a core-augmented Phillips curve and inflation	278
48	Current issues in macroeconomic theory	284
	Answers	286

Instructions for Use

There is a chapter in the *Workbook* for all chapters in *Positive Economics*, except Chapter 12. The chapters in the *Workbook* fall into two categories: first, those accompanying analytic chapters of the textbook and, second, those accompanying discursive chapters. The former are in the great majority, and have two sections:

(1) The study guide and questions to be answered in the text;
(2) Questions for essay or class discussion.

The latter have only section (2).

HOW TO ANSWER THE QUESTIONS

Where alternative answers are printed in the text, e.g. raise/lower/indeterminate or T/F (True/False), you should circle the answer you consider correct. Longer multiple-choice questions use letters, rather than numbers, to mark the alternative answers. Again, you should circle the letter of the answer or answers you consider correct. For questions which require a written answer, space appropriate to the length of the correct answer is left in the text.

For the benefit primarily of the student working alone, some parts of the *Workbook* are written in a programmed form, and the student is asked to check each answer after attempting the question. These sections can also be used for class work, in which case some of the instructions, for example 'If you answered Q9 wrongly, re-read pp. 306–11,' can be ignored or replaced by explanation from the class tutor.

Where reference is made in the text to e.g. 'table 3.3' or 'page 87', unless it is stated otherwise the reference is to R. G. Lipsey, *An Introduction to Positive Economics*, sixth edition.

In the graphical questions, if your answer is not exactly the same as the answer given, but is very near, you should first check that the discrepancy does not arise from slight inaccuracy in reading the graph, which is not an important mistake.

CHAPTER 1

Introduction

In this chapter in Lipsey you are counselled, first, against confusing certain different classes of statement—primarily, the *positive* statement, the *normative* statement, and the *analytic* statement—examples of all of which are—'North Sea oil saves oil imports', 'North Sea oil revenues should be used in Scotland' and 'If North Sea oil helps Scotland, then it helps Britain'. Some statements might contain both positive and normative elements—for example 'North Sea oil belongs to England' tells us, given a known legal framework, certain facts about the position of North Sea oil wells—but it may also express approval of these laws.

Q1   Here are six statements. Which are *positive*, which are *normative*, which are *analytic*, and which contain elements both of the *positive* and the *normative*?

    (1) Microprocessors can replace the human element in
        many technical processes.   P/N/A/P+N

    (2) Microprocessors are only as good as the people who
        program them.   P/N/A/P+N

    (3) The inventors of microprocessors deserve knighthoods.   P/N/A/P+N

    (4) Unless alternative jobs can be found for the redundant
        workmen, labour-saving microprocessors will increase
        unemployment.   P/N/A/P+N

    (5) The microprocessor revolution will increase the quality
        of life of us all.   P/N/A/P+N

    (6) Microprocessors are too expensive to incorporate in
        domestic equipment such as washing machines.   P/N/A/P+N

Check your answers so far. If you answered (6) incorrectly, remember that a proposition can be positive, but wrong—indeed, if it couldn't be wrong, it wouldn't be positive. Carry on, now, with Q 1.

    (7) Gothic architecture is better than Norman architecture.   P/N/A/P+N
    (8) Gothic churches are nicer than Norman churches.   P/N/A/P+N
    (9) The Concorde shatters greenhouse windows.   P/N/A/P+N
   (10) The Concorde is a better aeroplane than the Jumbo-jet.   P/N/A/P+N
   (11) England ought to go ahead with developing a Jumbo-jet.   P/N/A/P+N

Check your answers. If you had any difficulty, especially with (7) and (10), read on. If not, jump to Q 2. Sometimes a statement which seems to use purely normative words depends for its meaning upon some already accepted set of aims. To take (7), it might be an aim of architecture to minimize the weight of materials used to enclose a given space, and the Gothic system of crossed arches might be better at this than the older system of parallel arches. So Gothic architecture is better—more efficient—at achieving a desired goal. But the proposition of (7) also contains evaluative, normative, elements—for example, it might be denied on the grounds that other aims of architecture, normatively considered more important, are defeated by Gothic architecture. Carry on:

   (12) The Falkland Islands belong to Britain.   P/N/A/P+N

(13) Alsatian dogs are large, fast and have big teeth.   P/N/A/P+N
(14) Alsatians are vicious.   P/N/A/P+N
(15) Alsatians should be locked up.   P/N/A/P+N

Q 2   Is economics a natural science or a behavioural science?

Natural/Behavioural/Neither

Q 3   Which of the following use the concept of theory in the sense explained in Lipsey?

(1) 'The origins of the Great War can be explained in terms of Marxist theory.'
(2) 'A. J. P. Taylor's theory of the origins of the Great War is that it was caused by inflexible train timetables.'
(3) 'Theoretically, Korchnoi should not have lost a pawn to Karpov.'
(4) 'Theoretically, after a good harvest the price of apples should drop.'

QUESTIONS FOR DISCUSSION

1   In November 1982 Prime Minister Thatcher and Chancellor Howe asserted that every-one must 'shoulder a fair share of the burden of reducing unemployment'—including the unemployed and old-age pensioners. They meant that living standards should fall. Pensioners' leader Jack Jones claimed that no measure which did not involve a substantial increase in the pension could be called fair.

Is 'fairness' a positive or normative concept?

2   Some psychologists believe that there are noticeable differences between the mean intelligence of certain ethnic groups. Read reports in *The Times Educational Supplement* of 20 and 27 September 1974, or *The Times Higher Educational Supplement* of 27 September 1974.

The exponents of this view were subject to hostile demonstrations by students and lecturers. Do you consider that political demonstrations are ever a proper way of expressing disbelief in positive hypotheses? Or do you think that the demonstrators considered that the psychologists in question had made value judgements?

3   Read the correspondence page of a popular daily newspaper. Is there a single letter which does not contain a normative element?

4   'If the scientist finds that the issue is framed in such terms that it is impossible to gather evidence for or against it, he will then try to reword it, so that it can be answered by an appeal to the evidence.' How might you begin to do this in the case of the following general assertions?

'British justice is the best in the world.' 'More guilty people are given proper punishment, and more innocent ones freed in Britain than anywhere else.' 'British justice doesn't provide enough deterrence.'

CHAPTER 2

The Tools of Theoretical Analysis

The main point of this chapter is the importance of mathematics in economics. Most economic theories can be expressed mathematically, and the language of mathematics makes it easier to deduce predictions by means of which a theory can be tested.

Q 1   (1) Express on Fig. 1 the proposition 'In any one year, the number of replacement engines sold by the group always equals the number of new cars produced, whether 10,000 or 20,000.' Check your answer.

        (2) Express on Fig. 1 (cross out what you have already written) the proposition 'For every new car produced, two new batteries need to be made.'

Q 2   Solve the following problem geometrically, on Fig. 2.

Apples cost 10p a pound, oranges 15p. I always spend $1\frac{1}{2}$ times as much on apples as oranges, and this week I spend 100p in all. How many pounds of apples do I buy?

Hints—the quantities along the two axes should be 'amount spent on apples' and 'amount spent on oranges'. For one line, draw the relationship 'amount spent on apples' = $1\frac{1}{2}$ × 'amount spent on oranges'. For the other line, plot a graph of every point for which the sum of the values on each axis is 100p. That is, choose a distance along one axis, subtract that value from 100, travel the distance of your answer along the other axis and plot the resulting point on the graph. After you have done this three or four times you will not need to continue—you might like to consider why the line is straight.

Q 3   Imagine that you are going to solve geometrically the following problem: A slow car sets out along a road at 2 pm and travels at 25 mph. A faster car starts the same journey at 3 pm, and travels at 35 mph. When does the faster car overtake the slower?

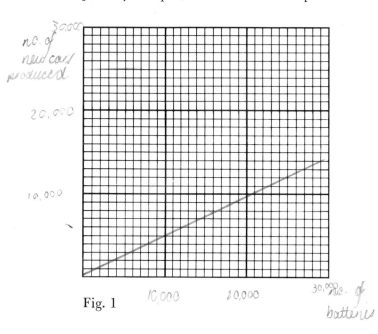

Fig. 1

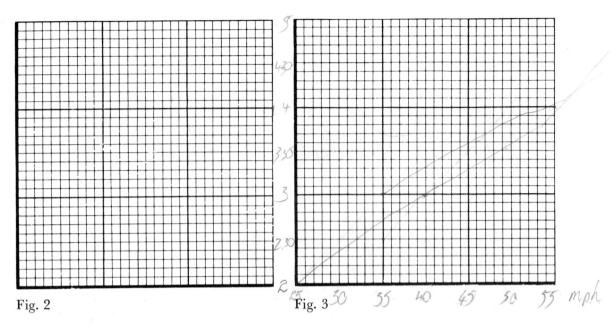

Fig. 2   Fig. 3

What would you measure along each axis of your graph?

(a) Speed along one, time along the other
(b) Miles from the start along one, time along the other
(c) Speed of one car on one axis, speed of the other on the other

Q 4   Set up a geometric solution to the problem of Q 3 on Fig. 3.
      Check your answer algebraically.
      What is your answer? _____

QUESTIONS FOR DISCUSSION

1   A leading British weekly contained the following statement in an editorial:
  'So far space research has only found a belt of radiation round the earth, and that had
already been proved mathematically.'
  Can the existence of anything be proved solely by mathematics?

2   'The quantity of ice-cream cornets a group of children buy depends upon the heat,
expressed in degrees centigrade, the price of an ice-cream cornet, and their average pocket-
money.'

  (a) Write the foregoing statement in the functional notation that you have learned in
       this chapter. Be sure to explain what any symbols you use mean.

  (b) Will the quantity they buy vary directly or inversely with the heat? Directly or
       inversely with the price of an ice-cream cornet? With average pocket-money?

  (c) Can you predict what will happen if the temperature falls by 10° and the average
       allowance rises by 5p? If not, what further information about the function would
       you need?

3   State a precise equation that is a specific example of the general hypothesis: 'The
lower are A-level achievements at comprehensive schools, the greater will be the number of
pupils entered for public school.'

4   Consider the hypothesis, 'Students with one A at A-level obtain at least a lower second
in their degree examinations.' If, out of a sample of 100, four exceptions were found, would
you say the hypothesis is refuted?
  If you believe that the hypothesis predicted well, would you say that high A-level scores
cause good degrees? If you do not think this is correct, what would you say?

4

Appendix to Chapter 2

Q 1   Write down the functions which correspond to the following rules (use 'x' for 'a number', — the first part of the question is answered as an example):

(1) Take a number, double it and add 3 $y = 2x + 3$

(2) Take a number, add 5, and multiply the
    result by 4 $y = $ _____

(3) Take a number, divide it by 5 and
    square the result   _____

(4) Take a number and add it to four times
    its own square root   _____

Q 2   Express verbally the following, where

P = price, Q = output, and a time period is one month:

(1) $Q_t = Q(P_{t-2})$ _____

_____

(2) $P_{t+3} = P(Q_t, P_{t+1})$ _____

_____

Q 3   Complete the following, such that it means the same as

$Q_t = Q(P_{t-2})$

_____ $= Q(P_t)$

Q 4   (1) In agricultural economics, rainfall is an exogenous/endogenous variable.
       (2) In a theory concerning the determination of market price and quantity sold of a
           commodity, market price is an exogenous/endogenous variable.

Q 5   Which of the following are identities?

(1) $4x + 3 = (6 + 8x) \div 2$
(2) $8x + 4 = 2x + 16$
(3) Mary's mother's father is Peter's uncle's brother.
(4) Peter's father's mother is Peter's brother's grandmother.

Q 6   (1) A sufficient condition for rain is the presence of clouds.   T/F
       (2) A necessary condition for rain is the presence of clouds.   T/F
       (3) A necessary condition for no-rain is the absence of clouds.   T/F

CHAPTER 3

The Tools of Statistical Analysis

The purpose of this chapter is to show how empirical data can be used scientifically even in subjects such as the social sciences in which laboratory experiments are impossible.

You should now read the whole of the chapter.

Let us assume that we wish to test the hypothesis that the larger the housing estate a person lives in, the less communication he will have with other people.

Q 1   First, we have to take a large/random/haphazard sample of people living on housing estates.

        Check your answer. Pause a moment and consider what is meant by a 'random sample'.

Q 2   Which of the following must be true of a random sample?

    (a) Before the actual sampling method is chosen, no one knows which members of the population will appear in it.
    (b) Every member of the population has an equal chance of being chosen.
    (c) A random sample is an accurate microcosm of the population.

Q 3   If you know the exact characteristics of the population, can you deduce the exact characteristics of a random sample of that population? Yes/No

        Check your answer. If you were wrong, do Q 4. If not, carry on with Q 5.

Q 4   Can we deduce whether the method by which a sample has been taken was random by inspecting the sample? Yes/No

The point of all this is that the randomness of a sample has to do with the method by which the sample is chosen. Just seeing what the sample looks like does not tell us about this. Of course, if we happen to know what the population is like, and we know that the sample is in fact very unrepresentative, then we may *suspect* that our selection procedure was not random, especially if, when the same procedure is used to select other samples, they are also similarly unrepresentative.

Q 5   Why would you reject the method of selection by sticking pins in a telephone directory? _____

_____

We decide on a suitable method, and pick out our sample. We are aware of the size of the housing estate the members of our sample live on, and the number of their acquaintances.

(For the purposes of this example we will take the unrealistically small sample size of 12.)

We then tabulate our information: we arbitrarily number the persons sampled from 1 to 12, for reference only.

Individual no.	Size of estate (in no. of houses)	No. of acquaintances
1	30	50
2	100	32
3	100	28
4	72	32
5	65	34
6	90	17✓
7	60	42
8	82	35
9	38	44
10	50	43
11	137	17
12	65	55

We now express the information in a scatter diagram. Label the axes, and plot the points in Fig. 1.

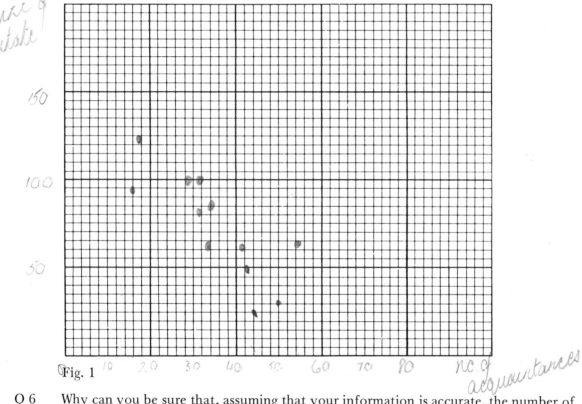

Fig. 1

Q 6   Why can you be sure that, assuming that your information is accurate, the number of one's acquaintances is not completely explained by the size of one's housing estate?

We formulate the second hypothesis, therefore, that the number of one's acquaintances also depends on the number of gardens which one's own back garden joins. We return to our sample, and find the following data.

Individual no.	No. of neighbouring gardens	Individual no.	No. of neighbouring gardens
1	3	7	3
2	3	8	3
3	2	9	3
4	3	10	2
5	2	11	3
6	1	12	4

As we had hoped, we see that the number of gardens backed on by individual no. 3 is less than those backed on by individual no. 2; that the number is higher than average for 12, and lower for 6. We can classify this data as in table 3.3, p. 41.

Q 7   Complete this table.
Average number of acquaintances known, classified by estate-size and no. of neighbouring gardens.

		No. of gardens			
		1	2	3	4
	0–40				
Estate	41–80				
size	81–120				
	121–140				

Q 8   Read down column 3, and interpret the information verbally.

_____

Q 9   Now do the same, reading across row 3.

_____

This is really as far as we can go without statistical techniques. If we used multiple regression analysis we could find out what would be the likely effect of a change in the number of back-gardens, keeping estate-size constant, or vice versa. (By the use of various results and assumptions we can also form a measure of the reliance which we can place upon the representativeness of our sample.)

Statistical methods can be very useful indeed. But, like most techniques, they have limitations; here is a quotation, not from some exasperated, antediluvian civil servant, but from a prominent professional statistician writing in an elementary textbook:

'There was a time when popes and kings had astrologers at court to help them plan for the future. Nowadays government departments have statisticians for the same purpose. One day they will be relegated to the Sunday newspapers to displace the astrologers from their last refuge.'[1]

Many statisticians—especially those at the UK Treasury—would disagree. But the warning note is sounded—it's as wrong to expect statistical machinery to churn out infallible predictions as it is to believe the adage, 'Lies, damn lies, and statistics'.

Q 10   Chemistry, astronomy, anthropology, physics, metallurgy, psychology, economics, physiology, geology and social psychology all lay claim to being sciences. What problems do astronomy, geology, anthropology, social psychology and economics meet in testing their theories which are not encountered by the others? _____

_____

[1] M. J. Moroney, *Facts from Figures*, Penguin 1956.

QUESTIONS FOR DISCUSSION

1   In September 1978 Dr Rhodes Boyson, a Conservative Party spokesman on education, revealed that A-level results per head of children in the appropriate age group were better in Trafford, where schools are selective, than in Manchester, where they are comprehensive. He inferred from this that selection is better than non-selection. Do you think this inference was justified? (Trafford is a middle-class suburban district, Manchester is an inner city.)

2   This was written to the *Financial Times* (18.4.74):
    'Sir,—The news that the Treasury has built a computer model of the economy prompts me to inquire how the most important part of the economy— the individual—has been incorporated in the model.
    'Treasury forecasting has been so disastrous that one is driven to the conclusion that no provision has been made for the individual—so long regarded by Whitehall and the Treasury as an administrative inconvenience.'
    What is meant by the assertion that a statistical model should 'incorporate the individual'? What point is the correspondent probably making?

3   The National Opinion Poll of the *Daily Mail* used to show public opinion more pro-Conservative than the *Telegraph's* Gallup Poll. The method used by the *Mail* was to entrust their samplers to approach a fixed number of people in the street and ask them their politics—their samplers were usually young ladies. Gallup selected names at random from a voters' register. Can you offer an explanation for the discrepancy?

4   'He seems to have known the world by intuition, to have looked through nature at one glance' (Pope on Shakespeare). How far can social investigation follow Shakespeare's lead?

5   'If you want to know the effects of a tax cut on unemployment in the UK there is no sense in studying what happened when taxes were cut in other countries or in the UK in the past; the circumstances were bound to be different so that these experiences are of no relevance to what will happen in the UK if taxes are cut now.' Comment on this view in the light of what you have studied in this chapter.

Appendix to Chapter 3

Q 1   Here are some observations, made in a biochemistry laboratory, of the length of time taken to process a batch of samples. (The observations are being used to estimate average and marginal costs of certain biochemistry tests.)

Length of time (in minutes) taken to process batch	*Number of tests in batch*
103	21
110	24
102	18
105	32
98	30
125	40
91	12
80	10
97	22
90	18
100	17
120	38

Plot them on a scatter diagram on Fig.1.

(1) How long would you expect 26 tests to take? 80/100/120

(2) Are these observations consistent with the conclusion that the machinery involved needs a warm-up period before the tests can be started? Yes/No

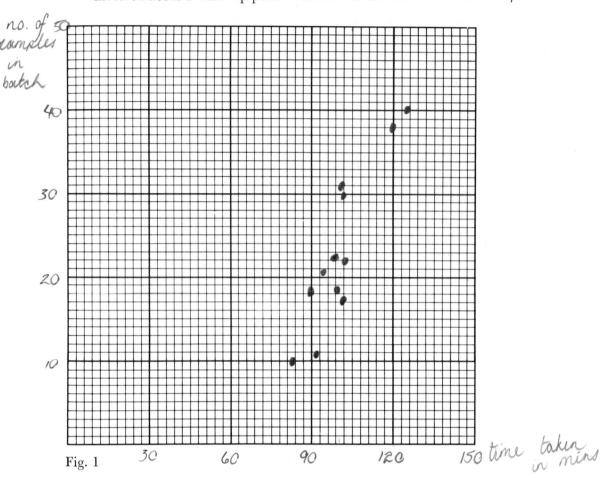

Fig. 1

Q 2   Here are the prices of goods in a 'representative shopping basket' for two different years.

		Year 1 £	Year 2 £
Potatoes	(2 kilos)	0.18	0.36
Bacon	(500g)	1.50	1.90
Beans	(3 tins)	0.60	0.68
Chicken	(1 frozen)	2.20	2.25
Butter	(250g)	0.80	0.90
Detergent	(1 box)	0.70	0.85

(1) With year 1 as base, what is the value of the price index at year 2? _____

(2) Which commodity changed in price the most between the two years? _____

(3) Which commodity caused the price index to change the most? _____

(4) If, between the two years, households increased their consumption of chicken and decreased their consumption of bacon, the change reflected by the price index of (1) would be too high/too low.

10

CHAPTER 4

The Problems of Economic Theory

THE NATURE OF ECONOMIC PROBLEMS (Read up to page 53.)

Q 1   (1)   What are the three divisions into which resources are classified? _____

_____

      (2)   Sometimes a fourth is added—what? _____

_____

      (3)   If the fourth category is not used, in which of the other three is it subsumed?

_____

Q 2   Which of the three categories of factors are involved in the production of the following commodities?
    (1)   Wild blackberries
    (2)   Motor-cars
    (3)   Haircuts in a shop
    (4)   The advice of an accountant
    (5)   Cultivated blackberries

Q 3   Is it important whether a house is classed as a commodity, or a stream of services?
Yes/No
Check your answer; if you were wrong, re-read Lipsey, page 52.

Q 4   What is the function of production in our society? _____

_____

SCARCITY

Some economists use the concept of 'bliss' as the ideal state of society, when everybody has everything he wants. No society approaches this—people's wants seem to expand quite as fast as production—so the problem of scarcity is still paramount, entailing in a market economy *choice* and *cost*.

Q 5   What is the economist's term for cost measured by forgone alternatives? _____

_____

BASIC ECONOMIC PROBLEMS (pp. 53—6)

Most problems involving scarcity—problems about *cost*, problems about the procedures by which a *choice* can be made—can be placed into one of the seven categories described in Lipsey, pp. 53—6.

Q 6   (1)   Complete this list of problems:
      (1)   What commodities are being produced and in what quantities?
      (2)   By what methods are these commodities produced?
      (3)
      (4)

(5)

(6)

(7) Is the economy's capacity to produce goods and services growing from year to year, or is it remaining static?

(2) Here are some headlines from the daily newspapers. Classify them according to their category.

(1) Priority of agriculture vital

(2) Will Italian economy outstrip British?

(3) 'State aid only for the needy' say Tories

(4) Unofficial strike hits Chrysler's again

(5) Container berths at Tilbury still lying idle

(6) 'Index-linked savings a confidence trick' says Building Society manager

(7) Sugar rationing still imminent?

(8) No conductors in new pay-as-you-enter buses

(9) A production line to be bought by British Leyland from Honda?

Q 7 In some countries, the commodities which are produced, and the quantities in which they are produced, are decided for years in advance by a central authority. By what mechanism do free-market economies avoid the necessity for such an authority?

_____

Q 8 List the 4 main questions in microeconomics

(1) _____

(2) _____

(3) _____

(4) _____

You must know these by heart. Read on to the end of the chapter.

Q 9 Refer to Fig. 1, which is a guns-butter production-possibilities graph.

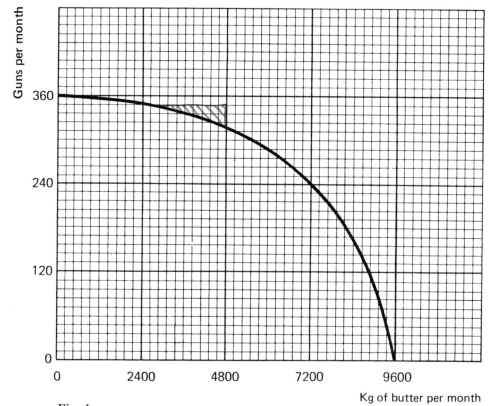

Fig. 1

(1) If 240 guns are produced, what is the maximum amount of butter that can be produced? 4800/8400/7200

(2) Assume that a change occurs which increases unemployment. How will the curve shift? _____

_____

(3) Can we represent reallocation of resources between the production of guns and butter? Yes/No

(4) How many extra guns can we get if we drop from consuming 4800 kg to 2400 kg of butter? 20/50/30/60

(5) What is the cost of the extra guns in (4), measured in terms of butter forgone?

_____

Q 10 (1) If the total output of an economy grew by 6% in one year at the same time as the percentage of unemployed resources fell from 7% to 4%, what was the real growth rate? (Assume that a 1% fall in unemployment causes a 1% rise in output.) 2%/3%/4%

(2) Would you predict that the 6% rise in output was likely to continue for the next year? Yes/Could be/No

(3) For the next two years? Yes/Could be/No

Q 11 In Germany in 1939 a very large increase in the production of armaments could be achieved by means of a decrease in the production of consumer goods, whereas in the USA between 1940 and 1942 it was accompanied by an increase. Can you explain why this difference in behaviour occurred? _____

_____

QUESTIONS FOR DISCUSSION

1   In the summer of 1982, the UK economy was in dire straits, with high inflation and appalling unemployment. Government ministers were refusing to sanction any of their civil servants' plans which might involve extra expenditure. Yet when the Falkland Islands were invaded by Argentina, the fleet was despatched and an army transported, at a cost which was estimated by the Government, in response to Parliamentary Questions, of about £1.5 billion.
   What does this sort of cost figure mean?
   What was the opportunity cost of the Falklands war?

2   When Peugeot took over Chrysler (UK) in 1978, a British shop steward from a notoriously unproductive and strike-bound factory was taken on a trip to a Peugeot factory in France. He was full of admiration for the high wages, the physical conditions of work, the modern machinery and the standard of the finished cars. Upon learning that Peugeot employ many immigrant workers, an internal security force of armed guards, and adopt a rather harsher attitude to unionization and the right to strike from that prevalent in the UK, he decided that British workers would prefer to remain lower paid.
   Discuss his attitude within the framework of economics outlined in this chapter.
   The table below was compiled by the *Sunday Times* (30.7.78) from *Social Indicators 1960–1975*, EEC (Brussels 1978). Would the economist have a different viewpoint from the sociologist (for example, with regard to women at work)? What do you think about this method of compiling an overall rank order?

3   Economists use the term *free goods* for commodities that are so plentiful that every household can have as much of them as it could conceivably use. How many free goods can you think of?

Britain's rung on the ladder of social success

(The *lower* the rank number, the better)

out of 9 EEC countries

for	rank
short working week	6
night and Sunday work	5
women 35-60 in work (the *more* the better)	1
working conditions	1
fatal accidents	3
money spent on leisure	2
healthy diet	7
car ownership	8
fridge ownership	6
pensions	2
family allowance	7
suicides	3
deaths from car accidents	2
deaths from infectious diseases	4
life expectancy at birth	4
perinatal mortality	6
deaths from heart and lung disease	9
hospital beds	3
patient/doctor ratio	7
children in compulsory schooling	1
housing	1

Overall rank order
(excluding housing)

Denmark
Germany
France
Holland
UK, Belgium
Luxembourg
Italy
Ireland

4   The banks of the river Clyde west of Glasgow are very beautiful. Unemployment in these areas is very high. Assuming that industrial development would mar the beauty of the countryside, what is the opportunity cost of this industrial development? What is the opportunity cost of the beautiful countryside? Do you think that a middle-class car-owner with a safe job might evaluate these costs differently from an unemployed labourer in Renfrewshire?

CHAPTER 5
A General View of the Price System

Economics began when society started to organize in the way described by Lipsey on pages 59 and 60.

Q 1   The following paragraph is a précis of an article in a Sunday colour supplement. Which of the economic concepts listed below are applicable to the community described?

'An ecological community has been started on a Welsh farm by some people who are dissatisfied with many elements of modern economic life. The girls look after the hens and cattle, the men do the heavy work in the fields. They make their own clothes, in part from leather from their own cattle tanned in the nearby town, in a tannery owned by a friend who accepts poultry in payment. The same method is used to pay the thatcher whose skill is sometimes required—other building jobs they can all manage. It's a hard life, but they all say that they enjoy it, although, especially in the spring, they would like more spare time for leisure.'

(a)   Surplus and specialization

(b)   Money

(c)   Factor services

(d)   Division of labour

(e)   Scarcity

There are three essential concepts introduced in this chapter:

(1)   Consumer
(2)   Producer
(3)   Market mechanism

The market mechanism is the means by which the behaviour of consumers and producers interacts to determine what is produced, and how it is allocated. This it does by establishing a price for each commodity. Consumers are people who demand goods, producers those who supply them—that consumers are pretty well always producers and vice versa presents no difficulties here (it will later); we merely choose to separate these two functions for the purpose of our analysis. This sort of abstraction is a part of all theory building.

A CHANGE IN DEMAND (remember, we assume that all factors affecting demand, other than the one in question, remain constant)

Q 2   Tape-recorders suddenly become more popular than record-players. Which of the following will result?

(a)   A shortage of tape-recorders
(b)   A shortage of record-players
(c)   A surplus of record-players

(d)   A surplus of tape-recorders
(e)   Increased production of tape-recorders
(f)   Increased production of record-players
(g)   A fall in the price of tape-recorders
(h)   A rise in the price of record-players

A CHANGE IN SUPPLY

Q 3   Oil from the North Sea makes oil production cheaper, the cost of producing coal stays the same.

The immediate results are:

(a)   A glut of coal
(b)   A glut of oil

The subsequent results are:

(c)   An increase in the price of coal
(d)   A decrease in the price of oil

Q 4   During the Korean war in 1950 and 1951 the United States attempted to purchase for its reserves very large supplies of most raw materials. What would you have predicted would happen to the prices of raw materials imported into Britain? They would rise/ be unchanged/fall.

Q 5   Now consider the markets for (i.e. the demand for and supply of) cricket bats and tennis racquets. Assume that many people play both games. Give explanations for the following events, or say why you cannot.

(1)   More people prefer tennis this summer, and the price of tennis racquets has gone up. _____
_____

(2)   There are fewer people who now have the patience to make cricket bats, and more tennis is being played this summer. _____
_____

(3)   Cat-gut has become more expensive, so more cricket bats will be sold this summer.
_____
_____

(4)   The changes described in (3) will bring about an increase in the supply of cricket bats, so to prevent surpluses accumulating the price will have to fall. So cricket bats will become cheaper, tennis racquets more expensive.
_____

Now check your answers.

If you get (2) or (3) wrong, remember that the initial change in each question will cause the price to change and this change in price will induce further reaction on the part of consumers and producers.

If you got (4) wrong, remember that an increased supply of a commodity may be *caused* by an increase in demand and therefore price, or *may cause* a decrease in price in order to avoid unsold stocks—but not both!

Q 6   A decrease in the price of a good, accompanied by a larger sale of that good, might mean:
(a)   Demand has increased so people have bought more.
(b)   Supply has increased so the price has had to drop.
(c)   An increase in demand has caused an increase in supply and a subsequent drop in price.

Check your answer. It is essential that you should understand this, and if you are still worried you ought to re-read Lipsey Chapter 5 to the end of Change in Supply.

Remember, an increase in the quantity sold may be caused by a rise in demand, in which case prices will rise as well, or by an increase in the quantity producers wish to sell at each price without there being any change in consumers' tastes, in which case prices must fall.

QUESTIONS FOR DISCUSSION

1   Trace out, in a manner similar to the analysis in this chapter, the effect of a change in consumers' demand away from pork and toward lamb resulting from a successful advertising campaign on the part of lamb producers.

2   What will happen, according to the theory of this chapter, if there is a rise in the cost of producing barley relative to the cost of producing other agricultural products?

3   What will happen if, on a particularly fine day in April, there is a sudden and temporary increase in the demand for ice-cream? What will happen if the exceptionally good weather and the exceptionally high demand continues this way all summer?

4   If goods are expensive because they are scarce, why are rotten eggs not high-priced?

5   A gentleman of the pseudonym 'Simple Lifer' wrote the following letter to the Glasgow *Evening Times* (5.3.71): ' "Soapy Hudson" suggested in a recent letter that washing machines are a mixed blessing.

'I suggest that we would be happier if we got rid of the whole jingbang—washing machines, fridges, carpet sweepers, dish washers, carpet shampooers, TV sets, radios, and motor-cars!

'Maybe then we would have room to live! There would be no air pollution, no noise, no accidents, and fewer of the frustrations arising from present day technology!'

Is he saying that the market mechanism doesn't work? Or that it might work, but doesn't achieve a desirable objective?

CHAPTER 6

Basic Concepts of Price Theory

THE HOUSEHOLD

Economics is concerned with the behaviour of people, individuals or groups, when they are doing such things as buying, selling, producing, consuming. Actual decisions must be taken— whether to buy this or not, whether to consume or save. The basic decision unit for the theory of demand is the *household*, and whenever any person, or group of people, makes an effective consumption decision, we say that he, or it, is acting as a household. So when, for example, a firm makes a consumption decision (perhaps about the furniture for its executive suites) it is fulfilling the economic function of a household.

Q 1   What is the minimum number of members of a household? _____

Q 2   Is a hospital a household? Yes/No

Q 3   If it is, is then a hospital ward a householder? Yes/No

Check your answer.

If you answered Q3 wrongly, remember that if we have decided that X (which is comprised of $x_1, x_2, \ldots, x_n$) is a household, then x_1 or x_2 cannot be households since the decision taken for X is the decision for all x_i.

THE FIRM

As we did with consumption, we select from the full set of activities of individuals, businesses, governments, public corporations and the like, those activities which have to do with the production and sale of commodities. Whenever an individual or a group is engaged in such activities we say that he (or it) is acting as a firm.

Q 4   A steel company produces as much steel as the government stipulates, and sells it all at the market price. Is it a firm? Yes/No

Q 5   Could Robinson Crusoe be a firm? Yes/No

Q 6   Is a privately owned television company a firm? (If so, what is its product?)
Yes/No _____   _____

Q 7   What do we assume is the basic motive behind a firm's behaviour? _____
_____

There is an essential link between households and firms, without which the economic system would be quite different.

Q 8   Households are the main owners of_____ , of which _____
_____ are the main purchasers.
Firms act in order to_____
Households act in order to_____ .

18

THE CENTRAL AUTHORITIES

Q 9　A firm is considered as one unit; so is a household. Are they central authorities?
Yes/No _____

_____

THE MARKET

Q 10　Define a market. _____

_____

Q 11　What is the probable market for Lancashire evening papers? _____

Q 12　What is the market for gold? _____

Q 13　What is the market for right-hand-drive motor-cars? _____

Q 14　What is the English market for gold? _____

Q 15　What do we call a market where there is a large number of buyers and sellers, such that no one has an appreciable influence on price? Free/competitive/open

Q 16　Can the market for one commodity be identical to the market for another? Yes/No

Q 17　List the factors which separate the Argentinian market for beef from the French market for veal. _____

_____

Q 18　In a goods market, _____ are sellers, buyers can be _____
_____ . In factor markets, sellers are usually _____ ,
and buyers are _____ .

Q 19　Is the English market for antibiotics free or controlled? _____

Q 20　Do the following 'firms' occupy the market sector, the non-market sector, or both?

(1)	Rolls-Royce aero-engines	M/NM/B
(2)	Rolls-Royce motor-cars	M/NM/B
(3)	Preston Comprehensive School	M/NM/B
(4)	Cadbury Schweppes	M/NM/B
(5)	British Steel—in theory	M/NM/B
(6)	British Steel—in practice	M/NM/B

Q 21　What do we call a collection of markets? _____

Q 22　In war-time, economies generally become less _____ , or in other words
more _____ , since the government needs to direct resources
toward specific ends.

Q 23　Is British Petroleum in the private sector, the public sector, or both? _____

QUESTIONS FOR DISCUSSION

1　In Kent, in 1978, a pilot study was carried out by the Education Authority into *Education Vouchers*—a system designed to give parents a greater choice in the schooling of their children, and to introduce competitiveness between schools in order to improve standards. Argue for and against such a system. Is it obviously true that parental choice is the most important consideration?

2　The majority of economists tend to be liberals in the sense defined by John Stuart Mill, that is they tend to believe in the value of leaving adult individuals free to decide their own fate including allowing them to spend their money as they wish. Yet many also believe that the central government is right in forcing comprehensive education, not only on parents but also on dissident local authorities. How can these views be compatible?

3   There is a lot of evidence that if you are wearing your seatbelt in a car, you are less likely to receive serious or fatal injury if the car crashes. Yet most people do not bother to wear their seatbelts, and the government has now introduced legislation to make it illegal not to wear a seatbelt. Argue for and against such legislation. Can you detect any difference between such legislation and the existing legislation about manufacturing safety standards which, in effect, make it difficult, if not impossible, to choose to buy a car which is more likely to kill you but costs less than safer cars?

4   What do you think are some of the differences between British Leyland (a public-sector firm) and Fords (a private-sector firm)?

5   It is assumed in standard economic theory that all firms behave in similar fashions in similar situations whatever their size or internal organization. Some critics say this is not so; that the size and organization of a firm significantly affect the way it will behave in a given situation. What do you think at this stage? We shall return to this question again after we have studied the standard theory and the criticisms made of it.

CHAPTER 7

The Elementary Theory of Demand and Supply

We now start developing our formal theory of demand and supply.

DEMAND

Seven hypotheses were given on pp. 74ff. Although it was not at this stage asserted that demand is affected by all seven factors—it was rather suggested that, in view of their *a priori* plausibility, they were all worthy of testing—we do, in fact, as we shall see, have a lot of evidence to support these hypotheses.

Here is a list of the variables assumed to influence quantity demanded:

(1) Price of the commodity
(2) Prices of other commodities   An individual house-
(3) Income of the household   hold's demand   Market
(4) Sociological factors   demand
(5) Tastes of the household
(6) Size of the population
(7) Income distribution

Consider the quantity of fresh asparagus demanded.

Q 1   Into which of the seven categories do the following factors fall?

    (1)   Dislike of cabbage and butter beans_____

    (2)   The football pools _____

    (3)   War indemnity payments to the government and subsequent decreased taxation

        _____

    (4)   The price of celery and leeks _____

    (5)   A tax of 10p per bunch of asparagus sold _____

    (6)   A successful birth-control campaign _____

    (7)   The National Asparagus Week organized by the Association of Asparagus Growers _____

    (8)   Accelerated-freeze-drying, which makes satisfactory dried vegetables cheaper

        _____

    (9)   A shower of manna _____

   (10)   The fact that the Princess of Wales likes asparagus _____

Check your answers. If you got more than three wrong, do Question 2.

Q 2   Consider the demand for telephones in houses or firms. Into which of the seven categories do the following fall?[1]

(1)   The wages of typists _____

(2)   The progressiveness of income tax _____

(3)   The number of public telephones _____

(4)   The installation charge for a telephone _____

We now want to study the various relationships which we have postulated, and it will be convenient if we can study them one at a time. We have a simple technique which helps us to express our knowledge concisely and clearly. This is a graph which plots the relation between one of the factors and market demand, under the condition that *all the other factors remain constant*. We concentrate mostly on the relation between price and demand because we are interested in developing a theory of price.

Assume that we want to plot quantity of beans purchased against their price. *We must first decide on our units.*

This is not quite as simple as it seems. For example, 'kilos' and 'pence' won't do at all.

Q 3   To decide on the units to use, we would have to add two words after both 'kilos' and 'pence'. Give an example of such words:

_____ _____ and _____ _____

If you were wrong, re-read Lipsey p. 74.

Q 4   Whereas the number of pens in people's pockets at any one time is a stock/flow, the demand for pens is a stock/flow.

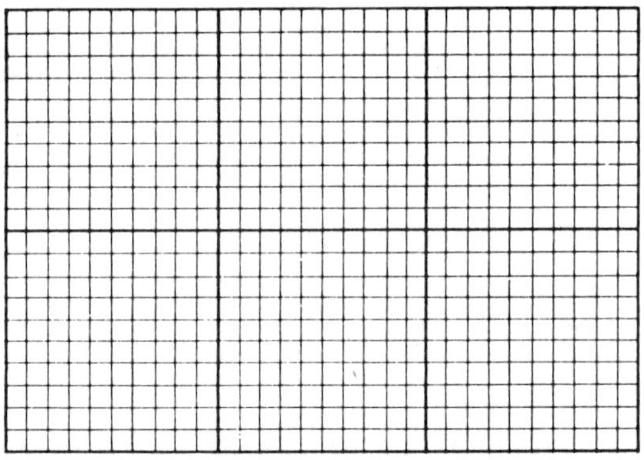

Fig. 1

On the horizontal axis of Fig. 1 write in '£s per kilo'. On the vertical axis write in 'kilos per week'. Have the zero point for both where the axes meet—let the units run to £10 per kilo and 1000 kilos per week.

Now make the explicit assumption that as price *rises*, quantity of beans purchased *falls*. (This is an *assumption*, not a rule. Intuition tells us that it is plausible, but it is not scientific to trust intuition—it certainly helps us to decide which theories to test, seldom helps us to test them.) In this case, of course, there is plenty of evidence. Now before reading on, draw in on Fig. 1 a demand curve which exemplifies this assumption. It should share with Fig. 2 one quality—it should slope downwards. If it doesn't, you shouldn't continue until you realize why whatever you have drawn is wrong.

Now refer to Fig. 2.

Q 5   At what price will 10 be bought? _____

_____

[1] They may fall into more than one.

Q 6   At what price will 14 be bought? _____

Q 7   How much will be bought at £4? _____

Q 8   How much will be bought at £1? _____

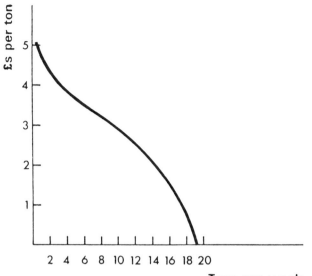

Fig. 2

You will notice that the curve which we have drawn is smooth—'continuous'—that is, it purports to show the quantity demanded for *every* price—ignoring the indivisibility of money below the unit of the halfpenny. This is an obviously convenient approximation—it is much easier to draw,

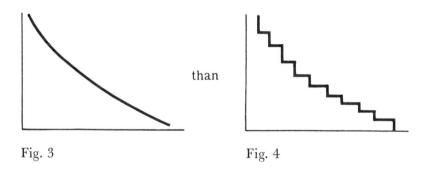

Fig. 3   than   Fig. 4

Moreover, a demand curve which is constructed in this way, from a series of observations, is usually built up from fewer observations than one for every halfpenny change in price, because most commodities do not change price by the halfpenny. We will have a set of observations such as this:

Price	Q demanded (to nearest 125)
10p	20,125
12½p	15,000
17½p	13,500
21p	12,125
25p	10,000
27½p	9,500
35p	8,750
40p	8,000
43½p	8,000
50p	7,750
55p	7,500

23

Q 9   Label the axes, and plot the points on to Fig. 5.

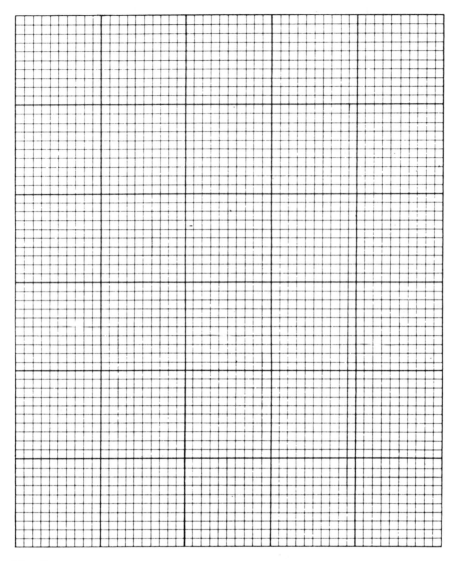

Fig. 5

Now draw a smooth curve, keeping as close to the points as possible. *You have made the assumption that, if price were to be between any of the actual observations taken, quantity demanded would fall in with the pattern suggested by these observations.*

Q 10   (1)   If 15p were the price, how many would be demanded? _____

       (2)   If 18,000 were demanded, what would the price be?_____

       (3)   If 11,250 were demanded, what would the price be?_____

If you were wrong, rub out your graph and try again.

Q 11   Show on Fig. 6 the following demand curves:

       (1)   200 demanded whatever the price;

       (2)   As much as possible demanded at 20p, but none at all at 20½p.

D_1 on Fig. 7 is a market demand curve for a given set of conditions other than price. By moving *along* the curve we observe the effects of a change in price. We want to show the effects of changes in the other conditions (population, tastes, etc.). *Each set of other*

24

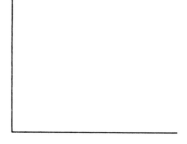

Fig. 6

conditions has a separate demand curve. So we show these effects by drawing different curves — or 'shifting' the original curve.

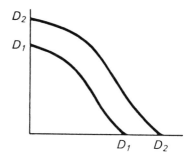

Fig. 7

D_1D_1 might be a demand curve for one level of 'prices of other goods', D_2D_2 for another. D_2D_2 shows higher demand at each price.

Q 12   Assume that, in Fig. 5, demand increases by 1000 at *every* price. Draw the new curve on Fig. 5.

(1)   How much is demanded now at 35p? _____

(2)   How much is demanded now at 15p? _____

Make sure that you understand pp. 82–3.

Q 13   How will the market demand curve of a 'normal' good shift if

(1)   The price of substitutes falls? right/left/not/indeterminate

(2)   Population rises? right/left/not/indeterminate

(3)   Tastes shift away from the commodity? right/left/not/indeterminate

(4)   The prices of complements fall? right/left/not/indeterminate

(5)   Distribution of income becomes more even? right/left/not/indeterminate

(6)   National income rises? right/left/not/indeterminate

(7)   Complements become more expensive? right/left/not/indeterminate

(8)   Substitutes become more expensive? right/left/not/indeterminate

Q 14   (1)   Define an 'inferior good' _____

(2)   Can a market good be inferior over the whole range of income?
Yes/No   Explain _____

_____

25

Q 15   Which of the curves in Fig. 8 might be an income-demand curve for an inferior good over the levels of income plotted? (Note the labelling of the axes.)

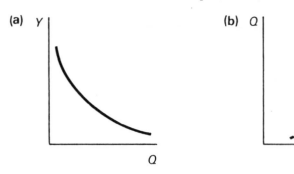

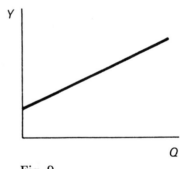

Fig. 8

Q 16   Here is a household's income-demand curve for a normal commodity:

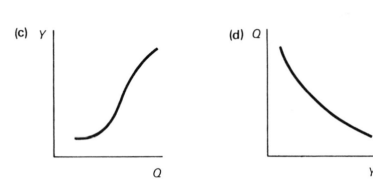

Fig. 9

How will it shift if

    (1)   The commodity's price falls? right/left/not at all

    (2)   Substitutes become more expensive? right/left/not at all

    (3)   The household's wage-earners gain a pay rise? right/left/not at all

    (4)   Complements become cheaper? right/left/not at all

    (5)   Substitutes become cheaper? right/left/not at all

    If you got Q 16 (3) wrong, re-read p. 84. Then do Q 17. Otherwise, go to Q 18.

Q 17   You are considering a price-demand curve for cotton.[1] (If the cost of producing cotton changes, assume that its price changes.) Which of the following would result in a shift, and which a movement along the curve?

———————————

[1] Which is imported.

(1) A change in the price of nylon   shift/movement along

(2) A change in the wages of cotton pickers   shift/movement along

(3) A rise in national income   shift/movement along

Q 18 Any good that is inferior for some levels of income *must* be normal at some lower levels of income. True/False. Explain _____

_____

Q 19 The demand for a good declines if the prices of complements increase. T/F

Q 20 Demand curves are usually drawn with quantity on one axis and price on the other, because price is without doubt the most important determinant of demand. T/F

Q 21 The market demand curve is derived from individual demand curves by vertical summation. T/F

If you were wrong, re-read Lipsey page 70, footnote 1.

Q 22 The demand for a good increases if the price of substitutes falls. T/F

Q 23 The statement in Q 19 might, in some possible world, be wrong. T/F

If you were wrong, re-read Lipsey page 77.
Remember, it is just the effect that the price of one good has on the demand for another that *defines* whether they are complements or substitutes.

Q 24 'Since in the United States, *per capita* income is higher than that of France, Americans use more petrol than Frenchmen.' A sound or unsound argument?

Q 25 The demand for inferior goods increases as household income increases, but at a slower rate. T/F

Q 26 A rightward shift of the demand curve means that more of the good will be demanded at every price. T/F

Q 27 When we say that the demand curve for a commodity is downward-sloping to the right, we mean that

(a) more of the commodity will be demanded as income rises.
(b) more of the commodity will be demanded as the price of a substitute good rises.
(c) more of the commodity will be demanded as its own price falls.
(d) more of the commodity will be bought as population increases.
(e) All of the above answers are correct.
(f) None of the above answers is correct.

Q 28 If the price of lamb rises and that of pork falls

(a) more lamb will be bought.
(b) more beef will be bought.
(c) more pork will be bought.
(d) less lamb and pork will be bought.

SUPPLY

Q 29 Which of the following questions are aspects of the main question 'What determines the quantity of wheat supplied?'

(a) How much fertilizer is needed to grow wheat?
(b) How much wheat is needed to bake bread?
(c) Are steam ovens more efficient than hot-air ovens?
(d) How attractive is the agricultural life to modern workers?

Make sure of p. 86. Remember, they are *hypotheses*, not rules.

Q 30   Consider the supply of metal girders. Which of the four factors mentioned on p.86 do the following exemplify?

   (1)   The increased use of computers _____

   (2)   A rise in the wages of coal miners _____

   (3)   The nationalization of the steel industry _____

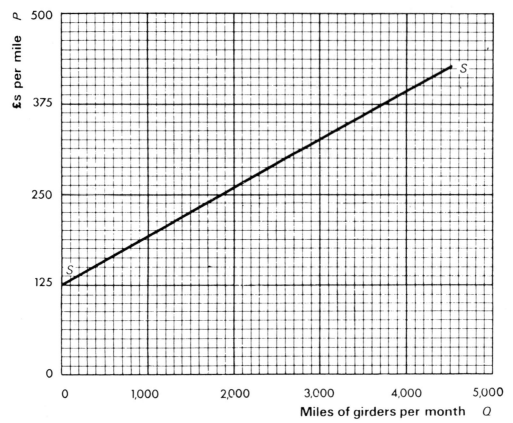

Fig. 10

   (4)   The price of girders _____

   (5)   Increased ore costs _____

Look at Fig. 10. As in the last chapter, we can plot quantity supplied against one of these factors. Again we single out price—just the price of the one commodity considered, and again we make the standard continuity assumption.

Q 31   What do we call this sort of graphical relation, where the supply curve is straight?

   _____

Q 32   Will more or less than 4,000 miles be supplied at £375? More/Less

Q 33   Build up on Fig. 11 a continuous supply curve from the following data. (You will have to write in your own axes.)

Price	Q supplied
17½p	11
32½p	20
30p	18
21½p	13
10p	7
15p	10

28

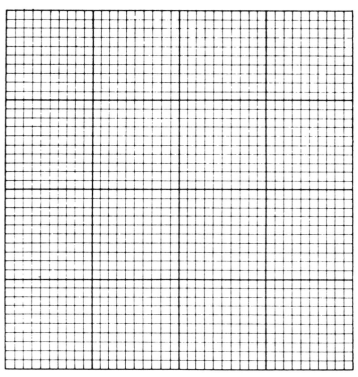

Fig. 11

(1) How many will be supplied at 26p? _____

(2) Interchange the axes of Fig. 11 and redraw the graph on Fig. 12.

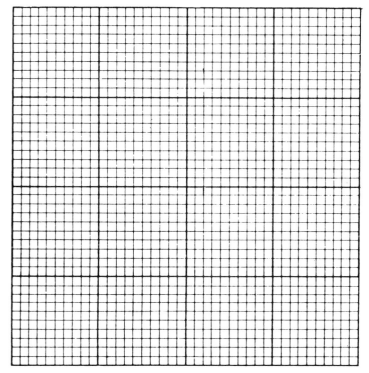

Fig. 12

Q 34 At what price will 9 be supplied? _____
       Again, we portray a change in conditions other than price by shifting the curve.

Q 35 What portrays the effect of changing prices? _____

If you are wrong, you must re-read Lipsey, p. 84. Remember, we are aiming to derive a theory of price.

Assume that other conditions change so that SS in Fig. 10 shifts $\frac{1}{2}''$ to the right.

Q 36   What does this mean? _____

Q 37   How much will now be supplied at £310? _____

Q 38   What price will be needed now to cause 250 to be supplied? _____

Q 39   How will the supply curve in Fig. 10 shift if

    (1)   The cost of iron ore falls? right/left/not at all

    (2)   The Government awards OBEs to the producers of metal girders? right/left/not at all

    (3)   The price of girders rises? right/left/not at all

    (4)   A new smelting process is invented and employed? right/left/not at all

Did you get Q 39 (3) right? If not, you must go back to page 29 in the workbook to remember how you satisfied yourself about the difference between movements along and shifts. This point may seem tiresome, but it is very important not to be confused about it.

Q 40   How will the supply curve in Fig. 10 shift if

    (1)   A new method of house construction means that local authorities want to buy many more girders? right/left/not at all

    (2)   The wages of furnace-men rise? right/left/not at all

    (3)   Devaluation means that all supplies are temporarily diverted overseas, since foreign purchasers can offer more money? right/left/not at all

If you got (1) wrong, you're failing to make the all-important theoretical distinction between demand and supply. All right, you may know that price depends on both of them, *but at the moment we're just making 'if' statements about each of them separately.*

Q 41   Place Q 39, sections 1, 2 and 4 in their categories of influencing factors.

    1 _____ 2 _____ 4 _____

Q 42   An increase in the wages of the men making cars will shift the supply curve of cars to the right. T/F

Q 43   In the theory of supply, we aim to explain the goals of firms. T/F

Q 44   A discovery that reduces the cost of producing a commodity will usually, *ceteris paribus*, increase its supply. T/F

Q 45   A supply curve is predicted to shift to the right if the prices of all other commodities rise. T/F

Q 46   The fact that a supply curve slopes upwards to the right is consistent with the fact that the more of a good is made, the more it costs to produce. T/F

Q 47   The fact that a supply curve slopes upwards to the right means that the more of a good is made, the more money the suppliers require for each unit. T/F

Q 48   A supply curve which was a horizontal straight line would mean

    (a)   whatever the price, only one amount is ever produced.
    (b)   below a certain price, none is ever produced.
    (c)   above a certain price, none is ever produced.
    (d)   above a certain price, so much is produced that the graph is not big enough to show it.

Q 49   A supply curve that was a vertical straight line would indicate that

    (a)   there was a maximum price below which no supply would be forthcoming.
    (b)   every increase in price would increase the quantity supplied.
    (c)   the quantity supplied was very responsive to price.
    (d)   the same quantity would be supplied, whatever the price.
    (e)   none of the above answers is correct.

Q 50   The supply curve of wheat tells us how much wheat

    (a)   has been produced each year during the last 20 years.
    (b)   would be produced this year at each possible price of wheat.
    (c)   would be sold this year at each possible price of wheat.
    (d)   would be produced at each possible level of farm income.
    (e)   Either (b) or (c) is satisfactory.
    (f)   Either (c) or (d) is satisfactory.
    (g)   None of the above answers is correct.

Q 51   A rightward shift in a supply curve indicates that

    (a)   a higher price is necessary to call forth any given quantity supplied than before the shift occurred.
    (b)   less will be supplied at each possible market price.
    (c)   the willingness of producers to supply the commodity has diminished.
    (d)   more will be supplied at each possible market price.
    (e)   None of the above answers is correct.

QUESTIONS FOR DISCUSSION

1   When we draw a market demand curve for a commodity, showing the quantity households wish to purchase at various prices, what things do we assume remain constant?

2(a)   If there is a rise in the price of margarine, what do you expect will happen to the demand for butter? What term would you apply to the relationship between butter and margarine?

(b)   Draw a figure illustrating both the original demand curve and the new demand curve for margarine. Which way does the demand curve shift, to the right or to the left? Explain why a shift of the curve in this direction illustrates this change in demand.

(c)   What would be the effect on the demand curve for margarine of a relaxation in the rule of the UK advertising authority that margarines high in polyunsaturates may *not* advertise themselves as healthier than butter, although there is considerable evidence that they are?

(d)   Combine your answers to (a) and (c) with the two assumptions

(1)   margarine of any type is cheaper than butter
(2)   all incomes rise

Can you tell which way, if any, the demand curve for margarine will shift? Why or why not?

3   What would you predict would happen to the market demand curve for oranges as a result of the following?

(a)   A rise in average income.
(b)   An increase in the birth rate.
(c)   An intensive advertising campaign that convinces most people of the importance of a daily quota of natural Vitamin C.
(d)   A fall in the price of tangerines.
(e)   A government programme that raises the income of the poor people in the country by taxing richer people, but leaves total income the same.
(f)   A fall in the price of oranges.

4   Name a few changes that you would expect to increase the demand for petrol; a few that would decrease it; a few that would not affect it. What about the demand for one particular brand of petrol?

5   As average income rises, what do you expect to happen to the demand for videos, cars, used cars, books, university education, public transport, newspapers, rice, television sets, magazines, whisky, fur coats, salt?

6   The following news item appeared in the *Sunday Times* of 28.2.71: 'Mrs Doris Pearsall has good reason to be cheerful. In March last year she became the first lady to be elected president of the Birmingham Butchers' Association. Now the meat trade has made another breakthrough by becoming one of the very few jobs in which women get equal pay. Every employer should be paying equal rates by 1975, but some have a lot of ground to make up. The chances of meeting the deadline are revealed in an exclusive survey on page 52.'
    What are the long-term implications for the demand curve for cosmetics?
    In Scotland (you may be surprised to learn) relatively more women are butchers than men. What would you predict would be the relative effect on the meat supply curves in England and Scotland?

7   During the first half of 1974 the price of animal feedstuffs rocketed. What effect do you think this had (by the next year) on the numbers of prime animals brought to market?

8(a)   What do you think has been the effect on the supply curve of chickens of the innovation of large-scale cost-saving methods of broiler production (often referred to as factory farms)?

    (b)   Suppose a successful campaign by the RSPCA convinces chicken farmers of the cruelty of their ways, and many abandon the new methods despite some loss of profits. What will happen then?

    (c)   Suppose there is an increase in the price of land suitable for broiler production. What is the effect on the supply curve of broilers?

9   What will happen to the supply of cars if the following occur?

    (a)   An increase in the price of trucks.
    (b)   A fall in the price of steel.
    (c)   Introduction of a better assembly-line technique.
    (d)   An increase in the desire of car manufacturers to be highly esteemed by the nation, rather than to earn as much money as possible.
    (e)   An increase in the price of cars.
    (f)   An increase in the number of man-hours lost through strike action.
    (g)   Increased wages because of (f).
    (h)   Productivity bargains which combine (g) with more efficient production techniques.

10   What do you think have been the main changes in the conditions of the supply of cars since the industry started?

11   Refer back to question for discussion 7. What effect did the increase in feed prices have on the numbers of store[1] calves brought to market in mid-1974? Check some contemporary newspaper reports.

---

[1] Immature cattle, too old for veal but too young for beef.

CHAPTER 8

The Theory of the Behaviour of Individual Competitive Markets

THE DETERMINATION OF THE EQUILIBRIUM PRICE

In the last chapter we have expressed demand as a function of price, holding constant all the other factors which influence demand, and supply also as a function of price, holding constant all the other factors which influence supply.

For any given value of all the other factors (variables) that influence demand and supply, therefore, we can show on one diagram the various amounts supplied and demanded at any price.

Fig. 1 shows the market demand and supply schedules for a commodity:

Price (£s per ton)	Quantity demanded (tons per year)	Price (£s per ton)	Quantity supplied (tons per year)
5	0	1	0
4.50	2.25	1.50	0
4	3.35	2	0
3.50	4	2.50	1.6
3	4.75	3	3
2.50	5	3.50	4
2	5.5	4	4.75
1.50	5.75	4.5	5.5
1	6	5	6.25
0.50	6.25	5.5	6.9
0.00	6.5	6	7.7

Fig. 1

Plot the schedules of Fig. 1 on to Fig. 2. Choose your own scale for the axes.

Q 1   Define equilibrium price. _____

_____

Q 2   What is the equilibrium price in our example? _____

_____

Q 3   What is the equilibrium quantity? _____

So far we have no theory to explain why the equilibrium price should prevail—why the market mechanism works, in fact. We will first introduce the concepts of *excess demand* and *excess supply*.

Excess demand is the difference between quantity demanded (q^d) and quantity supplied (q^s), i.e. excess demand = $q^d - q^s$.

Excess supply is merely $q^s - q^d$ and hence is just excess demand with the sign reversed.

Often people talk about excess demand when $q^d > q^s$ and excess supply when $q^s > q^d$, but it is also acceptable to speak only of excess demand allowing it to be positive when $q^d > q^s$ and negative when $q^d < q^s$.

Q 4   To make a statement about the amount of excess demand, is it necessary to mention a price? Yes/No

Q 5   In, and only in, equilibrium, excess demand equals negative excess supply. T/F

If you got Q 4 or Q 5 wrong, you should re-read this chapter of the Workbook up to Q 4. Look at your completed Fig. 2 and see how you would measure excess demand at £3 per ton. Then, see how you would measure excess supply at £3 per ton. You are just measuring the same distance, calling it positive in one case and negative in the other, and this is true at any price.

Now do Q 6 and 7.

Q 6   Excess demand minus excess supply equals zero. T/F

Q 7   Excess demand plus excess supply equals zero. T/F

The theory of the causes of changes in price is simple. It is described on pages 91–94.

Q 8   When there is negative excess supply there is upward/downward pressure on price.

Q 9   When there is positive excess supply there is upward/downward pressure on price.

Q 10   In Fig. 2 what is the excess demand at:

     (1)   £2 per year _____

     (2)   £3 per year _____

     (3)   £4 per year _____

     (4)   £5 per year _____

Assume now that two extra tons are demanded at each price.

Q 11   What is the new equilibrium price? _____

Q 12   What is the excess demand at the old equilibrium price? _____

Q 13   What is the new equilibrium quantity? _____

Q 14   What supply shift would be needed to restore the original equilibrium price? right/left/impossible

Q 15   What supply shift would be needed to restore the original quantity? right/left/impossible

Q 16   What supply shift would be needed to restore the original price *and* quantity? left/right/impossible

Q 17   Assume that there is a further change in taste such that 2 more tons are demanded at each price (making an increase of 4 tons at each price over the original demand). What is the quantity bought, when price has reached its new equilibrium? _____

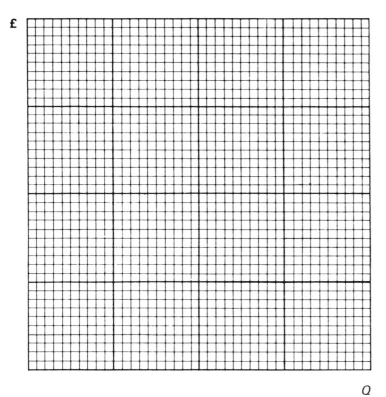

£

Q

Fig. 2.

Q 18   What, therefore, is the change in the quantity bought over the original equilibrium?

_____

Q 19   Why is the change less than 4? _____

_____

Q 20   Is it possible, taking our hypotheses as assumptions, that price could be at any level other than the equilibrium level? Yes/No

Q 21   Is it possible, given our assumptions, that price could remain for a considerable time at any one level other than equilibrium? Yes/No

Q 22   Consider the market for coal. What would be the effect of the following changes on the equilibrium price and quantity of coal?

(1)   The change-over that occurred in the 1920s and 30s from coal to oil firing of ships' boilers.
price up/down/indeterminate; quantity up/down/indeterminate

(2)   An autonomous population shift from the coalfields.
price up/down/indeterminate; quantity up/down/indeterminate

(3)   The introduction of lower-cost mining machinery.
price up/down/indeterminate; quantity up/down/indeterminate

(4)   An increase in the efficiency of coke for central heating.
price up/down/indeterminate; quantity up/down/indeterminate

(5)   The eventual exhaustion of many good coal seams.
price up/down/indeterminate; quantity up/down/indeterminate

(6)   The running out of the North Sea gas resources, and the subsequent increased cost of producing the extra coal required in place of gas.
price up/down/indeterminate; quantity up/down/indeterminate

(7) The more efficient use of labour in the coal industry, and the obsolescence of the steam locomotive, both of which occurred in the 1950s in Britain.
price up/down/indeterminate; quantity up/down/indeterminate

Q 23 In the above seven situations, which curves would shift?

(1) Supply: right/left/no shift. Demand: right/left/no shift

(2) Supply: right/left/no shift. Demand: right/left/no shift

(3) Supply: right/left/no shift. Demand: right/left/no shift

(4) Supply: right/left/no shift. Demand: right/left/no shift

(5) Supply: right/left/no shift. Demand: right/left/no shift

(6) Supply: right/left/no shift. Demand: right/left/no shift

(7) Supply: right/left/no shift. Demand: right/left/no shift

If you answered 23 (6) incorrectly, re-read page 84 in Lipsey. It is *essential* to distinguish between movement along a curve, and shifts in the curve.

Q 24 Consider Fig. 3:

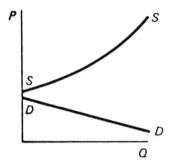

Fig. 3

(1) Will an equilibrium price and quantity be reached in this case? Yes/No

(2) If not, why not? _____

Q 25 Excess demand is a stock, not a flow. T/F

Q 26 Excess supply causes price to rise. T/F

Q 27 A rightward shift in the demand curve will lead to a rise in price and a rise in the equilibrium quantity bought and sold. T/F

Q 28 A leftward shift in the demand curve will lead to a fall in the price and a fall in the equilibrium quantity bought and sold. T/F

Q 29 A leftward shift in the supply curve will lead to a rise in the price and a rise in the equilibrium quantity bought and sold. T/F

Q 30 Excess demand curves usually slope from north-west to south-east. T/F

Q 31 A fall in quantity supplied causes an increase in equilibrium price. T/F

Q 32 If the demand curve slopes down and the supply curve slopes up (i.e. they are normal),

(a) excess demand increases as price increases.
(b) excess supply decreases as price increases.
(c) excess demand increases as price falls.
(d) None of the above is correct.

Q 33 A rightward shift in the demand curve and a leftward shift in the supply curve will

(a) increase price
(b) decrease price
(c) leave price unchanged
(d) have an indeterminate effect on price

Q 34   A leftward shift in the demand curve and a rightward shift in the supply curve will

(a) increase price
(b) decrease price
(c) leave price unchanged
(d) have an indeterminate effect on price

Q 35   A rise in the price of corn (the main food used for pigs) is predicted to

(a) lower the equilibrium quantity of pork
(b) lower the price of pork
(c) have no effect on the market for pork
(d) raise both the equilibrium price and quantity of pork
(e) None of the above answers is correct.

QUESTIONS FOR DISCUSSION

1   Do identical goods have to sell for the same price in one market? If they do not, describe what might be happening. (*Hint*: how is an equilibrium price reached?)

2   Who are the participants in a market? What information about each do we assume? What effect on the adjustment-to-equilibrium process does the conventional 'three tier' system of manufacturer, wholesaler and retailer have, compared with a simple economy of single markets?

3   How do you reconcile the hypothesis that the quantity demanded varies inversely with the price, with the statement that a rise in demand will lead to a rise in price?

4   'The effect of price changes often eludes analysis. For example, two of the food groups that have shown absolute decreases in consumption *per capita* — flour and potatoes — have also shown decreases in price relative to the prices of all goods. Consumption of meat *per capita* has been rising in the face of an increase in relative prices.' This statement about American consumption changes since the 1930s comes from the report of a full-scale investigation into the future patterns of US resource allocation made for the American Government. Do the changes elude your analysis? (Remember that demand depends on variables other than price. Remember also that shifts in demand induced by changes in variables other than the commodity's own price will cause the price to change.) How would you re-word the passage to make clear what you think did happen?

5   Assume that the price and sales of a commodity in 1967 were 25p and 12,000, but in 1968 were 30p and 20,000. How might this have arisen? Illustrate your answer diagrammatically.

CHAPTER 9

Elasticity of Demand and Supply

Assume that a producer can adopt a different method of production which will enable him to produce a larger output, at a lower cost per unit. In order to decide whether or not to change to this method, he wishes to find out how far he will have to drop the price in order that demand will equal his new, larger supply. In other words, he is interested in the responsiveness of *quantity demanded* to changes in price.

Take now the case of a number of purchasers, who, for some reason or other, want more of a commodity that they have been consuming. How much will they have to raise the price which they offer to the producers in order to persuade them to produce the extra amount they want? What, in fact, is the responsiveness of *quantity supplied* to changes in price?

We are so interested in this that we have a special terminology in which we describe all such responsiveness.

We could merely measure the ratio of the actual change in one (e.g. 'a drop in price of 4p') to the actual change in the other (e.g. 'an increase in demand of 1,000 per week'), but it is in fact more useful to measure *proportional* changes.

'The percentage change in x brought about by a percentage change in y' defines the term 'y-elasticity of x'.

In the first paragraph we discussed the 'price elasticity of demand'; in the second the 'price elasticity of supply'; We could also have the 'income elasticity of demand', the 'population elasticity of demand', the 'factor cost elasticity of supply'.

(Price) Elasticity of demand is defined as $-\dfrac{\text{the percentage change in quantity demanded}}{\text{the percentage change in price}}$

Q 1   Define income elasticity of demand. _____

If you were wrong, re-read the explanation above. Then do Q 2.

Q 2   Define price elasticity of supply. _____

Q 3   From which of these sets of information can you deduce the elasticity of either demand or supply for the given commodities, over the relevant range? What are the elasticities, if you can make the deduction?

(a)   At a total level of production of ten tons per day, a change in price of 5p will produce a change in the quantity demanded of ten lb per day.

_____

(b)   An increase in price from 5p to 6p will cause the amount offered by suppliers to double. _____

(c)   An extra 1p per lb will be needed to reduce the demand for butter at 10p per lb by 30 cwt per day. _____

(d)   At a price of £5 per article, we will need to drop our price by 5p in order to sell one tenth as many again. _____

If you had difficulty with these, you are probably not adopting a sufficiently systematic approach. Although it may seem a bore, you should draw rough tables like tables 9.2 and 9.3 on pages 100 and 101 of Lipsey. When you can't fill an element in table 9.3, it will be obvious that you can't deduce the elasticity. Try again.

Q 4   An increase in price of 1p on 5p to 6p is either 20% of 5p or 16.7% of 6p. We seem to have two rival claimants to represent 'the percentage change in price'. How do we circumvent this difficulty? _____

_____

If you couldn't answer Questions 1–3, read pages 100–1 again. This just *has* to be learned. In order to answer the next question you need to have read the Appendix to Chapter 9.

We want to be able to award a unique elasticity to each point on a curve. The result which we get when we use the formula, however, will depend upon how large a ΔP we choose. For example

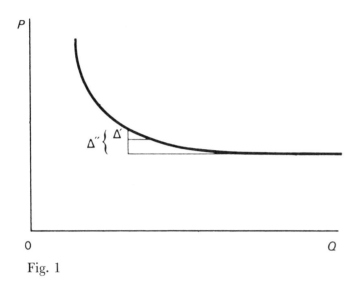

Fig. 1

in this diagram the choice of Δ' will clearly give us a different result from Δ''.

But how big a ΔP should be chosen? Let us take a curve where we know in advance what the elasticity is. We choose a curve where elasticity is always 1—i.e. where the percentage change in quantity demanded always equals the percentage change in price, and where revenue, therefore, remains constant (consider—if the price of Fords increases by 1%, and the number sold drops by 1%[1], Fords will receive the same revenue). Since revenue equals price × quantity, the formula for such a curve (do you remember what it is called? Read Lipsey, p. 102, if not) can be written $p \times q = k$, where k represents the constant revenue.

The formula for the demand curve in Fig. 2 is $pq = 1440$.

TABLE I

Initial price	Change in price	Initial quantity	Change in quantity	Elasticity
12	+5	120		
12	+2	120		
12	+1	120		
12	−1	120		
12	−2	120		
12	−5	120		

_____

[1] Strictly speaking, 0.99%.

Q 5   Now use the method to calculate the elasticity at $p = 12$, $q = 120$ (we know, of course, that it should be 1 – at that point, and at all others). Calculate the elasticity for the 6 price changes in Table I, filling in all the blanks. Calculate the change in quantity to 1 decimal place.

Therefore, the smaller the ΔP, the better is the approximation to the value of the elasticity. The techniques of calculus enable us to assign a unique value to the elasticity. (See Appendix – Lipsey, pp. 109–11.)

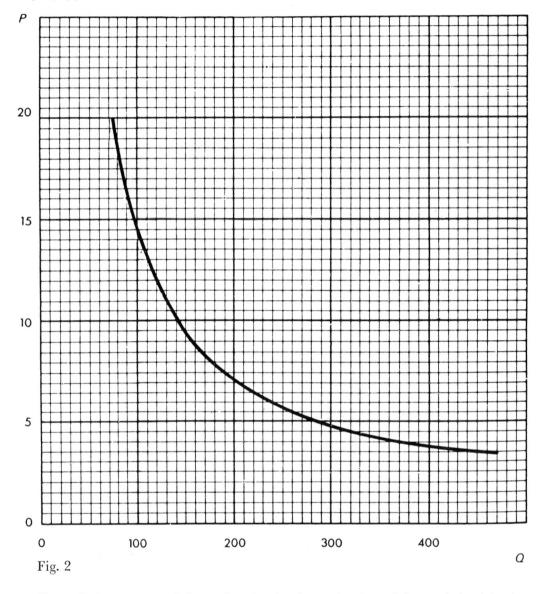

Fig. 2

Since all the necessary information for the determination of demand elasticity is contained in the demand curve, we can deduce elasticity from it.

Q 6   Fig. 3 shows us a demand curve for a commodity:

   (1)   Can we assign a single elasticity to the whole curve? Yes/No

   (2)   What is the elasticity of demand at £3 ? _____

If you answered Q 6 (1) wrongly, do Q 7. Otherwise, go to Q 9.

Q 7   In Fig. 3, (1) what is the elasticity of demand at £2 _____

   (2) and at £4 ? _____

Which demonstrates fairly clearly that you were wrong! Now do Q 8.

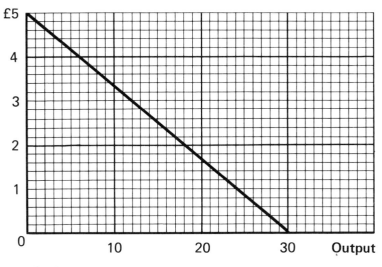

Fig. 3

Q 8   When the demand curve is a straight line, part of the elasticity formula_____ (fill it in) is a constant. Which part?_____

If you were wrong, go back to Q 7, and work through it again.

Q 9   What does a perfectly elastic supply curve at price x mean? _____

_____

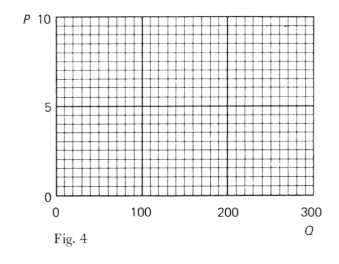

Fig. 4

Q 10   Draw in Fig. 4 a supply curve of infinite elasticity at price 5.

Now draw in a demand curve of infinite elasticity at price 4.
        Will this commodity be traded, and if so, what will be the equilibrium price and quantity? Yes/No _____

Q 11   Given that quantity previously demanded was 100, change in quantity demanded 5, change in price +25p and elasticity of demand is 1.2, what was the price before the change? _____

Q 12   Given that price was £100, quantity demanded 1000 tons, change in quantity demanded is 340 tons and elasticity of demand 17, what is the change in price?

_____

Q 13   Price rises—elasticity of demand is 0.8. Does revenue (i.e., price × quantity) rise or fall? Rise/Fall

Q 14   Price falls—elasticity of demand is 2.3. Does revenue rise or fall? Rise/Fall

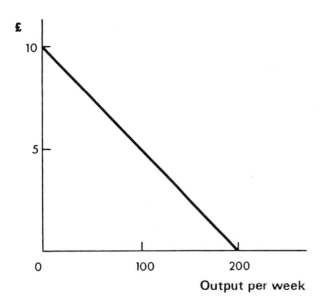

Fig. 5

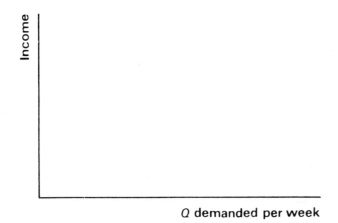

Fig. 6

Q 15   Over what price range does the demand curve in Fig. 5 have less than unit elasticity?

_____

(*Hint*: Calculate $\Delta Q/\Delta P$, which is a constant, and substitute into the elasticity formula to discover the price and quantity for which elasticity equals 1.)

Q 16   Over what price range does the demand curve in Fig. 5 have more than unit elasticity?

_____

Q 17   In Fig. 5, how would elasticity at £7.50 be altered if the figures on the output axis were doubled? doubled/halved/not changed

Q 18   The greater the ease with which other goods can be substituted for it, the greater/less its price elasticity of demand.

You should now read to the end of the chapter.

Q 19   Sketch on Fig. 6 a possible income-demand curve for keg bitter.

Q 20   Define cross-elasticity of demand. _____

Q 21   Consider Ford Fiestas and Vauxhall Chevettes.[1] Will their cross-elasticities probably be
        > 0 or < 0? _____

Q 22   When two supply curves pass through the same point, the flatter is less elastic at that
        point. T/F

Q 23   When a demand curve is of such a shape that, as price changes through the whole of its
        range, quantity demanded changes in such a way that sales revenue (i.e. quantity ×
        price) remains the same, we can assign a single elasticity to every point on the curve,
        and that elasticity is one. T/F

Q 24   A curve has greater than unit elasticity at point x when quantity demanded changes by
        a higher percentage than does price. T/F

Q 25   If the Government subsidizes egg farmers in an effort to reduce drastically the price of
        eggs, economic theory predicts that this policy will be more successful if the demand
        curve is very steep than if it is very flat. T/F

Q 26   If the Government subsidizes egg producers in an effort to increase greatly the con-
        sumption of eggs, economic theory predicts that this policy will be more successful
        if the demand curve for eggs is very steep than if it is very flat. T/F

Q 27   If the elasticity of demand for a commodity exceeds unity, a fall in its price will result
        in an increase in the total amount of money spent by consumers on purchases of that
        commodity. T/F

Q 28   The elasticity of a linear demand curve increases as you travel down the curve. T/F

Q 29   The steeper the demand curve for cigarettes, the more successful an increase in the
        tobacco tax will be, if

        (a)   the aim is to increase government revenue
        (b)   the aim is to reduce government revenue
        (c)   the aim is to reduce diseases caused by smoking

Q 30   A supply curve that is a vertical straight line has an elasticity that is

        (a)   zero
        (b)   more than zero, but less than one
        (c)   one
        (d)   greater than one
        (e)   negative

Q 31   A rightward shift in the supply curve of some product will reduce the equilibrium price
        to a greater degree

        (a)   the more elastic is the demand curve
        (b)   the less elastic is the demand curve
        (c)   the more the elasticity of demand diverges from unity in either direction
        (d)   the closer the elasticity of demand is to unity

Q 32   A rightward shift in the demand curve for a commodity is predicted to increase the
        equilibrium quantity to a greater degree

        (a)   the more inelastic is the supply curve
        (b)   the more elastic is the supply curve
        (c)   the closer the elasticity of supply is to unity
        (d)   the more the elasticity of supply diverges from unity in either direction

_____

[1] Similar cars in the Ford and Vauxhall (General Motors) range.

Q 33   A demand curve which is a horizontal straight line has an elasticity that is

   (a)   zero
   (b)   greater than zero, but less than one
   (c)   one
   (d)   greater than one
   (e)   between one and infinity
   (f)   infinite

Q 34   A good with negative income elasticity is inferior/normal over that range of income.

QUESTIONS FOR DISCUSSION

1   Why do we use percentage changes rather than absolute changes in measuring elasticities? What examples can you think of to illustrate the advantage of this definition?

2   During the Second World War, many families were forced to use margarine for the first time. After the war, laws which had existed in several Allied countries forbidding the colouring of margarine were repealed and manufacturers invested large sums of money to make their product more attractive and to advise consumers of what they had done. In 1957, estimates for the pre- and post-war elasticities of demand for butter were published. One was approximately 1.35 and the other was approximately 0.35. Which do you think was which? What do you think happened to the cross-elasticity of demand between butter and margarine?

3   What do you think the elasticity of supply of fresh fish would be on any one day (i.e., if we related a change in the price on that day to any induced change in the quantity supplied on the same day)? How is this elasticity likely to be influenced by the available methods of refrigeration?

4   If the demand for food is inelastic, does it follow that the demand for sausages is inelastic?

5   At the beginning of 1971 a report was published in the UK by an association of doctors which demonstrated that the link between cigarette smoking and lung cancer is established beyond any reasonable doubt. On the assumption that the possession of tobacco is not made illegal, what recommendations might the Minister of Health make to the Chancellor of the Exchequer? Given that the major part of the cost of cigarettes is taxation, and that revenue from this tax is very substantial, how might the aims of the Minister of Health conflict with those of the Chancellor? Under what price-elasticity-of-demand conditions would they not come into conflict?
   Does the following table, which gives the price of cigarettes, consumption per year per person, and personal disposable income, show any effect of the doctors' report?

	Price for 20 (1963 prices) p	Cigarettes per year per person	Personal Disposable Income (1970 prices) £m
1964	23.1	3,740	30,584
1965	24.5	3,580	31,381
1966	24.2	3,640	32,121
1967	23.6	3,740	32,752
1968	23.5	3,850	33,240
1969	24.1	3,790	33,696
1970	22.9	3,910	34,775
1971	21.5	3,710	35,354

Applications of Price Theory: Price Controls and Agriculture

In this chapter we discuss some of the predictions of the theory of supply and demand which we have already developed, and in doing so, by using the graphical analysis of Chapters 2 to 9, we see how conveniently our conclusions can be expressed. At this stage we can test our theory, for if we can deduce from the theory conclusions which we can show do not correspond to the facts, then we know that some part of our theory is wrong.

Q 1   Which of the following diagrams show in continuous lines the parts of the supply and demand diagram which determine quantity traded in disequilibrium?

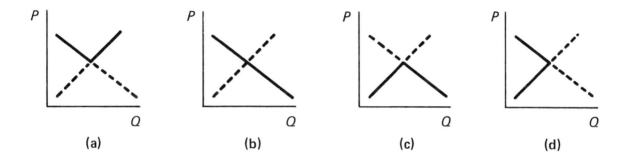

(a)   (b)   (c)   (d)

Fig. 1

MAXIMUM PRICES

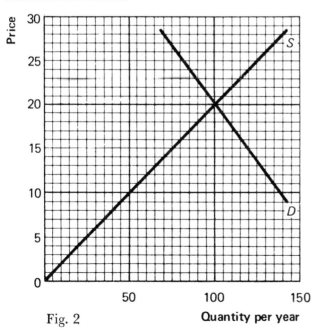

Fig. 2   Quantity per year

Refer to Fig. 2

Q 2   Over what range will a maximum price be ineffective? _____

Q 3   When the maximum price is set at £16, the excess demand will be _____
       _____ per year.

Q 4   What price would consumers be willing to pay for the amount actually supplied at
       the controlled price of £16? _____

Consider now the setting of a MINIMUM price, using the example of labour.

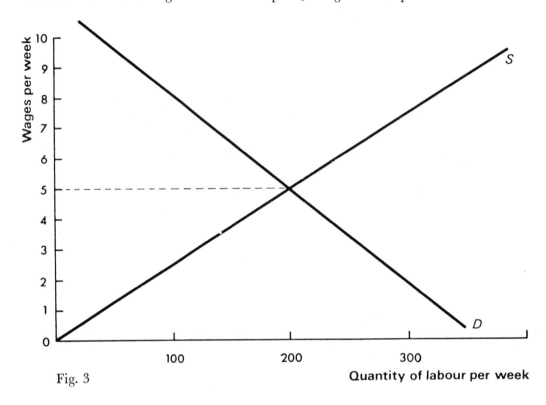

Fig. 3

Refer to Fig. 3.

Q 5   Over what range will the minimum price be ineffective? _____

Q 6   If the minimum wage is set at £7.50, the wages of those employed will fall/rise.

Q 7   Is it possible that the *total* wage bill will rise? Yes/No. If so, under what conditions?
       When the elasticity of demand is _____

Q 8   Under what conditions will the total wage bill fall? _____
       _____

Q 9   Will a black market in labour arise? Yes/No

Q 10   By how much will the minimum wage reduce employment in our example?
       _____

Q 11   Fig. 4 shows a market for private rented accommodation.

       (1) Label the curves. (Check in Lipsey p. 119 if necessary.)

       (2) Illustrate the effect of an increase in population.

       (3) The SL curve is flat because the long-term supply of rented accommodation is
            relatively elastic/inelastic.

       If the rent is set by law at r_c:

       (4) What will be the short-run supply of accommodation? _____

46

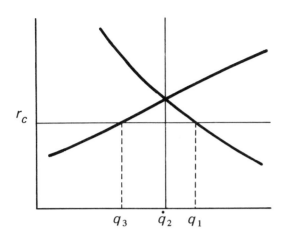

Fig. 4

(5) Would you expect landlords to ask tenants for "key money"?

(6) What will be the long-run supply of accommodation? _____

(7) What will be the eventual housing shortage? _____

Q 12   Fig. 5 shows the demand and supply curves of an agricultural product.

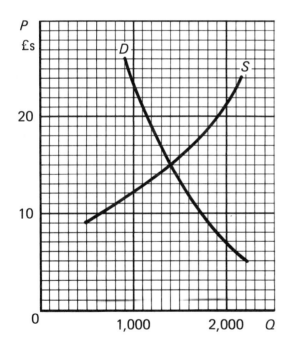

Fig. 5

(1) What is equilibrium revenue to farmers from this crop? _____

Assume that good weather causes an increase in the crop to 1,750.

(2) What is the drop in revenue to the farmers? _____

(3) How much will the Government have to buy in order to restore farmers' income?
Approx. _____

If you had difficulty with Q 12 (3), the way to do it is as follows:
Mark the point on Fig. 5, above the output of 1,750, where price will have to be in order to

yield a revenue of £21,000. Then read off the non-Government demand at that price (the Government will have to buy the rest).

Q 13   Will a *price change* after a supply fluctuation be greater, the greater the elasticity of demand? Yes/No

Illustrate your answer by drawing in the space below a supply-demand diagram with two different supply curves passing through the same equilibrium point. See Fig. 10.6 in Lipsey.

Q 14   What form will the demand curve have to take in order to keep farmers' total revenue constant, whatever the unplanned fluctuations in supply? _____

QUESTIONS FOR DISCUSSION

1   All political parties in the UK agree that rents should be subject to some control. Why do you think the Labour Party believes in more control than the Conservatives? Why should there be any rent control? What do you think might be the effects of rent control on the availability of houses to let?

2   In 1977 the hot summer in the UK caused pretty well all strawberries to ripen during the last week in June and the first in July. Why was this bad for strawberry growers? What industry benefited?

3   Make a list of the apparent absurdities of the Common Agricultural Policy. Then justify (if you can) the policies leading to each.

4   The following article appeared in the Cookery column of the *Guardian* (21.2.69): 'Skate knobs are the jaw muscles of the skate in translucent nodules from an inch to two inches across. They make a delicious substitute for scampi at a fraction of the cost. Being in great demand and short supply, look for them from your fishmonger early in the day.' What does our theory predict will happen to the price of skate knobs? Suggest a reason why this hasn't happened already.

5   In 1974 a scheme was introduced in the UK by which old-age pensioners were supplied by the Government with coupons which they could exchange for purchases of butter and beef. The Government would then refund the face value of the coupons to the shops. What sort of policy was this a substitute for? Why old-age pensioners—why not everybody?

6   Why are agricultural stabilization schemes easier for commodities like wheat than commodities like lettuces?

7   What is wrong with Cup Final ticket touts?

Appendix to Chapter 10

Comparative statistics is the comparison of different states of equilibrium. *Dynamics* is the study of the movement from one position—and not necessarily an equilibrium position—to another. Comparative-static analysis might tell us, for example, that the equilibrium price of strawberries is 12½p a lb in June and 175p in December. Dynamic analysis would study the movement in the actual prices between those times, and if, for example, through a failure in the crop in June there was persistent excess demand at 12½p a lb, it would study behaviour of producers, consumers and market price, assuming that the reactions of each to the disequilibrium situation took time to occur so that the disequilibrium persisted for some period of time.

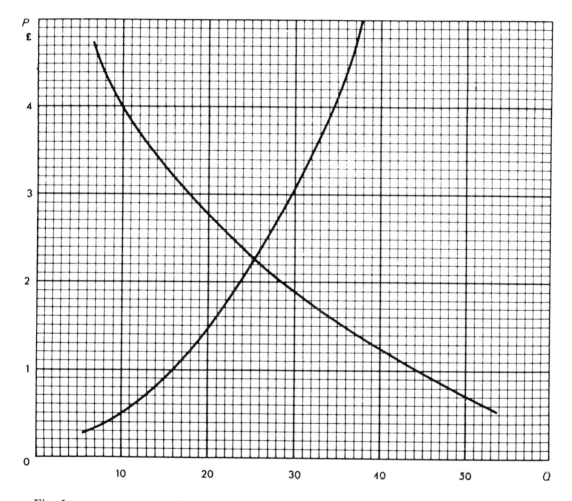

Fig. 1

THE COBWEB

Assume that Fig. 1 is a cobweb diagram of a market for strawberries. Assume also that suppliers expect that the present market price will prevail next year, and that the size of one year's crop must be planned a whole year in advance.

Q 1　A drought in year t causes 10 tons to be supplied instead of $25\frac{1}{2}$.

　　(1)　What is the price in year t ? _____

　　(2)　In what year will price be £2.65p ? $t +$ _____

　　(3)　In what year will quantity supplied be 24 ? $t +$ _____

49

Now go back to the static equilibrium, and assume that, instead of the drought, marvellous weather in year t causes 35 tons to be supplied.

        (4)   What price will clear the market?_____

        (5)   What quantity will be supplied in year $t + 1$?_____

        (6)   What price will clear the market in year $t + 1$?_____

        (7)   How much will be supplied in year $t + 2$? _____

        (8)   What price will clear the market in year $t + 2$?_____

        (9)   What quantity will be supplied in year $t + 3$?_____

Q 2   Is this a stable or unstable adjustment mechanism? _____

Q 3   A demand curve which is flatter than the supply curve will yield a stable/unstable adjustment mechanism.

Q 4   If the slope of the demand curve is equal to minus the slope of the supply curve, prices and quantities will alternate between 2/4/3 levels each, and will _____ reach equilibrium.

Q 5   If the supply curve is, over the relevant range, less elastic than the demand curve, the process is stable/unstable.

Q 6   The stability of the process depends on the relative slopes of the demand and supply curves, and on nothing else. T/F

QUESTIONS FOR DISCUSSION

1   What is the difference between static and dynamic analysis? What are some of the limitations of statics?

2   Draw a graph from the following equations:

$$D_t = 100 - 6p_t$$

$$S_t = 4p_{t-1}$$

where S and D are supply and demand and where the subscripts t refer to time-periods. Is the system stable or unstable? Formulate a different demand equation that would change your conclusion.

3   In 1976 a 25% shortfall in the potatoes crop trebled their price. (What was the elasticity of demand for potatoes?) Strawberries, however, were plentiful and cheap. One farmer, known to one of the authors, decided to plant fewer potatoes and more strawberries for 1977. Was he wise or foolish?

4   The simple cobweb assumes that producers base their production plans for next year's output on this year's prices. They are not assumed to learn anything from previous price fluctuations. One way of changing this assumption to one perhaps more realistic is to introduce the idea of a 'normal' price, and to assume that future production plans are based upon some average of actual market price and this 'normal' price.

    Construct a supply-demand schedule on graph paper, and let the 'normal' price be the equilibrium price. Start off a cobweb with an unforeseen drop in supply, caused perhaps by unusually bad weather, but assume that the price which producers expect to receive in the next time-period equals actual price + normal price, all divided by two.

    Trace out the cobweb process. Is it more or less stable than the simpler version? What are the stability/instability conditions now?

CHAPTER 11

Applications of Price Theory: International Trade

Q 1   What term do economists use for a situation where countries do not trade with each other? _____

Q 2   The Terms of Trade are measured by: $\dfrac{\text{the (a) _____ of (b) _____}}{\text{the (c) _____ of (d) _____}}$

Q 3   Fig. 1 shows a Production Possibility Set for a country producing two (bundles of) commodities.

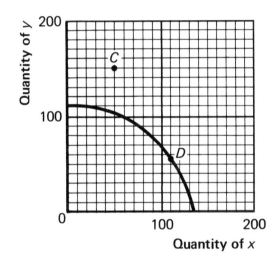

Fig. 1

(a)   In autarky, this is coincident with the _____ .
(b)   If 100 x are produced, what is the most y that can be produced? _____
(c)   If this country exports x, and the Terms of Trade are 0.5, can the country consume at point C? Yes/No
(d)   Whatever the Terms of Trade, since a country can choose what to export and what to import, international trade can always expand the Consumption Possibility Set. T/F
(e)   Assume initial production to be at point D on Fig. 1. If the x–y Terms of Trade are 2 (i.e. the price of y is twice that of x), what production of x and y will maximize the country's Consumption Possibility Set?_____

Q 4   Fig. 2 shows the domestic Supply and Demand for a typical traded good.

(a)   If the world price is 13, how much will be imported/exported? _____
(b)   If the world price is 8, how much will be imported/exported? _____
(c)   What will be the change in domestic price of the imported good in (b)? Increase/decrease of _____

(d) If the domestic demand curve shifts 400 units to the left, and the world price is 7, what will be the change in domestic price, and quantity imported?_____

Q 5 (a) When exports exceed imports, a country has a Trade _____ .
     (b) When imports exceed exports, a country has a Trade _____ .
     (c) If the exchange rate changes from $1.6 = £1 to $1.75 = £1, the pound has appreciated/depreciated.

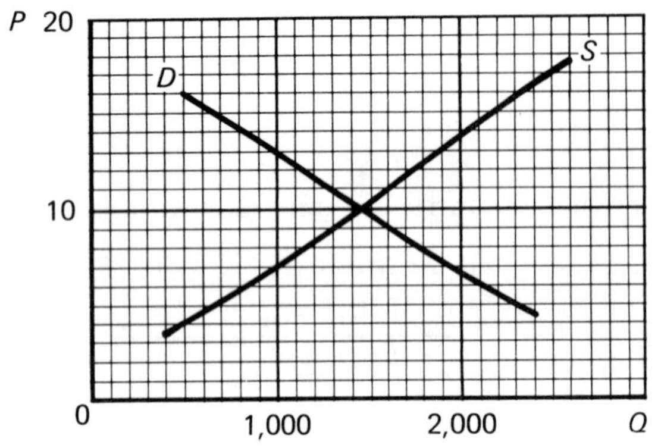

Fig. 2 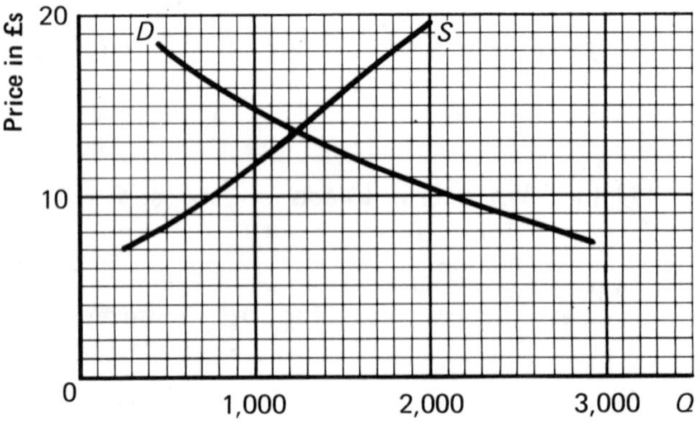   Fig. 3

Q 6 Fig. 3 shows the domestic Supply and Demand for an imported good. The world price (in dollars) of this good is $16. How much will be imported if the exchange rate is:

     (a) £1 = $2 _____
     (b) £1 = $1.5 _____
     (c) £1 = $1.25 _____

Q 7 For a country whose total production and consumption is small in world terms:

     (a) An appreciation of the domestic currency increases/decreases exports and increases/decreases imports.
     (b) A depreciation of the domestic currency increases/decreases exports and increases/decreases imports.

Q 8 If at current prices Germans are indifferent to whether they buy identical peaches from France or Italy, and if peaches cost 5 francs a kilo in France, and $12\frac{1}{2}$ lire a kilo in Italy, what information does this contain about the franc-lire exchange rate?

_____

_____

Q 9 If at current prices Italians are indifferent to whether they buy identical tyres from France (where they cost 60 francs) or Germany (where they cost 35 marks), what information, *assuming the answer to Q 8*, do you now have about the lire-mark exchange rate? _____

Q 10 Assume a two-country world (Britain and America) and that each country's demand for imports from the other country has an elasticity greater than unity. Assume a diagram plotting the demand and supply curves of dollars.
      In which direction will the stated curves shift, and what will happen to the equilibrium exchange rate in each of the following circumstances?

     (1) There is a large inflation in Britain while the US price level is steady.
          The demand curve for dollars shifts left/right and the pound rises/falls in value.

52

(2)   Americans develop a strong taste for British sportscars.
      The supply curve for dollars shifts left/right and the pound rises/falls in value.

(3)   The Americans put a heavy import duty on all British goods.
      The supply curve for dollars shifts left/right and the pound rises/falls in value.

(4)   As a result of a rise in the short-term rate of interest in London, there is a greatly increased desire to make short-term loans in London.
      The supply curve for dollars shifts left/right and the pound rises/falls in value.

(5)   As a result of the election of a radical government, people holding pounds become convinced that the pound will soon fall in value.
      The demand curve for dollars shifts left/right and the pound rises/falls in value.

(6)   Experience shows that, in spite of some fluctuations in the rate over a month or two, the long-term expectation under (5) was mistaken.
      The supply curve for dollars shifts left/right and the pound rises/falls in value.

We can see from the last question that the analysis of the effect of shifts in the supply and demand of currency, and the mechanism which exists to establish an equilibrium exchange rate, is analogous to the analysis of the market for any commodity.

Q 11   What do the following people demand and supply in the foreign-exchange market?

(1)   An American importer of English antiques _____

(2)   A London businessman who wishes to invest on the New York Stock Exchange?
      _____

(3)   A Swiss banker who holds pounds as a reserve currency for international payments and believes that the pound will be devalued _____

(4)   An American couple holidaying in Scotland _____

(5)   A German importer of American-made refrigerators that are transported in Norwegian ships and insured with Lloyds of London _____

(6)   An American company that wishes to use its accumulated profits to establish branch plants in Canada and France _____

(7)   American firms located in Canada and France that need to pay interest to bond-holders who are residents in the United States _____

QUESTIONS FOR DISCUSSION

1   In 1964, when devaluation was being contemplated in the UK, two eminent bankers wrote to *The Times* (21.11.64). They said that devaluation would be 'demoralizing to the whole nation, would represent a permanent and substantial movement of the terms of trade against us, and would give, at best, only a very temporary fillip to our competitive position'. You should not continue until you have worked out how their argument is inconsistent.

2   During early 1979, the British exchange rate improved slightly when OPEC put the price of oil up, and rather more when the Labour government fell in March. Provide explanations.

3   If you return from a trip abroad you will find you get a lower rate of exchange on the foreign coins in your pocket than on the foreign paper money in your wallet. Can you think why? There is a limit to the amount by which the rate on coins can sink below the rate on paper money. Can you think what might set this limit? You may also find that your bank will not even accept some heavy low-value foreign copper coins. Why? You will also receive a worse rate for exceptionally high value notes. Why?

4   'It finds itself in the extraordinary situation of being like a well-established business whose directors *think* it is doing well, but can't tell you for sure because there is no breakdown of profits between the various departments, nor is there any accurate measure of how rapidly the departments are growing. In short the Isle of Man has no set of national accounts, and it couldn't with any degree of certainty tell you whether it's heading for a balance of payments crisis, or to what tune it is in the black.'

This is taken from an article about the Isle of Man which appeared in *The Times* (27.9.70). How can part of the UK have its own 'balance of payments crisis'? What might happen to correct it? If the Isle of Man were to close its frontiers and mint its own currency, in what different manner might it correct this 'crisis'?

CHAPTER 13

Effects of Changes in Prices and Incomes

Behind every market demand curve—and remember, all the demand curves in the workbook so far have described the total, i.e. market, demand for a commodity—there are all the independent decisions made by all the people who form the market.

Q 1   What do we take as the basic decision unit for the theory of demand? _____

_____

THE BUDGET LINE

Q 2   The price of *x* is £5 each, of *y* 50p each. These are the only goods that I consume, and I receive an income of £15 a week. I neither borrow nor save. Construct a budget-line diagram for one week's purchases on Fig. 1.

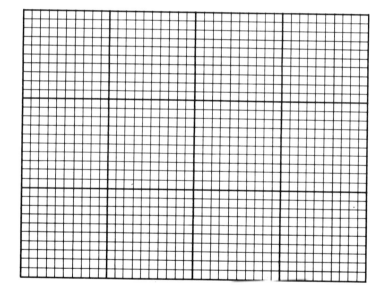

Fig. 1

(1)   Can I buy any combination of *x* and *y* that does not lie on the budget line? One lying above/below the line/neither

(2)   My income rises to £20 a week. Which good, or goods, will have to change price in order to restore my original budget line? *x*/*y*/both

(3)   On the original budget line I decided to consume 10 *y* (how much *x* did I consume? _____). My income then fell by £5. Draw in my new budget line. By how much will the price of *x* have to change (given that *y* remains constant) in order to make it possible for me to consume the same amount of *x* and *y* as before? up/down by £ _____

(4) What would the new price of y have to be, if x had remained at £5, for me to be able to consume the bundle of goods described in (3)? _____

(5) If I still consume 3 of x after the price of x changes by the amount required in (3), what does this imply about my elasticity of demand for x? _____

_____

(6) The budget line shifts its intercepts to $5x$ and $20y$. Could this be the consequence of one price change from the original data in (2) above? Yes/No

(7) ... of an income change only? Yes/No

(8) ... of two price changes? Yes/No

(9) ... of one price change and an income change? Yes/No

Q 3   'The relative price of x has risen, but that of y remained constant.' Could you illustrate this on a diagram? Yes/No

Q 4   If all money prices are multiplied by p, by what must income be multiplied in order to restore your original command over goods? _____

Q 5   In the budget line of Q 2(6) what is the cost, in terms of x forgone, of $10y$? _____

Check your answers, and if you got any wrong, re-read pp. 155–9, and do Q 6.

Q 6   Construct a budget line on Fig. 2.

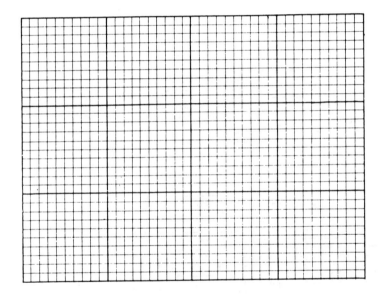

Fig. 2

(1) Assume that the price of the good measured along the horizontal axis doubles. The budget line will cut the horizontal axis

    (a) half the previous distance from the origin
    (b) twice the previous distance from the origin

(2) Assume that the change in Q 6 (1) takes place, but income doubles.

    (a) The original budget line will be restored
    (b) The new budget line will cut the vertical axis half the original distance from the origin, and the horizontal axis at the original distance
    (c) The new budget line will cut the vertical axis twice the original distance from the origin, and the horizontal axis at the original distance

Consider for a moment why budget lines are straight. If you understand this, do question 8. If not, do question 7.

Q 7   First of all, re-read Lipsey pp. 155—7. Now look at Fig. 3.

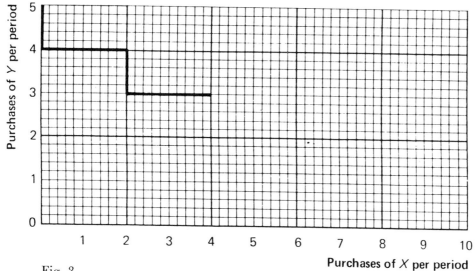

Fig. 3

The price of Y is £2, the price of X is £1. My income is £10 per consumption period. Assume I start by consuming 5 Y.

(1)   How many X do I consume?_____

(2)   Now I decide to consume one less Y. How many X can I consume? _____
_____

(3)   Now I decide to consume 3 Y instead of 4. How many more X can I consume?
_____

(On Fig. 3 the lines representing the drop in consumption of Y and the increase in consumption of X are filled in.)

(4)   Now I decide to consume 2 Y instead of 3. How many more X can I consume?
_____

Check your answers. Sketch on Fig. 3 the lines representing the drop in consumption of Y from 3 to 2, and the increase in the consumption of X. Continue until no Y are consumed, and 10 X. The line joining the outside points of the staircase is the budget line. It is straight, just like a staircase, because the 'tread' and 'riser' of the staircase are always in the same relation to each other. This is because relative prices are constant; one Y always trades for $2X$. Now do Q 8.

Q 8   Assume a *budget* line as in Fig. 4:

This would mean

(a)   the more of one good I consume, the cheaper it gets
(b)   the more of one good I consume, the more expensive it gets
(c)   the goods' relative prices are constant, but my income is changing.

Check your answer. If you were right carry on. If not, back to Q 7.

So one individual's budget line is straight because prices are what he finds in the shops, and do not change according to the level or pattern of his purchases.

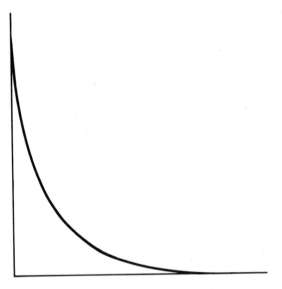

Fig. 4

REAL AND MONEY INCOME

Money income of a household is the amount of money that a household receives per period—measured, of course, in the appropriate currency.

Real income is the purchasing power of that money income—or, to be rigorous—the set of all combinations of goods that it is possible for the household to purchase.

It is sometimes impossible to tell when a household's real income has risen or fallen. Consider a fall in the price of records, together with no other price change. You can now buy more records, or the same number of records and more of something else with what you save on your previous record bill. This is a clear rise in real income—as an increase in the price of records would be a clear fall. But now consider a fall in the price of records but an increase in the price of books—the price changes being such that, in order to consume the same amount as before of one of them, you have to consume less of the other. Perhaps this suits you; you like records, and can now buy more of them. Perhaps however, you would prefer to buy more books, and now have to make do with less, or cut down on your records. All we can say is that real income has changed—the set of possible bundles of commodities now contains some that it did not before, and no longer contains some that it used to. To talk about a rise or a fall is inappropriate (at least without further tools of analysis).

Q 9   Prices double, money income rises by 25%. What is the change in real income?
up/down by _____

Q 10   Real income drops by $\frac{2}{7}$, prices rise by $\frac{1}{6}$. What is the change in money income?
up/down by _____

We have seen that the effects of a change in absolute price can be completely compensated by a change in the absolute level of income.[1] It cannot therefore be absolute prices which determine the allocation of resources, since we have just implied that it is possible that a change in absolute price need have no effect at all on the real components of the economy. The allocation of resources is determined by the *ratios* of absolute prices.

Q 11   These are called _____ prices.

INFLATION AND DEFLATION (pp. 160–1)

Three concepts are introduced here.

---

[1] Provided that you have no cash balances or other assets whose value is fixed in money terms.

(a)   The price level. This is the average level of money prices.
(b)   Inflation. This is a rise in the price level.
(c)   Deflation. This is a fall in the price level.

Q 12   When the price level is constant, a rise in the money price of a good means that it has become more expensive in terms of other goods. T/F

Q 13   There is no change in income that can duplicate a fall in the prices of some goods, other prices remaining constant. T/F

Q 14   The slope of the budget line indicates the opportunity cost of one commodity in terms of other commodities. T/F

QUESTIONS FOR DISCUSSION

1   Draw a budget line for a teenager whose total consumption out of her allowance is for cokes and records. Cokes cost 12p each, records cost £1.44p, and her allowance is £3.80 a week. Draw a new budget line illustrating what happens when the price of cokes increases to 18p. Assume that her allowance is cut to £3.33p. Draw her new budget line and determine what price increases would have had the same effect as the cut in her allowance.

2   Explain why an increase in money income shifts the budget line outward and an increase in prices shifts it inward.

3   What is the significance of the slope of the budget line?

4   Smith and Jones each have £50 and each plans to buy a tent and a sleeping bag for a camping trip they intend to take next month. The price of the tent is £30 and the price of the sleeping bag is £10. Smith buys his equipment now and stores it in the basement. Jones keeps his money in the bank, but when he goes to buy his equipment in a month's time he finds that prices have changed. The price of the tent has gone up to £33 and the price of the sleeping bag has gone up to £11. Who is better off, Smith or Jones? Which of the boys would have been better off if the price of the sleeping bag had gone up to £12, but if the price of the tent had fallen to £26? If the price of the sleeping bag has risen to £15 and the price of the tent has fallen to £25, which of them is better off? Who is better off if the price of the sleeping bag has fallen to £9 and the price of the tent to £24?

5   In 1977 the price level in Britain rose by 8%, and the earnings of Ford workers rose by 16%. In 1978, Ford workers negotiated a pay rise of 17%. What was the real rise in Ford wages over the two years if inflation in 1978 was

(a) 8%   (b) 10%   (c) 12%?

CHAPTER 14

Theories of Household Demand

You should read now up to page 175; that is, the whole of the section on Utility Theory.

The theory of diminishing marginal utility is one of the cornerstones of economics. It provides the explanation for the downward slope of the demand curve.

Q 1   The hypothesis of diminishing marginal utility states that for any individual consumer the value that he attaches to successive units of a particular commodity will diminish steadily as his total consumption of that commodity increases, given one assumption. What is that assumption? *the consumption of all other commodities held constant.*

Q 2   'The hypothesis of diminishing marginal utility implies that I gain six times as much satisfaction from my first bun at tea time as from my sixth.' T/F✓

Q 3   'The hypothesis of diminishing marginal utility implies that I gain six times as much satisfaction from my second car as I do from my third television.' T/F✓

We must now make a step from 'attaching value' to commodities to predicting actual market behaviour. We do this by means of the hypothesis of utility maximization.

Q 4   Define the hypothesis of utility maximization. _____

_____

Q 5   Does the prediction that free goods will be consumed until their *MU* is zero mean that my behaviour in not going now for a free service on the car, when I should quite like to, is inconsistent with the hypothesis of utility maximization? Yes/No

If you answered this incorrectly, then you have forgotten what economics means by cost. Read p. 53 again.

Q 6   Derive from the total utility map on Fig. 1 the implied marginal utility map, and draw it in on the second graph.

(1)   What is the marginal utility of the third unit? _____

(2)   What is the marginal utility of the fifth unit? _____

(3)   Does the behaviour of the individual support or oppose our hypothesis?

_____

Check your answers. If you got Q 6 wrong (or are not confident that you know why you got it right), do Q 7. If not, go on to Q 8.

Q 7   (1)   The hypothesis of diminishing marginal utility states that, as you add to your consumption of a particular good, the *extra* utility which you derive gets progressively larger/smaller.

(2)   Which of the two diagrams in Fig. 2 represents diminishing marginal utility? (a)/(b)

60

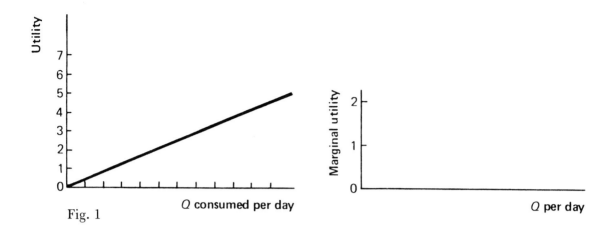

Fig. 1

(3) Diminishing marginal utility means that total utility

    (a)   rises at a constant rate
    (b)   rises at first, then falls
    (c)   rises, but at a decreasing rate

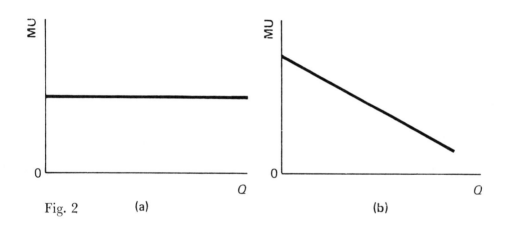

Fig. 2   (a)   (b)

Check your answers. If you got part (3) wrong, read Lipsey, page 166 again. Diminishing marginal utility means that additions to total utility get smaller as consumption is increased, and may become negative.

As long as total utility is increasing—that is, as long as marginal utility is positive, however small—the curve which represents total utility will of course go on rising, however slowly.

    (4)   Which of the two diagrams in Fig. 3 corresponds to diminishing *marginal* utility?

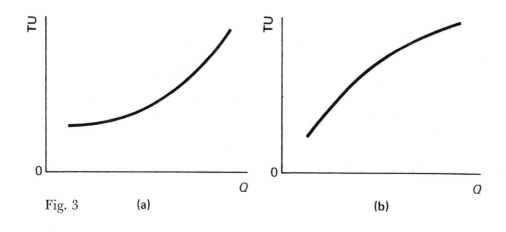

Fig. 3   (a)   (b)

Q 8   (1)   Draw on Fig. 4(b) the approximate total utility curve derived from Fig. 4(a).

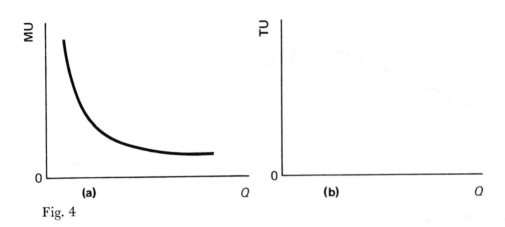

Fig. 4

(2)   Draw on Fig. 5(b) the approximate total utility curve derived from Fig. 5(a).

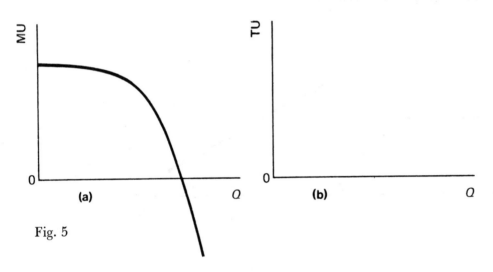

Fig. 5

You should now re-read carefully pages 169 and 170.

Q 9   Write down the utility maximization rule for *n* commodities

$\underline{MU \text{ of good } 1} =$ _____ . . . = _____

Assume that a consumer is *not* in the above utility-maximization position. This means that there is some commodity (including money itself) from the additional consumption of which more utility could be derived than cost incurred, *which implies that* there is some commodity where marginal utility is lower than the price being paid for it.

Q 10   The reason why *at least two* commodities must be involved in this way in any out-of-equilibrium behaviour is because the cost of one commodity *is* the amount of _____ sacrificed, measured in terms of money. Therefore 'too much' of one *means* '_____' of another.

Q 11   Given the information below and given a continuity assumption, construct the two *MU* curves on Fig. 6 (*x* and *y* account for a small proportion of the consumers' total expenditure). *Hint*: let your *MU* scale run from 0–150. You can represent higher *MU*s roughly by allowing your *MU* curve to become almost vertical out of the top of the graph. So do not bother to plot points higher than 150 accurately.

62

Good x MU	Unit consumed (per day)	Good y MU	Unit consumed (per day)
∞	1	200	1
500	3	150	2
70	4	110	3
60	5	50	5
51	6	10	6
50	8	5	8
47	10	0	10

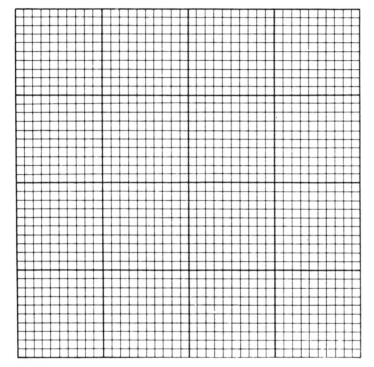

Fig. 6

(1) If at a price of 50p each 8 x are consumed, how many will be consumed (the price of all other goods being constant) if the price of x rises to 60p?

_____

(2) If good y costs 7p and good x costs 84p, how many x will be consumed given that 8 y are consumed? _____

If you answered Q 11 correctly, go to Q 13. But if you could not see how to do question 11, parts (1) and (2), look again at Q 9. (If you have not done this correctly, re-read Lipsey p. 170). This gives you the utility-maximization formula

$$\frac{MU \text{ of good 1}}{\text{price of good 1}} = \frac{MU \text{ of good 2}}{\text{price of good 2}}$$

If you have enough information to fill in three of these quantities (the two marginal utilities and the two prices), then you can calculate the fourth. It merely means working out a simple equation like, for example, $\frac{6}{4} = \frac{z}{3}$. The tables in Q 11 give this information. Look again at Q 11 (2). Straightaway we can fill in the price of y and the price of x (call x good 1 and y good 2):

$$\frac{}{84} = \frac{}{7}$$

63

The table for the *MU* of good *y* says that if 8 *y* are consumed daily, the *MU* of *y* will be 5. So we have now:

$$\frac{}{84} = \frac{5}{7}$$

We can work out by algebra that the *MU* of good *x* must be 60.

Looking back at the *MU* table for good *x*, we see that if the *MU* is 60, then 5 units are consumed daily. And this is the answer. Answer Q 11 (1) again, and do Q 12.

Q 12 (1) Using the data of Q 11, what is the *MU* of *x* if at a price of 11p three *y* are consumed per day, and *x* cost 5p each? _____

(2) What is the daily consumption of *x*? _____

As you can see, the part of the graph where the curves shoot up and away is irrelevant to these considerations. This illustrates one of the reasons why bread is cheaper than caviare.

CONSUMERS' SURPLUS

Q 13 The figure below is a typical demand/supply diagram. What, approximately, is consumers' surplus per period of time? (1) _____

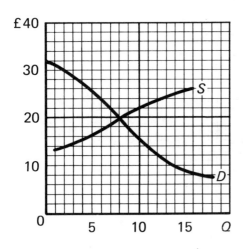

Here is how you calculate it. The demand curve tells you that if the price were £31, one item would be bought. Since the price is (2) _____ the person who would have been prepared to pay £31 is receiving a surplus of £31 − £20 = £11. The second item would have sold for £30, so the person who would have been prepared to pay £30 receives a surplus of £10. The third item would have sold for (3) _____ , with a consequent surplus of (4) _____ .

The total consumers' surplus is the sum of all the surpluses up to where the curves cross — so the eighth unit sold is accompanied by no surplus.

INDIFFERENCE THEORY

Q 14 A utility-maximizing household may allocate its weekly income between the purchase of *X* and *Y*. It chooses to buy 22*Y* and 10*X*.

(1) It is questioned about the bundles of *X* and *Y* which would leave it better off, or worse off, than its choice of 22*Y* and 10*X*. The questions, and its answers, are tabulated in Table 1. 'W' in the 'Evaluation' column means that the bundle would leave it worse off—i.e. it would prefer 22*Y* and 10*X*—'B' means that the bundle would leave it better off, and 'I' means that it would be indifferent between that bundle, and its original choice of 22*Y* and 10*X*.

64

From the data in Table 1, construct its *indifference curve* on Fig. 7, plotting the bundles of X and Y which would give it equal utility to 22Y and 10X.

(2) From the data given so far, can you infer the relative prices of X and Y? Yes/No
If Yes, X cost about _____ as much as Y.

(3) The price of Y doubles, and the price of X falls to one-third of its previous value; the household's money income remains the same. Can the household move to a higher indifference curve? Yes/No
Are you able to say that the household will definitely decrease its consumption of Y? Yes/No
If Yes, can you say that it will fall below any particular level?
If Yes, below (roughly) what level? _____

TABLE 1

Amount of Y	Amount of X	Evaluation
5	34	W
26	7	W
18	11	W
24	6	W
16	12	W
8	28	W
25	11	B
14	18	B
12	22	B
24	8	W
7	33	B
6	37	B
13	16	W
25	12	B
17	13	W
21	10	W
19	14	B
11	18	W
28	8	B
15	15	W
25	9	B
17	15	B
12	20	W
8	18	W
13	24	B
9	30	B
21	11	I
11	22	W
6	40	B
9	22	W
6	32	W
15	17	B
20	12	B
13	23	B
9	25	W
17	17	B
7	28	W

Amount of Y	Amount of X	Evaluation
11	25	B
7	31	I
22	12	B
12	28	B
29	7	B
6	33	W
5	37	W
5	36	W
9	28	B

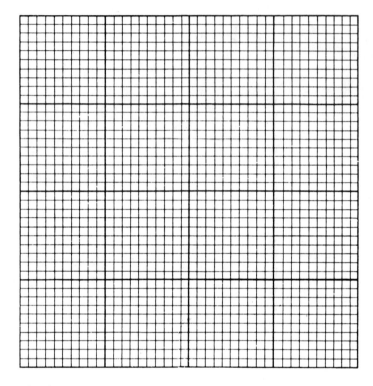

Fig. 7

Q 15 The following bundles of clothes and food give a household the same level of satisfaction, when consumed during a given period of time.

Bundle no.	Quantity of food	Quantity of clothes
1	30	10
2	25	12
3	20	14
4	15	17
5	12	20
6	7	40

(1) Construct the appropriate indifference curve on Fig. 8.
(2) The household would prefer any point to the right/left of the curve.
(3) Assume that the household is a utility maximizer, and consumes 10 units of food
and 23 units of clothes. What are the relative prices of clothes and good?
Clothes are roughly _____ as cheap as food.
(4) Draw in a budget line which corresponds to a consumption of 35 units of food if
no clothes are consumed, given that food and clothes cost the same price per unit.

(a) If the household is a utility maximizer, will it consume on the indifference curve which you have already drawn? Yes/No

(b) Have you enough information to tell where the new point of utility-maximizing consumption will be? Yes/No

(c) Can you at least say that there are any parts of the budget line which cannot contain the new point of consumption? Yes/No

(d) If your answer to (c) was Yes, what parts are they?_____

If your answer was No, look again at Fig. 8. All points on the budget line to the left of Clothes, 14 and to the right of Clothes, 26 are below even the old indifference curve. So they must be inferior to all points on the new, superior, indifference curve.

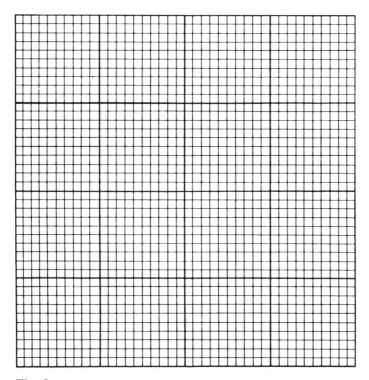

Fig. 8

You should now re-read the section on the derivation of demand curves from indifference maps.

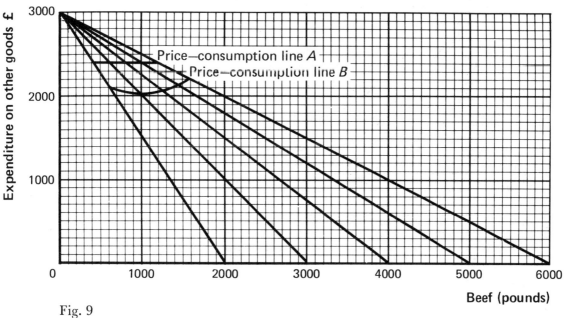

Fig. 9

Q 16 On Fig. 9 sketch in (using two different colours) indifference maps that could lead to price-consumption lines A and B.

From the price-consumption lines, derive demand curves A and B and enter on Fig. 10 below.

(1) For the demand curve derived from price-consumption line B, how much beef will be consumed if its price is £0.80? _____

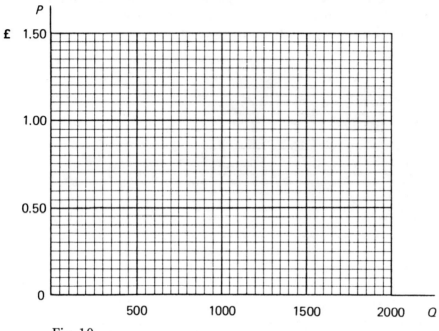

Fig. 10

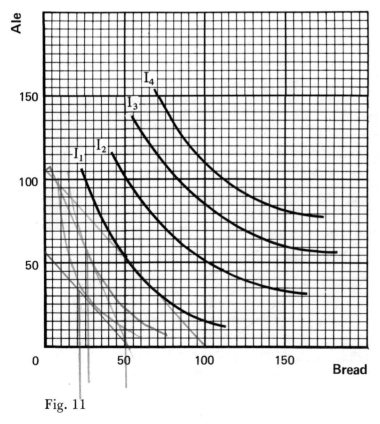

Fig. 11

68

(2) For the demand curve derived from price-consumption line B, how much beef will be consumed if its price is £1.25? _____

Q 17 An indifference curve includes

  (a) constant quantities of one good with varying quantities of another.
  (b) the prices and quantities of two goods that can be purchased for a given sum of money.
  (c) all combinations of two goods that will give the same level of satisfaction to the household.
  (d) combinations of goods whose marginal utilities are equal.

Q 18 Households may attain consumption of a higher indifference curve by all but which of the following?

  (a) an increase in money income
  (b) a reduction in absolute prices
  (c) a proportionate increase in money income and in absolute prices
  (d) a change in relative prices caused by a reduction in one price.

THE INCOME EFFECT AND THE SUBSTITUTION EFFECT

No one reacts to a drop in the price of eggs by going into a supermarket and saying to himself 'Half a dozen more eggs this week because of the substitution effect, and an extra couple because of the income effect'. In order to make an operational difference between these two reasons, economists examine what *would* have been his change in purchases, had his money income also changed in such a way that he would have remained on the same indifference curve. This hypothetical change is called the Substitution Effect, and the difference between the hypothetical position and the new actual position is called the Income Effect.

Q 19 Assume that an individual consumes two commodities, bread and ale. His income is £30 per week, ale costs 30p a pint, and bread 15p a loaf. (He does not save.) Construct his weekly budget line on Fig. 11, which is an indifference map.

  (1) How much bread does he eat? _____

Now assume that a shortage of wheat causes the price of bread to double. Draw in his new budget line, and construct the notional budget line required to analyse his change in consumption into its two components.

  (2) What is the substitution effect on his consumption of bread? _____

  (3) What is the income effect on his consumption of bread? _____

  (4) What is the substitution effect on his consumption of ale? _____

  (5) What is the income effect on his consumption of ale? _____

QUESTIONS FOR DISCUSSION

1   Draw a budget line assuming some given income and money prices of two goods X and Y. Show a 10% rise in the money price of X. Show a 10% fall in the money price of Y. Compare these two cases with respect to the substitution effect, the income effect, and the total effect of the change.

2   The original good for which it was asserted that the demand curve sloped upward was that of wheat in the diet of farm labourers in England in the last century. Explain why more wheat might be consumed when its price rose, and less when its price fell. What conditions are necessary for such 'Giffen goods' to exist?

3   Would you say that the behaviour of a heavy cigarette-smoker, whose consumption of cigarettes increased, despite increased tax levels on cigarettes, as he got older (but not richer) was consistent with the hypothesis of diminishing marginal utility? We have a special word—

'addiction'—for such behaviour. Does this suggest to you that we implicitly expect the hypothesis of diminishing marginal utility to be true for most commodities?

4   When the Department of the Environment, which is the UK Ministry responsible for building and improving roads, evaluates the effects of, for example, a road improvement on a route from a city to a seaside town, it looks, among other things, at the saving in journey time which will benefit those already using the route. It calculates this benefit by multiplying the number of existing users by the value of the time saving. There will also be some *extra* travellers, attracted by the faster journey. Benefit to them is calculated by multiplying the number of new users by the value of the time saving, *and dividing by two*. What assumption about the demand curve for journeys along the road is being made here?

CHAPTER 15

The Theory of Demand: Measurements and Tests

QUESTIONS FOR DISCUSSION

1   Why are we interested only in refutable theories? Shouldn't we prefer irrefutable ones? (*Hints*: What good is a theory that predicts that anything can happen? A theory that says that only some things can happen must say that other things cannot happen.)

2   What do we mean when we say that there is a ready-made alibi to explain away any apparent refutation of some theory? Why do we say that tastes provide such an alibi in demand theory? What would we need to do in order to remove this particular alibi?

3   After the price of coffee quadrupled in 1976, due initially to adverse weather conditions in the producing countries, the price of cocoa increased by almost as much. Provide an explanation for this. Do you think that cocoa is a substitute for coffee? Might it be a complement?

4   Make a detailed list of your purchases of consumer goods—other than 'consumer durables' like tape-recorders—for two weeks for which you have the same amount of money to spend. After you have done this, go over the list and look for possible inconsistencies—where one evening one week, for example, you have had two pints of beer, an Indian meal and a rear stalls cinema seat, whereas in the other week you might have had three pints of beer, a meal and a front stalls seat. See how many 'inconsistencies' were real inconsistencies, and how many were just due to a fluctuation in taste, or a change in conditions like the weather. Using hindsight, do you think you could have derived more satisfaction from a different allocation of your budget?

5   When real incomes have risen to the extent that every household has one car and most have two, what would you then think would happen to the income elasticity of demand for automobiles?

6   Use some of the following propositions to develop a framework within which you might attempt to identify an income demand curve for beer or discuss how they complicate such an attempt.

   (1)   British miners' incomes have risen three times as much as the average in the last three years—by 20% in real terms.

   (2)   Consumption of beer in South Wales, Nottinghamshire and South Yorkshire has increased by 4% in the last three years.

   (3)   Although Czech miners are much poorer than British miners, they are at least 25% richer than any other Czech skilled workers—even those in the steel industry.

   (4)   30% more beer is drunk in Czech mining areas than in steel producing areas.

   (5)   Czech beer (mainly from Pilsen) is of far better quality than British beer.

7   Draw a diagram that illustrates the identification problem in the measurement of demand and supply curves.

8   Criticize both of the following statements:

   (a) 'Since I have calculated that the elasticity of demand for reproductions of the Mona Lisa is 0.89, I intend to corner the market, and sell them at a high price, thereby becoming very rich.' (A fictional entrepreneur.)

   (b) 'Those financiers who . . . most pride themselves on their ability to predict what is going to happen are the very ones who jump out of the highest windows of skyscrapers. Economic forecasting, like weather forecasting in England, is only valid for the next six hours or so. Beyond that is sheer guesswork.' (A real lecturer in mathematical statistics.)

What will probably happen to the entrepreneur of (a)?

9   Criticize each of the following statements:

   (a) 'The great changes in output in the British economy over the last 20 years show the important influence on the allocation of resources of changes in the conditions of supply.'

   (b) 'The great changes in household consumption in the British economy over the last 20 years show the important influence on the allocation of resources of changes in the conditions of demand.'

   (c) If you drew up two tables, one for changes in consumption for the last 20 years, and one for changes in production for the same time-period, would you expect the two tables to show any relation to each other?

CHAPTER 16

Background to the Theory of Supply

Q 1   Debenture holders are actually creditors/owners/managers/debtors of the firm.
They have claim to the firm's assets if it goes into liquidation after/before/along with
the shareholders.

Q 2   Which of the following groups of claimants would be the last to have their claims
honoured in a bankruptcy?

    (a)   debenture holders
    (b)   commercial creditors
    (c)   common stockholders
    (d)   preferred stockholders.

Q 3   Which of the following always have limited liability?

    (a)   single proprietorships
    (b)   partnerships
    (c)   joint-stock companies
    (d)   the owners of all are fully liable.

Q 4   Among the disadvantages of the corporate firms are

    (a)   limited liability
    (b)   difficulty in raising capital
    (c)   the taxation of corporate income and again of shareholders' dividends
    (d)   all of the above are disadvantages from the point of view of the investor.

Q 5   A disadvantage to the joint-stock companies of raising a great deal of capital through
the sale of debentures is that

    (a)   the debenture market is much less stable than the stock market.
    (b)   debenture holders must be paid in good times or bad but stockholders do not
       have to receive dividends.
    (c)   debenture holders have unlimited liability.
    (d)   the interest on debentures is tax deductible for corporate income taxes.

QUESTIONS FOR DISCUSSION

1   List a few businesses best suited to each of the following forms: single proprietorship,
partnership and company.

2   The directors of a corporate firm decide to raise some more money for an investment
scheme, too large to be financed out of retained profits. They have the alternatives of issuing
more equity or borrowing from a bank. Under what conditions might

  (a)   the former be more beneficial to the *present* shareholders;
  (b)   the latter be more beneficial to the *present* shareholders?

3   In 1982, the total capitalized value of the giant British Leyland was less than the

market price of one office block in suburban Birmingham. Explain this apparently extra-ordinary, but actually quite reasonable, phenomenon.

4 In late 1974, the City of London was full of rumours of impending economic doom, especially that some large firms were in financial difficulties, or were about to be nationalized upon unfavourable terms.

Some firms raise capital by means of unsecured loan stock—this carries a higher rate of interest than bonds, but in the case of bankruptcy its owners have no claim upon the break-up value of the firm.

In view of the situation described in paragraph one, what would you predict would have happened to the relative values of unsecured loan stock, bonds, and ordinary shares? Look at the *Financial Times* for a few dates in October and November 1974, and observe the relative changes in value of such securities issued by one or two large firms, including British Leyland.

5 Victorian novels, like Thackeray's *Vanity Fair*, were full of wealthy businessmen who went bankrupt because their businesses failed. Why is this less common today?

Do you think that the shift in the last thirty years from firms owned by men trained in the same skills as their labour force to corporations run by accountants might have something to do with this? Do you think that many firms aim at excellence *in itself*, rather than as an investment to ensure a future demand for their product?

6 What is the primary function of the stock market? Do you think that the market for the shares of a very large company is similar to the *competitive* markets we discussed earlier? Why or why not?

7 If a lull in business in the economy is expected, which prices do you think will fall further, car shares or bonds issued by a car company?

CHAPTER 17
The Theory of Costs

Q 1   (a) What principle does the profit-maximizing firm use to assign costs to inputs?
_____
_____

(b) What is the minimum cost of money to a firm? _____
_____

(c) What are bygones? _____
_____

(d) What is profit? _____
_____

(e) Spell out the principle of opportunity cost _____
_____
_____

Check your answers; if you were wrong in substance, re-read Lipsey pp. 206–8.

Q 2   If a firm invests from surplus cash, the opportunity cost of this is zero because the
firm does not have to pay interest on its own money. T/F. Explain_____
_____

Q 3   A firm buys a machine for £5,000 which can produce at a constant rate of output for
5 years, after which it is worn out completely. The machine's potential output is
unimpaired if the machine stands idle. The second-hand price of the machine depends
solely on the amount of production which the machine is still capable of rendering
(i.e. value = £5,000 $(1 - \frac{1}{5} t)$ where t is the number of years the machine has been used.
(The market price of a unit of output is expected to remain constant into the
indefinite future.)

(1) What is the depreciation cost of the first six months' use of the machine?
_____

(2) What is the depreciation cost of the last six months' use of the machine?
_____

(3) What is the depreciation cost of six months when the machine lay idle?
_____

Now assume that the machine wears out whether or not it is used(e.g. it rusts away) so
that in the expression above for second-hand value t is the lapsed time from date of
purchase.

(4) What is the depreciation cost of the first year's use of the machine?
_____

(5) What is the depreciation cost of six months when the machine lay idle?
_____

Check your answers so far. If you answered any parts of Q 3 wrongly, re-read Lipsey pp. 206—7 and go back to the start of Q 3. If you got it right, go on.

(6) The value of a motor-car drops much more in the first two years of its life than in any subsequent year. Provide an explanation for this which does not depend on any idiosyncratic factors. _____
_____
_____
_____

(7) Assume in addition to the assumptions of Q 3(1), (2) and (3) that the firm cannot sell the machine. What is the depreciation cost of the first six months' use of the machine? _____ Of the last six months'? _____
_____

At the end of two years of continuous use the purchase price of an identical new machine falls to £2,500, owing to a technical innovation in the capital goods industry (ignore the assumption of part (7)).

(8) What happens to the resale value of the existing machine? _____
_____

(9) The firm, therefore, suffers a once-and-for-all capital loss. T/F

(10) Will the depreciation cost of using the old machine for the rest of its working life be changed? Yes/No. If so, by how much? _____ _____
If not, why not?

Check your answers. If you answered part (10) wrongly you might have been vaguely confused by the apparent paradox that although the firm has clearly been unfortunate in paying £5,000 for a machine which drops in price to £2,500, it is then lucky to find that its annual costs have actually decreased. What you are forgetting is your answer to part (9). The firm suffers a once-and-for-all capital loss, then adjusts immediately to the new position. Re-read Lipsey p. 206—7 and remember—bygones are bygones. If you haven't already, do Q 3 part 6.

Q 4   The opportunity cost of mining labour is lower than the miners' wage rate because there is little alternative employment for them. T/F. Explain.
_____

Q 5   Explain why the cost to the farming community of using manure as a fertiliser might be negative. _____
_____

THE PRODUCTION FUNCTION

Q 6   Define production function _____
_____

Q 7   The production function will be affected by changes in the prices of inputs/outputs/neither

Check your answer to Q 7. We are at the moment only concerned with the physical relationship between, for example, tons of steel and motor-cars, not the price of either.

Q 8   If a firm uses three factors of production, what is the minimum number which must be fixed in the short run? _____

Q 9   Modern motor-cars do not have chassis, but the whole body is built as the stress-taking member. When this change occurred, manufacturers had to change their capital equipment. Would this be analysed in the short, long, or very long run?
_____

Check your answers. If you were wrong, re-read Lipsey pp. 211–12. It is quite straight-forward.

Q 10   (1)   Can you complete Table 1 as it stands without any further information?
Yes/No

Look at the answer, and do the rest of the question. If you cannot, re-read Lipsey pp. 212–14.

TABLE 1

(1) Quantity of labour	(2) Total product	(3) Average product (to nearest whole number)	(4) Marginal product
1	10		
2	27		
3	49		
4	73		
5	96		
6	112		
7	119		
8	121		
9	122		

Variations of output per week with one fixed, one variable factor (land and labour). Land fixed at 1,000 acres.

     (2)   Is this short or long run? _____

     (3)   Fill in columns (3) and (4) of Table 1.

     (4)   Plot the average and marginal product curves on Fig. 1 (label the vertical axis *Product*, the horizontal axis *No. of men*).

     (5)   Are the data in Table 1 consistent with the law of diminishing returns? Yes/No

     (6)   After what level of *total output* do diminishing *marginal* returns set in?
_____

     (7)   After what level of total output do diminishing *average* returns set in?
_____

Check your answers. If you feel the need for more practice at this sort of curve-building, take the marginal product column given for Table 1 in the Answers section and derive the other two columns from it. Total product for any given quantity of labour input is just the sum of all the marginal products up to that point. For example, total product of the first 3 men is 10 + 17 + 22 = 49.

SHORT-RUN VARIATIONS IN COSTS

Inputs have a cost; we assume that the unit cost is always the same to the firm. In terms of the example of Table 1 this means that if the wage rate for the first man is £18 per week, so is the wage rate for the tenth man.

You should now re-read Lipsey pp. 215–19.

Q 11   Average variable cost is always equal to or below average total cost. T/F

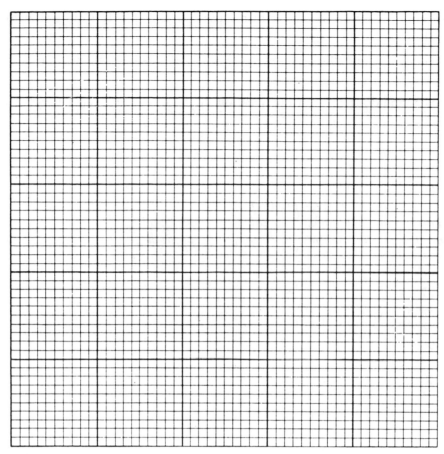

Fig. 1

Q 12 (1) Given that land costs £26 per acre per year rent, and that the weekly wage rate is £20, fill in the following weekly cost schedule on Table 2 using the data in Table 1.

TABLE 2

Quantity of labour	Total output	Total fixed cost	Total variable cost	Total cost	Average fixed cost	Average variable cost	Average total cost	Marginal* cost
1	10	500	20	520	50	2	52	2
2	27	500	40	540	18.5	1.5	20	1.18
3								
4								
5								
6								
7								
8								
9								

* For a working method of arriving at a figure for marginal cost, in this situation where inputs of the variable factor are not infinitely divisible (that is, they come in man-weeks only), divide the cost of each unit of labour by its marginal product. For graphical purposes, plot this at the level of output halfway between total output *including* the marginal unit, and *excluding* it. E.g. MC of 1.18 should be plotted against an output of 18.5.

(2) Plot the average and marginal cost curves on Fig. 2.

(3) After what level of total output do increasing marginal costs set in?

_____

(4) After what level of total output do increasing average total costs set in?

_____

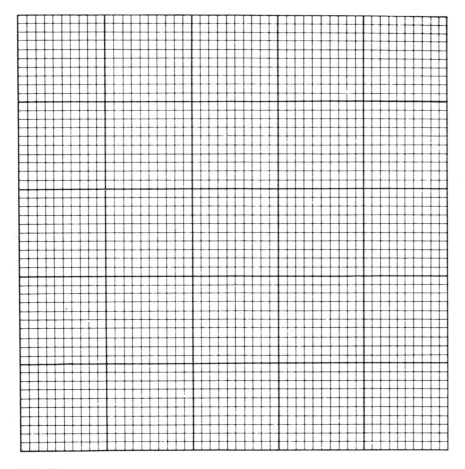

Fig. 2

(5) After what level of total output do increasing average variable costs set in?

_____

(6) After what level of total output do increasing average fixed costs set in?

_____

Check your answers; the answers to Q 12 parts (3) and (5) are the same as the answers to 10 (6) and (7). If you do not see why this should be, you should re-read Lipsey pp. 216–17.

(7) If you have plotted your graph correctly, the marginal cost curve should cut both *AVC* and *ATC* curves at their _____ point. If you find it difficult to see why this must always happen, and not be coincidence, you might think of cricket batting averages. So long as a batsman scores more runs than his previous average, his average rises. When he scores less, it falls. So if the average is falling, the marginal score must be below it, and if the average is rising, the marginal score must be above it. This means that when the average changes from falling to rising the marginal must change from below to above it—in other words it must cut it. And of course, the point where the average changes from falling to rising is the lowest point on the curve. This is true whatever is added in to start with to the sum to be averaged. With average total costs, it is the value of the fixed costs; with average variable costs, it is zero. The principle is not affected. Average total cost will go on falling longer than average variable cost because the marginal increment which served to turn the *AVC* curve upward would not be so

79

influential on the *ATC* curve, heavily weighted as it is by the initial fixed costs. But the *MC* curve will cut it at its lowest point.

Q 13   What is capacity output from Table 2? _____
The definition of capacity is on Lipsey p. 218.

THE LONG RUN

You should re-read Lipsey pp. 219–30.

Q 14   Profit maximization is a sufficient condition for cost minimization. T/F

Q 15   Re-arrange the following symbols such that they state the condition for cost minimization (in an industry whose two factors are labour and capital)

$$P_L, =, MP_K, MP_L, P_K$$

Do Q 16 before checking your answer to Q 15.

Q 16   Re-arrange your answer to Q 15 in order to give a different expression to the cost-minimization conditions.

Q 17   A movie film processing laboratory, whose output is 5,000 films per week, uses 50 units of capital per week and 100 units of labour. Its marginal product curves are given in Fig. 3 (a) and (b).

(1)   Capital costs £10 per unit per week, labour £15. Is the firm in a cost-minimizing position? Yes/No

(2)   The firm expands its output by 106 films per week. In order to remain in a cost-minimizing position, it will employ _____ extra units of labour, and _____ of capital.

Check your answer. If you were wrong, work through the following demonstration. If you were right, go to *.

The firm needs to employ more factors. It looks at the two marginal product curves and calculates from Fig. 3 (a) that one extra unit of capital will yield 19 extra units of production at a cost of £10.

So $\dfrac{MP_K}{P_K} = 1.9$ – or, alternatively, one extra unit costs 52.6 pence. One extra unit of labour will yield 29.5 extra units of production, at a cost of £15. So $\dfrac{MP_L}{P_L} = 1.96$ – or, one extra unit costs 50.8 pence. For the first 29.5 extra units (of the aimed-for 106) therefore, extra labour is employed. The firm then calculates that the next unit of extra labour will yield 29 extra units of production: $\dfrac{MP_L}{P_L} =$ _____ (Q 17 (3)). $\dfrac{MP_K}{P_K}$ is still _____ (Q 17 (4)) so for the next 29 extra units, extra labour is employed. The firm has now increased its production by 58.5 units, out of a desired 106. Continuing, therefore, with the same process, the next unit of labour will yield _____ (Q 17 (5)) extra units of production. $\dfrac{MP_L}{P_L} =$ _____ (Q 17 (6)). *The firm is therefore indifferent between employing extra labour and extra capital.* The managing director tosses a coin, and employs extra labour. Total extra production is now 87. Continuing, the firm again calculates $\dfrac{MP_L}{P_L}$, which now equals _____ (Q 17 (7)). *Check your answer.* Since $\dfrac{MP_K}{P_K}$ remains at 1.9, it is now in the interests of the cost-minimizing firm to employ extra capital. The extra production is 19, the derived total extra of 106 is achieved, $\dfrac{MP_K}{P_K} = \dfrac{MP_L}{P_L}$, and the firm is therefore producing 5,106 units in the cheapest possible way. (In order to produce this demonstration simply and clearly we have

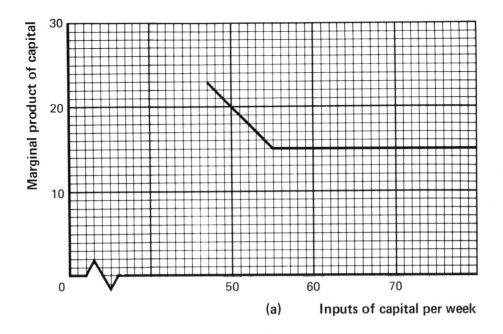

(a) Inputs of capital per week

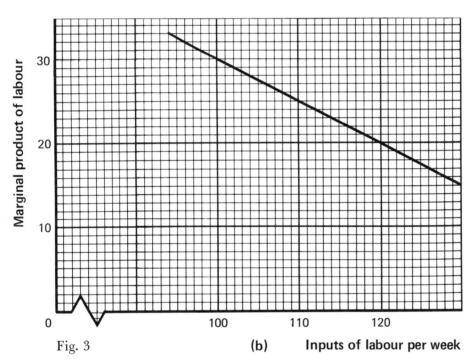

Fig. 3 (b) Inputs of labour per week

dealt in discrete terms—i.e. in 'lumps' of labour and capital—and chosen convenient figures).
You should now work out that the same conclusion would have been reached if the managing
director had employed extra capital after he had tossed his coin.

*Q 18 'A long run average cost curve might be sloping down, then up, because as output is
expanded—

(a) the necessary machines get cheaper, then more expensive.'
(b) spare floor space gets used up, thus spreading overheads better, but then runs
out, and the consequent overcrowding produces inefficiency.'

Only one of these is right. Which one? _____

If you were wrong, you must remember that since this is a long-run (minimum) cost curve
it is drawn to show costs when all factors are adjusted to be used in their cheapest
combination for each rate of output.

So, for points on the *LRAC* curve, there could *never* be any un-needed floor space. Could there be overcrowding? Yes, if we define overcrowding as a higher ratio of 'other factors' to floor space than for some lower level of output; no, if we define it as a situation in which the other factors are too close together to produce maximum efficiency for that level of output. The former possibility merely says that optimal factor proportions vary as output varies which is quite possible, while the latter implies that the optimal proportions are not being employed. In this case we are not on the *LRAC* curve.

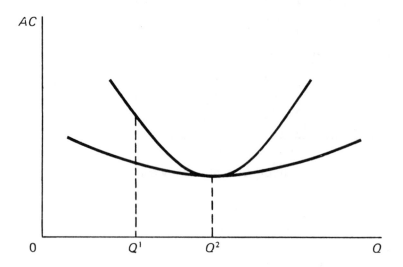

Q 19 (1) One of these curves is a *LRATC* curve, the other a *SRATC* curve. Which is the one underneath? _____

(2) How many levels of capital does the *SRATC* curve apply to?

_____

(3) Why is it more expensive to produce Q^1 on the *SRATC* curve than on the *LRATC* curve?_____

_____

Q 20 Look at Fig. 4

(1) The lines drawn on the figure each represent different combinations of labour and capital which will produce the same output. The lines are called _____ _____ . They represent outputs of 10, 20, 30, 40, 50, 60, 70, 80, 90 per unit of time. Label them appropriately.

(2) Should the 90 label be on the extreme right or left curve? right/left

Check your answer to 20 (2) — and if you were wrong, think about it and correct your diagram.

(3) Labour costs £10 per unit, capital £20. Construct a set of isocost curves on Fig. 4 which will yield the cost-minimization points for the production levels of each isoquant. As output increases, relatively more capital/labour is used.

(4) What is the lowest cost at which an output of 30 per unit of time can be produced? _____

Check your answer to 20 (4). If you were wrong, or could not do it, read on and do 20 (5) and 20 (6). If not, go on to 20 (7).

All you have to do is to look at the point where the isocost curve, which you drew in order to answer 20 (3), touches the 30 isoquant. You read off from this that $8\frac{1}{2}$ units of labour are used, and 9 units of capital. The cost is therefore $8\frac{1}{2}$ × £10 + 9 × £20 = £265.

(5) What is the lowest cost at which an output of 50 per unit of time can be produced? _____

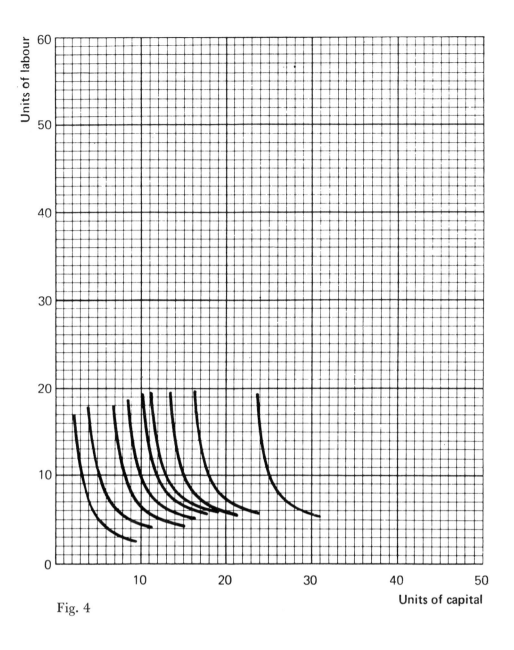

Fig. 4

(6) What is the greatest output which can be produced for a total cost of £200?

_____

(7) If the price of labour doubles — to £20 per unit — what will be the lowest cost at which 40 can be produced? _____

(8) What has been the change in the use of capital and labour in the production of 40 units, caused by this doubling of the price of labour? _____

capital up/down by _____ units

labour up/down by _____ units

(9) The effect shown in 20 (8) exemplifies the principle of _____

Q 21   Plot a long-run average cost curve for the firm represented in Fig. 4 (with capital costing £20, labour £10) on to Fig. 5. Remember — it is an _average_ cost curve, so you divide each total cost by the appropriate output.

(1) What is the minimum average cost of 60 units? _____

(2) Up to what output does this firm enjoy increasing returns? about

_____

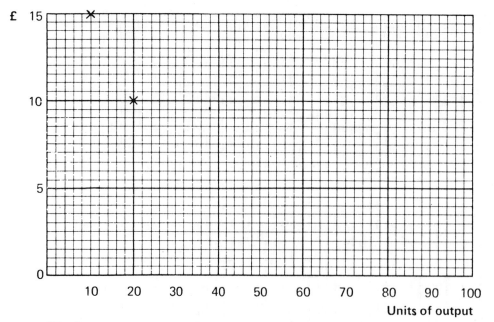

Fig. 5

(3) Can 50 units be produced at an average cost of £10? Yes/No

(4) Can 80 units be produced at an average cost of £4.5? Yes/No

(5) If the firm were, in the short run, producing an output of 20 with a capital stock which gave a capital consumption of 9 units, and with $7\frac{1}{2}$ units of labour, what would be its average cost? _____

(6) How would the firm in Q 21 (5) adjust its capital stock in the long run, in order to reduce its costs? _____ its capital stock until it would be using _____ units less/more of capital per period.

Read on now to the end of the chapter.

In this section on the very long run, two concepts are introduced, productivity and innovation.

Productivity is concerned with the rate of output per unit employed. Where there is more than one type of input, there is more than one productivity measure, depending on which input, or combination of inputs, is considered. Since all output of non-capital goods is consumed by people, we usually consider output per man hour, since we can then draw general conclusions about the standard of living from our knowledge about productivity.

Innovation is quite simply the introduction of a change into the production function.

On pp. 232–3 five different hypotheses about the origin of invention are outlined.

Here is a list of them:

(1) Invention is a random process.
(2) Invention is a response to the institutional framework.
(3) Invention and innovation are the product of the inherent logic and momentum of science.
(4) Necessity is the mother of invention.
(5) Profits are the spur.

Q 22 Which hypothesis do the following propositions support?

(1) There is no way of telling where the next thousand inventions are likely to occur.

_____

(2) Doctors are bound to find a cure for the common cold, because so many working days are lost through it. _____

(3) Leibniz and Newton both invented the techniques of differential calculus at the same time, and without collaboration. _____

(4) LSD is manufactured illicitly from flower seeds. _____

(5) Lower-cost large-scale industrialized building is now being used all over the country. _____

Q 23 Assume that there is full employment of skilled manufacturing workers and heavy unemployment amongst unskilled ones, and that an economist states that if only the union would allow the wages of the unskilled to fall sufficiently they would all find employment in manufacturing. What must this economist be assuming?

_____

Q 24 Of two firms similar in all but one respect, the one which owns its buildings is incurring lower costs than the one which rents them. T/F

Q 25 The marginal cost curve cannot be deduced from the average cost curve, but can be deduced from the total cost curve. T/F

Q 26 If the AC curve is rising, the MC curve must be above it. T/F

Q 27 If the AC curve is above the MC curve, the latter might be either rising or falling. T/F

Q 28 The production function relates

(a) cost to input
(b) cost to output
(c) wages to profits
(d) inputs to outputs
(e) all of the above.

Q 29 Each short-run average cost curve

(a) never touches the long-run curve
(b) always crosses the long-run curve
(c) always lies above all points on the long-run curve
(d) coincides with the long-run curve at one point

Q 30 A change in factor prices

(a) changes long-run cost-curve positions
(b) changes short-run cost-curve positions
(c) alters the optimal factor proportions
(d) is likely to do all of the above.

Q 31 (Optional)
An isocost line for two factors C and L (their respective prices are P_c and P_l) could have which of the following equations?

(a) $LC = £100$
(b) $£100 = P_c + P_l$
(c) $£100 = P_l L + P_c C$
(d) $£1,000 = P_l C$

QUESTIONS FOR DISCUSSION

1 How much is it costing you to attend university?

2 Why can supermarkets undersell small grocery stores and still make large profits?

3 The firm's short-run cost curve can never be below its long-run curve. Why not? Is our statement a testable one?

4   At the time of writing (1983) the microprocessor, or 'chip', is hailed as the greatest technical advance of the decade. Can you think of any industrial or commercial sectors where the use of microprocessors represents a *long-run* rather than a *very-long-run* shift?

5   Explain what 'spreading one's overheads' means in terms of the cost terminology of this chapter.

6   Many hospital laboratories are criticized for installing automatic sample analysers before they can use them to capacity. Provide a possible refutation to this charge using the analysis of this chapter.

7   In the last ten years or so the laundry industry has been undergoing what is popularly known as a 'major shakeout'. In other words, lots of laundries are going out of business, or merging into larger units. The average life of laundry machinery such as washers and tumble driers is about twelve years. It was about twelve years ago that major developments in the technology of laundry processes took place. New washing and ironing machines were developed, which are cheaper than the old type of machine if utilized to maximum or near maximum capacity. This capacity is greater than that of the largest of the old machines.

(a)   Draw possible *LRAC* curves appropriate to laundries using

(1)   the old machinery
(2)   the old machinery or the new machinery, depending on output.

(Draw in, in a dotted line, that part of the *LRAC* curve which would correspond to the new machinery being utilized where it ought not to be.)

(b)   Why do you think that the laundry 'shakeout' has been happening over the last ten years, rather than twelve years ago?

CHAPTER 18

The Equilibrium of a Profit-maximizing Firm

TOTAL, AVERAGE AND MARGINAL REVENUES

You have by now encountered total, average and marginal quantities enough to make short work of this section.

Q 1   What is the relation between average and total revenues? *average revenue AR = $\frac{T.R.}{output}$*

Q 2   Define marginal revenue. *revenue gained from producing 1 more unit*

The three rules for all profit-maximizing firms:

Rule 1   For a given output to be the profit-maximizing output, it is necessary that total revenue is equal to or greater than total variable cost.

Q 3   Why is rule 1 equivalent to '. . . it is necessary that average revenue be equal to or greater than average variable cost'?
     Because in order to obtain average revenue you divide/multiply marginal/total revenue by price/output, and in order to obtain average cost you divide/multiply marginal/total cost by price/output. The output is of course the same for both, and if you divide two quantities by the same amount you leave their relationship one to the other unchanged.

Rule 2   For a given output to be the profit-maximizing output, it is necessary that at that output $MC = MR$.

Q 4   Assume that the firm whose MC curve is given in Fig. 1 gets a price of £1.50 for each

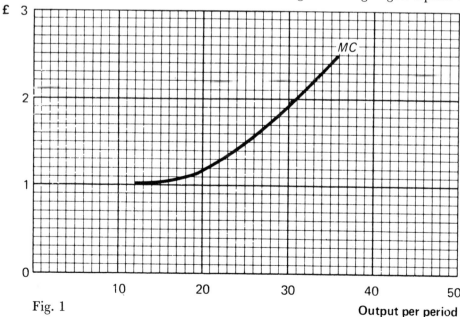

Fig. 1   Output per period

of its products, however many it sells. Draw in the appropriate marginal revenue curve (re-read Lipsey p. 237, if you can't).

(1) What is the profit-maximizing output? _____

(2) If the firm were producing 20 units per period, how much extra profit could it make by producing one extra unit per period? _____

(3) If the firm were producing 30 units per period, how much loss would it be making on the 30th unit? _____

Check your answers to 4 (1), (2) and (3). If you were right, skip 4 (4) and (5). If not, re-read Lipsey pp. 237–9, and carry on.

(4) How much loss could the firm avoid per period by moving from an output of 35 per period to an output of 33? _____

Check your answer. If you were wrong, try again, remembering that all you have to do is to add up the loss made on the 35th unit and the loss made on the 34th unit.

(5) How much more profit could the firm make by producing 21 instead of 18? _____

Rule 3   For a given output to be the profit-maximizing output, it is necessary that for slightly smaller outputs $MR > MC$, and that for slightly larger outputs $MC > MR$.

Sketch in on Fig. 1 an MC curve sloping down from left to right, which cuts the MR curve. You will immediately see what nonsense it would make to say that the point of intersection is at a profit-maximizing output. Indeed, MC curves might slope downwards, but if they do, the point at which they cut the MR curve is of no significance.

Q 5 $MR = MC$ is a condition for the profit-maximizing firm only in a situation in which factor prices do not change and technology is constant. T/F

Q 6   Average cost is more important than marginal cost in defining profit-maximizing conditions. T/F

Q 7   Variable cost is more important than fixed cost in defining profit-maximizing behaviour. T/F

Q 8   Any firm that cannot cover total costs cannot be a profit-maximizing firm. T/F

Q 9   Which of the following statements is correct for a profit-maximizing firm? TR greater than or equal to TC is

(a)   necessary but not sufficient
(b)   sufficient but not necessary
(c)   necessary and sufficient
(d)   neither necessary nor sufficient.

Q 10   Which of the following statements is correct for a profit-maximizing firm? TR greater than or equal to variable cost is

(a)   necessary but not sufficient
(b)   sufficient but not necessary
(c)   necessary and sufficient
(d)   neither necessary nor sufficient.

QUESTIONS FOR DISCUSSION

1   In February 1983 Arthur Scargill, the President of the National Union of Miners, was faced with a management plan to close a number of pits. He asserted that the only policy acceptable to the union was closure of a pit if it was exhausted of coal. What closure criteria would the management have been trying to adopt? Do you think 'exhaustion' is an economic concept?

At the time of writing (Feb. 1983) it is clear that the Government wants to appoint as Chairman of the National Coal Board a well-known devotee of 'hard-nosed' economics, who will close mines if they are loss-making. Scargill argues that a mine which is loss-making in the short run may be profitable in the long run, and that since it is impossible to close a mine temporarily they should be kept going (unless exhausted). What might happen in the long run to bring about this turnaround? How might the Board respond to this argument? (*Hint*: Is any new investment being undertaken anywhere by the British coal industry?)

What has actually happened since the beginning of 1983?

2   A common method of pricing items on a restaurant menu is to multiply the cost of the ingredients by a factor—often three—which is found to yield enough revenue to cover costs. This explains the wide difference between the price of, say, plaice and chips and fillet steak and chips. If you were to open a grill-bar where your competitors used this policy, and if you felt that your potential customers usually much preferred steak to fish, but were put off by the high prices charged in the other restaurants, what pricing policy might you adopt? What might you expect the response of your competition to be? Is a rule such as 'ingredient cost × 3' a profit-maximizing rule?

CHAPTER 19

The Theory of Perfect Competition

If we make two simplifying assumptions about the behaviour of firms, and the conditions under which they operate, we can use our previous supply and demand analysis together with the assumption of profit maximization to spell out in detail, but extremely succinctly, the logical implications of our theory. The use of the word 'perfect' to qualify the theory does not imply that a world in which the assumptions are true is a better world than one in which they are not true; it is merely meant to indicate a situation of 'extreme competition' or 'as much competition as is logically possible'.

Q 1   The theory of perfect competition is based upon two assumptions, one about the firm, the other about the industry.

The firm is a _____ *price – taker* _____

The industry has _____ *freedom of entry + exit* _____

TOTAL, AVERAGE AND MARGINAL REVENUE OF THE FIRM IN PERFECT COMPETITION

You should first of all make sure that you know why, when price is constant, $MR = AR$. If you are uncertain, re-read Lipsey, Chapter 18, p. 236.

Q 2   In perfect competition the average revenue curve, the marginal revenue curve, and the firm's demand curve are all the _____

_____

Q 3   Given the information that 200 units sell for £100, how many demand curves could you draw satisfying this condition for a firm in perfect competition? Draw them on Fig. 1.

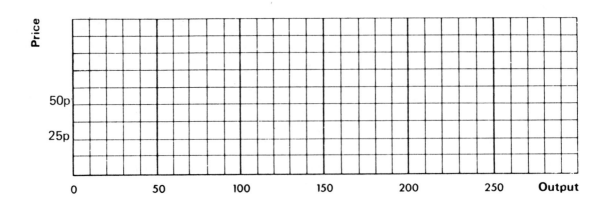

Fig. 1

Q 4   Construct the total revenue curve, corresponding to the above diagram, on to Fig. 2.

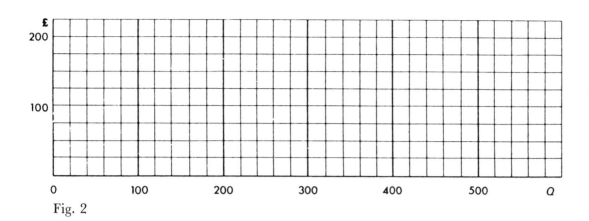

Fig. 2

     (1)   Can a *TR* curve in perfect competition be anything but a straight line? Yes/No

     (2)   What is *TR* at an output of 500? _____

SHORT-RUN EQUILIBRIUM OF THE COMPETITIVE FIRM

Q 5   If a firm maximizes profits, then in equilibrium marginal _____
is equal to marginal _____

     If a firm is perfectly competitive, market price equals marginal revenue. Therefore, when a perfectly competitive, profit-maximizing firm is in equilibrium, price equals marginal/average/total cost.

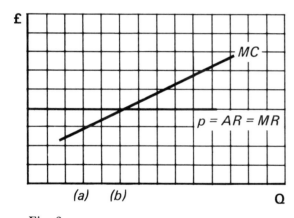

Fig. 3

Q 6   Given that a firm to whom Fig. 3 applies is producing at (a), and that it does not intend to move to (b), what can you say about it? _____

_____

THE FIRM'S SUPPLY CURVE

Refer to Fig. 4.

Q 7   (1)   If the market price is £10, how large will the firm's output be?

        _____

     (2)   If the firm's output is 30, what is the market price? _____

     (3)   Below what price will the firm not produce? _____

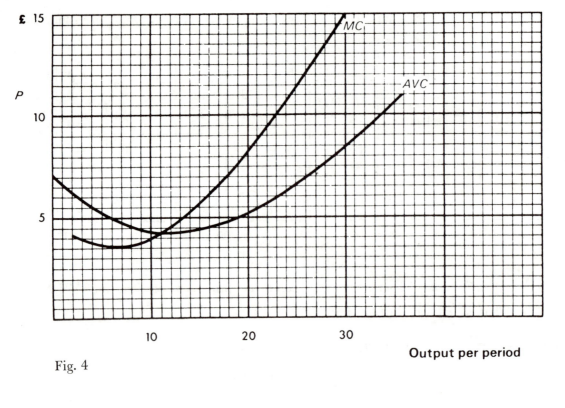

Fig. 4

(4) When the price is £8.25

what is *A VC*? _____

what is output? _____

what is, therefore, the total return on *fixed* costs? (i.e., excess of revenue over *VC*) _____

THE SHORT-RUN SUPPLY CURVE FOR A COMPETITIVE INDUSTRY

Q 8   There are 520 firms in the schmoo industry. 200 have a supply curve as in Fig. 5, and 320 have a supply curve as in Fig. 6:

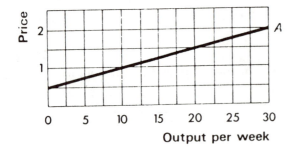

Fig. 5

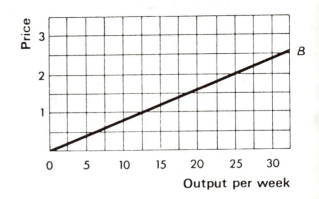

Fig. 6

Construct the industry supply curve for schmoos on Fig. 7:

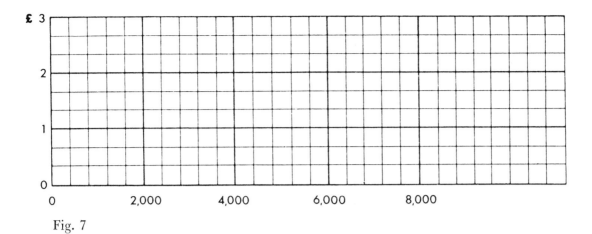

Fig. 7

The industry is faced with a straight-line demand curve which is defined by the two points that at $p = 3$: 0 is demanded, and at $p = 2$: 3,000 are demanded.

(1)   What is the equilibrium price and quantity? _____

(2)   How much will each firm with supply curve A offer? _____

(3)   How much will each firm with supply curve B offer? _____

PROFITS AND LOSSES IN THE SHORT RUN

The condition for short-run equilibrium is that price should equal marginal cost. This says nothing about total cost. In the short run, therefore, total cost may be less than total revenue, equal to it, or greater than it. In competition, it is *possible for a firm to make a loss in the short run*. This may seem odd; why doesn't the firm stop producing immediately? Because, although it is making a loss, it is making the minimum possible loss. Were it to close down it would still have to meet all its fixed contractual payments.[1] So long as variable cost is less than revenue, it will pay the firm to remain in operation in order to offset some at least of its potential loss.

SRATC (Short-Run Average Total Cost)

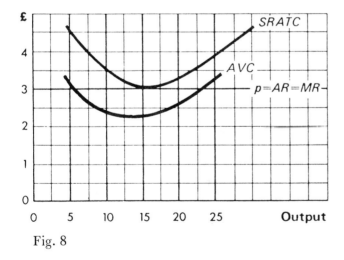

Fig. 8

Q 9   Have you enough information in Fig. 8, which is the cost diagram for profit-maximizing a firm, to deduce immediately the output of the firm? Yes/No. If so, what is it? _____

---

[1] Unless, of course, it went bankrupt.

LONG-RUN EQUILIBRIUM

Q 10   What is the second key assumption of perfect competition? _____
_____
_____

Q 11   This position (Fig. 9) is possible in the short run for the firms of a particular industry.

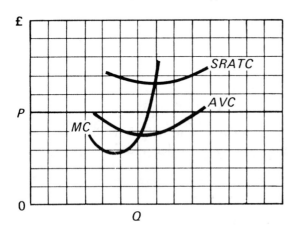

Fig. 9

So is this:

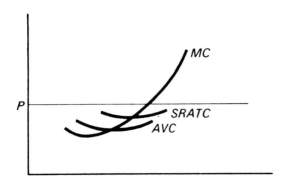

Fig. 10

(1)   In the long run, which of these positions can persist? The first/second/neither.

(2)   In the first case capital will move out of/into the industry.

(3)   In the second, capital will move out of/into the industry.

(4)   Sketch in on Fig. 10 a *SRATC* curve which could persist in the long run, given that price remains constant.

Q 12   Have we enough information here to predict the ultimate movements in price in Figs. 9 and 10? Yes/No

Remember, the *SRATC* curves correspond only to one level of plant; *nothing* has been said about the *LRAC* curve.

Q 13   (Optional)

(a)   You are given the information that an industry is in full long-run equilibrium. There is then a rise in demand for the product of that industry.

What will happen to the prices in the long run if all inputs are bought from perfectly competitive firms, themselves in LR competitive equilibrium? Rise/fall/ no change

If you don't understand this, re-read the final paragraph on pp. 258–9, and do Q 19 (b).

(b)   The total output of a perfectly competitive industry depends on the _____ of _____ individual firms in the market.

Q 14   'The *only* reason why Shropshire farms are more profitable than nearby Welsh hill farms is quite simply the depth of topsoil'—quote from farming item on television documentary.

(a)   Is this an economist's use of 'profitable'? Yes/No
(b)   In Shropshire the imputed cost of farm land is higher/lower than in the Welsh hills.

Q 15   In short-run competitive equilibrium, we predict that:

(a)   marginal cost is rising
(b) $P = MC$
(c)   there is no incentive for firms to enter the industry
(d)   all of the above answers are satisfactory
(e)   both (a) and (b) are satisfactory
(f)   none of the above answers is satisfactory.

Q 16   If more firms enter a competitive industry, our theory predicts that

(a)   marginal cost curves rise
(b)   the industry supply curve shifts to the right
(c)   output of all existing firms increases
(d)   product price falls
(e)   all of the above answers are correct
(f)   both (b) and (d) are satisfactory
(g)   none of the above answers is satisfactory.

Q 17   In long-run competitive equilibrium, the theory predicts that

(a) $TC = TR$
(b)   firms operate at a minimum total average cost
(c) $MC = MR$
(d)   there is no incentive for entry or exit of firms
(e)   all of the above answers are satisfactory
(f)   none of the above answers is satisfactory.

Q 18   If firms are suffering losses in a short-run competitive equilibrium, we predict that

(a)   production will be stopped by the industry
(b)   some firms will exit from the industry
(c)   more efficient new firms will enter the industry
(d)   both (b) and (c) are satisfactory.
(e)   none of the above answers is satisfactory.

Q 19   For a price-taker, $P = MR$. T/F

Q 20   The industry supply curve is the vertical summation of the individual firms' supply curves. T/F

Q 21   Demand curves in competitive industries are very nearly infinitely elastic. T/F

Q 22   Firms in short-run competitive equilibrium may be suffering losses. T/F

Q 23   Firms in long-run competitive equilibrium may be earning economic profits. T/F

Q 24   The number of firms in an industry is important to the application of the competitive model because it affects the applicability of the assumption that firms are price-takers. T/F

Q 25   (Before attempting this question, work through Table 19.1, page 244.)

(1)   Define the firm's elasticity of demand.

_____

(2)   What symbol is given to firm's elasticity of demand?

_____

(3)   What symbol is given to elasticity of market demand?

_____

(4)   Given: $\eta_m = 0.5$
World output = 5,000,000
Firm's output increases from 100 to 200 units (*ceteris paribus*)
What is η_F? _____

(5)   Given $\eta_F = 1,000$
Firm's output increases by 25%
World output increases from 10,000,000 to 10,000,100
What is η_m? _____

QUESTIONS FOR DISCUSSION

1   State and explain the two critical assumptions of the theory of perfect competition.

2   'Marginal cost need not *necessarily* equal price in conditions of perfect competition, because there might be a situation where *every* firm in an industry is operating with diminishing costs. In these conditions price would have to be above m.c., otherwise all the firms would be operating at a loss.' Explain why you agree or disagree.

3   Draw supply and demand curves illustrating what will happen if, in a perfectly competitive industry, firms are not covering their total costs. Draw a diagram showing what will happen to firms remaining in the industry.

4   Why do we say that perfect competition and decreasing costs (over the entire relevant output) are incompatible in long-run equilibrium? If we observed an industry with many firms, each one of which had unexploited economies of scale, would you conclude that the industry was not perfectly competitive? Would your answer be affected by the added information that (a) the industry was not growing in size, or (b) the industry was growing in size?

5   The following two paragraphs appeared in an article by the *Daily Telegraph* Air Correspondent (22.2.71): 'There is no doubt that the world's airlines would prefer not to have to buy the costly supersonic aircraft. The giant, subsonic airliners, they feel, would be more certain earners.

   'But if one has Concorde, the other major airlines will have to buy it, too, or go out of business. It will meet the needs of a substantial proportion of passengers wanting fast and comfortable travel, while the jumbos concentrate on the cheaper bulk tourist trade.'

   Does the writer consider that airlines are competitive? The argument is presented in a confusing manner. Sort it out by distinguishing between the two essentially different services being provided. Do you think that the reasoning is consistent?

   After a long legal battle, the dynamic entrepreneur Freddie Laker was finally allowed, in 1978, to operate wide-bodied aeroplanes on trans-atlantic routes. His fares were cheap, and the other airlines immediately followed suit by lowering their fares. Before Laker was allowed to operate, what condition for competition was unfulfilled?

Subsequently, Laker went bankrupt, but only after another round of fierce price competition. Laker's lawyer claimed that a conspiracy among his competitors had caused the bankruptcy. What sort of conspiracy could this have been? Why didn't his competitors go bust too? (Careful—the reason may not be obvious.)

CHAPTER 20

The Theory of Monopoly

This chapter should seem simpler than the previous one. This is because by now you should be thoroughly familiar with all the important concepts used in our analysis.

Q 1   In order to review your understanding of these, you should provide one-sentence definitions of each of the following:

(1)   Demand = AR _____

(2)   Marginal revenue _____
_____

(3)   Average total cost (short-run and long-run) _____
_____

(4)   Average variable cost _____
_____

(5)   Marginal cost _____
_____

(6)   Profits _____
_____

All the conclusions of the theory of monopoly that differ from the conclusions of the theory of perfect competition stem from the alteration of one assumption. *Whereas a competitive firm faces a flat demand curve, a monopolistic firm faces a downward-sloping demand curve.* In other words, the monopolist is *not* a price-taker. We see from the argument of Chapter 19 that, given normal assumptions about the shape of the various cost curves, a monopolist can make a profit in the long run. Long-run profits can only exist if capital is prevented from being transferred into the industry making them. *Barriers to entry* are therefore an implication of the assumption that the monopolists' demand curve does not shift in the long run.

Q 2   In perfect competition, $AR = MR = P$. In monopoly, are these all different?

_____

Q 3   Look at Fig. 1.

We will now construct the marginal revenue curve. Let us look at the marginal revenue of the fifth unit. Total (weekly) revenue from the first four units would have been $4 \times £24 = £96$. Total revenue from the first five units, however, is $5 \times £22.50$, since in order to sell the extra unit price has had to drop by £1.50. $5 \times £22.50 = £112.50$. The marginal revenue of the fifth unit is, therefore, $£112.50 - £96 = £16.50$. This point is plotted on the graph. Let us now look at the MR of the eighth unit.

(1)   Total revenue of the first 7 units _____

(2)   Total revenue of the first 8 units _____

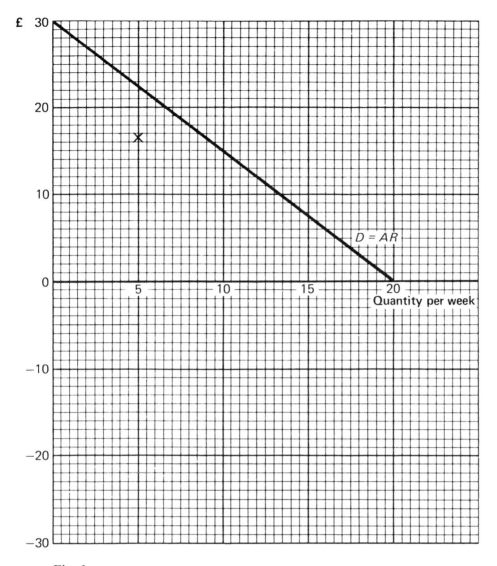

Fig. 1

(Check these answers—if you were wrong, work them out again.)

      (3) ∴ Marginal revenue of the eighth unit _____

            Plot this point on the graph.

            Now, the *MR* of the 11th unit.

    (4) *TR* of the first 10 units _____

    (5) *TR* of the first 11 units _____

(Again, check these answers)

      (6) ∴ *MR* of the 11th unit _____

      Now, draw a straight line through these points, and continue it below the horizontal
      axis. This is the *MR* curve. (N.B. Those who happen to know the theorem which
      states that all the *MR* points should lie on a straight line, which bisects exactly the
      distance from the origin to where the *AR* curve cuts the horizontal axis, should
      remember that our analysis here is discrete, not continuous.)

      (7) In our example, therefore, between any two outputs up to 10, the drop in price
            is sufficient to cause an actual drop in total revenue. Elasticity of demand is
            therefore, over that range, greater than/less than one.

Check your answer to Q 3 (7). If you were wrong, look again at Fig. 1. If price drops anywhere in the output range 1–10, enough extra units are demanded to cause an increase in revenue — so % change in quantity is greater than % change in price, i.e. $\eta > 1$.

(8) Between any two outputs above 10, the drop in price causes a drop in total revenue. Elasticity of demand over that range is greater than/less than one.

In order to understand the theory of monopoly, it is essential to understand elasticity of demand. We will consider the proposition 'The price charged by the profit-maximizing monopolist will never be where a demand curve has an elasticity of less than one.'

Q 4 (1) An elasticity of less than one means that proportionate change in quantity demanded is less than/greater than proportionate change in price.

(2) If proportionate change in quantity demanded is less than proportionate change in price, a decrease in quantity supplied will result in a decrease/increase in total revenue.

Check your answers to Q 4 (1) and (2).

Since a decrease in quantity supplied must obviously (*ceteris paribus*) decrease the total costs of the monopolist in the short term, no profit-maximizing monopolist will choose an output where he could *increase* revenue and *decrease* costs by decreasing quantity supplied. We will now consider the same point graphically. Fig. 2 shows a monopolist's demand curve:

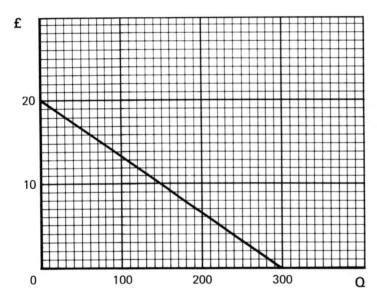

Fig. 2

(3) What is the level below which price will not be set?

Check your answer.

(4) On a straight-line demand curve, elasticity falls/rises as the curve falls.

(5) The point of unit elasticity is halfway down/a quarter from the top/a quarter from the bottom.

(6) Write down the formula for elasticity _____

(7) What is elasticity at £8? _____

(8) What is elasticity at £12? _____

(9) What is the change in total revenue from a reduction in quantity supplied from 180 to 150? _____

100

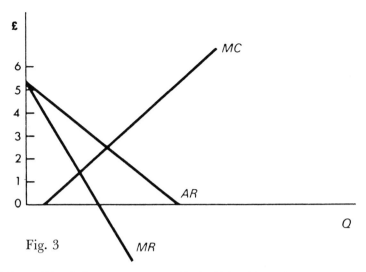

Fig. 3

Q 5   Fig. 3 shows a monopolist's MR, AR and MC curves. What is the equilibrium price?

_____

Q 6   Does the marginal cost curve cut the $SRATC$ curve, or the AVC curve, at its lowest point? _____

If you were wrong, re-read Lipsey pp. 216–17.

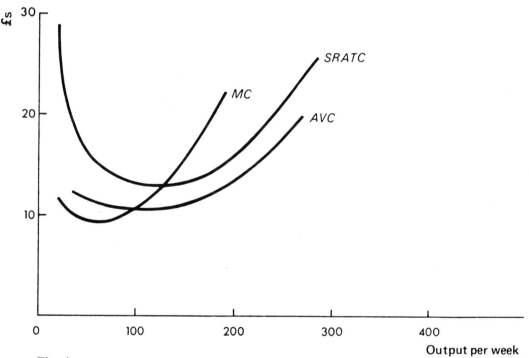

Fig. 4

Q 7   Superimpose on Fig. 4 the straight-line demand curve defined by the two points (0, £30) (300, £0). The marginal revenue curve corresponding to this is defined by the two points (0, £30), (150, £0). Draw this in also.

(1)   What is the profit-maximizing quantity? _____

(2)   What (approximately) is the total amount of profit? _____

Assume that the demand curve shifts until it is defined by (0, £20) (200, £0). Its MR curve is now defined by (0, £20) (100, £0).

(3)   What will be the new price? _____

101

(4) For how long will it persist? _____

(5) Assume that the demand curve shifts until it is defined by 0, £21; 200, £0. What will be the new price? _____

(6) What will be the new level of profits? _____

(7) So a monopolist must/need not make profits.

THE ABSENCE OF A SUPPLY CURVE IN MONOPOLY (Read p. 264).

What is a supply curve? A supply curve joins all the points which show the quantity offered for sale by a supplier at a given price. One can therefore say, for a firm in competition, 'If the price is *x*, *q* will be offered for sale'. Why can this not be said for a monopolist? To start with, the monopolist is *not* faced with a market price to which he reacts. It is his behaviour which helps *make* the price. Secondly, different *shaped* demand curves (facing the monopolist with unchanged costs) might well result in different outputs but the *same* price. To summarize: in competition, only one output is associated with one price and vice versa. In monopoly, two or more prices may be associated with one output, or two or more outputs may be associated with one price.

Q 8   Patent laws, franchises, molotov cocktails and membership of the Royal Institute of British Architects have one thing in common. What is it? _____

PRICE DISCRIMINATION

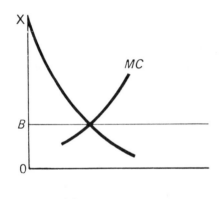

Fig. 5(a)

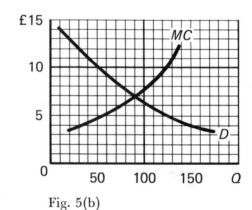

Fig. 5(b)

The demand curve in Fig. 5(a) contains the information that, at prices between *OB* and *OX*, there exist potential purchasers for the commodity. Ordinarily, when the price is *OB*, all those who were willing to pay *more* than *OB* will derive a surplus equivalent to the difference between what they were prepared to pay, and what they actually pay.

If the firm can exploit this by identifying these consumers, and charging them the highest price which they are prepared to pay, then the firm can appropriate this surplus to itself.

Q 9   What, therefore, must the supplier be able to prevent? _____

Q 10   If the seller in Fig. 5(b) were a discriminating monopolist who could separate his purchasers into three groups—those purchasing items 1–40, 41–70, and 71–90— approximately how much surplus could he appropriate? (i.e. how much extra money would he receive per period of time above what he would receive if he could not discriminate?) _____

Q 11   Does the elasticity of demand of those parts of the demand curve which fall below the intersection with the *MC* curve affect potential gain? Yes/No

Q 12   Does the elasticity of demand of those parts of the demand curve which fall above the intersection with the *MC* curve affect potential gain? Yes/No

Q 13   Will the potential gain to the supplier be the higher or lower, the greater the elasticity of demand above the point of intersection? Higher/lower

Q 14   Electricity suppliers commonly charge each consumer a lower rate the more he consumes (i.e., £X for the first A kilowatts, £Y for the next B kilowatts, etc.). Is this price discrimination? Yes/No

Q 15   Soap firms often have promotions in which you pay the full price for the first package or bar of soap that you buy and only 20p for the second. Is this price discrimination? Yes/No

Check your answers to Questions 10–13. If you were wrong, look at Fig. 5 again. The steeper the demand curve above *B*, the higher the prices the discriminator may charge. And the steeper a demand curve, the less elastic it is—as you know!

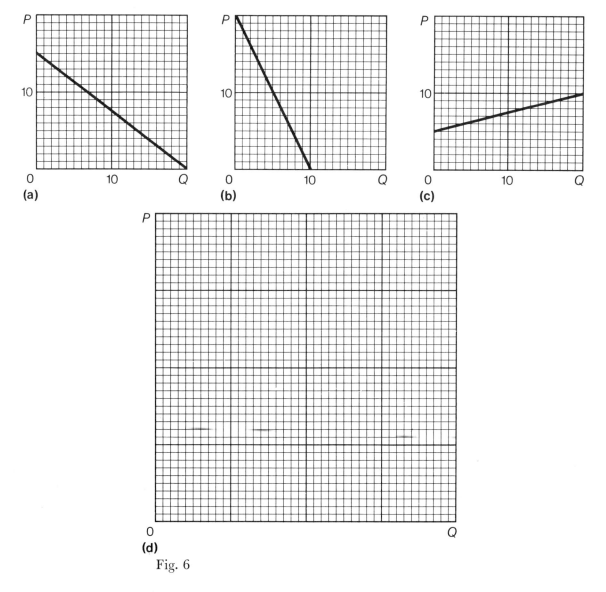

Fig. 6

Q 16   The monopolist whose *MC* curve is given in Fig. 6 (c) sells in the two separate markets whose demand curves are given in Fig. 6 (a) and (b). Construct on Fig. 6 (d) the diagram which will show his equilibrium output.

    (a)   What is the price in market (a)? _____

(b) What is his price in market (b)? _____

(c) What are his sales in market (a)? _____

(d) What are his sales in market (b)? _____

Q 17   Marginal revenue is less than average revenue for a monopolist because the monopolist

(a) must advertise in order to sell his product.
(b) must reduce the price on units he could sell at higher prices in order to increase his sales.
(c) worries about the entry of new firms.
(d) All of the above answers are satisfactory.
(e) None of the above answers is satisfactory.

Q 18   Equilibrium of the monopolistic firm

(a) occurs where $P = MC$.
(b) occurs where $MR = MC$.
(c) occurs where $P = MR$.
(d) necessarily is profitable.
(e) Both (c) and (d) are satisfactory.
(f) Both (a) and (d) are satisfactory.
(g) None of the above answers is satisfactory.

Q 19   The theory of price discrimination predicts that in comparison to single-price monopoly

(a) output will increase, and average revenue will decrease.
(b) output will increase, and average revenue will increase.
(c) output will decrease, and average revenue will decrease.
(d) output will decrease, and average revenue will increase.
(e) None of the above answers is satisfactory.

Q 20   For a monopolist, MR is not equal to price. T/F

Q 21 $MR = MC$ is a condition for a monopolist's profit-maximizing equilibrium. T/F

Q 22   Any good that has substitutes cannot be produced under conditions of monopoly. T/F

Q 23   The Kensington shop 'Sleepeasy' has the only UK concession to import 'Töste' mattresses from Sweden. It is, therefore (in the UK) a monopolist. T/F

Q 24   The larger a firm's profits, the greater will be its monopoly power. T/F

Q 25   Price is greater than MC for a monopolist. T/F

Q 26   It is useful to think of monopoly power as a variable that is subject to empirical measurement. T/F

Q 27   In our theory, monopolists are assumed to be profit-maximizers. T/F

Q 28   Output under price discrimination is predicted never to be larger than output under perfect competition, nor smaller than output under single-price monopoly. T/F

Q 29   Price discrimination can occur under perfect competition as well as under monopoly. T/F

Q 30   If all buyers have identical demand curves, price discrimination based upon quantity of purchase may still be possible and profitable. T/F

Q 31   One of the points (a) and (b) in Fig. 7 could never be taken by a profit-maximizing monopolist. Which one? (a)/(b)

If you couldn't work this out, work through Q 4 again.

104

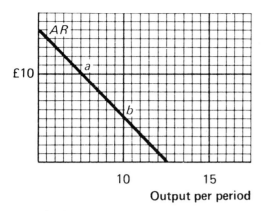

Fig. 7

QUESTIONS FOR DISCUSSION

1   Comment on the monopoly power of the following sellers:

British Leyland
British Gas
British Telecom
British Rail
British Sugar Corporation

How many of these price-discriminate? In what ways?

2   It is sometimes asserted that 'monopolies are creatures of the state'. What do you think is meant by this, and to what extent do you agree?

3   Since there is, by law, only one coal-mining industry, could it, if it were not regulated, maximize profits by setting very high prices? How would it set prices, and what information would you want to have if you were to give advice on the most profitable prices to set?

4   Producers of mechanical and electronic calculating equipment used to give a substantial 'educational discount' to universities purchasing such equipment for academic work. What might lead these firms to choose to abandon this practice, other than legal restrictions? (*Hint*: ask an academic how important computing equipment was to universities years ago and how important it is today.)

5   Here is a terrible warning not to patronize expensive restaurants. This advertisement for one of the most prominent makes of ice-cream appeared in the *Caterer* (22 May 1969): 'THE MOST PROFITABLE SWEET YOU CAN SERVE—Profit: up to £7 per gallon. You get 64 portions (size 20 scoop) from a gallon for no more than 1½p per portion. Charge from 5p to 15p depending on your kind of clientele and your profit on a gallon of ice-cream can be between £2 and £7. The sweets you make yourself can't match that kind of profit! No other sweet can.'

Explain how all the criteria for successful price discrimination are satisfied.

CHAPTER 21

Theories of Imperfect Competition

In the UK, an apple producer sends his apples to market and takes the going price. The processed-food giant Lyons turns the apples into apple pies and sells them to supermarkets at a price which they quote to the supermarket chain. In the first instance, the market is competitive and the firms are *price-takers*, in the second the market is not, and a system of *administered prices* prevails.

MONOPOLISTIC COMPETITION: THE EXCESS CAPACITY THEOREM

A firm in monopolistic competition faces a downward-sloping demand curve. Although its product is differentiated from those of manufacturers of similar goods, its demand curve is very sensitive to changes in the prices of these other goods.

Q 1   How do we represent the effect on the firm's demand curve of changes in the prices of closely competing products? _____

Here is a short-run equilibrium diagram of a microcomputer company (Fig. 1).

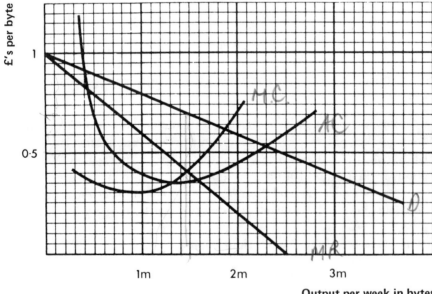

Fig. 1

Q 2   (1)   Label the curves.

           (2)   What is the *SR* equilibrium price? _____

           (3)   What is the *SR* equilibrium quantity? _____

           (4)   What is the *SR* equilibrium profit? _____

Q 3   Because the company is now making profits, what will be the reaction of at least some other firms? _____

Q 4   (1)   The increase in the number of firms among whom total demand has to be shared will cause the company's demand curve to shift to the right/left.

       (2)   The immediate influx of new firms means that, to start with, the *AR* curve shifts £1m to the left, parallel to its old position. Will there be an incentive for even more firms to enter the industry? Yes/No

       (3)   Assume that the next influx causes an additional shift to the left of £1.2m. Now what will some firms do? _____

Q 5   What will the price be when the firm is in equilibrium, assuming that the demand curve shifts parallel to its previous position?

    We know that if a firm maximizes profits, then marginal revenue equals marginal cost (this holds for competition and monopoly, but in competition $MR = AR$).
    This gives us one condition that must be satisfied in equilibrium—i.e. $MR = MC$.

Q 6   This is a necessary/sufficient condition for profit maximization.

    Check your answer to Q 6. Unless you are quite confident that you understand this point, do Q 7. Otherwise, go to *.

Q 7   (1)   '$MR = MC$ is a necessary condition for profit maximization' means that if MR does not equal MC, then profits might not be/are not being maximized.

       (2)   *But*, it is possible that $MR = MC$, yet profits are not being maximized. This would be true in which of the diagrams in Fig. 2?

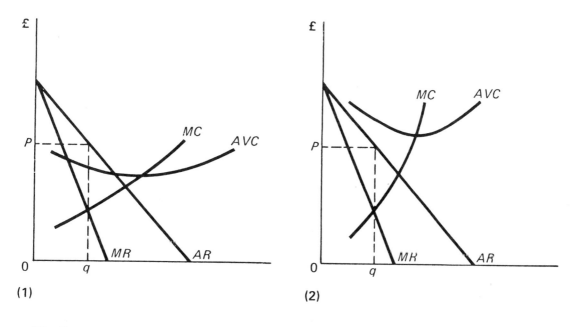

(1)   (2)

Fig. 2

    Check your answer to Q 7. If you were wrong, then you should re-read Lipsey pp. 235–9.

    *We have just studied one necessary condition, that $MR = MC$. We also know that in a competitive equilibrium—and monopolistic competition is, of course, competitive—profits will be zero. This gives us a second condition.
    The second condition is, in fact, a sufficient condition—that is, if it is satisfied the first must be satisfied also. This may not seem obvious; a diagrammatic representation will help, but you must follow the argument of the next five paragraphs closely.

107

As long as the demand curve cuts a segment of the *SRATC* curve, it is possible to make a profit. (Read pages 273–4 again, if this is not clear.) Therefore no such demand curve can persist in equilibrium, because of the incentive to other firms to enter the industry.

If, however, the demand curve were to fall below the *SRATC* curve—e.g. *D'''* in Fig. 3—the firm will not be able, in the short run, to find a point where it may produce and cover its costs. (Ignore the *LRAC* curve at the moment.)

So this cannot be an equilibrium demand curve. The only possible short-run equilibrium position is where the demand curve is _____ (Q 8) to the_____ _____ (Q 9) curve. We know, however, that output is set where *MR* cuts *MC*—therefore this intersection must be vertically below the point of tangency. We provide a brief (and optional) demonstration that this is the case.

At the equilibrium position, the *AR* and *SRATC* curves pass through the same point, and have the same slope. This in turn means that at this point the *total revenue* and *total cost* curves will also be tangential. (They must obviously pass through the same point, yet since

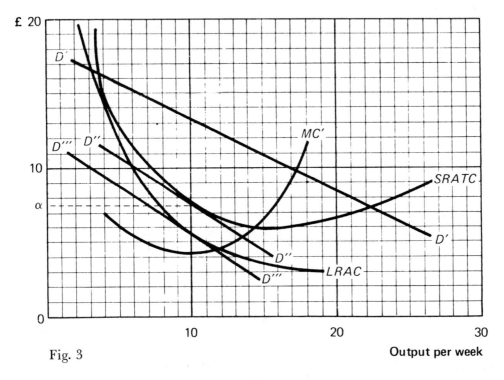

Fig. 3

SRATC is everywhere else above *AR*, the *TC* curve must be everywhere else above the *TR* curve.) Make sure now that you know what we have established so far.

The final stage is to remember what the *MR* and *MC* curves measure. They measure the rate of change of *TR*, and of *TC*—and that is, of course, the slope of the curve. So at the equilibrium point they must be *equal*. They are clearly not tangential, since the rate of change of the *TC* curve is first below that of the *TR* curve, and then above it (check this on the diagram), so *they must cut*. And this is what we set out to establish.

Q 10   Look at Fig. 4, which shows the equilibrium of a firm in monopolistic competition.

Draw in a possible marginal cost curve. It must pass through two points.
These points are

(1) £ _____   Q _____

(2) £ _____   Q _____

Check your answer. If you were wrong, then re-read Lipsey pp. 216–17. You should know that *MC* curves always cut *AC* curves at their lowest point—look again at p. 79 of the Workbook. And in any position of equilibrium, *MC = MR*, otherwise the firm would make more profits by simply producing more, or less.

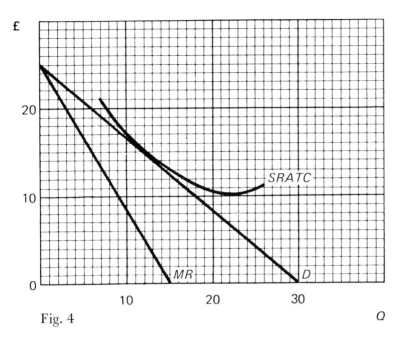

£

20

10

0

10   20   30

SRATC

MR   D

Fig. 4   Q

Q 11   Assume that the firm has reached the position α in Fig. 3 by the process we have
described. It has remained on its *SRAC* curve, since it has retained the same capital
equipment. It now has an incentive to move on to its *LRAC* curve, in order to
produce an output of 10 units p.w. more cheaply.

(1)   When it has done this, what will be its *SR* profit? _____

(2)   What will be its *LR* profit? _____

If you answered Q 11 incorrectly, then you haven't realized that the new *SRAC* curve is in
the same position relative to the new demand curve as the previous one was to the old
demand curve. So the process will start again, and will continue until _____
_____ (Q 12).

This implies that there will be overcapacity in the industry, *both in the short and long run.*
If you do not completely understand why this is the implication, first of all re-read note 1
p. 223 on the *LRAC* curve, then do Q 13. Otherwise go to †

Q 13   (1)   In long-run equilibrium, the demand curve to the firm must be tangential to
the upward/downward sloping part of the *LRAC* curve.

(2)   This means that the firm will want to move to a position where it is at the
minimum point of a different *SRATC* curve. T/F

Check your answer to Q 13 parts (1) and (2). Monopolistic competition leads to excess
capacity, both in the short and the long run. In the short run it is easy to understand; a
profit-making firm, with the optimal capital equipment, finds that its profits _____
_____ (3) other firms into the industry and this causes its sales to _____ (4).
(This means that its demand curve shifts to the right/left) (5). Its capital stock is therefore
appropriate to a larger output than its equilibrium output. So it has excess capacity because
it has *not* got the optimal capital stock.

But in the long run, as it seeks to reduce costs, it must move to its _____ (6)
curve. And, as we have seen, it must move to that part of this curve where it is best to use a
capital stock which could be operated even more cheaply at a higher level of output. (This is
the point made on Lipsey p. 223, which you should re-read if necessary.) So in this case,
although the firm has excess capacity, it is on its optimal *SRATC* curve.

(7)   Why doesn't the firm use its equilibrium capital stock to produce a higher output,
since we have deduced that the higher output will have a lower average cost?

_____

†We have, therefore, derived three closely linked predictions.

Q 14   (1)   Prices will be lower/higher than if the industry were competitive. Why?

        (2)   Prices will be above average cost/marginal cost.

        (3)   The industry will, both during the equilibrating process and at equilibrium, suffer from over/under capacity.

        (4)   We refer to this as the _____ theorem.

OLIGOPOLY

Q 15   Label the curves in Fig. 5. Point b is referred to as (1) _____ , and point c as (2) _____

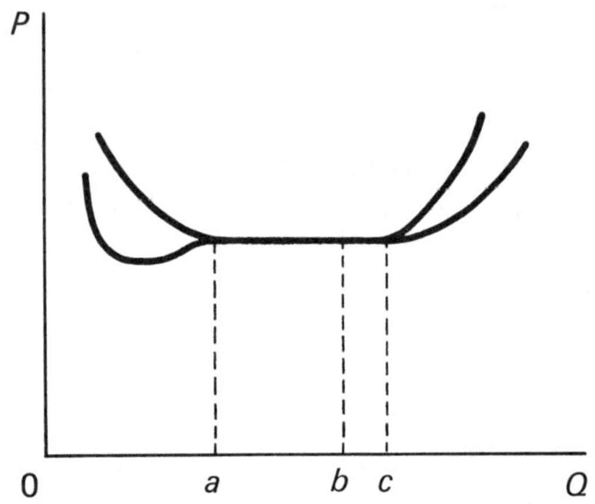

Fig. 5

Q 16   In which of the following situations would it be least likely that the cost curve would be as shown in Fig. 5?

        (1)   A typing agency?

        (2)   A computer bureau using a main-frame computer?

        (3)   A firm providing a computing service using micros?

        Why? _____

PROFIT-MAXIMIZATION WITH COSTLY PRICE CHANGES

Fig. 6 applies to the conditions described in Lipsey p. 280.

Q 17   (1)   Label the curves. (Ignore the dotted line.)
           The normal profit-maximizing output is _____ , and price _____ .

        (2)   The normal mark-up is _____ over average variable cost.

        (3)   If the demand curve shifts and becomes the dotted line, what will be the new output? _____ and the new price? _____

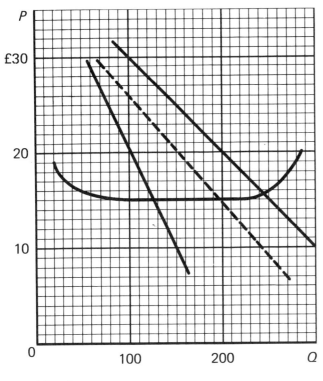

Fig. 6

QUALIFIED JOINT PROFIT-MAXIMIZATION

The reasoning behind this hypothesis is not difficult to understand; if all the firms make an agreement to act as a single monopolist, the total profit to the industry will be maximized. But it will still be in the interests of the *individual* firm to lower its price and increase its sales at the expense of the others, if it can get away with it.

But the recognition of the importance of its competitors' reactions differentiates this case from the case of the perfectly competitive producer. Unfortunately there is no simple theory that predicts precisely how close a group of oligopolistic competitors will come to the monopoly position of joint profit-maximization. What we do instead is to outline some of the conditions which, it is hypothesized, will permit the firms to move in the direction of joint profit-maximization.

Q 18   Which of the total cost curves of Fig. 7 (a) and (b) will inhibit the entry of new firms more?

Q 19   Firms in an oligopolistic industry have production costs as in Fig. 7(c). They decide to embark on an advertising programme in order to raise the barriers to entry which new firms would face. Assume that they each undertake £200,000 worth of advertising per year. Sketch in their *new ATC* curve. (*Hint*: draw in the average advertising cost curve first, then add the two curves vertically.)

(1)   What is the new *ATC* at an output of 2 per year? _____

(2)   What is the new *ATC* at an output of 3 per year? _____

(3)   What is the new *ATC* at an output of 5 per year? _____

(4)   What is the new *ATC* at an output of 10 per year? _____

Brand proliferation provides an explanation for the multitude of different brand-names for one firm's product. The explanation (p. 287) depends upon a hypothesis that there are some products where consumers value a change, even if it is only a change in packaging.

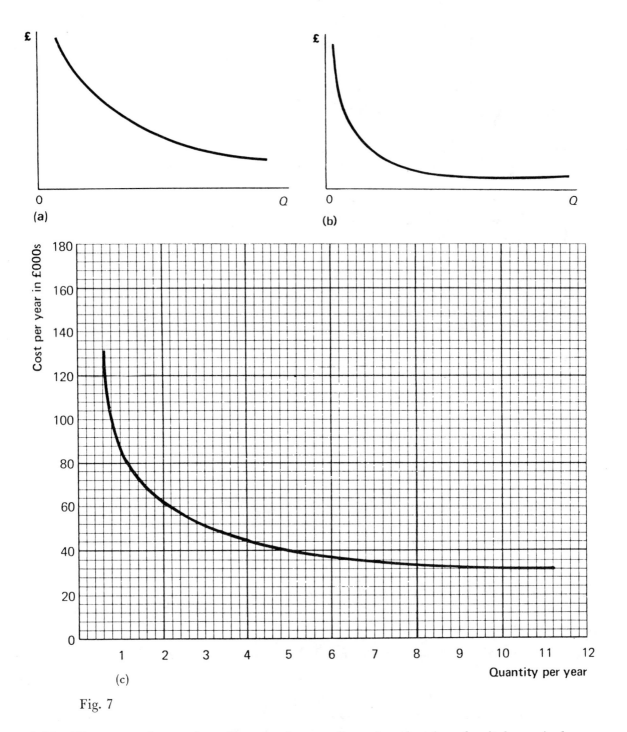

(a)

(b)

Cost per year in £000s

Quantity per year

(c)

Fig. 7

Q 20   The greater the number of brands, the more/less of random brand switches a single new firm can expect to pick up.

Q 21   The important difference between our assumptions for monopolistic competition and those for perfect competition is that monopolistic competitors

(a)   don't try to maximize profits.
(b)   worry about their influence on the market.
(c)   have an inelastic demand curve facing them.
(d)   sell similar but not identical products.

Q 22   Which of the following conditions are met at long-run equilibrium in monopolistic competition?

(a) $MR = MC$
(b) $P = ATC$

(c) $P = MR$

(d) $P = MC$

(e)   all of the above

(f)   (b) and (c)

(g)   (a) and (b)

(h)   (b) and (d)

(i)   none of the above.

Q 23   Long-run profits are possible in an oligopolistic industry primarily because

(a)   firms can always set the profit-maximizing price and output.

(b)   oligopolistic firms use the most efficient production methods.

(c)   the demand is typically quite elastic.

(d)   entry of new firms is difficult.

Q 24   The cigarette industry appears to be poorly analysed by the theory of monopoly because

(a)   it has three major firms.

(b)   it has excessive price competition.

(c)   it has enormous amounts of non-price competition.

(d)   smoking is now considered a threat to health.

(e)   Answers (a), (b) and (c) are satisfactory.

(f)   None of the above answers is satisfactory.

Q 25   The hypothesis of qualified joint profit-maximization implies that firms

(a)   are profit-maximizers.

(b)   are unselfish.

(c)   will act as if they had a monopoly.

(d)   are able to exploit the gains from limiting competition in some respects, but not in all respects.

(e)   All of the above answers are satisfactory.

(f)   None of the above answers is satisfactory.

Q 26   Among the essential aspects of oligopoly is

(a)   excess capacity.

(b)   non-price competition.

(c)   a large number of firms.

(d)   mutual recognition of interdependence.

(e)   Both (a) and (b) are satisfactory.

(f)   Both (b) and (c) are satisfactory.

(g)   None of the above answers is satisfactory.

Q 27   The excess-capacity theorem predicts that there will be many firms, with each producing less than the amount that would minimize its costs. T/F

Q 28   Because monopolistic competition has a zero-profit equilibrium, profits play no role in the theory. T/F

Q 29   In oligopoly, the firm does not have a single demand curve that is independent of the behaviour of rival sellers. T/F

Q 30   Oligopoly is impossible if there is no product differentiation. T/F

Q 31   The number of sellers is hypothesized to affect, but does not fully determine, the behaviour of oligopolistic industries. T/F

Q 32   If there is evidence of price cutting in an industry, it is clear that the industry is not oligopolistic. T/F

QUESTIONS FOR DISCUSSION

1   'In a slump most cartels break down because members rat on each other by special sales below the ring prices' — *Daily Mail* City Editor (13.12.74).

Suggest a behavioural mechanism which might explain why price agreements fail when demand falls. Can you devise a set of supply and demand conditions such that price agreements are more likely to fail when the demand curve shifts to the right instead?

2   In 1982 one of the few expanding markets was that for microcomputers. With which model would you analyze the microcomputer market? Why are new micros often marketed before the manuals to explain how to use them are ready? When IBM eventually marketed a Personal Computer, why did they charge more for it than other, smaller, firms did for similar machines?

Was this perhaps price discrimination? Argue the case why it might have been in the interests of IBM to charge less than the other firms.

3   Explain Lancaster's resolution of the excess-capacity theorem debate. Argue against his explanation from the viewpoint of an economic planner in the Soviet Union.

4   In what ways is the retail filling-station industry monopolistically competitive and in what ways is it perfectly competitive? Can you think of any of the predictions of either theory that would be refuted by the behaviour of the firms in this industry?

5   In 1949, the Vice-president of the McGraw-Hill Book Company wrote, in an article in the *American Economic Review*, that, if there were only two firms in an industry, and if they were of the 'hard-driving, fiercely independent type . . . [that] has played such a large part in the industrial development of the USA, two of them would be enough to create a ruggedly competitive situation'. Are two competitors sufficient to guarantee non-monopolistic behaviour? Discuss this argument.

6   It is often claimed that oligopolistic prices are sticky (i.e. that they do not adjust rapidly to market changes). Why do you think this claim is made? How might you go about testing it?

7   In the previous edition of this book, readers were asked to comment on the way in which lawyers charge for their house-purchase services. Here is an excerpt from *Which?*, March 1970, reporting on the system.

'It is illegal for anyone other than a lawyer or owner to prepare the deed transferring ownership of a house, unless that person can prove he didn't do it for gain.

'*Solicitors' scale fees—buying and selling*. The scale charge—the same for buying and selling—depends upon the price of the property registered.

'The buying-selling scales are set (indirectly by Parliament) by a statutory committee, which has to include two solicitors. They set the maximum charge which a solicitor can make for conveyancing.

'The profession itself has made rules to prohibit solicitors from holding themselves out to undercut the scales.

'*Reduction in fees*. About one in five members were given a reduction of some sort.

'Of the members who got reductions, one in three said it was because they were friends or relatives of their solicitors. A few said it was because of business connections, because it was a standard practice of their solicitor, or because they shopped around. Half didn't know why.'

Since 1970, fee scales have been made illegal. What would you predict would have been the effect on solicitors' charges for house transfer in the past twelve years?

In fact, such is the efficiency of the solicitors' old-boy network, charges have hardly altered. Solicitors disapprove of price competition. To test this, telephone a sample of solicitors from your local 'Yellow Pages' and ask them to *quote* for the sale of a £30,000 unregistered title house. When the authors tried this they got an 80% refusal (60% polite, 20% rude).

114

8   Messrs. Rank Xerox have kindly given permission for us to reproduce one of their recent advertisements.

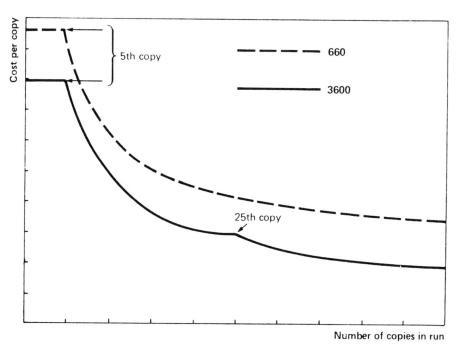

This firm does not sell its machines, but installs them in the customer's office, and charges according to the number of copies made, which the machine records. The graph in the advertisement represents exactly the relationship between cost and numbers in a run of copies from one original.

(1) Make a check that at no point is marginal cost negative. (If at some point it were, what would this imply about the cheapest way to get that number of copies?)

(2) Most large institutions which need document-copying facilities have two possible methods. First, the photocopy, made by such a machine as Rank Xerox produce, and secondly, the stencil, which requires that the document be re-typed on special paper. This is therefore a longer process and is generally used when a large number of copies is required, but the machinery involved is itself less expensive to manufacture. Interpret Rank Xerox's pricing policy in the light of this information.

CHAPTER 22

Competition, Oligopoly and Monopoly: Some Comparative-static Predictions

In this chapter the logical implications of the two sets of assumptions that constitute the basis of the theory of perfect competition and the theory of monopoly are examined.

THE DRIVE TO MONOPOLIZE PERFECTLY COMPETITIVE INDUSTRIES

An implication of the theory of perfect competition is that, at the equilibrium industrial output, price equals marginal cost. Fig. 1 shows such an equilibrium.

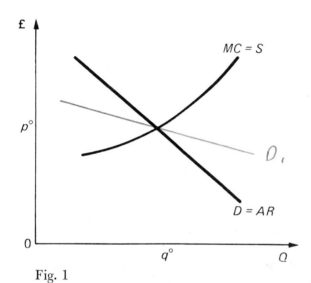

Fig. 1

Q 1   Total revenue to the industry equals _____$p^{0} \times q^{0}$_____

Q 2   Must there *necessarily* be a different price, such that when it is multiplied by its corresponding quantity, total revenue is larger? Yes/No

Check your answer to Q 2. If you were wrong, remember that if an industry is monopolized profits are earned—but revenue might fall. *Costs*, of course, fall *further*, and this is how the profit is earned.

Q 3   Assume that the members of the industry represented by Fig. 1 form a restrictive co-operative. Sketch in how the industry would make a profit.

    (1)   Under what conditions would total revenue fall? _____

Check your answer to Q 3 (1). If you were wrong, do parts (2) and (3), If not, go on to Q 4.

    (2)   If two demand curves pass through the same point, which is the more elastic, the steeper or the shallower? steeper/shallower

(If you can't answer (2), you must re-read Lipsey pp. 100–3 on elasticity. You cannot afford to be unsure about this.)

(3) Sketch in on Fig. 1 a shallower demand curve, passing through point $p°, q°$. You can see immediately that for a change from $q°$ to any q less than $q°$ total revenue from the shallower increases ~~more~~/less than that from the steeper curve. And if the curve is so shallow as to have elasticity greater than one, total revenue actually decreases.

If you still find this confusing, try and think of it 'in reverse'. Elasticity greater than one means that if a producer *drops* his price he sells enough more to *increase* his revenue. It therefore also means that an *increase* in price is accompanied by a *decrease* in revenue. And now, to drive the point of this section home,

(4) If revenue decreases after monopolization, how can it be to the firm's advantage? _____

Q 4   Seven years ago a number of farmers were prosecuted for growing too many potatoes. Why was it in their interest to flout the law? _____

_____

Q 5   In England in the nineteenth and twentieth centuries many powerful suppliers' co-operatives were built up, all in the same sort of market. Can you think what they were? (*Hint*: in the general election of May 1979 the Conservative Party promised to decrease their powers.)

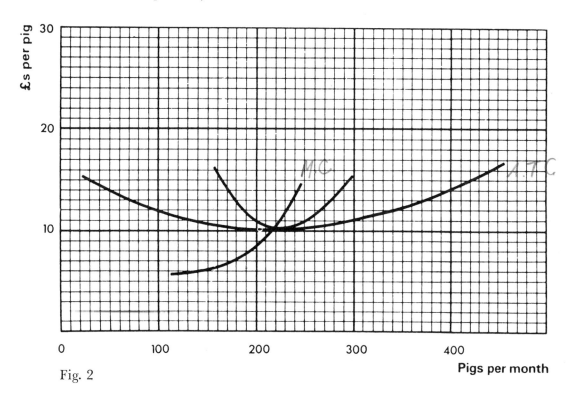

Fig. 2

Q 6   Here is a pig farm in competitive equilibrium (Fig. 2).

(1) Label the curves.

(2) Assume a quota of 140 pigs per month is imposed on this farm. By how much *must* price rise for the farm to stay in business in the long run?

_____

(3) Assume price actually rises by £3 per pig. How much long-run profit will this farm now make? _____

117

(4) How much short-run profit *could* it make (on the original short-run curves), if it could successfully deceive the quota-imposing authority and no one else did so?

_____

A CHANGE IN DEMAND: COMPETITION

Q 7   Here is a firm in competitive equilibrium.

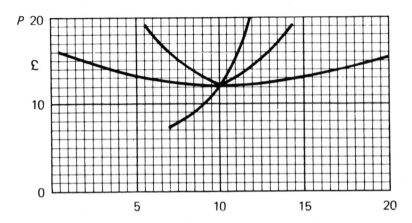

Fig. 3

(1)   Label the curves in Fig. 3. You should be able to do this without any hesitation — check up in Chapter 17 if necessary.

(2)   Construct the *industry* short-run supply and demand schedule on Fig. 4, for the industry of which the Fig. 3 firm is a member, given that the S and D schedules are straight lines, and defined by

$$S; p \text{ (in £s)} = \frac{Q}{250}$$

$$D; p \text{ (in £s)} = 27 - \frac{Q}{200}$$

You are also given that the long-run supply curve is defined by $p = £12$. What is the short-run equilibrium price and quantity? _____

(3)   Assume a rise in demand of 1,000 units at every price.

(1)   With what new equation do we replace the demand equation in Q 7 part (2)? _____

(2)   Draw in the new demand curve on Fig. 4 (extend graph if you need).

(3)   What is the immediate change in price? _____

(4)   Construct a new price line appropriate to this on Fig. 3.

The firm depicted on Fig. 3 is now making profits.

(5)   Approximately what will be its total profits *in the short run*?

_____

The firm will now seek to maximize its profits, and it will do this in the long run by moving to the right along the *LRAC* curve. Say this means that it produces at 15 units per day. Draw in an *AVC* and a *MC* curve for this output. There are, however, two reasons why this cannot be an equilibrium position. One is that this increase in production, and that of other firms in a similar position, must itself lower the price from the level to which it rose initially.

118

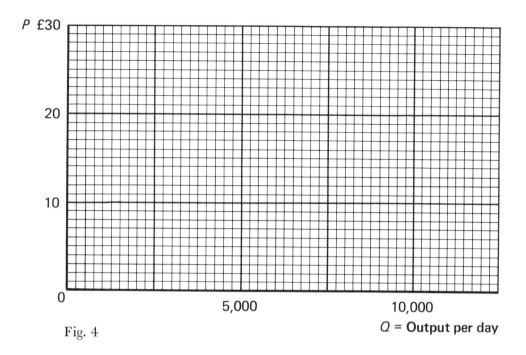

P £30

20

10

0

5,000   10,000

Fig. 4

Q = Output per day

Q 8   What is the second reason? _____

_____

The new price line therefore falls, and, as it falls, in order to continue making profits the firm will be moved along its *LRAC* curve until, when the price line eventually merges with the original one, it will have returned to its old position.

Recap: as long as the price line lies above the minimum point of the *LRAC* curve, profits can be made. As long as profits are made, firms will enter this industry and lower the price line.

Q 9   What assumption in Q 7 has excluded the possibility that the firm's *LRAC* curve might have *shifted* during this process? _____

_____

Q 10   Since each firm is now producing at its old output, how is the increased output necessary to meet the increased demand attained? _____

_____

Q 11   The theory of perfect competition implies, therefore, that in a constant-costs industry an increase in demand will be followed by a change/no change in price, and an increase in the size of the firm/the number of firms in the industry.

Q 12   In competition, the only cause of profits is access by particular firms to superior technology. T/F

Q 13   In competition, a necessary and sufficient reason for a rise in price is a rise in factor costs. T/F

Q 14   A fall in demand in competition will result in no long-term change in price if costs remain constant. T/F

Q 15   A fall in demand in competition will result in a long-term rise in price if factors are bought from firms who experience external economies of scale. T/F

Check your answers so far. If you answered any of the last seven questions wrongly you should re-read pp. 296–9.

The analysis of the effect of a fall in demand is not completely symmetrical with that of the effect of a rise in demand. (This means that one cannot use exactly the same description of the process, replacing the word 'fall' with the word 'rise'.) This is because the adjustment

119

to long-run equilibrium does not necessarily take the same length of time. For a rise in demand, the length of the transitional period depends on how long it takes to go through the process of increasing the capital stock of plant and equipment in an industry. For a fall in demand, it depends on how long it takes to reduce the capital stock in an industry. It might for example take two years to build new capital, but twenty years for existing capital to wear out.

Q 16   It pays a firm to remain in production in the short run even though it is making losses as long as total revenue exceeds total fixed/variable cost.

Q 17   In an industry which encounters economies of scale, a decrease in demand will result in a rise/fall in price.

Q 18   In an industry with an upward-sloping long-run supply curve, a decrease in demand will result in a rise/fall in price.

A CHANGE IN DEMAND: MONOPOLY

You might like to try constructing in the space below a diagram for a monopolist, showing an *increase* in demand, at all prices, but a *fall* in equilibrium price. *Hints*: make your *MC* curve shallow, your initial *AR* curve steep and your subsequent *AR* curve shallow. (Don't spend too long over this, and don't worry too much if you can't do it.)

CHANGES IN COSTS

Q 19   Fig. 5 shows the short-run industrial supply and demand diagram for a competitive industry (ignore the *MR* curve).

(1)   Costs increase by £2 per unit. Draw in the new *MC* curve. What is the change in the short-run equilibrium price and quantity? _____

_____

(2)   Now assume instead that the diagram represents the demand and marginal cost curves of a monopolist. Again, costs increase by £2 per unit. What is the change in the equilibrium price and quantity? _____

(3)   Conclusion—a cost change produces a greater effect on price and quantity in monopoly/competition.

120

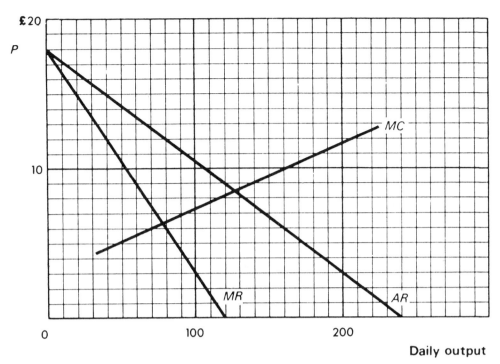

£20

P

10

MC

MR

AR

0   100   200

Daily output

Fig. 5

TAXES

Q 20   What are the three sorts of tax considered? *lump-sum, per-unit*
       profits

Q 21   In the long run, the whole burden of a per-unit tax must fall on the producer.
       True/False

Q 22   What will be the short-run effect of a lump-sum tax levied on a competitive industry?
       Raise price/lower price/neither

Q 23   What will be the total long-run effects of a lump-sum tax on a competitive industry?
       All passed on/none passed on/some passed on

Q 24   Explain your answer to Q 23 _____
       _____
       _____

Q 25   A monopolist's cost and revenue curves are shown in Fig. 6 (label the curves).

       (a)   At what level of sales is elasticity unity? _____

       (b)   At what level are profits maximized?_____

       (c)   What level of specific tax would be required to drive him out of business?
             _____

Q 26   Since a competitive industry does not make profits, what is the use of a profits tax
       on such an industry? _____
       _____

Q 27   A monopolist has control of the price he charges for his product. He will thus be able
       to maximize his profits by:

       (a)   raising his price by the whole amount of a tax, thus passing it all on to his
             customers.

       (b)   absorbing the whole of any cost reductions into his profits, thus passing on to
             his customers none of the benefit.

121

(c) Neither (a) nor (b).

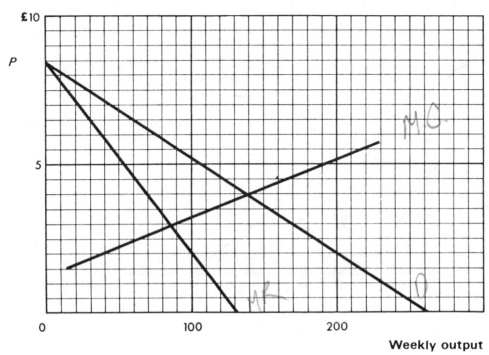

Fig. 6

Q 28 A rise in unit costs is predicted to cause a

(a) rise in price in monopoly, but not in competition.
(b) rise in price in competition, but not in monopoly.
(c) rise in price in both competition and monopoly.
(d) None of the above answers is satisfactory.

Q 29 A fall in demand for the product of a competitive industry is predicted to lead to

(a) a fall in price.
(b) a decrease in the output of each firm.
(c) a decrease in the number of firms in the long run.
(d) All of the above answers are satisfactory.
(e) Only (a) and (b) are satisfactory.
(f) None of the above answers is satisfactory.

Q 30 A fall in demand for the product of a monopolized industry is predicted to lead to

(a) a fall in price.
(b) a decrease in the output of each firm.
(c) a decrease in the number of firms in the long run.
(d) All of the above answers are satisfactory.
(e) Both (a) and (b) are satisfactory.
(f) None of the above answers is satisfactory.

Q 31 Other things being equal, the output change in response to a change in costs is predicted to be

(a) less in competition than in monopoly.
(b) less in monopoly than in competition.
(c) equal in monopoly and competition.
(d) The theory does not yield a prediction on this subject.

Q 32 In competition, in equilibrium, a price change is a sufficient condition for a cost change. T/F

122

Q 33 In monopoly a cost change is a necessary condition for a price change. T/F

Q 34 In monopoly a cost change is a sufficient condition for a price change. T/F

Q 35 If demand rises for a monopolist's product, a sufficient condition for a price rise is that the new demand curve is not more elastic than the old one at the same prices. T/F

Q 36 The market demand curve plays a role both in the theory of competition and in the theory of monopoly. T/F

Q 37 The market supply curve plays a role both in the theory of competition and in the theory of monopoly. T/F

Q 38 No profit-maximizing firm will produce where its own elasticity of demand is less than 1. T/F

Q 39 No profit-maximizing monopolist will produce where demand is inelastic. T/F

Q 40 If you are merely told that the demand for the product of a monopolized industry has increased, then you cannot make a clear prediction about the direction of change of the output of that industry. T/F

QUESTIONS FOR DISCUSSION

1   In February 1983 the British Minister of Health instructed hospitals to ask outside firms for tenders to provide hotel services such as laundry and catering. Why might he have done this? Was it a good idea?

When the Chairman of one Health Authority proposed that his hospital laundry would advertise its services to the private sector and that he was confident that it would rapidly become the largest laundry operation in the area, he was swiftly told to forget it. Why was he so confident? Why was he prevented? (Remember, the government was Conservative, favouring private firms.)

2   Potato farmers in the UK often complain that government restrictions actually prevent them from growing as many potatoes as they want—indeed, they say that productive land is left idle.

(a)   For what might the government's action be a substitute?
(b)   Under what conditions will it benefit the farmers?
(c)   Why do individual potato farmers complain?
(d)   Can 'productive' land where planning permission for non-agricultural use will not be granted ever remain fallow in the long run? If it can, how much competition will there be in the farming industry?

These two paragraphs appeared in the same article in the *Financial Times* (1.10.70):
'This season the Potato Board, under pressure from growers, allowed the acreage to be grown to be increased to 90 per cent of the basic allotment. The acreage planted rose from 536,000 to 589,000 acres. At the same time the average yield is believed to have been boosted to a near-record level of between 10 to 10½ tons per acre average as a result of very favourable weather for potatoes in certain key growing areas. This more than offset poor crops in other districts and total production should be over 6 m tons.'
'A support-buying programme for potatoes to lift the present low prices being received by producers is likely to be started early in this month because of a surplus of potatoes.
'The Potato Marketing Board confirmed yesterday it was discussing with the Government the introduction of a buying programme in the near future.'

Assume that the voice of the 'growers' referred to in the first paragraph was in fact the voice of the largest and most efficient growers.

(1)   Outline how these growers might benefit, even if there were no support programme, from an increase in permitted production.

(2) Given that every grower were allowed the same percentage increase, under what demand conditions would even the most efficient grower suffer from increased production?

3   'We regret that we can no longer absorb the increased price of flour, and we intend to raise the price of a standard loaf by 1½p. Other firms will no doubt follow this signal'—a spokesman for a very large bakery firm, October 1974.

(a) Is the baking industry competitive?
(b) If the large firm is a monopolist, is it a profit-maximizing monopolist?

4   'A government policy that increases the costs of all firms is unfair because it is easier for monopolists who set their own prices to pass on cost increases to the consumer than it is for perfect competitors whose prices are given.' Comment on this assertion, ignoring the normative issues.

5   France is occasionally beset by 'artichoke wars'. When good weather produces a bumper crop, prices fall sharply and angry farmers from Brittany storm into Paris, even barricading the streets with artichokes in protest. Assuming that not many artichokes are used up in pelting the citizenry of Paris, what would you say to the farmers if called upon to advise them? You are expected to be honest with them, and to explain the difficulties as well as the advantages of your plan.

CHAPTER 23

Competition, Oligopoly and Monopoly: Some Predictions about Performance

Q 1 Under perfect competition, in equilibrium, *price* equals *marginal cost*. Under monopoly, price is greater than/lower than marginal cost. Let us examine in detail why (upon first acquaintance, at least) the former situation is better for consumers than the latter.

Fig. 1 shows demand, marginal revenue and marginal cost curves for an industry (label them), producing a good, *x*.

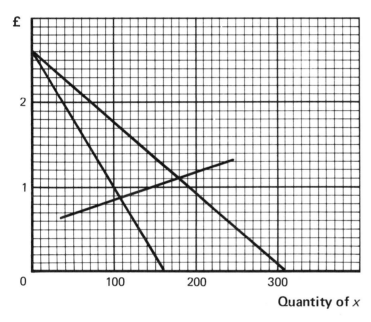

£

2

1

0   100   200   300

Quantity of *x*

Fig. 1

Q 2 (1) Under competition, equilibrium price is _____ , equilibrium quantity is _____ .

(2) Under monopoly, price is _____ , quantity is _____
_____ .

We shall focus attention on the part of the demand curve which lies between the competitive and the monopolistic prices. The demand curve tells us that, if the price of *x* were £1.50, for example, _____ would be demanded (Q 2 (3))—25 more than at the monopoly price of £1.70. (There would either be new consumers, or old consumers buying more.) *Yet each of these extra items would still be produced at less than marginal cost.* If the price were £1.40, 140 would be demanded—and the 10 extra would still be produced at less than marginal cost. Until the price of *x* falls to £1.10, the extra items would be produced at less than marginal cost.

We now have to analyse exactly what it means when the price which people are prepared

125

to pay is greater than marginal cost, and we must first of all remember what economists mean by cost. *They mean* _____ (Q 2 (4)). So, 'price of x is greater than marginal cost' *means* 'price of x is greater than the value of what has to be given up in order to produce x'. This implies that, to maximize value, resources should be switched from the production of alternatives to the production of x, until the value of the extra x is no longer greater than the value of what has to be given up in order to produce it. So at every point of the demand curve to the left of its intersection with the marginal cost curve, which is the position of _____ equilibrium (Q 2 (5)), it is worthwhile switching resources into the production of x, since by doing so overall value is increased.

Q 3   Plot the following observations of quantity *demanded* for the product of a competitive industry, and construct the demand curve, by interpolation, on to Fig. 2.

Price	*Quantity demanded*
£1.00	43
£1.60	30
£2.30	15
£1.20	39
£0.50	54
£3.00	0

Now plot on Fig. 2 the industry supply curve defined by the equation $y = 2x$, where y represents quantity in units of 1, and x price in units of 10p.

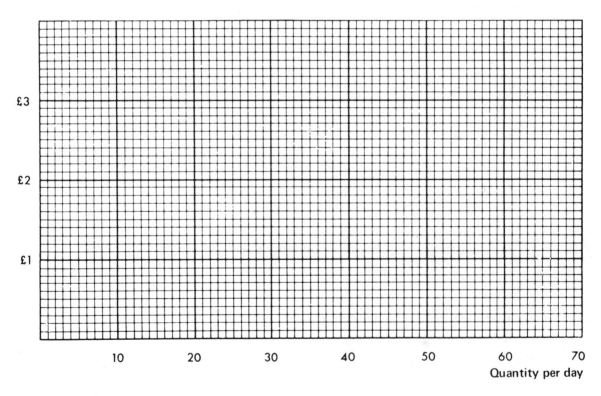

Fig. 2

(1) (Optional) What is the equation of the demand curve? _____

_____

(2) What is the equilibrium price and quantity? _____

_____

(3) Must £1.55 be the average cost for *all* suppliers in the short run?
Yes/No

(4) If the solution in (2) above is the equilibrium price in the long run, must £1.55 be the average cost for *all* suppliers in the long run? Yes/No

Assume now that the industry becomes a monopoly. Whereas previously the hidden hand of the market removed from the suppliers any element of choice about their activities, now the monopolist can actually choose any number of different profit-making positions. We assume that this monopolist is a *profit-maximizer*. This means that he equates marginal cost to average revenue/marginal revenue (Q 3 (5)).

Construct his marginal revenue curve on Fig. 2. (*Hint*: it must be a straight line.)

(6) What is the new equilibrium price and quantity? _____

(7) How much daily profit is the monopolist making? _____

(8) Is price higher or lower than in the competitive case? Higher/lower

(9) Is quantity supplied higher or lower than in the competitive case? Higher/lower

Check your answers to Q 3. If you did not answer it successfully, or if you would like some more practice in the construction of these curves, do Q 4. Otherwise, go on to *.

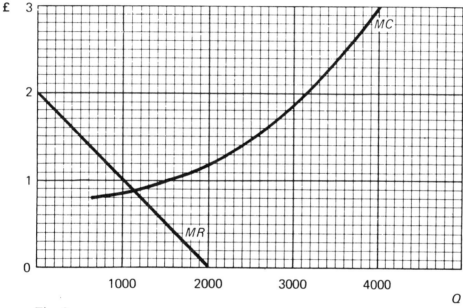

Fig. 3

Q 4   Fig. 3 represents the marginal revenue and marginal cost curves of a monopolist.

(1) What is the equilibrium quantity? _____

(2) What is the equilibrium price? _____

Check your answers to Q 4 (1) and (2). If your answer to (2) was £0.87, then you were being careless. If you did answer it correctly, and if you feel that you have the relationship between the *AR* and *MR* curves completely taped, skip to the *. If not, read on.

In Chapter 20 we constructed a marginal revenue curve from an average revenue curve, and we remember that if the *AR* curve is a straight line, so is the *MR* curve. It is also true that if the *MR* curve is a straight line, so is the *AR* curve. We will now construct the *AR* curve from the *MR* curve in Fig. 4.

We first notice that when quantity sold stands at one unit only, then *TR* = *MR*, since the marginal unit sold is the only unit sold. *AR*, which equals *TR* ÷ volume of sales, is therefore also the same. The first point to mark in on the *AR* curve is therefore the point £1.50, 1. Now *TR* at sales of one is £1.50. The *MR* curve tells us that the sale of the second unit brings an addition to *TR* of £1.00. So at sales of 2 units, *TR* = £1.50 + £1.00 = £2.50. *AR*, therefore,

127

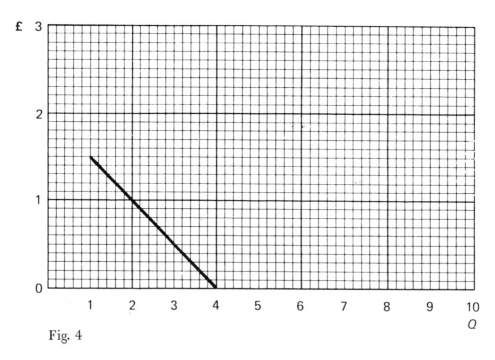

£ 3

2

1

0

1   2   3   4   5   6   7   8   9   10

Q

Fig. 4

which equals $TR \div Q$, equals £2.50 ÷ 2, = £1.25. So the second point to mark in on the AR curve is the point £1.25, 2.

The MR curve tells us that the sale of the third unit brings an addition to TR of _____ _____ (Q 4 (3)). So at sales of 3 units, TR = _____ (Q 4 (4)). AR therefore equals _____ (Q 4 (5)). So the third point to mark in on the AR curve is the point _____ (Q 4 (6)).

Check your answers, and work out AR at Q of 4 in the same way. Draw a line through the points, down to the horizontal axis. *You'll see that it cuts this axis twice as far along from $Q = 1$ as the MR curve does.* For convenience (and in order to deal with these lines mathematically) when we are dealing with large quantities, such as in Fig. 3, we start both lines at $Q = 0$, not $Q = 1$. So the AR curve in Fig. 4 cuts the horizontal axis at 4,000, not 3,999. We ignore the slight inaccuracy to which this leads.

*We assume that, when the industry changed from a competitive to a monopolistic structure, there were no changes in cost or demand conditions. We will now change this assumption. (Questions 5–7 refer to Fig. 2.)

Q 5   Assume that new economies of scale are exploited by the monopolist, and that over the output range 10 upwards the marginal cost curve shifts down by £0.50. What is the new equilibrium price and quantity? _____

Q 6   Assume also that a large advertising campaign by the new monopolist shifts the demand curve 6 units to the right at each price. What is the new equilibrium price and quantity? (You will have to construct a new MR curve.) _____

Q 7   Assume that instead of the exploitation of economies of scale, the monopoly runs into difficulties of managerial co-ordination, so that the MC curve shifts £0.46 up from the position of the competitive supply curve. (Assume that the demand-curve shift in Q 6 remains.) What will be the new equilibrium price and quantity? _____

The classical preference of competition to monopoly was based on the argument that competitive organization led to the best allocation of resources, that monopolistic organization led to a different allocation of resources and that monopoly was therefore inferior to competition.

THE EFFICIENCY OF PERFECT COMPETITION

Q 8   Are the following situations steps towards Pareto Optimality?

(1) Old-age pensioners receive a pension increase paid for by increased taxation. Yes/No

(2) Old-age pensioners receive coupons for issues of free fillet steak from the Euro-mountain. Yes/No

(3) My new wordprocessor enables me to write this book more quickly, and to save half the salary of a secretary. Yes/No

(4) My new wordprocessor enables me to write this book more quickly, and to enable my secretary to concentrate on the less tedious aspects of her job. Yes/No

Q 9 (1) For a firm to be productively efficient it must be operating with a rising marginal cost curve. T/F

(2) For a firm to be operating in a productively efficient industry, its marginal cost curve must not be declining. T/F

Q 10 Whenever firms face downward-sloping demand curves, marginal revenue will be (1) _____ than price. Since *MR* will be equated to (2) _____ , this will also be (3) _____ than price. So allocative inefficiency (4) will/will not occur, since an increase in production would lead to a (5) greater/lower value being produced than cost incurred.

Q 11 Which of conditions 1–3, pp. 313–14, would be unfulfilled if the following were true?

(1) The demand for shop leases in new shopping precincts is an example of a snow-ball effect. If Tesco takes a lease so will Boots, and then Marks and Spencer and Mothercare. With each new lease taken the number of circulating shoppers increases, thereby increasing the revenue of existing shops. _____

(2) The price of certain drugs is much higher to retail pharmacists than to hospitals.

(3) Very large 'Euro-size' lorries do more damage to the roads per ton of goods carried than smaller lorries. _____

The classical position was that, with a few exceptions, monopolies would hold production below the optimum level, which was in general the level reached by competitive organization. The few exceptions were of the sort which we have described in Q 4.

Q 12 What did the liberal economists say should be done with natural monopolies like railways? _____

The duplication of railway lines or water pipes, necessary to competition, was an obvious reason why costs would be lower in monopoly; but there was a much more general argument why long-run or very long-run productivity would be higher in the case of monopoly than competition. This argument is described on pp. 318–20, which you should now re-read.

Q 13 The classical proposition that monopolization of a competitive industry will lead to higher prices and lower output is

(a) a deduction from the fact that demand curves slope downward.
(b) a deduction from downward-sloping demand curves, provided that costs are unchanged.
(c) a value judgment.

Q 14 If one cannot say anything about the effect of monopoly and competition on costs, one cannot predict whether prices will be higher or lower under competition. T/F

QUESTIONS FOR DISCUSSION

1   In 1983 a report was made to the UK Department of Health recommending generic prescribing—this is the replacement of expensive branded drugs by their cheaper, unbranded,

equivalents. The drug companies strenuously objected, saying that in the long run the Government, which foots the drugs bill, would not in fact save money. Why would they object? Could their reasons be valid? Produce some arguments for and against the drug companies' claim.

2   'The patent laws should be revised so as to prevent monopolistic abuse of the patent grant without destroying the incentive to innovate.' Suppose you had to propose such a reformulation, what would you want your new law to provide for and what information might you want first?

3   State the classic case against monopoly as provided in this chapter. Is it sufficient to convince you of the value of anti-combine laws? What other considerations pro and con occur to you?

4   Many of the earlier inventors in the time of the industrial revolution earned very little for their simple but revolutionary inventions that transformed industries such as cotton textiles. Why do you think this was so?

5   Professor Steiner developed his theory concerning product differentiation (see p. 321) before either the introduction of the BBC second TV channel or the introduction of local radio stations in the UK.

(1)   Given that the largest group of listeners is interested in pop music, what does Steiner's theory predict about the nature of the programmes on all the local stations?

(2)   Would you expect the local stations to produce programmes which were in some sense 'between' those on the BBC Radio 1 and 2 and Radio 4 service, or to produce programmes that were even more pop-orientated than those on BBC 1 and 2?

(3)   If the BBC wishes to maximize its total TV viewing audience, how would you expect the programmes on BBC 2 to compare with those on BBC 1 and ITV? Would this be the result that satisfied most of the audience? Has this happened?

(4)   The Independent Television Authority is the statutory body in the UK which is responsible for 'standards' in the quality of programmes put out by the independent television companies. One of these companies, London Weekend Television, was in financial difficulties, which were exacerbated by quarrels between producers, who on the whole favoured 'high quality' programmes, and executives whose main concern was naturally some sort of vague approximation to profit maximization. Mr Rupert Murdoch, the well-known publisher of the *News of the World* which is a newspaper that few would accuse of sacrificing profitability for standards, was prepared to inject large quantities of money into London Weekend Television in return for virtual control. This scheme was vetoed by the ITA.

Account for the actions of the ITA. If you disapprove of their disapproval, might your attitude be changed if there were more than one independent television company broadcasting in London at the weekend? Is the nature of the programmes put out by the BBC relevant?

(5)   Recently the ITA has started a new channel—Channel 4. Why does it show programmes satirized by Les Dawson as 'Hamster breeding for retired quantity surveyors'?

CHAPTER 24

Criticisms and Tests of the Theory of Supply

In this section of the workbook we shall confine ourselves in the main to the Hypothesis of Full Cost Pricing, and the Hypothesis of the Separation of Ownership from Control. You should, of course, read the whole of the chapter, paying particular attention to pages 329–30.

Q 1   Is full cost pricing consistent with competitive behaviour? Yes/No

Q 2   Assume that a full cost pricer is a member of an industry whose equilibrium price is 50p per article. His conventional mark-up is $\frac{1}{7}$ of his average costs, and his output is 500 articles a day. What are his total daily costs? _____

Q 3   Fig. 1 shows the marginal cost curve, the average variable cost curve, the demand and marginal revenue curves of a monopolist.

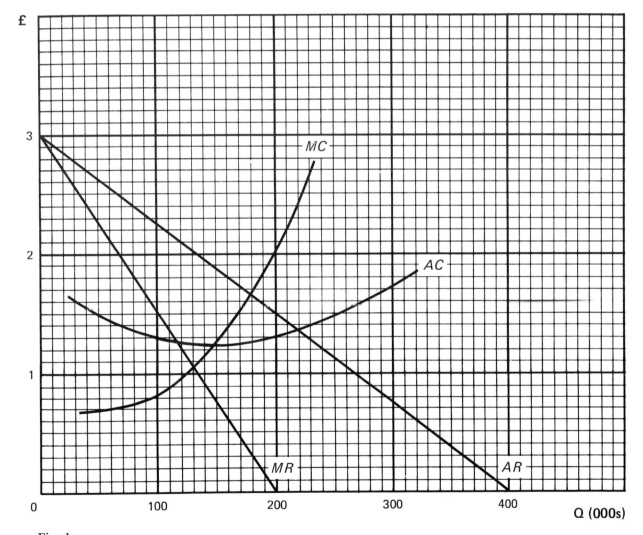

Fig. 1

(1) Assume that the only figures which he has tell him that, in the past, his variable costs have been about £1.30 per article. His conventional mark-up is 20%.

    (1) What quantity will he actually supply? _____

    (2) What will be his total excess of revenue over variable cost? _____

    (3) If his fixed costs (including interest payments) are £20,000, what will be the level of his 'monopoly profits'? _____

(2) How much extra profit could he make if he knew his cost and revenue curves and maximized his profits? _____

The Hypothesis of Separation of Ownership from Control can lead to a prediction that a firm will maximize not profits, but the level of sales.

Q 4   Could this prediction be made for a firm in perfectly competitive equilibrium? Yes/No

Q 5   If your answer to Q 4 was Yes, what difference would the managers make?

_____

Check your answers to Q 4 and Q 5. If you are confused about this, remember that in perfect competition a firm's behaviour is determined by market forces, and not the wishes of its owner.

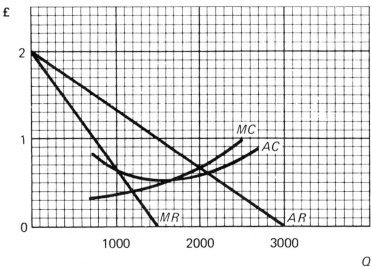

Fig. 2

Q 6   (1) Fig. 2 shows the usual data for a monopolist. (*AC* now includes a return on capital.) Assume that the wages of management increase with the level of sales, and that the management's interest is to maximize its own wages. What would be the difference in the level of sales between the profit-maximizing output, and the management's wages-maximizing output? _____

_____

    (2) Why would it not be in the interests of management for sales to increase to a steady level greater than 2,100? _____

Q 7   Is it possible for a businessman to maximize his profits without being aware that he is doing so? Yes/No

Q 8   'If a firm does not seem to be maximizing its profits, then we can always say that it is nursing its market position, and is really seeking to maximize its *long-term* profits.' Is this a useful approach? Yes/No. Explain.

_____

_____

If you were wrong, re-read p. 331.

Q 9   Which of the following hypotheses is likely to be untestable?

    (a)   sales-maximization
    (b)   profit-maximization in the long run
    (c)   short-run profit-maximization
    (d)   satisficing
    (e)   full-cost pricing
    (f)   all of the above
    (g)   none of the above.

Q 10   Which of the following hypotheses does not predict that output will necessarily rise in response to a decrease in cost?

    (a)   sales-maximization
    (b)   profit-maximization
    (c)   full-cost pricing
    (d)   both (a) and (b)
    (e)   both (b) and (c)
    (f)   both (a) and (c)
    (g)   none of the above.

QUESTIONS FOR DISCUSSION

1   Provide analogies for the following events, according to the 'evolutionary' theory of the firm.

(1)   Death
(2)   Survival of the fittest
(3)   Mutation
(4)   Genetically determined behaviour
(5)   Dominant characters
(6)   Recessive characters

2   In January 1979, supplies to petrol filling-stations were drastically reduced by a national strike by the drivers of petrol tankers. Some filling-stations sold their ration at the price which had prevailed before the dispute, and some added about 30%. (All filling-stations sold all their ration almost immediately.) Those who increased their price were denounced as 'profiteers'. They were not. Why not?

3   'We're doing very nicely out of the sugar shortage thank-you very much. We can sell all the German sugar we can get hold of—and we can get as much as we want at a price— and since it's much more expensive we make much more profit out of our mark-up'—the owner of a Birmingham wholesalers, reported on the local radio station in November 1974. What sort of pricing system is this an example of? What is the difference between a unit and an *ad valorem* mark-up?

4   In an article in *The Times* (29.11.68) seven criteria were outlined, which were used by Mr Arnold Weinstock, the chief executive of GEC and the apotheosis of modern managerial efficiency, to '. . . control the performance of divisions within his own group'. They are:

(a)   profits as % of capital employed
(b)   profits as % of sales
(c)   sales as multiple of capital employed
(d)   sales as multiple of fixed assets
(e)   sales as multiple of stock
(f)   sales per employee
(g)   profits per employee.

(1)   Are all these criteria independent—that is, could any of the ratios be deduced from any combination of the others? How many independent ratios are left?

(2)   For each ratio (deal with all the original seven, if you like), what action might Mr Weinstock take if it rose or fell (relative to its counterparts in other firms)? In which cases would he be pleased, and in which displeased? (State specifically any assumptions you might want to make.)

(3)   If you have the opportunity, read the whole article on page 27 of *The Times Business News* (29.11.68). Do you agree that the conclusions of the last paragraph follow from its premises 'by logic'? (i.e. *might* there be other reasons for higher US profits?) Treat this as a discussion of economic *reasoning*, not fact.

(4)   The article provoked the following response:

> *Profit not all*—From Mr K. H. Tuson. Sir,—I am horrified at your article last Friday describing Mr Weinstock's yardsticks of efficiency; if it correctly states his attitude towards the engineering companies he controls I am sorry for him and sorrier still for the engineers and technicians who are the mainstay of his activities.
>
> Does nothing but profit, expressed in terms of money, matter in the world today? What about the quality of the goods which his factories produce; what about the standing of his engineers in the world and their contribution to technical development?
>
> AEI used to be proud of their outstanding advances in steam turbine design and manufacture; are their engineers to go round in future boasting of their sales as a multiple of fixed assets? Another business potentate tried in the thirties to run an engineering company on financial considerations alone and came a sad crash.
>
> You appear to regard the G.E., of America, as a shining example, but in fact when all factors are given proper weight, it stands a long way down in the league table of world engineering firms. If your article indeed sets out the be all and end all of the present management I despair of the future of the group they control. Yours faithfully, K. H. TUSON, Pickhams, Hayreed Lane, Wilmington, Polegate, Sussex.

Restate this argument in the terminology of economic theory. (But do you really think its author is basically interested in profit, even long-term profit?)

5   'Rising costs will put up the price of whisky in the New Year . . . but the Distillers tell me that . . . they would not upset customers by putting up prices during the hectic pre-Christmas trade'—*Daily Mirror* (13.12.74).

Two possible reactions to this are:

(i)   Good old Distillers
(ii)   Typical—just expecting to make a packet from their customers *next* Christmas.

(a)   To what sort of scientist would you go to test which reaction is more correct?
(b)   Why might the hypothesis behind (ii), if included in the theory of long-run profit-maximization, detract from, rather than aid, the theory?

CHAPTER 25

The Demand for and Supply of Factors of Production

We can analyse the process by which factor prices and factor incomes are determined in exactly the same sort of way as we have analysed the determination of the equilibrium price and quantity in a market for final goods.

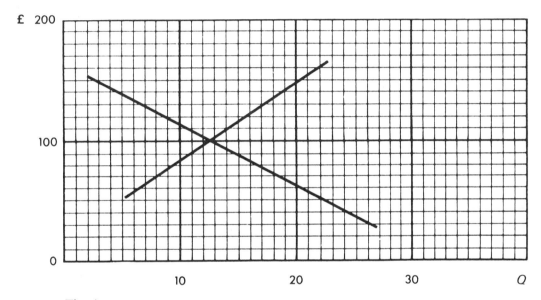

Fig. 1

Q 1   Fig. 1 is a demand and supply diagram for a factor of production. What is the equilibrium total income per period of that factor? _____

Q 2   Substitutes for the factor become much cheaper, with the result that the demand curve shifts right/left by 6 units. What is the new equilibrium income? _____

If you were wrong, then you need to go right back and re-read Chapter 7.

Q 3   What will happen to the home demand for cane sugar refining machinery if the UK is constrained by the wily French to increase its imports of raw beet sugar from Europe at the expense of raw cane sugar from the Commonwealth? _____

Q 4   This is an example of the general proposition that the demand for a factor of production is derived from _____

Table 1 shows how much the product of the *i*th worker can be sold for. All other factors of production are assumed to be fixed.

TABLE 1

Worker no.	Revenue (£s)	Worker no.	Revenue (£s)
7	30	16	19
24	15	35	11.5
12	22	41	10
28	13	50	9.5

Plot these points on Fig. 2, and construct by interpolation the curve fitting them. This curve is called the _____ (Q 5) curve.

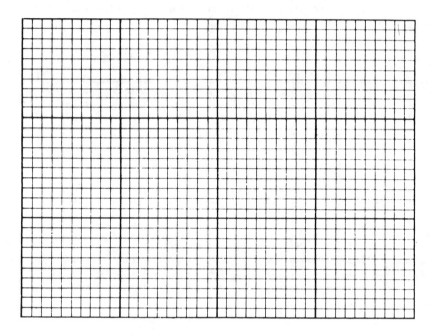

Fig. 2

Q 6   If the wage rate is £15, roughly how much profit per period will the firm make on the product of the:

(1)   5th man? _____

(2)   10th man? _____

(3)   15th man? _____

(4)   20th man? _____

(5)   25th man? _____

(6)   How many men will the firm employ in equilibrium?

Q 7   What will be the firm's excess demand for labour if it is employing 30 men, and the wage rate is:

(1)   £18? _____

(2)   £16? _____

(3)   £10? _____

(4)   £9.50? _____

Q 8   How many workers will be employed in equilibrium if the wage rate which the firm must pay is:

(1) £20? _____

(2) £16? _____

(3) £10? _____

(4) £30? _____

Q 9   In equilibrium, if a firm is maximizing its profit, the marginal revenue product of the variable factor is equal to the _____ of the variable factor. In competition this is merely the _____ . In equilibrium this relationship must hold for all/at least one/only one factor(s).

We have illustrated the cardinal proposition that the marginal revenue product curve of a factor is the demand curve for that factor.

But we have not yet explained how we can determine what the shape of the *MRP* curve is. We have assumed, for the purpose of questions 6—9, the data in Table 1, and we have seen that when this is translated into a graph, the *MRP* curve slopes downwards. But how are the data in Table 1 derived? This is what we shall now explain.

First of all, we will leave value aside, and look at the purely physical relationship between inputs and outputs. We already have a hypothesis which deals with this. Assume that the only variable factor is the factor whose *MRP* curve we wish to find, and the hypothesis of _____ (Q 10) predicts that the extra output produced by successive increments of the variable factor will decline. Examples jump to the mind—farm labourers and fields, detergent and washing machines, car workers and production lines.

So we have so far assumed and illustrated a declining marginal physical product curve. (Its actual shape, of course, depends upon the factual situation in the industry in question.)

The next step is to reintroduce value, and to derive the marginal revenue product curve from the marginal physical product curve.

We shall restrict our analysis to perfect competition, and our method shall be first to make a simplifying assumption in order to demonstrate the way in which the *MRP* is derived from the *MPP*, and then to relax this assumption and make the appropriate changes in our deduction.

The simplifying assumption (p. 354): The output of all other firms is constant.

Q 11 Changes in one perfectly competitive firm's output, as it employs more factors, cause price to change upwards/downwards/not at all.

Q 12 'Therefore the price of the firm's physical product will be the same at all points on the *MPP* curve, and the *MRP* curve is obtained by multiplying each *MPP* by the constant price.' Correct/Incorrect

If you were wrong, read pp. 352 and 353 again.

So far, the analysis has not really been very difficult. Translating a relationship between inputs and outputs, where the outputs are measured in physical terms, into one where the outputs are measured in value terms, presents no problems if, at any level of input and output, the value of the output remains the same.

It gets tricky now, when we relax this simplifying assumption. We now conclude that a change in the price of the variable factor will result in a change in the equilibrium market price of the final product. Indeed, in perfect competition anything else would be impossible. You should now make sure that you understand Lipsey pp. 352—7. We will go through this process step by step.

Step 1   Determine the market price of the commodity for some particular price of the variable factor. To determine the market price we need to know the industry supply curve, and the demand curve. Chapter 19 has taught us how to do this; what we have to do now is to show how the marginal cost curves which we need can be derived from the marginal physical product curves.

Fig. 3 is a *MPP* curve for a firm in a competitive industry. The only variable factor is labour. Fig. 4 is the graph on which we shall plot marginal cost. (We shall do it rather crudely, since the inputs of labour are not infinitely divisible, but come in chunks of one man-week.)

We will assume that the cost of labour is £10 per man-week.

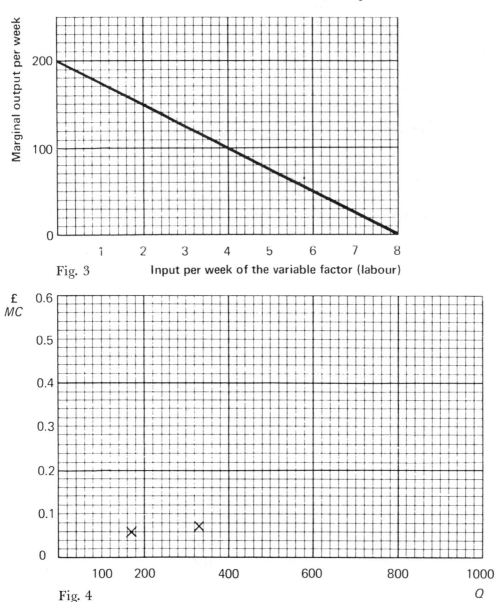

Fig. 3

Fig. 4

The first man yields an output of 175 articles. He costs £10, so we can say that each article costs £10 ÷ 175 = £0.06 (roughly). On Fig. 4 the point 175,[1] £0.06 is marked.

The second man yields an output of _____ (Q 13). He costs £10 also, so each article costs £10 ÷ 150 = £0.07. Total output is now 175 + 150 = 325, and between 175 and 325 the *MC* is £0.07. The point 325, £0.07 is marked.

The third man yields an output of _____ (Q 14). He costs £10, so each article costs £10 ÷ 125 = £0.08. Total output is now 325 + 125 = 450, and between 325 and 450 the *MC* is £0.08. Mark in the point 450, £0.08.

The fourth man yields an output of _____ (Q 15). He costs £10, so each article costs _____ (Q 16). Total output is now _____

---

[1] For ease of exposition we mark this at 175, not 87.5 (= 175 ÷ 2), and we follow this practice through during this demonstration.

138

(Q 17), and between 450 and 550 the *MC* _____ (Q 18). Mark in the point _____ (Q 19).

The fifth man yields an output of _____ (Q 20). Each article costs _____ (Q 21). Total output is now _____ (Q 22). Mark in the point _____ (Q 23).

For the sixth man, mark in the point _____ (Q 24). For the seventh man, mark in the point _____ (Q 25).

The eighth man produces nothing, in no circumstances would be employed, so we'll forget about him.

Draw a line through the points, making the continuity assumption which we explained on p. 23 of the workbook.

This is the firm's *MC* curve. Assume there are 100 firms in the industry, with identical *MC* curves. Re-label the horizontal axis of Fig. 4 to convert it to the industry short-run supply curve. (If you can't do this, re-read Lipsey p. 249.)

The demand curve for this industry is a straight line, defined by the two points demand = zero when price = £0.28, and demand = 24,000 when price is £0.20.

Equilibrium price is, therefore _____ (Q 26). (Check your answer and if you were wrong, find where your mistake was before going on.)

Step 1 is now complete.

Step 2   Multiply every point on the marginal physical product curve by this price, £0.10. All this means is that the output figures on the vertical axis of Fig. 3 are replaced by their value equivalents. So 100 articles at £0.10 each are worth £10, and £200 articles are worth £20. Pencil in on to Fig. 5 the Marginal Revenue Product curve. (Q 27) What is the *MRP* of the sixth man? _____ Do not continue until you are sure about the (very simple) relationship between Fig. 3 and Fig. 5.

This is the 'demand curve for labour' given that labour costs £10 per unit. A strange curve indeed! The only point on it which has any significance is the point £10, 4. All the others are pretty meaningless, at this level of analysis, since the only admissible point on the vertical axis is £10.

Nevertheless, we now have the information that when labour costs £10, the firm will employ 4 units. (If you're not sure why this is, then you haven't properly understood why an *MRP* curve is a demand curve, and you should look again at Qs 5–9.) So mark this point in. This is the end of Step 2.

Step 2½   Go out and have a drink and return fortified for:

Step 3   Go back to Step 1, and assume that the cost of labour is £20 per man-week. Construct the appropriate *MC* curve on Fig. 4. (You don't have to go through the whole tedious procedure, if you notice that £20 = £10 × 2. Each point you mark on the graph will be twice the height of the point for a cost of £10.) Find out the equilibrium price. (Q 28) What is the equilibrium price? _____ Check your answer (making allowances for difficulty in reading the graph).

Now go through Step 2, for a price of £0.15 and pencil in the appropriate curve on to Fig. 5. This time, the only point in which we are interested is the point _____ (Q 29). Check your answer. If you were wrong, and can't see why, then you should work through Step 2 again, making sure you've pencilled in the correct *MRP* line. In this case, of course, the only admissible point on the vertical axis is £20.

If you now go through Steps 1 and 2 again for a number of different labour costs and then join together the different 'admissible points', you will have built up a demand curve for labour.

Q 30   Because the change in the quantity of the factor demanded by a firm consequent upon a change in the factor's price is always reduced by the shifting of the *MRP* curve, the resulting demand curve must be flatter/steeper than any of the *MRP* curves.

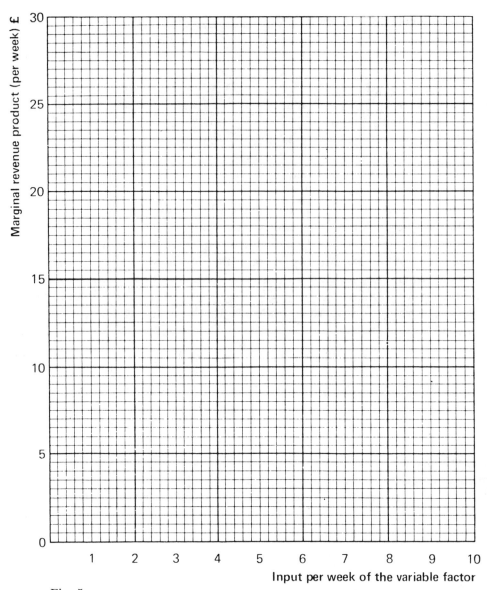

Fig. 5

Q 31   As factor price falls, the industry supply curve for the commodity will shift right/
        left. Price will therefore rise/fall, and the *MRP* curve will shift right/left.

Q 32   The slope of the *MRP* curve depends on the slope of the demand curve for the final
        product. T/F

A PERFECTLY COMPETITIVE INDUSTRY'S DEMAND FOR A FACTOR

There are two ways of deriving the industry's demand curve.

(1)   By aggregating all the individual demand curves obtained by the procedure outlined in
       the last section.
(2)   By aggregating all the marginal cost curves for one price of the factor, then for a second
       price, and so on, and then following the procedure described on page 356.

The only difference between these methods is that the aggregation is made at a different
stage of the analysis of the last section.

THE ELASTICITY OF DEMAND FOR A FACTOR

Q 33   If the price of a factor rises, its employment will fall by the more/less the higher is
        the elasticity of demand for its final product.

140

Q 34   You have the following data:

(a)   Around the prevailing price of £2, the elasticity of demand for good A is 5.

(b)   The supply curve is perfectly elastic.

(c)   The equilibrium quantity is 100 A per day.

(d)   The proportions of the three factors used in A's production are fixed, there is no innovation, and the total amounts spent on the factors X_1, X_2 and X_3 are £100, £25 and £75 respectively.

(1)   What will be the change in X_1's income if its price rises by 25%? (The elasticity formula is on p. 38 if you can't remember it. But you ought to be able to.)

_____

(2)   What will be the change in X_2's income if its price rises by 25%?

_____

Q 34 illustrates that, even if you know the elasticity of demand for the final product, you can say nothing about how a change in a factor's price will affect its income until you know the size of its share in the production of the final good. The smaller the share, the more elastic/inelastic (Q 35) the demand for that factor will be, therefore the more likely it is for a rise in that factor's price to increase/decrease (Q 36) its total income.

Q 37   You are told that, although a particular factor only accounts for 1% of the costs of production of a commodity, its elasticity of demand is very high. You deduce from this that other factors can be easily/only with difficulty substituted for it.

THE SUPPLY OF FACTORS OF PRODUCTION

In this section of the workbook we shall deal with two points:

(1)   The choice between income and leisure.
(2)   The hypothesis of equal net advantage.

Assume that the wage rate for a particular job is 50p per hour. Draw an individual's goods—leisure budget line on Fig. 6. (Ignore the fact that some sleep is physically necessary—this will admittedly mean that he never can choose some positions on the budget line, but this won't affect the analysis.)

Q 38   He chooses to work an eight-hour day. What is his daily income?_____

Q 39   His wage rate halves. Draw his new budget line on Fig. 6. He now chooses to work a ten-hour day. What is his new daily income? _____

Q 40   The hypothesis of equal net advantage (p. 361) would become testable as it stands if we could _____ non-pecuniary advantages. We cannot at the moment do this, so we make a particular assumption about monetary and non-monetary advantages.

Q 41   What is this assumption? _____

_____

Q 42   Fig. 7 shows a hypothetical supply curve of labour to the biscuit industry. How would you represent on this diagram the effects of:

(1)   A rise in the marginal product of labour in the cake-baking industry?

_____

(2)   The construction by the *owners of biscuit factories* of football pitches and tennis courts for their employees?

(3)   A fall in the marginal product of labour in the cake industry?

_____

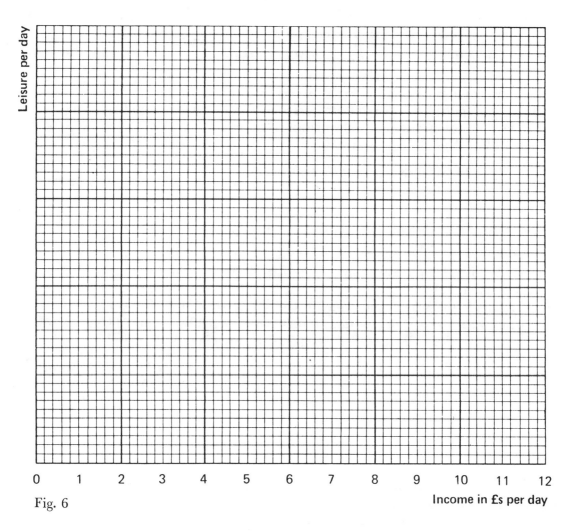

Fig. 6

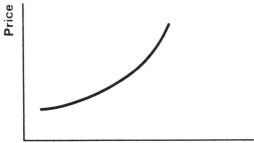

Fig. 7

(4) A rise in the marginal product of labour in the biscuit industry?

_____

(5) An increase in building costs in towns where biscuits are baked?

_____

(6) An increase in crime in cake-baking towns? _____

Q 43   We propose the following hypothesis(es) about factor demand:

(a) It is derived from product demand.
(b) It depends upon relative factor prices.
(c) It is usually inelastic.
(d) It is derived from the cost of production.
(e) All of the above answers are satisfactory.
(f) Both (a) and (b) are satisfactory.
(g) Both (c) and (d) are satisfactory.

142

(h) None of the above answers is satisfactory.

Q 44 Other things being equal, we hypothesise that elasticity of factor demand

(a) varies directly with the elasticity of demand for the final product it makes
(b) varies inversely with elasticity of final product demand
(c) is largely independent of elasticity of demand for the final products
(d) will be higher for factors without close substitutes
(e) Both (a) and (d) are satisfactory.
(f) Both (b) and (d) are satisfactory.
(g) None of the above answers is satisfactory.

Q 45 Marginal productivity theory leads to which of the following propositions?

(a) Wages in competitive markets are below wages in monopolized markets.
(b) The demand of an individual firm for a factor slopes downward.
(c) The total demand for the factor declines.
(d) All of the above answers are correct.
(e) Both (a) and (b) are satisfactory.
(f) Both (b) and (c) are satisfactory.
(g) Both (a) and (c) are satisfactory.
(h) None of the above answers is satisfactory.

Q 46 $MRP = MPP \times MR$. T/F

Q 47 The marginal revenue product of carpenters in two industries must be equal if they both receive the same wages and if the producers maximize profits. T/F

QUESTIONS FOR DISCUSSION

1   'It is necessary for our theory of distribution to have a downward-sloping demand curve for factors of production.' What do we need to know about the actual shape of the demand curve?

2   What assumptions do we need to derive the downward-sloping factor demand curve?

3   In the British National Health Service, the number of patients treated by each hospital specialist has risen only very slowly in recent years, whereas the number of patients treated by each dentist has increased faster. (Dentists have improved their efficiency by various changes in practice.) The members of one of these groups are paid a salary, the others are paid a fee for each procedure performed. Which do you think is which?

4   Assume that in the textile industry, which approximates to a perfectly competitive industry, there is a rise in the price of unprocessed cotton. Trace verbally and diagrammatically the reaction of the firms in the industry to this change, and show the final result on the quantity of cotton demanded.

5   The following remark was overheard at a tea party of the Neasden branch of the League of British Motherhood: 'The trouble with the British worker is that he's bone idle. You should see the absenteeism records of my husband's firm! You don't get it in Portugal, you know—there they really know how to work.'
    The average real wage in the UK is higher than in Portugal. Account for the phenomenon observed by this lady in somewhat less emotive terms.

CHAPTER 26

The Pricing of Factors in Competitive Markets

There is no difference between our analysis of the pricing of consumer goods and our analysis of the pricing of factors of production. In a free market the price of a factor will tend towards the point of intersection of the supply and demand curves.

THE GENERALITY OF THE THEORY OF FACTOR PRICES

All factors of production have a price, and in a free market prices are determined by supply and demand. So the theory is a theory about all factors of production in a competitive market.

CONDITIONS FOR EVERY UNIT OF ONE FACTOR TO BE PAID THE SAME PRICE

The process of the equalization of the returns to identical factors is analysed in the same terms as the equalization of the prices paid for identical consumer goods. In a competitive market in equilibrium no factor will remain in one job if it could earn more in another. So identical factors will move until all differentials are eliminated. As factors move, the 'gaining' firms should offer less as they obtain more factors, and the 'losing' firm offer more to those which remain (because marginal revenue product will fall in the expanding industry and rise in the contracting one).

Q 1   We have two categories for the causes of differences in factor prices (not necessarily identical factors). What are they? _____

_____

Q 2   Into what category might the following fall?

(1)   The difference between the pay of casual labour in the building industry and in agriculture. _____

(2)   The difference between the price of pig iron and sheet metal. _____

_____

(3)   The difference between the rent of a shop in a town and the rent of a house in the same street. _____

We now introduce the two extremely important concepts of Economic Rent, and Transfer Earnings. You should read pp. 368–73 in Lipsey at least twice.

Transfer earnings are defined as the payment necessary to prevent a factor from transferring to some alternative employment. *Economic rent* is defined as any payment made to a factor over and above that necessary to keep it in its present use.

How does this tie in with one's notion that rents are earned in conditions of scarcity? Consider an agricultural community, with everyone earning the same wage, all providing the same sort of labour. If any employer were to offer less wages, his labour would move away into similar employment elsewhere. So all earnings are _____ (Q 3)

Then an agricultural college is set up, and a small number of the most able farm workers are trained in more efficient agricultural techniques. All the farm owners compete for the services of the few graduates of this college, and bid up their wages. The other farm workers would have an incentive to acquire the training, but they are unable to do so. The graduates' *transfer earnings* are therefore the standard wage, and all their additional income is *rent*.

Q 4   Does the Queen earn rent? Yes/No

Q 5   Assume the rate of interest on safe securities is 5%, that repairs to my £10,000 house, plus insurance to cover the difference in risk between securities and the house, cost my landlord £500 per year, and that my rent is £1,000 per year. How much economic rent does he receive? _____

Q 6   Substitute repair and insurance costs of £250 a year in the above question. Now how much economic rent? _____

Q 7   Is it possible for an economic rent to be negative? Yes/No

Q 8   Paranoid Pig (a Punk group) are offered two contracts by agents, one at £50,000 a year and one at £100,000. They accept the larger. Their alternative employment would be on the buses at £60 a week (for all of them). How much rent, and how much transfer earnings do they receive (both inter and intra industry)?

_____

If you didn't get this question right, read pp. 368–73 again. If you did, you can skip the next question.

Q 9   Sykes of Denshaw worsted mill pays his expert spinners £88 a week, but Jagger of Dobcross can only offer £86 a week. All the other mills in the region only produce shoddy, not worsted, and pay their workers a uniform £84 a week. What are the transfer earnings, and what is the rent, of Sykes' workers? _____

_____

Q 10   Fig. 1 is the supply curve of a factor. What is the rent of the factor which would accept work at (1) £15 per week, when 200 are employed in equilibrium; (2) £20 per week when 300 are employed?

Once an oil well has been sunk, the machinery on the rig has no alternative use—all the income from it is rent. But, when the decision comes whether to replace the machinery and to continue pumping, the amount of income earned—which has been rent—is a major factor in the decision whether or not to use the new machinery elsewhere. If, during its life, it had yielded less than the current marginal return to capital, it will not be replaced. If it yielded more, then it was earning a _____ (Q 11) equivalent to the marginal return to capital, plus a pure rent equivalent to the excess, and it will be replaced.

Q 12   Define quasi rent. _____

_____

LAND RENTS AND LAND TAXES

Read up to the end of the chapter.

The essential point to remember is that, given a particular demand curve, the price of a commodity will only change if supply is changed. A tax on rents will not change the supply of the good earning the rent, since, so long as it is earning *some* rent, it is earning more than it could anywhere else (this follows from our definition of rent and transfer earnings).

Q 13   What is the economic attraction of a tax on rent? _____

_____

Q 14   In 1971, the UK government was considering giving tenants of furnished rooms—perhaps in the landlord's own house—security of tenure at a 'fixed rent', perhaps lower than the rent already being paid. They decided against it, because they believed that the result would be fewer rooms offered to let. All such 'rents' are

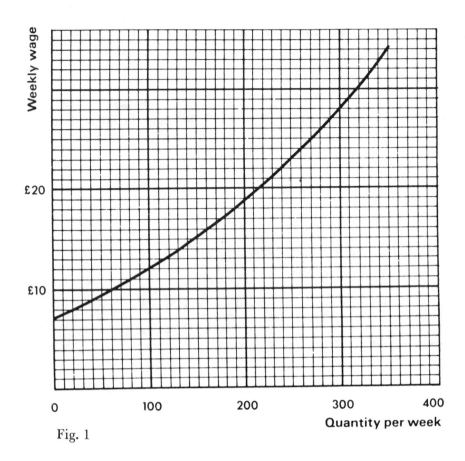

Fig. 1

subject to UK taxation. Would all such 'rents' be rents in the economic sense?
Yes/No Explain_____

QUESTIONS FOR DISCUSSION

1   In 1976–7, under pressure from women's rights groups, the UK Government introduced legislation to ensure that women doing similar jobs to men would be paid the same.
This legislation also made it illegal to specify sex when advertising for staff (except in certain
jobs, such as the fire service). Amusing advertisements now appear, such as this one taken
from the *Hereford Advertiser* (29.2.83)
     'Strong porter required for abattoir. Must be able to use chain-saw. Male or female appli-
cations accepted.'
     Discuss the possible effect of this legislation on wages and employment (of both sexes) in
jobs which used to be the prerogative of one sex, and in jobs (such as low-paid piece-work
done at home by housewives) where domination by one sex is a matter of convenience rather
than custom.

2   The following facts were recently alleged on a BBC Radio 3 discussion on how
students selected their university courses:

(a)   Since teachers' salaries do not vary much from year to year, short-term variations in the
      total market demand for persons with particular trainings are reflected in short-term
      variations in the *supply* of teachers with those particular trainings rather than in varia-
      tions in their wages (e.g. when the demand for physicists rises, their wages rise in non-
      academic jobs, more are attracted to these, and the supply of physicists available to
      teach in universities falls).

(b)   A very important factor influencing the students' choice of a particular subject is the
      quality of the teachers who instruct him.

      (i)   Show the working of the control system implied by these two assertions.

146

(ii)   Explain what is meant by negative feedback and positive feedback, and show which this control system has. (If you do not know what these terms mean, ask someone taking a science course.)

(iii)   How would you change this control system to introduce negative feedback into it?

3   The Association of University Teachers made a successful plea after the Second World War for all university salaries to be the same across different fields of specialization. Thus, for example, lecturers were to get the same salary whether they were in physics, economics or classics. This appeal was made on grounds of equity and it was largely successful (there were a few exceptions as, e.g., in the case of lecturers on medicine).

(a)   What effect would this have on the starting salaries and typical starting grades for university staff in various fields?

(b)   If the AUT was successful in imposing uniform starting salaries for all university staff irrespective of their fields of specialization, what effect would this have on the quantity and quality of teaching available in different university departments?

4   In 1965 the Labour Government instituted a tax on increases in land values, called a betterment levy. The main argument in favour of this tax was that it would appropriate for the state some of the unearned capital appreciation enjoyed by landowners. Some of the arguments against it were:

(a)   the tax would harm new tenants on re-developed land because it would be passed on in the form of higher rents.

(b)   the incentive to develop land would be lost, so 'blighted areas' would occur.

(c)   the tax would raise the cost of living, since retailers occupying new, high-rent (see (a)) premises would pass this on to customers in higher prices.

What do you think of these arguments?

The tax did not yield as much as was hoped, and it was very expensive to administer. It was abolished by the Conservative Government as soon as they came to office in 1970. They had always promised to do this; do you see any connection between this promise and the relative failure of the tax?

5   'A ticket to hear Roxy Music costs £10 because Roxy Music are paid such vast fees for their performance.' Do you agree?

CHAPTER 27

The Income of Labour

We have so far constructed a model which describes the forces that determine the prices of factors of production. Up to now we have treated labour no differently from, for example, machine tools. Yet it is easy to think of significant differences between labour and other factors, and of forces brought to bear in the labour market which are absent elsewhere. Men, unlike other factors of production, need income in order to live.

THE DETERMINATION OF WAGES WITHOUT UNIONS

Q 1   In these circumstances, can the individual worker affect

(a)   the amount of labour he will offer? Yes/No

(b)   the wage rate he will receive? Yes/No

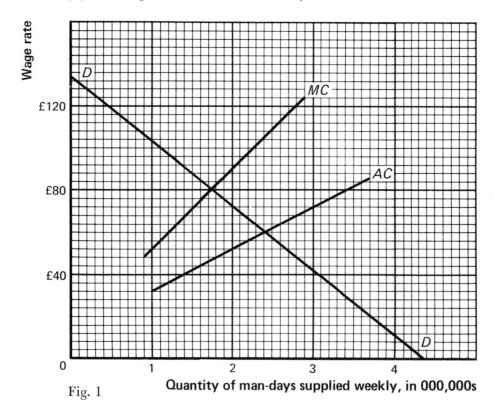

Fig. 1   Quantity of man-days supplied weekly, in 000,000s

Q 2   Look at Fig. 1.

(1)   Wages are £60. Is labour purchased by a monopsonist? Yes/No

(2)   What would be the wage rate under monopsony? _____

(3)   What would be the level of employment under competition? _____

(4)   What would be the level of employment under monopsony? _____

Check your answers. (If your answer to 2 (2) was £80, either you were careless or you need to read the chapter in Lipsey again.)

Q 3   If a monopsonist could make a separate contract with each worker, so that each worker received just the amount which would make him offer his services in that particular industry, *and no more*, then how much labour would the profit-maximizing monopsonist employ? _____

Check your answer. This question was intended to point to the fact that a monopsonist restricts employment because, if he increases the wage he offers in order to attract more labour, he has to pay that increased wage to all his existing workers as well. If you were wrong, re-read Lipsey p. 376. There is an analogy: if a *monopolist* could be a perfect price-discriminator, his output would be less than/greater than/equal to the output of the industry if competitive (Q 4). (Work out this for yourself later, if necessary.)

Q 5   In Fig. 1, why must the marginal cost be above the average cost?—i.e. put into commonsense terms the explanation 'because the average factor cost curve is rising'.

_____

_____

Here a word of warning is in order. Do not confuse the marginal cost curve of Fig. 1 with the *MC* curves with which we have dealt before. *Here* we are dealing with cost to the employer, *not* cost (in terms of leisure forgone) to the supplier of labour. The marginal cost curve shows how much extra the employer must pay on his total wage bill in order to employ one more unit of labour. The supply curve of labour is the *average cost* (to the employer) curve, which shows what wage is necessary to attract a given amount of labour.

THE DETERMINATION OF WAGES WITH UNIONS

Q 6   Do unions influence

(a)   the amount of labour offered? Yes/No

(b)   the wage rate? Yes/No

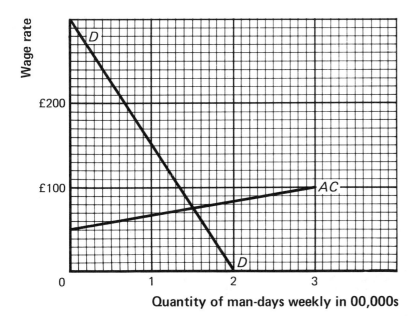

Fig. 2

Q 7   Assume that Fig. 2 represents a firm which purchases labour in competition with other firms. An effective union is formed, which negotiates a pay rise of £30 per week above the competitive equilibrium.

(1)   By how much will employment drop? _____

149

(2)   Is the new wage bill higher or lower, and by how much? _____

_____

(3)   Draw in the *MR* curve. At what point is the wage bill maximized?
       wage _____ employment _____

C Check your answers. If your answer to 7 (3) was £180, 80,000 then you misused the *MR* curve and should do Q 8. If you got it right, go to Q 9.

Q 8   'Marginal revenue is positive' means that an increase in sales must _____ total revenue. If the *MR* curve is _____ the horizontal axis, then it is positive. If the *MR* curve is _____ the horizontal axis, an increase in sales decreases total revenue. So at the level of sales where *MR* cuts the horizontal axis, total revenue must be at a _____

Q 9   (Optional) On the assumption that the rising *AC* curve of Fig. 2 is not caused by different workers requiring different minimum wages, but is instead a reflection of each worker's similar diminishing rate of leisure-income substitution, and assuming flexibility of working hours and a single hourly rate of pay, what is the union's surplus[1]-maximizing wage?

Q 10   Assume that the union sets up a pension fund out of employed members' contributions, so that workers out of a job because of the union's high wage policy are paid £85 per week. The union sets the wage at £170 per week. Overall, has the union been a success for the men? Yes/No. How much does each employed man have to pay to the pension fund? about _____

So you see, it is *in theory* possible for a union to increase the income of *all* those employed in a non-unionized industry.

Q 11   There is, however, one crucial condition, and that is one about the shape of the demand curve. What is it? _____

_____

The benefits of a union to its members are the most dramatic when labour is purchased monopsonistically. Fig. 3 represents the monopsonistic purchase of labour.

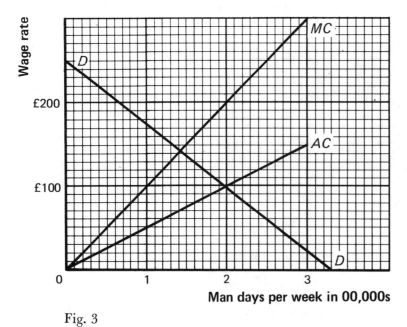

Fig. 3

_____
[1]The difference between what the workers would have worked for, and what they actually earn.

150

Q 12   (1)   What is the non-unionized wage rate? _____

       (2)   What is the non-unionized employment level? _____

Q 13   The union sets a minimum wage of £90. Sketch in on Fig. 3 the new *MC* curve. Between what wage rates is it a vertical line? _____ and _____

Q 14   At a wage rate of £90 what is the level of employment? _____

Q 15   If the employer wants to employ 200,000 man-days per week, what is the extra cost to him? _____

Check your answers. You might have worked out the answer to Q 15 by subtracting the total wage bill at a level of employment of 180,000 from that at a level of 200,000. Look now at the *MC* curve, between 180,000 and 200,000. Its average value is _____ (Q 16—check your answer) and 20,000 × £19 = £380,000.

Q 17   (Optional) On the same assumptions as Q 9, what would the union's surplus-maximizing wage in Fig. 3 be? _____

In order to avoid the problem of the conflict between a union's twin aims of high wages and high employment, collective bargains can be struck which remove from the employer the power to determine his own level of employment. He takes all, at a given wage rate, or nothing. This policy can be enforced only by very strong unions.

Q 18   Formulate in 'opportunity cost' terms the conditions under which the above policy will force an entrepreneur out of business.

       (a)   in the long run _____

       (b)   immediately _____

Check your answers. If you didn't understand the answers to Q 18, re-read Lipsey pp. 368—71 about transfer costs, and pp. 211 ff. about the short run and long run. This is important, so don't skip it.

Q 19   If a union is formed for labour purchased monopsonistically, both wages and employment can be increased. T/F
The wage can, however, never be higher than the competitive wage rate. T/F
If it is higher, it must result in a decrease in employment (a) from the monopsonistic level, (b) from the competitive level.

Q 20   Unions find it easier to gain wage increases under which conditions?

       (a)   The industry or firm is profitable/unprofitable.
       (b)   Labour costs are a small/large part of total costs.
       (c)   Firms are competitive/monopolistic.
       (d)   Demand for the product is increasing/decreasing.
       (e)   Labour supply is elastic/inelastic.

In Great Britain in 1979 there were many large wage increases. Public argument about these did not centre on the issues we have discussed in this chapter—*although they are all crucial*—because during this period the '*ceteris paribus*' assumptions which we have always made to examine a particular market did not hold. In particular, workers saw that since money prices of goods were rising all the time, they should demand more money for a given amount of work, in order to retain, over the length of time for which the wage bargain would be effective, at least the same real standard of living. (So, in theory they should save during the first half of the length of time covered by the wage bargain, while their wages were still relatively high, in order to spend *more* than their incomes during the second half of the length of time, when their wages would be relatively low.) This means, in effect, that the supply curve of labour kept shifting leftwards. Moreover, firms expected that the general rise in money incomes would mean that their demand curves would shift to the right, thus shifting the *MRP* curve of labour.

QUESTIONS FOR DISCUSSION

1   Use the theoretical models of factor markets to rank the following according to the probable magnitude of the equilibrium wage rate and the quantity of employment:

(a)   In a fairly isolated town, there is a large number of small sweet manufacturers. The workers in these plants have no union.

(b)   A union is organized that almost all the workers join.

(c)   After a few years, the union disbands due to lack of interest. At the same time, a large outside firm buys up most of the small sweet plants, hires the former owners as managers, and operates all the plants as one firm.

(d)   A large national union comes to town and reorganizes the union.

(If you have any doubts as to the ranking, do not hesitate to state them explicitly.)

2   Discuss the behaviour of the owner of a small decorating business in Wolverhampton who kept his men on his payroll during the recession of 1982–3 when he had no work for them, and went bankrupt in March 1983.

3   What economic problem does the union face in using its bargaining power to further its aims?

4   It is frequently charged that 'big labour' (the leaders of the large national unions) now have more in common with management than with their union members. Why might this change have occurred? How might you test the validity of the charge?

5   In the 1920s there were various attempts to set up Unemployed Workers' unions. Why do you think some of the unemployed didn't trust existing trades unions?

6   In the USA one of the very powerful car-manufacturing workers' unions has persuaded the employers to give pensions of up to £150 per week to 60-year-old employees. Can you see which two birds this one stone kills?

7   It is very difficult to form a strong union among agricultural workers, because they are so scattered. In the UK there is a minimum wage established by law for agricultural workers. Do you see any connection?

8   In 1982 doctors and senior nurses in Britain complained that the National Health Service was 'starved of manpower' (in fact, there were more nurses and doctors in Britain than ever before, and the complaint was merely part of an orchestrated attack on the Health Service by some doctors). Yet in the 1960s, doctors campaigned successfully to *restrict* entry to medical schools. Why do you think they did this?

CHAPTER 28

The Income of Capital

Karl Marx saw in the 'conditions of production that are objectified in capital' the roots of alienation in society. To those with a non-Marxian system, the use of *capital* in order to produce commodities is merely the hall-mark of any economy more advanced than that of pre-historic root-gatherers and animal hunters. Since capital is scarce, it has an opportunity cost, and can, therefore, be allocated by means of a price system.

Q 1   Why is the economic system of many communist countries referred to as 'state capitalism'? _____

Money is used to buy capital, and capital is productive. In order to measure how productive, the Present Value technique is used. This is Discounted Cash Flow, of which you may have read, and it is perhaps surprising that its use by businesses only became common in the last decade (and it is equally surprising what magic effects its use is expected to have).

If the annual rate of interest is 5%, and you were offered by a fairy godmother the choice of £100 now, or £103 in a year's time, you would choose £100 now, because even if you didn't want to spend it, it would accumulate to £105 in a year, and you'd be better off by £2 than if you accepted the £103. Conversely, if you were offered £100 now or £107 in a year's time you'd accept the latter; *if you wanted to spend £100 now you could borrow £100 for a year, pay back the £105 which you would owe your creditor in a year's time, and have £2 over.*

You would be indifferent between £100 now, and £105 in a year's time. *Either would give you exactly the same command over possible purchases, either now, or in a year.*

So if the rate of interest is 5%, £100 is worth £105 in a year's time.

Q 2   Write this in equation form, putting X equal to what £100 is worth in a year's time.
       $X = £100 \times$ _____ (Equation A)

       Check your answer.

Q 3   You leave this X invested for another year. Put Y equal to what X will be worth after this year has elapsed. $Y = X \times$ _____ (Equation B)

       (Check your answer)

Q 4   You leave this Y invested for another year. Put Z equal to what Y will be worth after this year has elapsed. $Z =$ _____ (Equation C)

       (Check your answer)
       Now, Equation A tells you that $X = £100 \times 1.05$. Substitute this expression into Equation B, and you get:

$$Y = (£100 \times 1.05) \times 1.05 = £100 \times 1.05^2$$

Q 5   Substitute this expression for Y in Equation C. $Z =$ _____

This states that, if the rate of interest is 5%, £Z in three years' time has the same value as £100 now. That is, the present value of Z is £100. We can state it more generally, putting i

for the rate of interest, and K for the sum invested:

Q 6 $Z = $ _____

   (Check your answer.)

   Often, we want to answer the question, 'What is the value now of £X in Y years' time?' In this case we know the values of Z, i and t, and have to solve the equation for K.

Q 7 $K = $ _____

   (Check your answer.)

   Sometimes we know the values of K, Z and t, and we want to find what interest rate makes K and Z have the same value. We can do this, solving the equation for i.

Q 8   The rate of interest is 10%.

   (1)   What is the PV of £100 received in 1 year's time? _____

   (2)   What is the PV of £130 received in 3 years' time? _____

   (3)   What is the PV of £90 received in 5 years' time? _____

   (Check your answer.)

   (4)   What is the PV, when i = 10%, of the following income stream? Received at end of:

Year 1	2	3	4	5	6	7 . . . ∞
100	0	130	0	90	0	0 . . . 0	_____

TABLE I

Years hence (t)	1%	2%	4%	6%	8%	10%
1	0.990	0.980	0.962	0.943	0.926	0.909
2	0.980	0.961	0.925	0.890	0.857	0.826
3	0.971	0.942	0.889	0.840	0.794	0.751
4	0.961	0.924	0.855	0.792	0.735	0.683
5	0.951	0.906	0.822	0.747	0.681	0.621
6	0.942	0.888	0.790	0.705	0.630	0.564
7	0.933	0.871	0.760	0.665	0.583	0.513
8	0.923	0.853	0.731	0.627	0.540	0.467
9	0.914	0.837	0.703	0.592	0.500	0.424
10	0.905	0.820	0.676	0.558	0.463	0.386
11	0.896	0.804	0.650	0.527	0.429	0.350
12	0.887	0.788	0.625	0.497	0.397	0.319
13	0.879	0.773	0.601	0.469	0.368	0.290
14	0.870	0.758	0.577	0.442	0.340	0.263
15	0.861	0.743	0.555	0.417	0.315	0.239

   (Check your answer. You shouldn't have had any difficulty, since it is just the sum of the three PVs you calculated in Q 8 (1)–(3).)

Q 9   Look at the irregular income flow of Q 8. What regular yearly flow, received *every* year from year 1 onwards, has the same PV? _____

Check your answer. It is just the yearly income you would get if you invested £244 at 10%.

Present Value calculations are usually made with the help of a table, part of which is reproduced in Table 1.

Present value of £1.0

$$PV = \left(\frac{1}{1+i}\right)^t$$

To calculate, for example, the PV, at 6%, of £4,328 in 13 years' time, you look for the entry common to the 6% column, and the 13-year row. It is _____ (Q 10). This is the PV of £1, so to get the PV of £4,328 you multiply 0.469 by £4,328, which is £2,030.

Q 11   You are given two income streams:

(a)   £50 per year for ever

(b)   £120 after 1 year
      £140 after 2 years
      £620 after 4 years

The rate of interest is 8%. Which is more valuable, (a) or (b)?

THE DEMAND FOR CAPITAL BY A FIRM

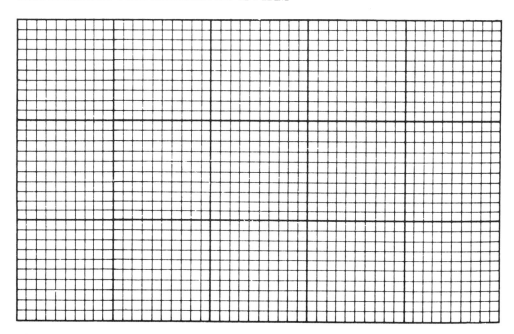

Fig. 1

Q 12   Construct a firm's marginal efficiency schedule for capital on Fig. 1 given

(a)   on its 1,500th pound invested it will earn 20%.
(b)   on its 3,500th pound invested it will earn 15%.
(c)   it is a straight line (the relation between quantity of capital and productivity is linear).

(i)   what is the marginal efficiency of the 5,000th pound? _____

(ii) at what point does marginal efficiency become zero? _____
      _____

(iii) How much will the firm wish to borrow at a rate of interest of 10%? _____
      _____

155

(iv) If the firm is rationed by its bank (the only source of its borrowing) to £7,000 credit, will an interest rate of 9% have any effect? Yes/No
Will an interest rate of 5% have any effect? Yes/No

Q 13 When comparing *capital cost* with *income stream* you should, in addition, deduct *depreciation* from the latter. T/F

THE AGGREGATE DEMAND FOR THE CAPITAL STOCK

Q 14 If the economy is at the equilibrium point $i = MEC$, and i falls and *remains* at a lower level, equilibrium can only be restored by a fall/rise in the capital stock.

Q 15 If technological innovation has shifted the *MEC* schedule to the right, this will have had a raising/lowering effect on equilibrium interest rates.

Q 16 With inflation at 15% per year, what is the real rate of interest on a mortgage at a nominal 12%?

Q 17 General medical practitioners can borrow money over a fixed period of years (up to 30 years) at a fixed (nominal) rate of interest, in order to acquire surgery premises. In November 1974 the rate of interest was fixed at 17%. Was it in their interests (in this respect) that the current 20% per year rate of inflation should continue? Yes/No

You might like to do some interesting calculations — assume that inflation runs at 20% per year for three years starting from now, 12% for three years, 6% for three years, and 3% thereafter. Should a doctor obtain a loan at 17% now, or at an expected 16% next year, or at an expected 15% the year after, or an expected 14% the year after that? Assume his income rises commensurate with inflation, and that he can alternatively rent premises at 15% of real market value.

Q 18 If interest rates can change quicker than the capital stock, the simple theory of Chapter 28 is more/less a theory of the determination of interest rates than capital stock levels.

Q 19 When the rate of interest was 5% I bought a perpetual bond for £2,000, giving me an income stream of £100 a year. The rate of interest now rises to 7½%. What has been my capital gain or loss? _____

Q 20 I have bought a bond for £1,000 which yields 2½% for ever — i.e. £25 per year. The government makes an issue of bonds at 5%. How much could I sell mine for now?

_____

The formula for calculating this is
$$\frac{\text{New price}}{\text{Old price}} = \frac{\text{Old rate}}{\text{New rate}}$$

Q 21 If you were a bank, would you charge a Ladbroke Grove junk shop a higher or lower interest rate than Marks and Spencer? Higher/Lower

Q 22 Why? _____

Q 23 If you lend money to a reliable building society which promises to pay you back at a fortnight's notice, will you expect a higher or lower rate than if you lend to a local authority which will only pay you back after two years? _____

Q 24 Why? _____

Q 25 Which one of the following statements is *not* a reason for a saver to desire interest on his savings account?

(a) The future is uncertain, so he would really prefer to spend the money now.
(b) He could have bought an income-earning asset instead.

     (c)   The bank will earn interest lending his savings to someone else.

     (d)   He wants to be able to get his money out quickly.

Q 26   The higher the rate of interest, *ceteris paribus*,

     (a)   the more investment opportunities will be profitable.

     (b)   the higher the necessary rate of return on any investment.

     (c)   the lower the amount of borrowing by the federal government.

     (d)   the greater the demand for investment funds.

Q 27   A hire-purchase salesman tells you that, by buying your car on the HP, you will pay 9% interest. 'You will', he says, 'borrow £1,000 for two years, and pay £180 interest, which is, of course, 9% per year. You will repay the loan in four six-monthly instalments of £295 (equals £250 principal plus £45 interest).' The *real* rate you are paying is in fact closer to 6%/14%/30%.

Q 28   A small firm of importers using *DCF* techniques finds that its bankers are reducing its possible overdraft facilities, because they have been instructed to lend more money to exporting firms instead.

       The firm of importers will raise/lower/not alter the rate of discount in its *DCF* calculations.

       The exporters, on the other hand will raise/lower/not alter their rates of discount.

Q 29   The *MEC* schedule slopes down because

     (a)   the additional labour needed to work with the additional machines is of progressively lower quality.

     (b)   capital is subject to diminishing returns.

     (c)   with fully employed resources, the opportunity cost of increments of capital rises.

Q 30   Explain why the price of a British government bond, redeemable for £1,000 in 1992, was £1,002 in 1983. 'Because the (1) _____ had (2) risen/fallen since the bond was issued.'

QUESTIONS FOR DISCUSSION

1   '. . . in low simplicity
He lends out money gratis and brings down
The rate of usance here with us in Venice.'

Shylock of Antonio, Merchant of Venice

In fact, of course, the Jewish religion forbade one Jew to take interest from another, just as Shakespeare implies was the practice among Gentiles.

    Discuss the economic characterization of a society where the rate of interest is zero. What are the implications for time preference and productivity of capital?

2(a)   For what purposes might you borrow? What types of consumer credit can you name?

 (b)   Why do businessmen borrow?

3   Many advertisements for British Savings Certificates carried, in mid-1974, the statement 'Invest £1,000 and make £340 tax free over four years'. This so infuriated the consumer magazine *Which?* that it invented this parody:

'The loss on National Dwindling Certificates — £260!'

Find out (a) the rate of interest offered on Savings Certificates, (b) the rate of inflation in mid-1974, and explain this assertion.

4   Building societies, who do not like to take risks, and who lend money for up to 25 years to a house-purchaser, sometimes change the interest which a borrower has to pay, so

that a person financing the purchase of a home through a building society when the interest rate is, say, 10%, might have to pay 12%, or 9%, in a year's time. Why does a building society not lend at a fixed interest?

CHAPTER 29

Criticisms and Tests of the Theory of Distribution

The predictions of the theory of distribution are logical implications of a small number of assumptions about the demand for and supply of factors of production.

The assumptions of the theory of distribution can be divided into one assumption about supply and two assumptions about demand:

(a) Supply — Factors will move among uses in such a way as to equalize the net advantage to their owners.

(b) Demand — (1) Factors are purchases under competitive conditions (do you remember how competitive conditions are defined? If you don't, re-read page 243).

(2) Firms maximize short-run profits.

So long as we consider factors other than labour, we observe the theory working well.

Fig. 1 shows the marginal revenue product curve for a factor in a *particular firm*.

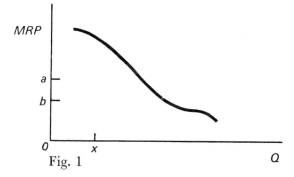

Fig. 1

Q 1   The price of the factor is Oa, and the quantity purchased Ox. What must this firm do if it wishes to maximize its profits? _____

_____

Q 2   Can you draw in the supply curve to the firm? Yes/No

If yes, describe it _____

If you were wrong, go back and look at pp. 352–3.

Q 3   The firm finds that the price of the factor has dropped to b in Fig. 1. In which of the following ways might this have come about? (More than one might be correct.)

(a) Supply fall
(b) Demand fall
(c) Supply rise plus demand fall
(d) Supply fall plus demand fall
(e) Demand rise plus supply fall
(f) Demand rise plus supply rise

(g)   Supply rise
(h)   Demand rise.

Pages 410–11 give examples of factors behaving as the theory predicts. You should be able to think of many more. You should now try to think of examples of

(1)   a fall in the price of a factor
(2)   a rise in the price of a factor

and you should see how successful the theory of distribution is in explaining your examples.

Q 4   How might British trade unions prevent the market mechanism from working as it would under perfectly competitive conditions? _____

_____

Q 5   If we had to reject the application of the supply assumption of the theory of distribution as applied to labour, does this imply anything about the marginal revenue product theory of demand for labour? Yes/No

Q 6   Assume that a new, cheaper method of growing rubber is discovered. Under what conditions will this result in a *reduction* in the revenue of rubber planters?

THE MACRO DISTRIBUTION OF INCOME (Read pp. 414ff.)

Q 7   If the amount of capital and land in an economy were fixed, whereas the labour force was growing, would you regard marginal productivity theory as refuted if the percentage of national income going to labour were to rise? Yes/No
Explain _____

_____

_____

Q 8   You are told that, in our example of Q 7, the percentage of national income going to land, which is in constant supply, is falling. Does this refute marginal productivity theory? Yes/No. Give your reason in a line.

_____

Q 9   Again in the example of Q 7, you have the information that the total income of capital has fallen. Does this refute marginal productivity theory? Yes/No. Explain in a line.

_____

QUESTIONS FOR DISCUSSION

1   Why do we say that the long controversy about the marginal productivity theory is, in many ways, a storm in a teacup? What common misconceptions help to stir up the storm?

2   Is marginal productivity theory a complete theory of distribution? If not, what is it? What is the standard theory of distribution?

3   Where do we find that our theory has the most predictive power? If we could collect more cases, would we succeed in proving the theory?

4   What do we mean by saying that the marginal productivity theory stands or falls with the theory of profit-maximization?

5   Of what value in testing our theory of distribution is a questionnaire that asks businessmen what they would do in response to a rise in wages?

6   'But a worker might consider the benefits of a job's working conditions adequate to accept exploitation, i.e. being paid less than his marginal value product. Marginal theory does not allow for this.' Comment fully on all the issues raised by this statement.

160

CHAPTER 30
International Trade and Protection

Some countries are better at producing certain commodities than other countries; Britain can produce Land-Rovers cheaper than Kenya, and Kenya can produce coffee beans cheaper than Britain. In this case, it is obvious that trade in coffee beans and Land-Rovers could benefit both countries.

Q 1   Look at Table 1. This shows the possible production of Land-Rovers and coffee beans in Britain and Kenya.

TABLE 1

	One unit of resources (e.g. 5 man-years) can produce:	
	Land-Rovers	Coffee beans (bushels)
Britain	10	50
Kenya	1	1,000

(1)   In order to increase *total* production of both Land-Rovers and coffee beans, Britain must transfer resources from _____ into _____ , and Kenya must transfer resources from _____ into _____ .

(2)   A transfer of *five* units by each country in the above directions will result in Britain producing _____ more _____ , and _____ less _____ , and in Kenya producing _____ more _____ , and _____ less _____ .

(3)   After the transfer of 5 units in each country, total (Kenyan and British) production of coffee beans rises by _____ , and of Land-Rovers by _____ .

Q 2   In the above example, the gains from specialization are clear—each country has an absolute/relative/proportionate advantage in the production of one commodity.

Q 3   These are called conditions of _____ .

In fact, the gains from trade do not depend upon reciprocal absolute advantage. Otherwise, there would be much less trade between East and West Europe.

Look at Table 2, which shows the resources required to produce hi-fi loud-speakers and amplifiers in Britain and Japan.

TABLE 2

	One unit of resources (e.g. 5 man-years) can produce:	
	Speakers	Amplifiers
Britain	800	600
Japan	1,000	2,000

Q 4   Does Table 2 represent a situation of reciprocal absolute advantage? Yes/No

Q 5   Since Japan is more efficient in the production of both speakers and amplifiers, specialization by each country cannot increase total production of *both*. T/F

Check your answers so far. It is explained on Lipsey p. 424 that gains from trade depend, not upon absolute advantage, but upon _____ (Q 6) advantage.

Q 7   In the example of Table 2, Japan has comparative advantage in _____ , Britain in _____ .

Q 8   By moving five units of resources in each country, Japan will produce _____ more _____ , and _____ less _____ , and Britain will produce _____ more _____ , and _____ less _____ .

Q 9   The net change in total production, after the transfer of Q 8, is _____ more/fewer speakers, and _____ more/fewer amplifiers.

In these circumstances a simple shift of the same number of resources in each country will not result in an increase in the production of *both* commodities. The less efficient country must shift more resources.

Q 10   In addition to the changes in Q 8, assume that Britain shifts another five units of resources from amplifiers to speakers. British production of speakers increases, again, by _____ and that of amplifiers falls by _____ .

Q 11   The net change in total production, after the shifts of Q 8 and Q 10, is_____ more/fewer speakers, and _____ more/fewer amplifiers.

Q 12   Look at Table 3.

TABLE 3

	One unit of resources (e.g. 5 man-years) can produce:	
	Wine (litres)	Olive oil (litres)
Greece	20,000	8,000
Spain	50,000	10,000

By shifting 15 units in Greece, and 10 in Spain, total production of wine increases by _____ and total production of olive oil increases by _____ .

On pages 424 and 425 of Lipsey it is explained that the theory of comparative advantage can be formulated in opportunity-cost terms—this formulation avoids the irrelevance (at this level) of the *absolute* efficiency of the countries concerned. It also avoids the difficulties of defining 'units of resources' when the countries may use different combinations.

Q 13   Fill in the following opportunity-cost tables, which you should derive from Tables 1, 2 and 3. Part of the first two tables have been filled in for you.

(1)   Opportunity cost of *one Land-Rover* and *one bushel of coffee beans*:

Britain   5   bushels of coffee beans _____ Land-Rovers
Kenya _____ bushels of coffee beans   0.001   Land-Rover

(2)   Opportunity cost of one speaker and one amplifier:

Britain
Japan   0.5 speakers

(3) Opportunity cost of one litre of wine and one litre of olive oil:

Greece

Spain

Q 14   In order to increase total production, countries should specialize in those commodities for which the opportunity cost is higher/lower.

In order to utilize this extra production possibility to the advantage of each country, trade must, of course, actually take place—otherwise there would be no point in specialization.

Q 15   What name is given to the amount of home-produced goods which must be given up in order to acquire one unit of foreign goods? _____

Q 16   In the example of Table 2, what terms of trade will make it worthwhile for Britain to sell speakers to Japan?

Below/above _____ speakers.

Q 17   In the same example, will trade benefit *both Britain and Japan* if international prices are such that:

(1) One speaker has the same value as 2 amplifiers?   Yes/No
(2) One speaker has the same value as 3 amplifiers?   Yes/No
(3) One speaker has the same value as 1 amplifier?   Yes/No

Q 18   A country can reduce imports by shifting the demand curve to the right/left, by means of devices such as 'secret' instructions to public-sector purchasers to add a notional percentage to the cost of foreign items when making purchase decisions. What are the other two main methods of reducing imports? _____ and _____

Q 19   If the French attempt to put a tariff on imports of Italian wine, as they have threatened to do, what would the Italians promptly threaten? _____
Might both countries end up worse off? Yes/No

Q 20   During 1977/8 the Taiwanese exported children's toys to England at very low prices. Some British toy manufacturers subsequently went bankrupt. Does this prove that low-price imports *can* be harmful? Yes/No

What should happen in England if at some stage comparative advantage were to reverse, or if the Taiwanese had been dumping goods at less than cost and stopped doing so? _____

Q 21   What are the three possible uses for foreign currency earned by exports detailed on Lipsey page 436?

_____

Q 22   (1) Which of these uses is exemplified by the recent British Leyland purchase of a Spanish engineering works? _____

(2) If the Spanish factory is used to assemble cars for the Spanish market which might otherwise have been exported to Spain ready assembled, complete the following simple explanation of how this acquisition by British Leyland might improve British living standards—'Assuming that the British and Spanish-assembled cars are identical, the British cars will earn more/less pesetas than the Spanish. But the Spanish may be produced at a lower overall cost, at the existing exchange rate. So British Leyland will make more profits. But British living standards will only rise if the *British* car-assemblers produce enough extra goods which are exported (or cause other goods to be exported) to earn enough foreign exchange to pay the Spanish assemblers and to _____

_____

Q 23   'Exporting one's unemployment' means that, in conditions of world full employment/ unemployment the beneficial/disadvantageous home multiplier effects of increased exports have, as their corollary, the effect of reducing, by means of the multiplier, the income of the country whose imports rise/fall relative to its exports.

Q 24   'Unemployment is well countered by an increase in exports.' Maybe—but suggest an alternative which can result in an even greater improvement in living standards.

_____

Q 25   Where there is not full employment, the loss through wasted resources will not/might not exceed the loss of income caused by imposition of a tariff. However, such a tariff might be nullified by other countries' _____

_____

Q 26   The real choices before the countries of the world do not concern free trade versus no trade, but somewhat _____ or somewhat _____ trade.

QUESTIONS FOR DISCUSSION

1   The citizens of underdeveloped Atlantis can weave two feet of cloth an hour or gather one basket of coconuts. Is there any point in their approaching the republic of Mu, whose inhabitants can weave three feet of cloth or gather two baskets of coconuts in the same period of time, and offering to trade? After all, they are inferior on both counts. A visiting economist advises the Atlantans to try. What possible opposition speeches do you imagine will be heard in the Senate in the capital of Mu? Appraise the validity of a few different arguments.

2   Why do German professional photographers use Nikon cameras (instead of Leicas)? Why do Japanese amateur photographers use Malaysian cameras?

3   It is generally agreed that America has a comparative disadvantage in the production of bicycles compared with British and European producers. If the present high tariffs on the importation of foreign bicycles were removed, what do you think would happen (a) to the average standard of living of US citizens, and (b) to the average standard of living of people now employed in the US bicycle industry?

4   'Japanese regulations [about the import of motor-cars] are not designed to make entry easy for the foreigner. The most common complaints are of bureaucratic delays, frequent changes of regulations relating to model specifications, and insufficient time to make model changes. Japan's pollution control standards are also very demanding.' *Financial Times* (30.1.75). In the world at present it is difficult for a developed country to impose tariffs without breaking international treaties. Do you see here a possible reason for the alleged Japanese obstructionism? However—'. . . Volkswagen figures show that Japanese regulations can be tackled effectively . . .' (the *Financial Times* continues) and '. . . British Leyland has never supplied its distributors with enough cars . . .' and '[in Japan] the price of the XJ12 [a British Leyland car costing £5,800 in Britain] is £13,425 . . .'

The *Financial Times* typically attributes the low volume of British car sales to disrupted deliveries due to labour disputes. This may be right, but suggest an alternative explanation which casts more credit on the sagacity of the British Leyland management. (*Hint*: there are few substitutes for the XJ12—and it is at least possible that British Leyland is a profit-maximizer.)

5   (This question requires a little background knowledge of late nineteenth-century history.)

The following table, taken from the 1903 Fiscal Blue Book, has been adduced by a famous historian as evidence of the proposition that, after the imposition of tariff walls against Britain by the developing countries of Europe in the 1880s, Britain switched her exports to these countries away from manufacturers to investment goods and fuel.

Do you think that the table bears this interpretation? (In your calculations of the differential changes in exports to the protected countries and the rest, don't forget to subtract columns 3 and 4 from 1 and 2.)

VALUE OF CERTAIN PRINCIPAL CLASSES OF BRITISH EXPORTS (IN THOUSAND £s)

	To all countries		To ten principal protected countries	
	1880	1900	1880	1900
Cotton Goods	75,564	69,751	15,990	13,840
Woollen and Worsted	21,488	21,806	13,526	11,475
Linen	6,814	6,159	4,895	4,052
Iron, Steel, and other Metals	32,000	37,638	17,626	15,171
Machinery and Mill Work	9,264	19,620	5,797	10,892
Coal, Coke, &c.	8,373	38,620	4,822	23,349

It is possible that Britain was short-sighted to export so many investment goods—explain. Why didn't she retaliate (a) with tariffs, (b) with export controls? (*Hint*: who exports, 'Britain' or British companies? And what economic doctrine held sway in Britain in the second half of the nineteenth century?)

CHAPTER 31

Less Developed and Developing Countries

Q 1   (Ignore for a moment the Malthusian aspects of increased health care.) When poor nations such as certain African countries suddenly acquire an oil revenue, they often want to buy the best in modern medicine. This often means that they buy 'off-the-peg' hospitals from Western countries, complete with CAT scanners and all the latest gadgetry. Comment on this policy. _____

_____

(When an international health-care planning team went to Bangladesh, the only purchases they recommended were certain antibiotics, vitamin tablets — and Land-Rovers.)

Q 2   Approximately what proportion of the world's income is enjoyed by the richest 40% of the world's population? _____

In the following exercise, the data are taken from a thought-provoking article by Professor J. E. Meade, entitled 'Population explosion, the standard of living and social conflict', which was published in the *Economic Journal*, Volume 77, in June 1967.

In 1959 Professor Meade and others were appointed by the Governor of Mauritius to make a survey of the economic and social structure of that country. Mauritius is a small tropical island, about the size of the county of Surrey, lying east of the island of Madagascar in the Indian Ocean. Its economy is centred on the production of cane sugar which forms 35% of its gross domestic production and 98% of its exports.

In the 1930s the population was virtually stationary. However, a malaria-eradication campaign combined with other measures of preventive medicine have changed the picture, as can be seen in Table 1 below. Malaria is a parasitic disease which is transmitted by certain species of mosquito. The main clinical symptoms are periodic attacks of chills and fever.

TABLE 1. POPULATION (THOUSANDS), BIRTH RATES AND DEATH RATES (PER THOUSAND) IN MAURITIUS

	Total population	Birth rate	Death rate	Rate of natural increase
1931–5[1]	401	31.1	29.6	
1944–8[1]	429	41.5	27.2	
1949–53[1]	484	47.4	15.2	
1954–8[1]	575	41.6	12.9	
1960	645	39.3	11.2	
1961	662	39.4	9.8	
1962	682	38.5	9.3	
1963	701	39.9	9.6	
1964	722	38.1	8.6	
1965	741	35.5	8.6	

[1] Average

These attacks are of varying length and frequency; at the onset of the disease, attacks may occur every few days but gradually the victim builds up a degree of resistance so that attacks become less frequent. However, this immunity is generally only temporary, lasting perhaps a few years. Malaria itself is rarely the cause of death but it is frequently an indirect cause, as malaria sufferers are weakened by attacks of fever and this weakness means that for some months after an attack they are more vulnerable to other diseases which may be fatal. There is some evidence to suggest that pregnant women who suffer from malaria are more likely to miscarry. In addition, as immunity is rarely inherited, infants are particularly vulnerable to the disease. Following the malaria-eradication campaign, we would therefore expect death rates to fall, live births to rise, and labour to be more productive. Now have a look at the figures for Mauritius.

Q 3   Complete the column headed 'Rate of natural increase'.

Q 4   At approximately what rate was the population growing in 1965? _____

Q 5   Declining infant-mortality rates combined with slightly increased fertility means that not only is population increasing in size but also that its age distribution is changing. Table 2 gives details of the *percentage* distribution by age groups—fill in columns 2, 4 and 6 to show the absolute numbers in each group. (You will have to approximate for 1944 and 1952.)

TABLE 2. POPULATION DISTRIBUTION BY AGE GROUPS

Age group	1944		1952		1962		European countries c. 1950
	% (1)	thousands (2)	% (3)	thousands (4)	% (5)	thousands (6)	
Under 15	35		40		46		25
15–64	62		57		51		66
65+	3		3		3		9
Total	100		100		100		100

Between 1944 and 1962 the number of children more than doubled. What were probable future trends? Making population forecasts is a tricky business; two possible projections, each based on different assumptions, are set out in Table 3. Projection A assumes that the 1961–3 levels of fertility will continue. Projection B assumes that fertility will decline rapidly from 1966 to 1972 when it is assumed that the maximum number of children born to each family will be three.

TABLE 3. PROJECTIONS OF NUMBERS IN AGE GROUPS (THOUSANDS)

Age group	Projection A		Projection B	
	1977	1987	1977	1987
Under 15	514	776	356	385
15–64	579	813	579	757
65+	37	51	37	51
Total	1,130	1,640	972	1,193

Q 6   What are the main resource implications of the changing age-distribution patterns as set out in Tables 2 and 3? (You may like to discuss this in class but you should note here the main points you would wish to raise.)

_____
_____
_____
_____

We now turn from population figures and look at what has been happening in the sugar industry which, as we have noted, is the main industry of the country. Table 4 gives details of output and employment.

TABLE 4. SUGAR INDUSTRY – PRODUCTION AND EMPLOYMENT

	Production (thousand metric tons)	Area (thousand arpents[3])	Employment (thousand persons)
1928–46[1]	267	137	—
1947–51[1]	419	156	56.7
1952–6[1]	517	178	54.2
1957–9[1]	556	189	56.3
1960	236[2]	202	56.7
1961	553	201	60.7
1962	533[2]	205	60.8
1963	686	204	(60.4)
1964	519[2]	207	(63.7)

[1] Average
[2] Production seriously reduced by cyclone damage
[3] 1 acre = 1.043 arpents

Q 7   Using the data provided in Table 4, complete Table 5 (as far as possible) to show: output per arpent (P/A), output per head (P/E) and employment per arpent (E/A).

TABLE 5. SUGAR INDUSTRY – PRODUCTIVITY

	Output per arpent	Output per head	Employment per arpent
1928–46			
1947–51			
1952–6			
1957–9			
1960			
1961			
1962			
1963			
1964			

QUESTIONS FOR DISCUSSION

1   Answer the following questions concerning the data in Table 5:

   (a) What do you think are the main reasons for the rise in productivity? Do you expect productivity to continue to rise?
   (b) What are the implications for employment?
   (c) What difference might it have made if the malaria-eradication programme had been accompanied by a successful family-planning policy?

2   In November 1974, at the opening of the UN World Food Conference, Kurt Waldheim, UN Secretary-General, said: 'If enough food is to be produced to keep up with the world population growth, if some improvement in living standards is to be achieved for the most underprivileged, and if adequate security stocks are to be established and maintained, then we must begin immediately to work for an expansion of food production in magnitudes never before undertaken or even achieved.' (Reported in *The Times*, 6.11.74.) At about the same time the EEC, having disposed of a butter mountain, was facing a beef surplus.

Is there really a food problem? Is the problem to be found not in production but in distribution? (Before you answer this you might like to have another quick look at Chapter 10.)

3   The following is an extract from a letter by Marc Ajakpo to the *Daily Times* of Lagos, published 8.9.78:

'I would like us to cast our minds on the happenings around us, for in them we can see the effects of a soaring population. We have been complaining about the decaying conditions of our public corporations like the National Electric Power Authority, the P & T, the Nigerian Railway Corporation and some others, but we seem not to consider the fact that the population they serve is not in proportion to the funds available.

'We have cried to the policy makers about the deplorable health facilities made available to the common man in our hospitals. (The privileged few attended private hospitals.) We have also made lots of noise about the falling standard of education of the younger generation. The fact that our population has been allowed to grow unchecked has contributed to these in no small measure.

'Naturally, men are polygamous. In the olden days they needed many wives and children to help them in their farms. But nowadays this is not so. But the situation still persists despite changes in socio-economic conditions.

'It is at this juncture that I would like to highlight the fact that the time is now ripe for us to find a solution to our population problem before we become a beggar nation. Nigerians lack the ability to plan and it is this inability to plan ahead in relation to our increase in population that has handicapped most of our projects in this country.

'Let us take for example the Universal Free Primary Education scheme which is no more free. It is a fact that our planners never quite worked out an estimation of its cost in relation to the country's population. As a result, we were faced with problems of inadequate class-rooms, lack of teaching materials, lack of teachers and the inability to pay teachers' salaries regularly.'

Here Mr Ajakpo is raising some of the problems, other than food, which face developing countries with expanding populations. You might like to think about the problems facing such countries in deciding how to allocate their resources between consumption and investment; within the category of investment it will be necessary to decide how much to allocate to education, medical care, etc. (i.e. investment in human capital) and how much to other forms of investment such as energy, transport as well as plant and machinery. In this context, if foreign aid is to be given to developing countries, what form do you think it should take?

4   What is meant by balanced growth? What are the arguments for and against?

5   'The problems of lesser developed countries are not predominantly economic, but are social and political in nature.' Do you agree?

CHAPTER 32

The Case For and Against the Free-market System

QUESTIONS FOR DISCUSSION

1   All new buildings in Britain must conform to the 'Building Regulations'. These set certain standards, both in construction and 'usability'. An example of the former is the minimum acceptable strength of floor joists, and of the latter the minimum headroom in a bedroom. Can you justify this interference with the free market? (You may find the first type of standard easier to justify than the second.)

2   With a glut of Middle Eastern oil (Feb. 1983), North Sea oil and North Sea gas, a thousand years of coal deposits and numerous new energy technologies in addition to nuclear power, why does there have to be a Minister of Energy? Why do we need state-owned energy companies? Why do we need an 'energy policy'?

3   Why does the Lada family saloon (a Russian car) not have a voice synthesizer to remind the driver to do up his flies?

4   If a new car-manufacturing plant were to be established in a fully planned economy (in which all decisions were made by the central authorities), what effects would the planners have to foresee? How would this process differ from what happens in a free-market economy?

5   There have been many headlines lately of the following sort: 'Poland To Try Profit Incentives', 'Russian Managers To Have More Initiative', 'Czechs Use Profits as Guides'. What do you think is the economic rationale for this?

6   The Road Research Laboratory has developed a method by which motorists could be charged according to their use of roads. Their use of congested roads would be taxed more heavily than their use of uncongested roads. The motoring organizations reacted violently against these proposals, and the government has announced that they will not be implemented. Yet this system could have benefited the 'motoring public' taken as a whole (admittedly, a brave theoretical construct). Demonstrate how. (*Hint*: what is the marginal social cost of a mile driven on a congested road? On an uncongested road? What causes congestion and what does it mean?) An alternative strategy was suggested by a correspondent of *The Times* (27.3.73):
'. . . a 30% charge on the cost of car advertisements should be imposed in order to create a fund for the moulding of further opinion to make it more receptive to the idea of using public transport'.
    Might this achieve a similar effect to charging motorists? How about subsidizing public transport?

CHAPTER 33

Aims and Objectives of Government Policy

QUESTIONS FOR DISCUSSION

1   Why doesn't the BBC show commercials? Why were the independent television companies more or less obliged by government pressure to establish a second commercial channel? Why does the new channel show such unpopular programs? (The reason may be rather devious.)

2   What are some advantages of the price system?

3   Why are taxi fares regulated? Why does jam have to have its ingredients' names on the label? Why aren't pubs open at breakfast time?

4   What justification might there be for government interference in the areas of education, medicine, defence, man-power training, public parks, egg production, electrical generation, foreign investment, child labour and the allocation of a privately financed toll highway?

5   Why is British Gas obliged by the government to increase its prices until they are roughly the same as the prices of electricity?
   Why is gas nationalized, but not oil?

6   If the government wishes to curtail the consumption of cigarettes, and believes the elasticity of demand to be very low, what other tools does it have at its disposal?

7   This was written to the *Daily Express* (13.12.74):

'How I agree about nationalizing farming. I have been married to a farmer for seven years and see my husband work every day—even when he is ill and should be in bed. If farming were nationalized he could work 40 hours a week.'
   What argument is this? Do you think that farm workers are strongly unionized? If the 40-hour week were adopted, whether by a nationalized industry or by a private agricultural sector, what might be the effects on the price of food?—on the employment of labour in agriculture?—on the size of farms?

8   In many countries, liquor is subject to heavy taxes. How would you test the hypothesis that the main incentive for levying these taxes is concern over public health and a consequent desire to severely limit—even if not stop altogether—the consumption of intoxicating liquors?

9   In a recent BBC television programme a couple who were living together unmarried, because one of them was unable to obtain a divorce, claimed that they had been unable to obtain a council flat because when their status was discovered they never seemed to get to the top of the waiting list. What point in this chapter is illustrated by this allegation?

10   Mr Enoch Powell believes in an unfettered price system. He doesn't believe in government interference, except to control 'natural monopolies'. His attitude can really be summed up as the belief that Gladstone was the last good Chancellor. He is, perhaps, even better

known for his attitude toward the immigration of foreigners.[1] Explain in what ways, therefore, he doesn't in fact believe that the market system functions properly.

---

[1] He wants it stopped.

CHAPTER 34

Macroeconomic Concepts and Variables

FROM MICRO TO MACRO ECONOMICS

One important lesson of this chapter is that the distinction between macro- and microeconomics is nothing like as clear-cut as it is sometimes represented. It is a platitude that a
distinction within a science is a distinction of convenience, but it is worth explaining that
although microeconomics and macroeconomics deal with some things that exhibit clear
differences of type (the distinction, for example, between the effect of a rise in income tax
on the income of the government and the effect on the price of peanuts of an improvement
in the cashew nut crop), much of their subject matter is drawn from the same category of
economic events, the difference being the level of aggregation at which they are treated. For
example, the national level of expenditure on consumer goods is treated as a macro variable,
whereas the expenditure of a family on a particular range of consumer goods is a micro
variable. But what of the expenditure of a village on consumer goods? It doesn't really
matter; we make a distinction between macro and micro variables because we have a hypothesis that variations in economic relations on the micro level are often cancelled out by
other opposite variations on the micro level, such that at a certain level of aggregation the
relation will be fairly stable. If this hypothesis is true for some level of aggregation, it will
enable us to do economics without having to find out every detail of individuals' economic
behaviour.

On p. 497 the micro-constituents of the macro concept of the Circular Flow of Income are
described. Make sure that you see why this is described as circular. Most of the problems of
macroeconomics can be formulated in terms of the income flow behaving in four ways:
increasing, decreasing, fluctuating or *remaining stable.*

SOME KEY MACRO VARIABLES

Unemployment

Look at Table 34.1 which shows UK unemployment rates since 1862. As you can see, the
unemployment rate has never been zero. Does this mean that we have never had full
employment? It is difficult to conceive of an economy in which everyone who wants to work
is in employment throughout the year. At any time there will be some people who are
temporarily between jobs—perhaps because they have given notice and are waiting to take up
their new job or are currently searching for a job that suits them. Other people may be
unemployed because they have been laid off but are expecting to be recalled. When people
are unemployed for relatively short periods between jobs, we call this frictional unemployment.
When the unemployment rate is high, only a small proportion of unemployment will be due to
people being out of work for fairly short periods between jobs, and when we talk of an
economy being at the full-employment level, we mean that any unemployment is frictional
unemployment.

Q 1   When we talk of the unemployed we mean all people who are not working. T/F

Actual and Potential Output

Q 2   The gap between actual and potential gross national product measures the difference between:

(a)   What the economy is producing and what it could produce if the unemployment rate were zero;

(b)   What the economy is producing and what it could produce if workers took shorter teabreaks, were more punctual and generally worked harder;

(c)   What the economy is producing and what it could produce if the economy were kept at full employment;

(d)   What the economy is currently producing and what it will produce in a year's time after investment plans have been completed.

Q 3   Potential national product is what could be produced if the economy were on its production-possibility frontier. T/F

Price Indices

We often use GDP figures to compare total real output in different years. However, if a country is experiencing inflation over these years, part—or possibly all—of any increase in GDP measured in current prices may be due to the rising prices. We must therefore measure GDP in constant prices in order to separate out the change due to inflation from the change due to increase (or decrease) in real output. Real GDP is a measure of output obtained by evaluating the current year's output in terms of the prices of some base year.

Q 4   Nominal GDP measures output in terms of current/constant prices.

On page 503 one form of price index, the implied GDP deflator, is mentioned. This is calculated as

$$\frac{\text{GDP at current prices}}{\text{GDP at constant prices}} \cdot 100\%$$

Q 5   Work out the implied GDP deflator for each year in the following table where the GDP figures are taken from CSO, *National Income and Expenditure*, HMSO 1982 (the 'Blue Book').

	Current prices (£ million)	Constant prices (£ million)	GDP Deflator
1975	94,339	94,339	_____
1976	111,566	97,793	_____
1977	127,050	99,190	_____
1978	146,079	102,284	_____
1979	167,937	103,711	_____
1980	194,538	101,488	_____
1981	210,788	99,291	_____

Q 6   What is the base year? _____

Q 7   By what percentage has real output risen between

(a)   1975 and 1978? _____

(b)   1978 and 1981? _____

(c)   1975 and 1981? _____

Q 8   If total UK population was 56 million in 1975 and $56\frac{1}{4}$ million in 1981, find whether real output *per capita* has risen. _____

Q 9   If GDP at current prices was £74,641 million in 1974 and the index was 79, find
       1974 GDP at constant prices. _____

THE NATIONAL ACCOUNTS

National income is the total market value of all goods and services produced in an economy
during some specific period of time. National income is also the total of all incomes earned
over the same period of time, so

$$\text{gross national product} \equiv \text{national income}$$

Gross national product is the sum of the value-added of all firms over this same period; that is,
the total value of *final* goods and sales. There is only one value of gross national product in
any period but we can calculate it in different ways. We can measure GNP by taking the value
of expenditure on goods and services produced (*the expenditure approach*). Alternatively, we
can value output in terms of factor incomes (*the factor-income approach*), and yet another
way is to measure GNP by summing value-added. These methods give us three different ways
of looking at the value of the nation's output. The important point to grasp is that, whatever
approach we use, the value of GNP will be the same because of the circular flow of income.

   The *income approach* to national accounting adds together all the kinds of income earned
by all households. The various categories of income are listed in column one of Table 34.2.

Q 10   Gross company trading profits (Item 4) are equal to dividends paid by companies to
       shareholders. T/F

Q 11   A firm's undistributed profits equal its receipts minus its payments. T/F

   In the *output approach* to measuring GNP, care must be taken to avoid double-counting
of products. Most commodities go through several stages of production which may be undertaken by different firms. A commodity may be a finished product for one firm and raw
material to another. Some commodities can be both intermediate and final products. In
macroeconomics a firm's output is defined as its value-added.

Q 12   Value-added = total value of sales less _____
       _____

Q 13   From the following information, calculate:
       (a)   value-added by each 'firm';
       (b)   total value-added;
       (c)   profits earned by each 'firm'.

       Last year,

       (1)   A group of fishermen sold their catch for £12,000. Materials purchased (nets, etc.)
             cost £900, wages paid totalled £8,000, interest on a loan (for their boat) was
             £500 and harbour dues came to £100.

       (2)   A nearby food-processing factory had a total sales revenue of £60,000. Costs of
             raw materials were: fish £10,000, packaging materials £1,000. Rent came to
             £7,000, interest payments £6,000 and wages £15,000.

       (3)   A fishmonger sold £7,000 of frozen fishfingers and £3,000 of fresh fish. The
             frozen fish cost £5,000, while he paid £2,000 for the fresh fish. He ran his shop
             single-handed, paid a rent of £1,000 and valued his labour at £2,000. Interest
             payment on a bank loan came to £100.

   The third way to measure GNP is based on categories of *expenditre*.

Q 14   List the categories of expenditure which must be included when calculating GDP
       by the expenditure approach. _____
       _____

Q 15   If you put some of your savings into an account with a building society, is this investment? _____

_____

Q 16   What are the three major components of investment? _____

_____

Q 17   Inventories are stocks of _____ goods held by the producer. If production exceeds sales, inventories are _____ . If sales exceed production and such sales have been accurately forecast, inventory disinvestment is intentional/ unintentional.

Q 18   As inventories are stocks of goods that have not been sold by the producers, their value must be deducted from GDP. T/F

We distinguish between the total value of all goods produced, whether consumed or not, and the same value minus the value of all capital goods which have worn out during this period. This latter concept is called *net national product*.

Q 19   NNP = GNP minus depreciation. T/F

Q 20   GNE minus capital consumption = NNE. T/F

When there are taxes on expenditure, VAT for example, the value of *national product at market prices* (i.e. sale price + tax) is not equal to national product valued in terms of income payments to factors of production. To find the value of *national product at factor cost*, expenditure taxes must be subtracted from national product at market prices.

Q 21   National income is equal to national expenditure at factor cost. T/F

Q 22   If instead of taxing goods, the government subsidizes them, national product valued at market prices will be greater/less than national product valued at factor cost.

At times we have referred to gross *domestic* product, and at other times to gross *national* product. Here are a couple of questions to check whether you understand the difference.

Q 23   GNP = GDP + exports. T/F

Q 24   Net property income = receipts by UK residents of overseas income less income from UK assets paid to UK citizens who live outside the UK. T/F

We need one further concept of income: *disposable income*.

Q 25   Disposable income = GDP minus _____
minus _____ , plus _____

Q 26   The following items appear in the 1981 national income accounts for an economy. Classify them into separate accounts of National Produce, Expenditure and Income. (*Note*: as there is no net property income from abroad, national product = domestic product.)

	£ millions
Wages and salaries	430
Imports of goods and services	220
Rent	50
Value-added in agriculture	100
Government current expenditure on goods and services	130
Capital consumption	70
Value-added in construction	120
Consumers' expenditure	450
Dividends	500
Income from self-employment*	60

*Gross of depreciation

	£ millions
Exports of goods and services	210
Undistributed profits*	110
Gross domestic fixed investment	150
Value-added in distributive trades	180
Value-added in manufacturing	700
Value-added in sectors not separately listed	290
Value of physical increase in stocks	10
Trading surplus of public corporations*	20

*Gross of depreciation

Q 27   Unfortunately, due to recent disturbances in the country, much information on Ruritania's national income and expenditure is missing. All the available information is given below. You are able to reassure the Chancellor of the Exchequer that this information is sufficient for you to compute the national product in one of the conventional ways.

     Find: (a)   gross national product and net national product at factor cost;
               (b)   gross national product at market prices;
               (c)   disposable income.

	£ millions
Dividends	40
Incomes of self-employed	780
Government expenditure on goods and services	300
Indirect taxes on expenditure	120
Value-added in manufacturing	1,000
Gross fixed capital formation	190
Wages and salaries	1,850
Gross trading profits of companies	170
Net fixed investment	150
Gross trading surplus of public corporations	40
Interest on the national debt	30
Rent	60
Retained profits of companies	130
Income tax	600

QUESTIONS FOR DISCUSSION

1   How do we distinguish between micro- and macroeconomics? Where do we draw the boundary?

2   What does microeconomics take as 'given' that macroeconomics considers? What would you say about the reverse question?

3   We noted that only final goods and services are included in GDP. Does this mean that earnings of people producing intermediate goods and services are not part of GDP?

4   Are education and medical care intermediate or final goods? When education and medical care are not sold in the market, are they excluded from GDP?

5   Can one compare standards of living in different countries using national-income data?

6   Comment on the following extract from a letter to *The Times* (28.11.78) by James Partridge:

'The absurdity of orthodox indices of "wealth" is clear: more road accidents mean more car repairs, more new car sales, more policing, more demand for safer, better-lit roads. "Wealth" in the form of GNP soars. Lead in petrol is apparently economic but none the less unhealthy. Meantime irreversible damage to health is treated by a Health Service which has been constrained precisely so that more "wealth" can be produced.'

7   A professor wrote to *The Times* that a letter posted in Britain to an address in Germany required a stamp for 5½p (in 1974). The same letter, if it had been posted inside Germany to the same address, would have required a stamp for 50 pfennig (roughly 8½p). What, he enquired, are the real costs of the two operations and who is losing on the difference? Can you throw any light on the question?

CHAPTER 35

National Income in a Two-sector Model

In this chapter we begin our analysis of the determinants of output and employment. In order not to have to think about many variables at once, we start by making some simplifying assumptions so that we can begin our study of the theory of national-income determination in a very simple economy; in later chapters we shall relax these assumptions.

Q 1   Which of the following propositions are incompatible with the basic assumptions discussed on pp. 519—20?

   (a)   Increased demand for a commodity will not result in a price rise because new techniques will enable it to be produced more cheaply.

   (b)   Even if the proportion of the population which constitutes the labour force increases, thereby increasing potential production, the price level will not fall.

   (c)   If employment increases, production *must* only increase in the same proportion.

Q 2   An increase in gross national expenditure always means an increase in both money and real gross national product. T/F

   If you answered this question wrongly, consider the following case:

Q 3   Total expenditure increases by 6% in one year. In the previous chapter you learned that GNE must be equal to GNP, therefore money GNP also increases by 6%. Now suppose that prices rose by 15% in the same period. Real GNP will have increased/ remained constant/decreased.

   If we want to find out about the behaviour of national income, we must start by separating out the change due to *price* changes so that we can concentrate on *output* changes—hence the important assumption on p. 520.

Q 4   When the aggregate supply schedule is perfectly elastic

   (a)   a rise in aggregate demand will raise price and income levels. T/F

   (b)   a fall in aggregate demand will cause output to rise and unemployment to fall. T/F

Q 5   When we say that income is demand-determined, we mean that the level of national income is determined by aggregate demand, firms producing whatever they can sell. T/F

THE BASIC MODEL

In the very simple model we study in this chapter, consumption and savings decisions are made by households; there is no business saving, no government expenditure and no government revenue from taxation. All consumption and investment goods are produced and sold within the country, so that there are no exports and imports.

Q 6   In this basic model, disposable income = national income = net national product = net domestic product. T/F

Q 7   What are the categories of expenditure which make up gross domestic expenditure?
(List them in symbols) _____

Q 8   There are two ways of expressing the equilibrium conditions. Can you remember what
they are? (Write them as symbols.)

(a)   _____

(b)   _____

In the last chapter we learned that expenditure is equal to income. This is an identity:
actual expenditure is equal to *actual* income through the circular flow of income. It is
important to understand that this identity holds whether or not an economy is in equilibrium.
For an economy to be in equilibrium, *desired* expenditure must be equal to income. To make
quite sure you understand this point, we will look at the circular flow of income in a very
simple economy where only one investment good is produced (canoes), all other goods being
consumption goods.

Q 9   Fill in the blanks in the following table:

(a)	OUTPUT (£000s)			EXPENDITURE (£000s)	
1.	Breadfruit	100	*Consumption*		
2.	Yams	80	1.	Breadfruit	100
3.	Pineapples	50	2.	Yams	60
4.	Fish	60	3.	Pineapples	40
5.	Canoes	120	4.	Fish	60
			Investment		
			5.	Planned fixed investment: Canoes	80
			6.	Planned inventory investment: Pineapples	10
			7.	Unplanned fixed investment: Canoes	____
			8.	Unplanned inventory investment: Yams	____

(b)   What is the value of GDP and GDE? _____

(c)   What is the value of planned expenditure? _____

(d)   What is the value of planned investment? _____

(e)   What is the value of unplanned investment? _____

(f)   Aggregate demand is less than/equal to/greater than aggregate supply.

The important point is that goods which have been produced, but not yet sold, still exist.
They don't vanish if nobody buys them; they pile up in firms' stockrooms and must be
counted as part of total expenditure. Through the circular flow of income, expenditure is thus
equal to national income.

Q 10   When aggregate demand exceeds aggregate supply, inventory investment is rising/
constant/falling.

Q 11   GDP = Planned expenditure plus unplanned inventory investment = GDE. T/F

On p. 522 it was stressed that savings and investment decisions are made by different groups
of people and that if, for example, firms wish to increase their investment, there is no automatic guarantee that households will be accommodating enough to increase their savings by a
corresponding amount.

Q 12   Return to the table in Q 9. What is national income in this simple economy? _____

Q 13   How much did consumers save? _____

Q 14   Saving is less than/equal to/greater than planned investment and saving is less than/ equal to/greater than actual investment.

In this example, actual expenditure is equal to national income (the identity of national-income accounts) but planned expenditure is not equal to income. For an equilibrium we require that planned expenditure equal actual output.

Q 15   In equilibrium, unplanned inventory investment will be positive/zero/negative and planned inventory investment may be positive/zero/negative.

This seems a good point at which to make sure you have grasped the difference between saving and investment. It is very important not to mix them up, so check your understanding by doing the following exercise.

Q 16   Group the following data as appropriate and check whether saving equals investment for the period concerned.

	£ million	Saving	Investment
Changes in business inventories	−10		
Expenditure on plant and equipment (net)	100		
Personal saving	90		
Total volume of transactions on the Stock Exchange	280		
Expenditure on residential construction (net)	50		
Undistributed business profits	60		
Value of individuals' building society deposits	120		

Q 17   Net investment in an economy can never be negative. T/F

EQUILIBRIUM IN THE BASIC MODEL

In equilibrium, desired expenditure is equal to national income. We will start by examining the two elements of aggregate expenditure: consumption and investment. You remember that every household will either spend its income on consumption or will save it.

Q 18   Fill in the gaps in the following table. (Figures are in £millions.)

National Income (Y)	Consumption (C)	Saving (S)
0	10	—
20	22	—
40	34	6
60	—	14
—	52	18
100	—	30
120	82	—
—	85	40

Q 19   Using the data in the table, plot on Fig. 1 the amount spent on *consumption* and the amount *saved*. Join up the points and label the consumption function *C* and the saving function *S*.

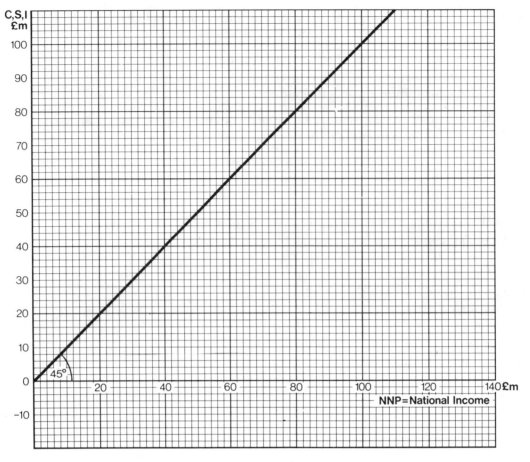

Fig. 1

Q 20   Investment is assumed to be fixed at a level of £8 million. Plot and label the investment function I on Fig. 1.

One way to find the equilibrium level of income is to find where aggregate expenditure is equal to income.

Q 21   How do we find aggregate expenditure? _____

Plot the aggregate expenditure function on Fig. 1 and label it E.

A 45° line has already been drawn on Fig. 1. This line shows all points at which annual expenditure is equal to annual income.

Q 22   The equilibrium level of national income can be found where intended consumption plus _____ equals NNP or national income; in other words, where _____ cuts the 45° line.

Another approach to finding the equilibrium level of income is to find the income at which intended saving equals intended investment. Find this point on Fig. 1 and check that both methods of establishing equilibrium income give the same result.

The consumption and savings functions which you have plotted on Fig. 1 are both straight lines. The equation for the consumption function is

$$C = 10 + \frac{3}{5}\,Y.$$

Q 23   Can you work out the equation for the savings function? _____
_____

Q 24   Now that we have a specific consumption function, we could work out what consump-

182

tion would be for any level of income. Find consumption when income is £80 million.
_____ (Check this on Fig. 1.)

Q 25   What is saving when income is £50 million? _____

Q 26   Write out the equation for aggregate expenditure. _____

Q 27   Now find the equilibrium level of income, using this equation for aggregate expenditure. _____

Q 28   Remember that there is another way of finding equilibrium income and work out the answer using this other method. _____

Check that your answers to Questions 26 and 27 are the same as you found in Fig. 1.
In order to make quite sure you understand how to find equilibrium income without having to resort to plotting graphs, here is another example for you to work out:

$$C = 0.75\,Y$$
$$I = 100$$

Q 29   Find the equilibrium level of income using (a) the aggregate-expenditure-equals-income approach, and (b) the savings-equals-investment approach.

(a)   _____

(b)   _____

We shall return to our analysis of equilibrium income in a little while, but now we must examine more carefully the nature of the relationship between consumption and income.

THE CONSUMPTION FUNCTION

Q 30   Have another look at the consumption and savings functions which you drew in Fig. 1 and say which of the following statements are correct for these functions:

(a)   As income falls, dissaving decreases.
(b)   As income rises, the proportion of income spent on consumption increases.
(c)   At no income level is consumption equal to income.
(d)   As income rises from £60 million to £100 million, the amount saved increases.

Q 31   From Fig. 1, you can see that as income increases, consumption also increases by more than/the same amount as/less than income.

The propensity to consume (save) is the relationship between income and consumption (saving) levels.

Q 32   The average propensity to consume, APC, is defined as:

(a)   (in words) _____
(b)   (in symbols) _____

Q 33   The marginal propensity to consume, MPC, is defined as:

(a)   (in words) _____
(b)   (in symbols) _____

Q 34   Fill in the columns headed APC and MPC in the following table:

(a) Y	C	APC	MPC	APS	MPS
0	50	___	___	___	___
100	130	___	___	___	___
200	210	___	___	___	___
300	290	___	___	___	___
400	370	___	___	___	___
500	450	___	___	___	___

(b) As income rises, the *APC* rises/remains constant/falls and the *MPC* rises/remains constant/falls.

(c) If income rises by £10, consumption spending will increase by £ _____

(d) If income falls by £30, consumption spending will fall by £ _____

Q 35 The average propensity to save, *APS*, is defined as:

(a) (in words) _____

(b) (in symbols) _____

Q 36 The marginal propensity to save, *MPS*, is defined as:

(a) (in words) _____

(b) (in symbols) _____

Q 37 Fill in the columns headed *APS* and *MPS* for the table in Q 34(a).

As $Y = C + S$, once we know what households decide to spend on consumption, we also know what they save. Any change in income (ΔY) must be allocated either to consumption, resulting in a change in consumption (ΔC), or to savings, resulting in a change in saving (ΔS). This means that

$$\Delta Y = \Delta C + \Delta S$$

Dividing this equation by ΔY, we get
$$1 = \frac{\Delta C}{\Delta Y} + \frac{\Delta S}{\Delta Y}$$

or
$$1 = MPC + MPS$$

Q 38 Find the corresponding *MPS* or *MPC* for the following:

(a) *MPC* = 0.75   *MPS* = _____

(b) *MPC* = $\frac{2}{3}$ *MPS* = _____

(c) *MPS* = 0.28   *MPC* = _____

Q 39 In Fig. 2 line *AC* is a community's consumption function.

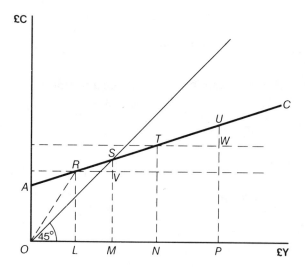

Fig. 2

Using letters, find:

(a) The break-even level of income _____ . At this income, the *APC* = _____ which is equal to the slope of line _____ .

(b) At income OL, the APC = _____ which is equal to the slope of line _____
At income OL, the APC is greater/less than 1.

(c) At income OP, the APC = _____ which is equal to the slope of a line _____
and is greater/less than 1.

(d) When income rises from ON to OP, the MPC = _____ which is equal to the
slope of line _____ .

(e) When income falls from OM to OL, the MPC = _____ which is equal to the
slope of line _____ .

(f) For the consumption function AC, the proportion of an increase in income spent
on consumption is increasing/constant/decreasing and is greater than/equal to/
less than 1, while the APC is falling/constant/rising.

(g) At the break-even level of income, the APC is greater than/equal to/less than 1.
At income levels below the break-even level of income, the APC is greater than/
equal to/less than 1, while at incomes above the break-even level, the APC is
greater than/equal to/less than 1.

The consumption function in Fig. 2 and the functions you plotted in Fig. 2 are linear
functions. The equation for a linear consumption function is $C = a + cY$ where

C is consumption

Y is income

a is autonomous consumption (i.e. that portion of consumption which is not determined by income. In other words, even if income is zero, consumption will
occur and a is thus the *intercept* of the C line with the axis along which
consumption spending is measured.)

c is the MPC and is thus equal to the *slope* of the C line on the graph.

Q 40   In Fig. 2,

(a) Autonomous consumption = _____

(b) When income is zero, dissaving is _____

(c) The MPC is equal to the slope of line _____

Q 41   The consumption function you plotted in Fig. 1 was $C = 10 + \frac{3}{5} Y$.

(a) What is autonomous consumption? _____

(b) What is the MPC? _____

Q 42   When the consumption function is given by $C = 0.75Y$,

(a) What is autonomous consumption? _____

(b) What is the APC? _____

(c) What is the MPC? _____

(d) What is the MPS? _____

(e) What is the APS? _____

Q 43   So far we have considered only linear consumption functions, which has meant that
the MPC rises/remains constant/falls as income increases.

Q 44   Consumption functions, however, are not necessarily linear and in Fig. 3 two
consumption functions of different shapes have been drawn. Which curve is consistent
with the following statements?

(a) APC and MPC fall as income rises;

(b) APC falls and MPC rises as income rises;

(c) *MPS* falls as income rises;
(d) *MPC* rises at low incomes and falls at high incomes.

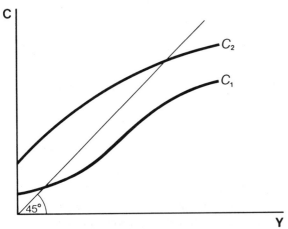

Fig. 3

Q 45   To sum up, we hypothesize that all/part of an increase in income is always spent and that the *MPC* exceeds 0/1 but is less than _____ .

CHANGES IN INCOME IN THE TWO-SECTOR MODEL

We now return to our simple model of the economy where there are only households and firms, and examine the causes of changes in the equilibrium level of income.

Q 46   When the consumption function is given by $C = 0.8Y$ and investment is determined exogenously so that $I = £20$ million, find the equilibrium level of income.

_____

Q 47   Suppose that producers are optimistic so that instead of producing at the equilibrium rate, they produce at a rate of £120 million. With national income at £120 million, aggregate expenditure would be £ _____ million. Firms would find they had sold less than they had produced by an amount equal to £ _____ million; this amount would be unintended investment in inventories. Saving would amount to £ _____ million and ex post investment (i.e. including the unintended investment) would be £ _____ million. In this situation firms would find it desirable to expand output/ contract output/leave output unchanged.

Q 48   Suppose instead that producers are pessimistic and decide to produce at a rate of £90 million. Intended consumption would be £ _____ million; intended saving would be £ _____ million; intended investment would be £ _____ million; and aggregate demand would be £ _____ million. Now if the firms are to meet all orders they would have to run down inventories by £ _____ million. If they were to do this, realized saving would amount to £ _____ million and realized investment would be £ _____ million. However, let us suppose that firms are unable to run down inventories (or are unwilling to do so). This means they will only meet orders amounting to £90 million, of which £20 million are orders for investment goods. In this event, realized consumption would be £70 million, so unintended saving would amount to £ _____ million. Total realized saving would be £ _____ million, and realized investment would be £ _____ million. Whether firms run down inventories or not, firms will find it desirable to expand output/contract output/leave output unchanged.

Q 49   The only level of income at which desired saving is equal to desired investment and at which desired expenditure is equal to output is £ _____ million.

186

We are now ready to consider what happens to the equilibrium level of income if there is a change in either or both of the two components of aggregate demand.

A shift in investment

Q 50   Suppose that investment increases from £20 million to £22 million. What happens to the equilibrium level of income? _____

Q 51   As a result of the rise in investment, the equilibrium level of income has risen. Suppose that producers continued to produce at a rate of £100 million. As a result of the shift in the investment schedule, aggregate demand is now £ _____ million of which intended consumption would be £ _____ million. Firms will find it desirable to expand output/contract output/leave output unchanged. As income rises, savings fall/rise/remain constant until in equilibrium saving is £ _____ million.

Q 52   Suppose that investment were to fall to £15 million. What would be the new equilibrium level of income? _____ At this new level, consumption is £ _____ million and saving is £ _____ million. The fall in investment of £5 million has resulted in the equilibrium level of income falling by £ _____ million.

A change in the consumption function

Q 53   Suppose that the marginal propensity to consume falls from 0.8 to 0.75. If investment is £20 million, the new equilibrium level of income will be £ _____ million and consumption has fallen from £80 million to £ _____ million.

Q 54   The fall in the *MPC* shifts down/changes the slope of the consumption function and shifts down/changes the slope of the aggregate expenditure function.

Q 55   When we examine a fall in investment, this shifts down/changes the slope of the investment function and shifts down/changes the slope of the aggregate expenditure function.

Q 56   A rise in the *MPC* from 0.8 to 0.9 will result in an aggregate expenditure function with a slope of _____ and an intercept of £ _____ million.

Q 57   Consider now a consumption function where $C = 10 + 0.8Y$. If investment is equal to £20 million, equilibrium income will be £ _____ million. The slope of the aggregate expenditure function will be _____ and the intercept will be at £ _____ million. If autonomous consumption fell from £10 million to £5 million, this shifts down/changes the slope of the consumption function and the aggregate expenditure function.

Q 58   If the *MPS* rises, this changes the slope of the savings function in a clockwise/anti-clockwise direction and increases/decreases equilibrium income.

Q 59   If the *MPS* falls, this changes the slope of the savings function in a clockwise/anti-clockwise direction and increases/decreases equilibrium income.

Q 60   If autonomous consumption rises but the *MPC* is unchanged, this shifts the consumption function up/down and the savings function up/down and equilibrium income increases/decreases.

Q 61   Aggregate demand rises as income rises at a rate equal to/greater than/less than the rise in income. This is because _____

_____

THE MULTIPLIER

So far we have discussed the *direction* of any change in equilibrium income. Can we say anything about the *magnitude* of such changes? Consider a change in investment: in Question 50, when $C = 0.8Y$ and $I = £20$ million, we found that a rise in investment (ΔI) of £2 million resulted in a rise in income (ΔY) of £10 million.

$$\frac{\Delta Y}{\Delta I} = \frac{\text{£10 million}}{\text{£2 million}} = 5$$

Thus a change in expenditure has led to a change in income five times the amount of the initial change in investment.

Q 62   The multiplier is defined as the ratio of _____ _____ to the _____ that brought it about.

Q 63   If the consumption function remains as $C = 0.8Y$ but investment falls from £20 million to £15 million, equilibrium income will fall by _____ million.

Remember, the multiplier describes the change in the *equilibrium* levels of national income between two different levels of expenditure. As it is a comparative-static theory, it does not say whether or not the new equilibrium level will actually be reached, or how long it will take to reach it.

Q 64   So far we have only defined the multiplier, but in the example above we found the value of the multiplier to be 5 when $C = 0.8Y$. The value of the multiplier is the reciprocal of the slope of the savings function.

     (a)   What is the savings function when $C = 0.8Y$? _____

     (b)   What determines the slope of the savings function? _____

     Check that the multiplier in this case is equal to 5.

In this simple basic model, the multiplier is easily derived. In more complicated models, it is not quite so easy to work out the value at a quick glance and it is important, therefore, that you should be sure you can also work out the multiplier's value by using a little algebra.

Q 65   As the multiplier describes the change in equilibrium levels of income, start by writing out the equilibrium condition when $C = cY$: _____

If investment changes, we know that the equilibrium level of income changes, so we can write

$$\Delta Y = c\Delta Y + \Delta I *$$

Re-arranging this we get $(1 - c)\,\Delta Y = \Delta I *$

$$\text{and} \quad \frac{\Delta Y}{\Delta I *} = \frac{1}{(1 - c)} = \frac{1}{s}$$

     What do c and s represent? _____

Q 66   The slope of the savings function, s, is $\dfrac{\Delta Y}{\Delta I}$. T/F

Q 67   If $C = 0.75Y$ and investment is £5 million, find:

     (a)   the value of the multiplier. _____

     (b)   the effect of an increasing investment by £1 million. _____

     (c)   the new level of equilibrium income. _____

Q 68   If $C = 5 + 0.75Y$ and investment is £6 million, find:

     (a)   the value of the multiplier. _____

     (b)   the equilibrium level of income. _____

     (c)   what would happen to equilibrium income if autonomous consumption fell by £1 million. _____

QUESTIONS FOR DISCUSSION

1   What assumptions underlie our theory?

2   Which variables are assumed to be endogenous and which exogenous?

3   Explain the process by which an economy will move towards the equilibrium level of income when

   (a)   aggregate expenditure exceeds GDP.
   (b)   withdrawals exceed injections.

4   What would be the value of the multiplier if the propensity to withdraw were (a) zero, (b) unity?

5   How can a household's annual consumption spending exceed its annual income?

6   Discuss the main factors, other than income, which might determine a household's consumption expenditure.

7   Why may a firm experience *unplanned* inventory investment? Why may a firm *plan* an increase or a decrease in its inventory investment?

8   The following is an extract from a letter to *The Times* (13.10.78) from Sir John Partridge:

'Since the end of 1973 industrial earnings have risen by 106 per cent; prices by 101 per cent; Gross Domestic Product by 4 per cent. Within GDP, industrial production (including North Sea oil activities) has risen by $1\frac{1}{2}$ per cent, and manufacturing production has fallen by 4 per cent. There are three elements in the equation: pay, prices, and output. It is the last of these which points most directly to the magnitude of our problems in the productivity field . . . a nation or a business which pays itself vastly more for a relatively static volume of production is playing ducks and drakes with its future.'

How can a nation pay itself more than the value of its production? Is not GDP $\equiv$ national income?

Appendix to Chapter 35; The Consumption Function

AGGREGATION PROBLEMS

Q 1   On p. 537 it was pointed out that if households have different *MPC*s, then the same total income will result in different levels of consumption depending on the distribution of income. Suppose that there are two regions, A and B. To keep numbers manageable, let us assume there are four families in each region.

   All families in region A have the same consumption function, details of which are as follows:

Y_d	C	MPC
£ 0	£ 600	_____
2,000	2,300	_____
4,000	3,900	_____
6,000	5,400	_____
8,000	6,800	_____

All families in region B have the following consumption function:

Y_d	C	MPC
£ 0	£ 500	_____
2,000	2,100	_____
4,000	3,700	_____
6,000	5,300	_____
8,000	6,900	_____

Fill in the gaps to show the marginal propensity to consume for each region.

Aggregate disposable income is £16,000 in each region. Consider three alternative ways in which this income might be distributed:

distribution I: each family has an income of £4,000,

distribution II: two families have £2,000 each and two have £6,000 each,

distribution III: two families have zero income and two have £8,000 each.

(a)   In region A, aggregate consumption would be:

    (1) £ _____ with distribution I

    (2) £ _____ with distribution II

    (3) £ _____ with distribution III.

(b)   In region B, aggregate consumption would be:

    (1) £ _____ with distribution I

    (2) £ _____ with distribution II

    (3) £ _____ with distribution III.

THE PERMANENT-INCOME AND LIFE-CYCLE HYPOTHESIS

Q 2   (a)   Suppose a man decides to become an accountant and calculates his life-time earnings will be as follows:

Age	Earnings per annum
19–23	£5,000
24–28	£8,000
29–34	£12,000
35–44	£15,000
45–64	£17,000
65–79	£8,000

Assuming that the interest rate is zero, calculate his annual permanent income.

_____

(b)   Now suppose that at the age of twenty-nine he wins £25,000 on the football pools. What effect will this have on his annual permanent income?

_____

(c)   Out of his winnings he buys a colour television for £500. Assuming the expected life of the set is ten years,

    (i)   in the first year, actual consumption of this set was £ _____ and saving £ _____

    (ii) in the second year, actual consumption was £ _____ and saving £ _____

(d)   As his career progresses, our man finds that he was over-cautious in his estimate of future earnings. He is so successful that he is able to set up his own firm when he is thirty-five. His income from then until he retires, at the end of his sixty-fourth year, is £25,000 p.a. On retirement his earnings are zero. What will be his new annual permanent income when he sets up in business on his own?

£ _____

QUESTIONS FOR DISCUSSION

1   Suppose the government were to:

    (a)   stipulate a higher minimum hire purchase deposit;
 or (b)   shorten the maximum repayment period,
what effect would this have on consumption and on the level of national income?

2   Many people today use credit cards, such as Access or Barclay cards. If the interest rate charged were to fall, how would this affect consumption?

3   Do you think the marginal propensity to consume of rich households is the same as that of poor households? What would be the probable effects on the equilibrium level of income of government policies redistributing income from the rich to the poor?

4   In permanent-income theories, you might expect to find a household's expenditure exceeding actual income when the household is first set up and also towards the end of its life. How does the household manage this?

5   Professor Duesenbery has suggested that consumption depends not upon absolute real income, but upon the *position* of the individual in the society's income scale—that is, upon relative income. This means, for example, that a person in the 10% of the population than whom 40% are richer and 50% are poorer consumes $1/x$th of his income, at one time. At another (perhaps later when everyone in the country is much richer) *as long as he is in the same 10%* he will still consume $1/x$th of his income. This position is often tacitly endorsed in the newspapers—cf. a letter to *The Times* (16.3.65): '. . . The emigrant (to the US) will almost certainly have greater purchasing power, but will he feel any richer? Eventually, his economic well-being depends distressingly on the level of other incomes in the community. What income do the Jones's have? What would they consider a good salary?'

    How might you go about testing this?

CHAPTER 36

National Income in More Elaborate Models

In the previous chapter we considered a very simple economy made up of two sectors: households and firms. We will now add a third sector—government—and, by the end of this chapter, we shall have added the fourth, and last, sector—foreign trade.

WITHDRAWALS AND INJECTIONS

A *withdrawal* is any income that is not passed on in the circular flow.

Q 1   Define an injection. _____

_____

_____

_____

Q 2   Which of the following are withdrawals, which injections, which are neither and which both?

    (a)   Payment to New Zealand for lamb imports? _____

    (b)   Firms increase the proportion of profits retained? _____

    (c)   Purchases of theatre tickets by foreign visitors? _____

    (d)   An actuarially based National Insurance scheme? _____

    (e)   The construction of a sugar beet refinery, financed by a bank loan? _____

    (f)   My decision to remove my savings from a building society, and to put them in the National Savings Bank. _____

    (g)   A decision by the banks to loan more to exporters, and less to producers for the domestic market. _____

    (h)   The payment by the government of a motorway-construction gang. _____

    (i)   Purchase of Rolls-Royce engines for German-built frigates. _____

Q 3   In the previous chapter, the only withdrawal in the basic model was _____ and the only injection was _____

Q 4   Withdrawals exert an expansionary/contractionary force on national income, while injections exert an expansionary/contractionary force.

Q 5   When withdrawals are greater than injections, the level of national income will rise/fall.

NATIONAL INCOME IN A THREE-SECTOR MODEL

If a government builds roads, hospitals, etc. it must raise money to do these things—either by borrowing, or by increasing the money supply or by levying taxes. To keep matters simple at this stage, let us assume that all saving is done by households and that all government expenditure is financed by an income tax. The amount paid in taxes will depend on the tax rate (t), and tax revenue (T) will be equal to the tax rate $\times$ national income, i.e. $T = tY$.

Q 6   If a person earns £5,000 and the tax rate is 30p in every £ earned, tax paid will be

_____

The government also levies taxes in order to redistribute income from the rich to the poor, the healthy to the sick, the employed to the unemployed.

Q 7   The government's budget is in deficit when tax revenue is less than/greater than the sum of _____

_____

Q 8   Disposable income (Y_d) is equal to _____

_____

Q 9   When Q stands for transfer payments, write (in symbols) disposable income as a function of national income. _____

We can now write consumption and saving functions as functions of either disposable or national income.

Q 10   If c is the *MPC* out of disposable income, and Q stands for transfers:

(a)   write consumption as a function of national income. _____

(b)   write saving as a function of national income. _____

_____

Q 11   If the *MPC* out of disposable income is 0.8, the tax rate is 30% and transfers are £10 million, write

(a)   consumption as a function of national income. _____

_____

(b)   If national income is £50 million, find consumption. _____

(c)   Is tax revenue sufficient to cover transfers? _____

_____

(d)   What are savings? _____

(e)   What is disposable income? _____

Equilibrium Income

Q 12   For equilibrium we require that aggregate desired expenditure equals national income. What are the components of aggregate expenditure in the three-sector model (in symbols)? _____

Q 13   Another way to find equilibrium is to see at what income level withdrawals equal injections. Write this condition (in symbols) listing each component. _____

Q 14   From the following information, plot consumption, investment, government expenditure and aggregate expenditure on Fig. 1. You may also find it helpful to complete the following table.

(1) $C = 0.8Y_d$	C is consumption
(2) $I = $ £78 million	Y_d is disposable income
(3) $G = $ £70 million	I is investment
(4) $Q = $ £40 million	G is government expenditure
(5) $T = 0.25Y$	Q is transfer payments
	T is tax revenue
	Y is national income

(a)   What is the equilibrium level of income? _____

(b)   Write out the equation for aggregate expenditure. _____

_____

Level of national income (£m)	Consumption (£m)	Investment (£m)	Government expenditure (£m)	Tax revenue (£m)	Aggregate expenditure (£m)
0					
150					
250					
350					
450					
550					
650					

    (c)   Its slope is _____ and its intercept is _____

    (d)   At equilibrium, consumption is _____ and saving is _____ while disposable income is _____

    (e)   At equilibrium is the government balancing its budget? _____

The other way of finding the equilibrium level of income is to find the income level at which withdrawals equal injections. Here $W = s(1 - t)\,Y + sQ + tY$, while $J = I + G + Q$. Note that Q (transfers) appears both as a withdrawal (sQ) and injection (Q). When solving for equilibrium income, we include the *net* effect as an injection of cQ in the injections equation and delete sQ from withdrawals.

    (f)   Write the withdrawals and injections equations and plot the functions on Fig. 1.

        Check that, at equilibrium, withdrawals equal injections.

    (g)   When national income is £250m, by how much do injections exceed withdrawals?

    (h)   When national income is £600m, by how much do withdrawals exceed injections?

At this point it would be a good idea if you worked out the answers to these questions using the algebraic method. If you find algebra a bit difficult, it is worth persevering as not only will it help you to answer questions more quickly but it will also help you to understand and remember the theory.

CHANGES IN EQUILIBRIUM INCOME IN A THREE-SECTOR MODEL

Q 15   Suppose now that the government were to raise the tax rate.

    (a)   What will happen to the consumption function? _____

    (b)   What will happen to the slope and the intercept of the aggregate expenditure function? _____

    (c)   What will happen to equilibrium income? _____

Q 16   If the government raises the tax rate to 30% but all other equations set out in Question 14 are unchanged:

    (a)   what will be the slope of the consumption function? _____

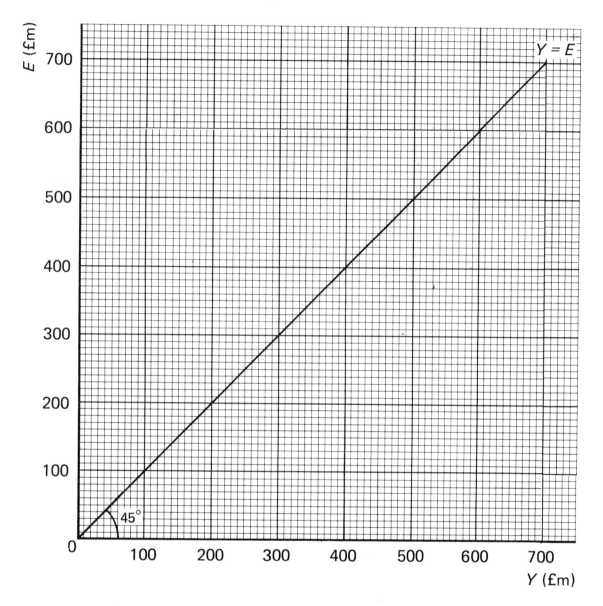

Fig. 1.

(b) what will be the slope and the intercept of the aggregate expenditure function?

_____

(c) what will happen to the level of equilibrium income? _____

_____

(d) At the original level of equilibrium income (£450m), withdrawals are less than/ greater than injections.

(e) At the new equilibrium what is tax revenue? _____

Q 17 Suppose that instead of increasing taxes the government decreases its expenditure.

    (a) What will be the slope and the intercept of the new aggregate expenditure function? _____

    _____

    (b) What will happen to equilibrium income? _____

Q 18 Assume that the government keeps the tax rate at 30% as in Question 16, but it also increases its expenditure by £12m.

    (a) What will be the new equilibrium level of income? _____

    (b) What will happen to the government's budget? _____

    _____

    (c) Has the additional government expenditure offset the effects of the higher tax rate on the level of income? _____

    _____

    _____

    _____

Q 19 Still keeping the tax rate at 30%, suppose that instead of increasing government expenditure by £12m, the government increases transfer payments by this amount.

    (a) What will be the new equilibrium level of income? _____

    (b) What will happen to the government's budget? _____

    _____

    (c) Compare your findings with your answers to the previous question. Why has income increased by a smaller amount when the injection took the form of an increase in transfer payments rather than expenditure by the government on goods and services? _____

    _____

    _____

    _____

    _____

Q 20 What would have happened to the level of income if investment had increased by £12m instead of government expenditure? _____

    _____

    _____

Q 21 A fall in the tax rate will mean that the *MPC* out of disposable income will rise/fall/ remain unchanged, while the amount of disposable income will rise/fall/remain unchanged, consumption will rise/fall/remain unchanged and national income will rise/fall/remain unchanged.

Q 22 A fall in transfer payments will mean that the *MPC* out of income will rise/fall/remain unchanged, disposable income will rise/fall/remain unchanged, consumption will rise/ fall/remain unchanged and national income will rise/fall/remain unchanged.

Multipliers in a Three-sector Model

We will start by reminding ourselves of the multiplier in the basic two-sector model we studied in the last chapter (remember: there was no government sector).

Q 23 If $C = cY$ and $I = I^*$, what is the marginal propensity to withdraw? _____

    _____

    _____

Q 24 In this simple economy, what is the value of the expenditure multiplier? _____

In the three-sector model where $C = cY_d$, $Y_d = Y - T + Q$, $T = tY$, $I = I^*$, $G = G^*$ and $Q = Q^*$, finding the multiplier is just a bit more complicated.

Q 25   Start by assuming there are no transfer payments, i.e. $Q = 0$.

     (a)   Withdrawals are equal to _____

     (b)   Injections are equal to _____

     (c)   Write savings as a function of national income. _____

     (d)   Write the equation for withdrawals (W). _____

     (e)   Write the equation for injections (J). _____

     (f)   When $W = J$, then Y equals _____

     (g)   The investment expenditure multiplier is $\dfrac{\Delta Y}{\Delta I} =$ _____

     (h)   The government expenditure multiplier is $\dfrac{\Delta Y}{\Delta G} =$ _____

Q 26   We will now do the same exercise for the case when there are transfer payments, i.e. $Q = Q^*$.

     (a)   Write down the savings function. _____

     (b)   Write down the withdrawals function. _____

     (c)   Write the injections function. _____

     (d)   Set withdrawals equal to injections and solve for Y.

            _____

     (e)   The transfer payments multiplier is $\dfrac{\Delta Y}{\Delta Q} =$ _____

Q 27   When $c = 0.8$ and $t = 0.25$, find the value of

     (a)   the expenditure multiplier. _____

     (b)   the transfer payments multiplier. _____

Q 28   When $c = 0.8$ but $t = 0$ (as in the two-sector model), what is the value of the multiplier? _____

Q 29   When $c = 0.8$ and $t = 0.25$,

     (a)   increasing government expenditure by £4m will result in income rising by _____

     (b)   increasing transfer payments by a similar amount will raise income by _____

     (c)   a fall in investment of £10m will change income by _____

Q 30   If the tax rate is cut, the value of the multiplier will rise/fall/remain unchanged.

Q 31   If people decide to save more of their income, the value of the expenditure multiplier will rise/fall/remain unchanged and the value of the transfer payments multiplier will rise/fall/remain unchanged.

Q 32   If we know that in a new equilibrium situation, brought about by a change in the rate of taxation, tax revenue has increased, then assuming no change in the propensity to save, we know that

     (a)   the level of income has risen/fallen.
     (b)   the level of saving has risen/fallen.

EQUILIBRIUM IN THE OPEN ECONOMY

Q 33   What are the four sectors that make up the open economy? _____ I^*, $G = G^*$ _____

_____

Q 34   In this economy, what are the main components which act as withdrawals from the system? Is any of them a declining function of income? _____

Q 35   What constitute injections? Are these variables exogenous or endogenous to our theory? _____
_____

Q 36   In this more complex model, what are the conditions for equilibrium? _____
_____
_____

Q 37   Express these symbolically. _____
_____

Q 38   In this chapter we assume that injections are unaffected by a change in income but withdrawals are affected by such a change. T/F

Q 39   Identify the following according to whether they are components of aggregate expenditure (C, I, G, X, M), factor payments (F), withdrawals (W), injections (J) or none of these (N):

		Expenditure/ Factor payment	W or J
e.g.	Construction of new motorway	G	J
(a)	Car hire by foreign visitors	_____	_____
(b)	Undistributed profits	_____	_____
(c)	Residential construction	_____	_____
(d)	Advice from a lawyer	_____	_____
(e)	Change in inventories	_____	_____
(f)	VAT	_____	_____
(g)	Your holiday abroad	_____	_____
(h)	Purchase of primary school computers	_____	_____

We now expand the model we used in Question 14 to include the foreign sector.

Q 40   The behavioural equations were:

(1) $C = 0.8Y_d$

(2) $I = £78$ million

(3) $G = £70$ million

(4) $Q = £40$ million

(5) $T = 0.25Y$

We now add:

(6) $X = £50$ million   where X is exports

(7) $M = mY = 0.1Y$ M is imports

(a)   What is m? _____

(b)   What is the equation for aggregate expenditure? _____

(c)   The equilibrium level of income is _____

(d)   What are net exports? _____

(e)   What is the expenditure multiplier? _____
_____

198

(f)   If exports were to increase by £10 million, by how much would income rise?

    _____

(g)   Assuming exports remained at £50m but the marginal propensity to import were 0.2, what difference would this make to

    (i)   income? _____

    (ii) net exports? _____

Q 41   The introduction into the model of the foreign-trade sector increases/reduces the value of the multiplier as imports are an injection into/leakage from the domestic circular flow of income.

Q 42   An increase in investment will cause national income to rise/fall. In an open economy the consequent change in national income will be greater than/the same as/less than a change in national income in a closed economy following an increase in investment of the same magnitude.

QUESTIONS FOR DISCUSSION

1   What would be the effect on national income of each of the following:

(a)   households save a greater proportion of their income;
(b)   a rise in exports;
(c)   a rise in imports.

Depict each graphically. Can you suggest any measures the government might adopt to offset any adverse effects on national income and employment of these changes?

2   What would be the effect on the value of the multiplier of:

(a)   a rise in the income-tax rate;
(b)   a fall in exports;
(c)   a rise in the marginal propensity to import.

3   'Increases in national income will increase revenue from taxes, both income and sales taxes, and decrease that part of public spending which is not cash limited, principally social security and other transfer payments.'
Are tax revenue and government expenditure endogenous or exogenous?

4   On 11.3.83 the *Guardian* reported Mr Peter Shore, the Shadow Chancellor, as advocating an increase in public expenditure of not less than £10,000 million.
'Mr Shore's proposals rest upon four main planks. The two most important are an increase in public spending of £5,000 million on goods and services . . . and an extra £4,000 million on measures to contain costs – such as action to tackle the National Insurance surcharge, or to cut VAT or to freeze rents.
'He also proposed a further £1,000 million spending in the coming financial year – £2,000 million in a full year – in increases on benefits and pensions. The fourth point in his programme is a self-financing tax package which includes a number of redistributive measures . . .'
Analyse carefully the effect of these proposals on the level of income and on employment. Would the multiplier effect be the same for each of the proposals? Which of the proposals would have the most immediate effect?

5   'If the consumer spending spree is sustained . . . then destocking will have to yield to an increase in actual output. This is bound to give some sort of boost to industrial production in the UK even if . . . a lot of the stocks will be replaced by imports. What matters with stocks is not so much the absolute level as the pace of change. Even if destocking merely slows down in the first half of this year it will have beneficial effects on output.' (Victor Keegan, the *Guardian*, 7.3.83.)
What is 'destocking'? Why might stocks be replaced by imports? Do you agree with Keegan

that it is not the level of stocks that is important but the rate at which they are rising or falling?

6   In the *Sunday Times* (6.2.83) Graham Searjeant wrote:

'. . . Britain is suffering from a chronic shortage of production . . . we have three million producing nothing at all and extra income going into imports.

'Crude reflation, for instance by cutting VAT or raising benefits, would probably make matters worse, if only because we have lost many factories and product lines. We have plenty of spare capacity but it probably does not match what people want to buy with extra income.'

What must be the value of the marginal propensity to import if extra income from reflation is spent on imports? Is this realistic?

CHAPTER 37

National Income, International Trade and the Balance of Payments

At the end of the last chapter we introduced the foreign-trade sector but did not explore in any depth the implications for our economy. Compared with, say, the United States, the UK economy is a relatively open economy, so that out of every pound spent on goods and services in recent years, about 30 pence have been on imports. Clearly, unless other countries are prepared to buy UK-produced goods and services, we will have a deficit on the trade balance. For any student of the UK economy it is very important to understand the causes of trade imbalances, together with the implications for national income and employment.

THE NET EXPORT FUNCTION

Q 1   If $X = £50m$ and $M = 0.1Y$, what is the equation of the net export function (N)?
_____

Q 2   At what level of income will there be trade balance? _____

Q 3   What will be the effect of the following:

(a)   Exports rise by £10m. At what income will there be trade balance? _____
_____

(b)   Exports remain at £60m and the marginal propensity to import rises to 0.2. Find where trade balance will occur. _____

(c)   Exports remain at £60m but the marginal propensity to import falls to 0.09. What will be the effect? _____

NET EXPORTS AND DOMESTIC ABSORPTION

Q 4   Define domestic absorption (A): _____

Q 5   When $C = 0.8Y_d$, $I = £78m$, $G = £70m$, $Q = £40m$, $T = 0.25Y$, $X = £50m$ and $M = 0.1Y$,

(a)   write the equation for aggregate desired expenditure. _____
_____

(b)   write the equation for consumption. _____

(c)   write the equation for domestic absorption. _____

(d)   write the conditions for equilibrium, using the absorption approach. _____
_____

Q 6   Using your answers to Question 5,

(a)   what is the slope of the absorption schedule? _____

(b)   what is its intercept? _____

(c)   what is the slope of the aggregate expenditure function? _____

(d)   what is its intercept? _____

(e)   The slope of the E line is less than/greater than that of the A line because imports fall/rise as income rises and net exports fall/remain the same/rise.

(f)   When national income rises by £10m, absorption rises by: _____
_____

(g)   Equilibrium income is at _____ when absorption is _____

(h)   Suppose that exports fell to £30m, find equilibrium income _____ and absorption _____

(i)   When domestic absorption exceeds national income, total demand for goods and services for domestic use is greater than/less than domestic output of such goods and services, and net exports are positive/negative.

Q 7   If the marginal propensity to import were to fall, this would shift the aggregate expenditure function upwards/downwards, while the absorption function would shift up/remain the same/shift down with the result that the equilibrium level of income would rise/fall.

Q 8   If exports were to fall, this would shift the aggregate expenditure function upwards/ downwards, while the slope of the absorption function would rise/remain the same/ fall and the net export function would shift up/down with the result that income would rise/fall.

Q 9   If the marginal propensity to save were to rise, this would shift the aggregate expenditure function upwards/downwards while the absorption function would shift up/remain the same/shift down with the result that income would rise/fall.

THE EFFECTS OF A CHANGE IN THE EXCHANGE RATE

Q 10   If £1 can be exchanged for $2 and American producers sell motorcycles for $4,000 while British producers sell motorcycles for £2,000, then an American motorcycle valued in sterling will cost _____

Q 11   Fill in the values of the following transactions:

	Transactions valued in £	valued in $
(a) UK exports 200 motorcycles to USA	_____	_____
(b) USA exports 200 motorcycles to UK	_____	_____
(c) UK and US net exports are positive/zero/ negative		

Q 12   Now suppose that the pound is devalued by 50% (it is not likely to happen—at least not at one go—but it will make the arithmetic simple), then £1 will be exchanged for $ _____

Q 13   Fill in the values of transactions if:

	Transactions valued in £	valued in $
(a) UK continues to export 200 motorcycles	_____	_____
(b) USA continues to export 200 motorcycles	_____	_____
(c) What has happened to the UK and US trade balances?	_____	
(d) The sterling price of American motorcycles has risen by _____ per cent.		
(e) The dollar price of British motorcycles has fallen by _____ per cent.		

(f)   Devaluation of the pound has resulted in the price of home-produced goods, in terms of dollars, rising/falling while the price of American goods, valued in sterling, has risen/fallen.

It is not very likely that exports and imports will continue at the same rate as before devaluation of the pound. When the price of a good falls, more will be demanded (other things being equal). You will remember that own price elasticity gives us a measure of the responsiveness of demand to price changes.

Q 14   Own price elasticity is defined as _____
_____

Q 15   We will now take different values for export and import elasticities and examine the effect on net exports:

Transactions valued in £

First, UK export elasticities:

(a)   If the UK export elasticity is $1\frac{1}{2}$: sales of motor-cycles to the USA will rise by _____ to _____ , value _____

(b)   If the UK export elasticity is 1: sales will be _____ , value _____

(c)   If the UK export elasticity is $\frac{2}{5}$: sales will be _____ , value _____

Now, UK import elasticities:

(d)   If the UK import elasticity is $1\frac{1}{2}$: US sales to UK will fall to _____ , value _____

(e)   If the UK import elasticity is 1: sales will be _____ , value _____

(f)   If the UK import elasticity is $\frac{2}{5}$: sales will be _____ , value _____

Q 16   Now have a look at the effect on the UK trade balance:

(a)   When both elasticities are equal to or greater than unity, the trade balance is in deficit/surplus.

(b)   When the *sum* of both elasticities is less than unity, devaluation has resulted in a deficit/surplus.

(c)   When the demand for imports is elastic and foreign demand for exports is not inelastic, the net export function shifts upwards/downwards and the aggregate expenditure function shifts upwards/downwards and income rises/falls.

Q 17   A rise in the income of other EEC countries will cause UK exports to increase/remain the same/decrease, the net export function will shift up/remain the same/shift down, with the result that the level of income consistent with trade balance will rise/remain the same/fall.

Q 18   Assuming that the sum of the import and export elasticities is not less than unity, a rise in domestic prices relative to foreign prices will cause the net export function to shift up/remain the same/shift down, so that trade balance will be found at a higher/same/lower level of income, the value of exports having risen/remained the same/fallen and the value of imports having risen/remained the same/fallen.

Q 19   As the level of national income rises, the net export function will shift up/remain the same/shift down and the trade balance will move from surplus to deficit/remain the same/move from deficit to surplus.

In the *non-tradeable goods model*, goods and services are divided into two categories: tradeable and non-tradeable.

Q 20 Define tradeable goods. _____
_____

Q 21 Oil is traded on world markets in US dollars. If the pound depreciates, this will cause the domestic price of oil to rise/fall, and the price of theatre tickets to rise/remain the same/fall. Resources will shift into/out of the non-traded-goods sector, output of tradeable goods will rise/fall, and domestic demand will shift from/towards non-traded-goods because of the change in the absolute/relative level of prices. As a consequence, exports/imports will increase and exports/imports will fall, shifting the net export function up/down and the aggregate expenditure function up/down, bringing about a rise/fall in national income.

Up to this point we have been assuming that the aggregate supply schedule is perfectly elastic, so that an upward shift of the aggregate expenditure function results in an increase in income at constant prices. In other words, producers can always meet increased demand without raising prices. In Question 13, following devaluation of the pound, we assumed that producers would continue to sell their motorcycles at £2,000: the traded price in foreign currency had changed but domestic prices remained constant.

Suppose now that the economy was at full employment. In this case it will be impossible to produce more, and domestic prices will rise. Say that the price of UK motorcycles rises from £2,000 to £2,500. We will start the analysis before devaluation occurs so that the rate of exchange was £1 for $2, and we assume that American producers continue to sell their motorcycles at $4,000.

Q 22 When UK motorcycles cost £2,000 and US motorcycles $4,000, the price was the same in terms of sterling, but when the price of UK motorcycles rose to £2,500, UK goods cost UK purchasers £ _____ more/less than US goods, and UK goods cost US purchasers $ _____ more/less than US-produced goods.

Q 23 As a result, British imports will rise/fall and British exports will rise/fall and the net export function will shift up/down.

Q 24 Assume, as before, the pound is devalued by 50%. This would mean that UK motorcycles will sell in the US for $ _____ and that US motorcycles would sell here for £ _____ . Under usual assumptions, this would cause imports of US goods to rise/fall and exports to rise/fall, so that the net export function will shift up/down and the aggregate expenditure function will shift up/down. Income will rise/remain the same/fall and prices will rise/remain the same/fall.

Q 25 In order to prevent price increases following devaluation when the economy is at full employment, it would be necessary for the government to offset any upward shift in the aggregate expenditure function. How might it do this ? _____
_____

QUESTIONS FOR DISCUSSION

1 Faced with a large trade deficit in 1982 and having had to devalue the franc three times since it came to power, in March 1983 the French Government introduced severe government-spending cuts and also increases in income tax. In addition, it restricted spending abroad by tourists to 2,000 francs per adult a year (approx. £190) and 1,000 francs per child.

(a) Trace out the effect of these measures on the French economy.
(b) Would any of these measures affect the British economy?

2 Analyse the effect of a rise in oil prices followed some years later by a fall in oil prices on the economies of

(a) oil-*producing* countries;

(b) oil-*importing* countries.

3   In the *Financial Times* (14.3.83) Ian Rodger presented the following gloomy picture:

'Three years of recession and the overvalued pound have taken a terrible toll in manufacturing output and employment. Production is down by 17 per cent since 1979 and the number of people employed has fallen by over 1.5m.

'Until about a year ago, it was widely believed that the shake-out was about fat rather than muscle—getting rid of overmanning, restrictive working practices and other inefficiencies. Many executives thought their companies were getting fitter as well as leaner.

'Since then, the relentless rise in import penetration in some major sectors has become widely recognized as a big obstacle to any widespread return to health.

'Since 1980, the volume of imports of manufactured goods has increased by 10 per cent while the volume of exports has dropped by 4 per cent. Last year, for the first time in over a century, Britain suffered a deficit in manufactured goods of £643m on an overseas trade basis.

'Almost every sector of manufacturing industry has been affected, with production volumes much lower than might have been expected. In turn, this has undermined efficiency and profitability.'

(a) Explain why 'recession and the overvalued pound' could have led to this situation.

(b) Use your micro theory to analyse why low production volumes undermine efficiency and profitability.

4   What is the difference between the absorption and component approaches to trade balance?

5   Suppose the government introduces import controls so that the marginal propensity to import is reduced. What will happen to national income, assuming

(a) other countries do *not* retaliate by cutting their imports from this country;

(b) other countries *do* retaliate?

6   This is an extract from the *Glasgow Herald* (22.2.71): 'Cocoa prices moved to new life-of-contract lows last week and the outlook is far from promising.

'Further evidence has emerged to show total world production this season has been badly under-estimated and the producer countries in West Africa have a lot of main-crop cocoa still to sell.

'The latest low Ghana purchase figure of less than 2,000 tons may be true of the particular week involved, but it is becoming obvious that there is a great deal more cocoa to come yet.

'Furthermore, the Nigerian crop has exceeded all expectations.

'At the same time consumer demand is at a very low ebb.'

We dealt with the problems of agriculture in a micro chapter—why have we then included this in a macro chapter? What might happen initially to the national incomes of the West African countries for whom cocoa is a major export (assuming that the market elasticity of demand for cocoa is less than unity over the relevant range)? (a) This year, (b) next year (c) the year after that? Make your multiplier and 'cobweb' assumptions explicit.

What action would you recommend to the governments of these countries, if they wished to stabilize their national incomes?

7   'Venezuela will ban luxury imports such as whisky, caviare and electrical goods for two months in an attempt to save foreign exchange, the Planning Minister said yesterday.

'On a yearly basis it would save about £30 million worth of whisky alone, this being Britain's main export to Venezuela and the Venezuelans being the world's largest *per capita* consumers of the product.

'Last year Britain exported £39 million worth of whisky to Venezuela in 18.5 million bottles—slightly more than one bottle for every man, woman and child.' (*Guardian*, 4.3.83.)

Examine the effects of this ban on the Venezuelan and the UK economies.

CHAPTER 38

The Money Supply

The main points brought out in Chapter 38 are:

(1)   The distinction between real and money income. Inflation means a general increase in the level of prices. While the cost of living of the average household has increased, its standard of living has also increased. Incomes and output have risen faster than prices so that the average household is better off in real terms.

(2)   The main effect of inflation is to redistribute income but there are also real effects, i.e. effects on the allocation of resources.

(3)   Anything can be money, so long as it fulfils the three functions of

    (a)   medium of exchange
    (b)   store of value
    (c)   unit of account

(4)   Money need not therefore be issued by anyone; it can be dug up (gold), or grown (tobacco) by private individuals. (In modern economies, however, the money supply is controlled by the central authorities as a matter of policy.)

(5)   The more confidence that members of a community have in the people or institutions issuing money, the less likely it is that the money will have any market value on its own, as does, for example, gold.

(6)   Any member of a community whom people trust to repay debts in the official currency can, if he is not legally prevented, issue claims upon himself which will then circulate as money.

THE NATURE AND HISTORY OF MONEY

Q 1   'A licence to print money.' We have seen that this was possessed by the old goldsmiths. Why was it, then, necessary for goldsmiths to keep any stock of gold at all?

_____
_____

Q 2   Given that the public's desired ratio of gold to paper money remained constant at 1:3, what was there to prevent goldsmiths, in whom confidence reposed, from paying all their bills with paper claims on themselves which then merely added to the circulating money supply, and therefore living free? _____
_____
_____

Q 3   'The natives of these parts use but the Cowrie shell for money, deluded into believing it valuable' (a missionary). Does the missionary understand the nature of money? Yes/No. Explain. _____
_____
_____

Q 4   'The greater the propensity to pay bills by cash instead of cheque, the lower the level of cash reserves which a bank need keep.' T/F

Q 5   The government creates as much money as it wants. What is this sort of currency called? _____

_____

THE UK BANKING SYSTEM

Q 6   What are the three *main* elements of the present-day banking system in this country?

_____

_____

Q 7   What are the main functions of the central bank? _____

_____

_____

_____

Q 8   If a commercial bank (or discount house) was faced with a run on its cash reserves, and it could not call in enough loans quickly, what would it do? _____

_____

_____

THE CREATION AND DESTRUCTION OF DEPOSIT MONEY

You should read this section carefully; it is very easy for even experienced economists to make mistakes about the creation of money.

(a) *A system containing a single bank*

Q 9   Assume a legal reserve ratio (which is above the 'prudent' ratio) of 10%. If a cash deposit of £50 is made, how much extra can the bank lend? _____

Q 10   Express the final result in balance sheet form.

(1)	Assets	Liabilities
Initially	_____	
Subsequently	_____	

We have the assumption that there is

(a)   no drain to any other bank, since there isn't any, and
(b)   no drain of cash to the public.

If we add the assumption

(c)   the bank is a profit-maximizer, and
(d)   the marginal revenue from lending (taking into account risk of default) is always above the marginal cost (i.e. the rate of interest charged to borrowers is higher than the rate paid to depositors),

then it follows that a single bank will always adopt what policy in regard to its loans?

(2)   _____

_____

(b) *Many banks, a single new deposit*

Assumption (a) above is now removed. It is a very common mistake to assume that all deposit creation takes place instantaneously, any bank receiving an extra deposit immediately expanding by the reciprocal of the reserve ratio. But think what would happen; assume that individual k deposits £100 in bank A, which lends £900 to individual 1. He pays his creditors m and n, by cheques drawn on bank A; but they bank with B and C; so £900 in cash has to be paid by bank A to banks B and C. Bank A now has to contract its loans by an extra £7,200. Meanwhile, B and C then lend an extra £8,100 to individual o, but his creditors bank with D _____ and so on. The correct aggregate expansion is made, but goodness knows how many banks go into liquidation in the process!

Q 11   Assume that individual a places a deposit of £100 into bank A. Assume also that A lends what extra it can to individual b, who banks with B, which lends to individual c, and so on. (The reserve ratio is again 10%.) Fill in the changes in the banks' balance sheets above the line before they have expanded their loans, after, below it.

```
      A          B          C          D          E
   A   L      A   L      A   L      A   L      A   L
 ─────────  ─────────  ─────────  ─────────  ─────────

     100
 ─────────  ─────────  ─────────  ─────────  ──────────────────────────────

cash:
loans:  ─────      ─────      ─────      ─────      ─────
```

The series 100 + 90 + 81 + 72.9 . . . sums to £1,000, as the series 10 + 9 + 8.1 . . . sums to £100. This is, of course, no piece of mathematical luck—it is a straightforward implication of every bank's strict adherence to the 10% cash ratio.

If you got the answer wrong, try again, working it through on your own.

(c) Many banks, many deposits

This is easy, once you have mastered (b) above.

Q 12   (a)   Assume a system with 10 banks in which a deposit of £300 cash accrues to bank I. There is a 10% cash ratio.

(1)   Show the initial changes in the balance sheet of this bank.

```
        L   │   A
       ─────┼─────
            │
```

(2)   Assume that bank I expands deposits up to the maximum possible; that 90% of all new deposits to any bank find their way into other banks (as cheques are passed between individuals for various transactions) and that other banks do *not* expand deposits when they obtain extra cash. Show the final changes in the balance sheet of bank I.

Bank I

```
        L   │   A
       ─────┼─────
            │
```

(3)   *Conclusion*: One bank in a multi-bank system cannot engage in a large deposit expansion even when it gets new cash if the other banks do not do the same. T/F

(b)   Assume that all banks expand deposits as soon as they obtain new cash.

(1)   Show the final changes in the balance sheets of the system.

	Bank I				Banks II to X	
L		A		L		A

(2) *Conclusion*: If all banks expand deposits together, the final result is the same as the monopoly-bank case. T/F

Q 13 Suppose that the required reserve ratio is 15% and that a bank has cash reserves of £15m, loans and bonds of £85m, and demand deposits of £100m:

(a) By what additional amount can this bank expand its loans? _____

(b) If the reserve ratio is changed to 10%, the bank must reduce its lending by/can make additional loans up to _____

Q 14 Suppose that you cash £300 from your grant cheque at your bank and keep all the money under your mattress (this is *not* a good idea!). If the required reserve ratio is 15%, what will be the effect on deposit money? _____

Q 15 What have we assumed so far about the public's desired cash to deposit ratio?

_____

_____

Q 16 If the public's desired cash ratio is zero, and the banks' reserve ratio is 15%:

(a) A new deposit of £300 would increase deposit money by _____

(b) If the public's desired cash ratio is 10% instead of zero, the increase in deposit money would be _____

(c) If the public's desired cash ratio is 15%, the increase would be _____

Q 17 The higher the proportion of its money holdings the public wishes to take in cash, the larger/smaller the expansion of deposit money supported by new deposits.

DEFINITIONS OF MONEY

Q 18 What are P.O. savings accounts, building society deposits, American Express cards and gold wedding rings examples of? _____

Q 19 What is the difference between *near money* and *money substitutes*?

_____

_____

_____

_____

_____

Q 20 In the table overleaf are listed various items which may or may not be classified as money, according to which money function they fulfil. Put a tick (or a cross) in the appropriate column if you think that the item listed does (or does not) fulfil that function.

Q 21 Using the information in the previous question, what is the total value of the money supply under:

(a) the sterling M1 definition? _____

(b) the sterling M3 definition? _____

	Store of value	Medium of exchange	Value in £ million
Building society deposits	_____	_____	1,500
Company securities:			
– ordinary shares	_____	_____	867
– debenture and preference shares	_____	_____	105
Local authority bonds held by			
the private sector	_____	_____	340
Notes and coins	_____	_____	4,661
New domestic share issues	_____	_____	35
Deposits in current accounts at			
commercial banks	_____	_____	8,779
UK government bonds	_____	_____	477
Money held in deposit accounts			
at commercial banks	_____	_____	18,879

QUESTIONS FOR DISCUSSION

1   During the Second World War, cigarettes were used as currency in prisoner-of-war camps. How well do you think cigarettes fulfilled the functions of money, and how easy would it be to debase the currency?

2   Mr Kovari, in a letter to *The Times* (20.7.78) wrote: 'Mr William Rees-Mogg advocates a return to the gold standard. What conceivable objection is there to a realistic monetary standard based upon useful commodities?'

What do you think about Mr Kovari's idea? What useful commodities do you think he had in mind?

3   What do we mean when we say that banks can create money? Some people advocate that banks should be required to keep 100% cash reserves behind all their deposits. What would be the effects of such a policy?

4   Banking can be treated as business; shareholders in banks expect to receive dividends. A prominent British banker was quoted in the *Sunday Times* (28.2.71) as saying, 'There are times when we could pay more and charge more; the supply of advances would be rationed by price and those who can pay more are alleged to be the most efficient . . . much bank money is still lent at rates of interest below those generally attainable in the markets, since we have been reluctant to exploit usuriously a scarcity of essential money.'

What might you, as a shareholder in the bank of this particular banker, say at a shareholders' meeting? What sort of reply might you expect? The *Sunday Times* financial journalist, Nicholas Firth, commented (the article concerned the relationship between the Conservative Government of Mr Heath, and industry in general):

'Faced with an attitude like this, in which money-lending to maximize profit is equated with usury and the doubting word "allegedly" is put ahead of the key notion that those able to pay the highest price for their capital are the most efficient, the Government should pause and wonder whether the country is worthy of it. We just cannot live up to the rarified notions of capitalism prevalent in the inner circles of government; and it is useless trying to make us revert to our nineteenth-century archetypes. We're too decadent—or should one say civilized—for such barbarities.'

5   What is the difference between the real and the nominal money supply?

CHAPTER 39

Monetary Equilibrium

Q 1   Throughout this chapter we shall assume the money supply to be exogenously determined. What does this assumption mean? _____
_____
_____

THE DEMAND FOR MONEY

Q 2   Why do we say that keeping money under the mattress—or in a current account at the bank—has a cost? _____
_____
_____

Q 3   What are the three main reasons for holding money? _____
_____

Q 4   What determines the transactions demand for money? _____

Q 5   As income rises, the demand for _____
balances will rise/fall and, as the interest rate falls, the demand for _____
_____ balances will rise/fall.

Q 6   Define speculative balances. _____
_____

Q 7   When the price of interest-earning assets rises, the interest rate will rise/fall.

Q 8   If people consider current bond prices are low and they expect them to rise, then they will tend to buy/sell bonds. Explain why. _____
_____
_____

Q 9   The demand for money will vary directly/inversely with the level of income, directly/inversely with the level of wealth, and directly/inversely with the rate of interest.

Q 10   Into which of the three categories of demand for money do the following fall (if any)?

   (a)   Money I keep in my current account to pay my rent. _____

   (b)   Money to pay a bill for a new car engine in case my claim on the guarantee does not come through quickly enough. _____

   (c)   The money which is deducted from wages in PAYE. _____

   (d)   The large cash balance held by a bookmaker. _____

   The level of cash balances depends on income. The rich speculate more, spend more on their weekly grocery bill and have a larger number of uncertainly timed payments than do the poor.

Q 11   What effect, on which of the categories, would the following have?

(a) Belief that the rate of inflation will increase. Raise/lower _____ balances.

(b) All unemployment and social security payments to be paid on a monthly, instead of a weekly, basis. Raise/lower _____ balances.

(c) Expectations that interest rates are about to rise. Raise/lower _____ _____ balances.

(d) A salary rise. Raise/lower _____

(e) Go-slow by civil servants in settling firms' VAT returns. Raise/lower _____ _____

(f) Credit cards which grant you up to two months' credit. Raise/lower _____ _____

(g) Authors' pessimism about the punctuality of royalty receipts. Raise/lower _____

Q 12 When we talk about the liquidity-preference function of a firm we refer to the amount of cash held by the firm on its business premises instead of in the bank. T/F

Q 13 What determines the real demand for money? (Write in symbols) _____

Q 14 What is the difference between the real demand for money and the nominal demand for money? _____
_____
_____

Q 15 If the price level rises by 10%, the nominal demand for money rises by _____%/is unchanged/falls by _____%, while real demand rises by _____%/is unchanged/falls by _____%.

Q 16 In the short term, wealth is considered to be constant and the demand for money, therefore, depends on the level of income and the rate of interest.

(a) When income is rising, but the rate of interest is unchanged, the demand for money is rising/unchanged/falling.

(b) When income is rising and the rate of interest is falling, the demand for money is rising/unchanged/falling.

Q 17 If the demand for money function is $M_d = 0.3Y - 20r$ (r expressed as %), find the amount of money demanded when:

(a) Income = £500m, $r = 5\%$ _____

(b) Income = £500m, $r = 4\%$ _____

(c) Income = £600m, $r = 5\%$ _____

(d) Income = £600m, $r = 6\%$ _____

Q 18 Suppose that all workers are paid on a monthly, rather than weekly, basis. Income and the interest rate are unchanged.

(a) The demand for money rises/is unchanged/falls because the transactions/precautionary/speculative demand for money balances has risen/remained unchanged/fallen.

(b) If the demand-for-money function when workers were paid on a weekly basis was $M_d = 0.3Y - 20r$, which of the following functions is consistent with workers being paid on a monthly basis:

(i) $M_d = 0.3Y - 15r$;
(ii) $M_d = 0.4Y - 22r$;
(iii) $M_d = 0.4Y - 20r$;
(iv) $M_d = 0.2Y - 20r$.

212

Q 19 Fig. 1 shows the effects of the rate of interest on money balances. This refers to the marginal decision: 'is the extra liquidity gained from the addition of £x to my money balances worth the sacrifice of £rx per year?' It is assumed that the value to the individual of extra liquidity decreases with the amount held. This implies that the higher the rate of interest, the less cash will be held—*ceteris paribus*. (Note that the average level of money balances is a stock, not a flow—so we do not have to label the axis '. . . per period of time'.)

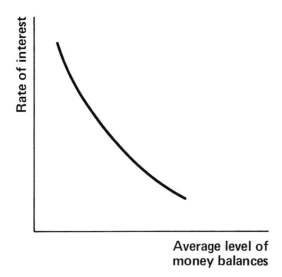

Fig. 1

(a) How would you represent on Fig. 1 an increase in the speculative demand for money? _____

(b) How would you represent a shortening of the payments period?

_____

(c) How would you represent the immediate effect of a rise in interest rates?

_____

Q 20 Equilibrium in the money market requires that the demand for money equal the supply of money. In our two-asset model, when this condition holds, it follows that

_____

Q 21 If the demand-for-money function is $M_d = 0.4Y - 20r$, and the money supply is £80m, find whether $M_d = \dfrac{M^*}{P}$

(a) when Y = £600m and r = 10%. _____

(b) when Y = £600m and r = 8%. _____

(c) when Y = £600m and r = 5%. _____

Q 22 If the demand for money exceeds the supply of money, firms and households will seek to buy/sell bonds. As a result, bond prices will rise/fall and the interest rates will rise/fall until _____

_____

Q 23 Following an increase in the money supply,

(a) the demand for transaction balances rises/falls/remains the same,
(b) which means there is more/less/the same money available for speculative purposes.
(c) The price of bonds will rise/fall as people attempt to sell/buy bonds and this causes a rise/fall in the interest rate.

213

Q 24 When the level of income rises but the interest rate and the money supply are unchanged,

    (a) the demand for money will rise/fall.

    (b) this means that the demand for money is now greater than/less than the supply of money (assuming that previously they were equal).

    (c) for a return to equilibrium, the interest rate must rise/fall.

    (d) Alternatively, if the interest rate is to be maintained at its original level, equilibrium could be achieved by raising/lowering the money supply.

Q 25 Let $M_d = 0.4Y - 20r$ and $\dfrac{M^*}{P} = £80m$. With current $Y = £600m$ and $r = 8\%$, $M_d = \dfrac{M^*}{P}$.

    (a) The level of income now rises to £625m, while r and $\dfrac{M^*}{P}$ are unchanged. Find M_d. _____

    (b) If the money supply is unchanged and $Y = £625m$, what is the interest rate at which $M_d = \dfrac{M^*}{P}$? _____

    (c) In order to maintain an interest rate of 8%, by how much would the supply of money have had to be increased? _____

THE LM CURVE

We have seen that different levels of income require different rates of interest in order to equate the demand for money with a constant money supply. More generally, we can now see that the rate of interest at which the demand for and supply of money are equal will depend on the level of income, the money supply and the size of the behavioural parameters of the demand-for-money function.

Q 26 The LM curve is the locus of all _____ combinations that yield equilibrium between the demand for and the supply of money.

Q 27 If the demand for money is $M_d = dY + er$, and the money supply is $M_s = M^*/P$, how is the LM curve derived? _____

Q 28 Suppose that the demand for money is given as $M_d = 0.4Y - 20r$ and $M_s = £80m$. Derive the equation for the LM curve. _____

_____

Q 29 What is the slope of this curve? _____ And the intercept? _____

Q 30 What would be the effect on the LM curve of the following:

    (a) A fall in the money supply. _____

    (b) A rise in the level of income. _____

_____

    (c) The demand-for-money function changes as a result of an increase in the speculative demand for money balances (e.g. $M_d = 0.4Y - 10r$ instead of $M_d = 0.4Y - 20r$). _____

_____

    (d) A fall in the demand for transaction balances (e.g. $M_d = 0.35Y - 20r$).

_____

When the position of the LM curve changes, monetary equilibrium can only be restored if the level of income and/or the rate of interest change. If the interest rate is held constant, the level of income must change. If the level of income is held constant, the rate of interest must change.

Q 31 When $M_d = 0.4Y - 20r$, $\dfrac{M^*}{P} = £80m$ and $Y = £700m$, what is the rate of interest at which there is monetary equilibrium? _____

214

Q 32 Now let the money supply fall to £79m. Keeping $Y = £700m$, the interest rate must rise/fall to _____ . (Before you work out the answer, see if you can predict the direction of change correctly.) Holding the interest rate at its previous level, income must rise/fall to £ _____ for equilibrium. Draw a diagram to illustrate your answer.

Q 33 Keeping $\dfrac{M^*}{P} = £80m$, let $M_d = 0.4Y - 10r$. Holding $Y = £700m$, the rate of interest must rise/fall to _____ . Holding r at its original level, income must rise/fall to _____ for equilibrium. Draw a diagram to illustrate your answer.

Q 34 With $\dfrac{M^*}{P} = £80m$, let $M_d = 0.35Y - 20r$. Holding $Y = £700m$, the interest rate must rise/fall to _____ ; holding r at its original level, income must rise/fall to _____ for equilibrium. Draw a diagram to illustrate your answer.

Q 35 If $M_d = 0.4Y - 20r$ and $\dfrac{M^*}{P} = £100m$.

(a) When $Y = £700m$ and $r = 8\%$, the demand for money is greater than/less than

215

the supply of money and, therefore, the rate of interest will rise/fall when income is held constant.

(b) When $Y = £500m$ and $r = 6\%$, the demand for money is greater than/less than the supply of money, and the rate of interest will rise/fall when income is held constant.

QUESTIONS FOR DISCUSSION

1   If you keep all your money in your current account at your bank you do not earn any interest on it. What could you do with your money in order to earn interest? What transactions costs are involved?

2   'A rise in bank base rates is always welcome news for investors. Seven-day deposit accounts are now offering 8 per cent compared with under 7 per cent a week ago.

'But this is still small beer compared with the more generous terms offered by the money funds . . . Save & Prosper is offering a high-interest deposit account (currently paying 11.25 per cent) with the flexibility of a cheque book facility for withdrawals of £250 or more. Customers earn money market rates on relatively small sums with no penalties on withdrawal and no requirement to give notice.' (Report in *The Times*, 15.1.83.)

(a) Are the 'investors' referred to in this report investors in the sense discussed by Lipsey?
(b) In what ways does the Save & Prosper high-interest deposit account discussed here differ from other savings and deposit accounts?

Do you think many people will transfer funds from existing accounts to this new account?

3   Outline the main forms wealth can take, and discuss the pros and cons of holding wealth in more than one type of asset.

4   On 19.3.79 Christine Moir reported in the *Financial Times* that British Rail's pension funds were to stop buying works of art:

'The Funds' purchases to date amount to £28m and include 12th-century candlesticks, Picasso's *Young Man in Blue* and Chinese and Egyptian antiquities.

'Since 1974 British Rail has been spending in the fine art auction rooms around 4 per cent of the new money flowing into its pension funds each year . . . BR defended (these purchases) on the grounds that it needed to diversify its investments as widely as possible and to seek the maximum shelter from future inflation.

'(The general manager) said: "the trustees have now decided that fine art should not represent a major diversification in a portfolio of this size". British Rail's pension funds already total £750m and are growing at around 10 per cent a year.

'At present the funds' budget is to keep about 10 per cent of their money in cash and fixed securities, 40 per cent in UK equities, 10 per cent in overseas securities and 25 per cent in property. A further 8 per cent has been in commodities and fine art, leaving 7 per cent flexible.'

(a) What factors do you think will be important in determining the type of asset the fund acquires? (Remember this is a *pension* fund.)
(b) What are the advantages and disadvantages of works of art when compared with other types of asset held by the fund?
(c) What factors might determine the proportion of the fund's budget allocated to different types of asset?

5   This is an extract from a letter to the *Financial Times* (30.11.74):

'Now that the government is actually minting gold sovereigns, would it not be possible for these to be designated as alternative legal tender to the pound sterling, albeit at their free exchange rate?

'Investment should quickly be revitalized by such a measure, because a would-be house purchaser, who today pays £105 per month for a £10,000 mortgage at 11%, could probably borrow at 4% from a holder of gold sovereigns who now receives no interest at all. The repayments on a £10,000 mortgage at 4% would be less than £50 per month (in sovereigns) which example illustrates the beneficial effect of honest money, with its endemic low interest rates, on the vital process of investment for the future.'

What do you think of this suggestion?

6   'The demand for money is positively related to national income valued in current prices.' How is the demand for money related to national income when there is inflation?

7   What do we mean by money market equilibrium? Which markets are in equilibrium along the *LM* curve?

8   What would happen to the *LM* curve if:

(a)   the money supply increases?
(b)   the price level rises?
(c)   the demand for transaction balances increases?

9   What would the *LM* curve look like if:

(a)   money and bonds were perfect substitutes?
(b)   money and bonds were non-substitutes?

10   Hamish McRae wrote an article for the *Guardian* (8.3.79) entitled 'Why some money is more "moneyish"'. Here are some extracts:

'Money, money, money. One of the most puzzling aspects of the present debate on the money supply, with all its references to M1, M3 and M5, is to try and see in what way the various definitions of money supply differ from each other and why the definitions should matter anyway.

'The key to understanding about money, in its various guises, is to grasp the fact that some money is more "moneyish" than others. To explain: money in our pockets, the notes and coins, is clearly money. It can be spent straight away without the bother of having to go round to the Post Office or bank to draw it out. Money in current account at the bank is also money, but you could argue that it is not quite as "moneyish" as notes and coin. Try and give a taxi-driver a cheque and you will see what I mean.'

What McRae is talking about is the ease and cheapness with which one asset can be exchanged for another. The usual term for this is 'liquidity'. Obviously money in the form of notes and coins is the most liquid of all assets. McRae goes on to list other assets with varying degrees of liquidity.

(a)   Here is a list for you to put in order of *decreasing* liquidity: shares in ICI; deposits with building societies; short-term government securities; time deposits with commercial banks; national savings certificates; long-term government securities; sight deposits with commercial banks; Picasso paintings, local authority bonds.
(b)   What are the costs of exchanging the following for pound notes: ICI shares; building society deposits, time deposits with commercial banks and Picasso paintings?
(c)   Which of the assets listed in (a) are included in the M1 and M3 definitions of money supply?
(d)   Some people argue for a broader definition of money supply to include deposits with building societies. What do you think are the arguments for and against a broader definition?

The IS-LM Model: the Determination of National Income and the Interest Rate with a Fixed Price Level

THE DETERMINANTS OF INVESTMENT

Up until now we have not considered what determines investment but have treated investment as an exogenous variable. We now have to examine the effect of the rate of interest on desired investment.

Any businessman making an investment decision has to weigh up many different factors. Clearly no one will undertake an investment unless the returns cover the cost. If these returns are yielded over a period of time, it is necessary to discount them to find the Present Value. The Net Present Value of any project is the difference between the capital cost of a project and the present value of the future cash flows to which the project will give rise. (If you cannot remember how to calculate the Present Value, you should have another look at Chapter 28 in the Workbook.)

Suppose that an investment project has a Net Present Value of zero when discounted at 13%. This means that 13% is the rate of discount which makes the expected stream of future net income equal to the cost of the investment. We say that the *rate of return* on this investment is 13% and this rate of yield is what Keynes called the *marginal efficiency of capital*. No project will be undertaken unless the rate of return is positive, but a positive rate of return is only a necessary, and not a sufficient, condition for investment. The firm must be sure that this rate is at least as high as the rate it could earn on any other asset. For example, a firm considering financing investment out of its business savings could use these savings to purchase government bonds, which yield a return, or it could deposit these savings in a bank account. Any investment project it undertakes must yield at least as much as these alternatives.

Q 1   If the rate of interest falls, the value of an asset producing a given stream of income will also fall. T/F

Q 2   The higher the rate of interest, the greater/smaller will be the amount of investment worth undertaking, other things being equal.

Q 3   When interest rates rise, the amount firms could earn on money not invested falls. T/F

It is not possible to forecast precisely the expected income streams of an investment project: there are many unknown factors such as the state of the economy, technological developments, etc. The longer the time horizon, the less accurate forecasts are likely to be.

Q 4   Suppose you are a producer of hosiery and are considering whether to introduce a new line of patterned tights. To do this you would need to purchase new and specialized machines. Would the following events be likely to *increase* or *decrease* the probability of your making this investment? When answering, make clear whether it is revenue or costs that are likely to be affected.

    (a)   Fashion magazines forecast a return of the mini-skirt.

    (b)   The Union of European Hosiery Workers has put in a claim for a 30% wage increase and threatens to strike if this is not granted.

    (c)   The Government announces that one of its major objectives will be to avoid any increase in the unemployment rate.

(d) There is a large explosion at the biggest nylon yarn producing plant in the UK.
(e) VAT on all clothing is cut by 2%.
(f) The rate of interest rises by 1%.
(g) You hear rumours that your main competitor has discovered a new technique which enables him to produce more hardwearing hosiery for the same price as his current products.

Q 5   The marginal efficiency of capital schedule falls as the stock of capital rises because the rate of interest falls. T/F

Q 6   The equilibrium amount of capital stock increases as the interest rate falls. T/F

Q 7   Referring to Fig. 1 below, complete the following:

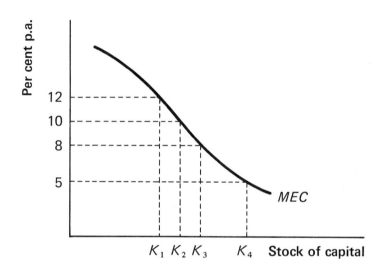

Fig. 1

(a) When capital stock equals K_1, the yield is _____

(b) If the rate of interest is 10%, the equilibrium amount of capital is _____

(c) A 2% fall in the rate of interest would require _____ of new investment to restore equilibrium.

(d) If the stock of capital is K_4, the yield is greater than/less than the new rate of interest (i.e. the rate in part (c)).

(e) If the rate of interest were to rise again to 12%, how can the equilibrium stock of capital be achieved? _____
_____

Q 8   Why may a fall in the rate of interest result in a *temporary*, and not permanent, increase in investment in plant and machinery? _____
_____
_____
_____

THE FINANCING OF INVESTMENT

Q 9   List the main sources of funds for investment. _____
_____

Q 10   What transactions take place when companies borrow directly from the public?

_____

Q 11   What two transactions take place when companies borrow *indirectly* from the public?

_____

_____

THE *IS* CURVE

Q 12   If aggregate expenditure is determined by consumption and investment, where
$$C = \quad 4 + 0.8Y$$
$$I = 180 - 10r$$
(*r* is rate of interest expressed as a percentage, i.e. 6% interest rate implies $r = 6$; all *C* and *I* are in £million.)

(a)   What is the equation of the aggregate expenditure function? _____

(b)   What is the equilibrium level of income when the rate of interest is 10%? _____

Q 13   The *IS* schedule represents all combinations of _____
at which desired aggregate expenditure is equal to national income.

Q 14   Your answer to Question 12 (b) gave you one *point* on the *IS* schedule.

(a)   How do we find the equation of the *IS* schedule? _____

_____

(b)   What is the equation of the *IS* schedule when the consumption and investment functions are as given in Question 12? _____

(c)   What is the slope of the *IS* schedule? _____

(d)   What determines the slope of the *IS* schedule? _____

_____

_____

_____

_____

Q 15   In Question 12 you found that when the rate of interest was 10%, the equilibrium level of income was £420m.

(a)   Now suppose that national income rises to £445m. What will consumption, investment and aggregate expenditure be, if the interest rate remains at 10%?

_____

(b)   Thus, with the rate of interest constant, the rise in aggregate expenditure is greater than/equal to/less than the rise in income.

(c)   For equilibrium at the higher level of income, the rate of interest must rise/fall, bringing about an increase/decrease in investment.

(d)   Find the rate of interest required to equate desired aggregate expenditure with national income at £445m. _____

(e)   What is investment now? _____

Q 16   Why is the slope of the *IS* schedule negative? _____

_____

_____

_____

_____

_____

Q 17   Suppose that the level of income is £430m, and the rate of interest is 9%.

(a)   Aggregate expenditure is greater/less than national income by an amount of_____

220

(b) For equilibrium at this level of income, the rate of interest must rise/fall to _____

(c) If the rate of interest were to remain at 9%, find the equilibrium level of income. _____

(d) Draw a diagram to illustrate your answer.

Q 18 Given the following consumption and investment functions:
$$C = a_0 + cY$$
$$I = a_1 + br$$

(a) What restrictions do you have to put on the behavioural parameters and the autonomous elements of expenditure to ensure a positive value of equilibrium income? _____

_____

(b) Derive the equation for the IS schedule. _____

What happens to the aggregate expenditure function and the IS schedule if:

(c) exogenous expenditure, A^*, falls? _____

_____

(d) the marginal propensity to save falls? _____

_____

(e) the value of b increases? _____

THE IS–LM MODEL

Q 19 The IS curve shows all combinations of interest rates and income levels resulting in equilibrium in the _____ market, while the LM curve shows similar combinations satisfying the equilibrium condition for the _____ market.

Q 20 For equilibrium in:

(a) the goods market we require: _____

_____

(b) the asset market we require: _____

_____

(c) both markets we require: _____

_____

_____

Q 21   If $C = a_0 + cY$ $0 < c < 1, \quad 0 < a_0$
           $I = a_1 + br$ $b < 0 < a_1$
           $M_d = dY + er$ $0 < d < 1, \quad e < 0$
           $\dfrac{M^*}{P}$ is money supply

(a)   What is the equation of the *IS* curve? _____

(b)   What is the equation of the *LM* curve? _____

(c)   Now set the *IS* equation equal to the *LM* equation and solve for *Y*.

       _____

       _____

(d)   What is the *interest-constant* multiplier? _____

(e)   What is the *interest-variable* multiplier? _____

Q 22   Suppose there is an increase in autonomous investment, i.e. a_1 increases.

(a)   At the original equilibrium values of income and rate of interest, desired aggregate expenditure is greater than/less than income.

(b)   The injection raises/lowers income through the multiplier, shifting the *IS* schedule outwards/inwards.

(c)   As income changes, the demand for transactions balances rises/falls.

(d)   With the money supply unchanged, the demand for money will exceed/be less than the supply.

(e)   As a consequence, the price of bonds will rise/fall and the interest rate will rise/fall.

(f)   The change in the interest rate will curb/encourage investment spending.

(g)   A new equilibrium level of income will be established that is higher than/lower than before but less high/low than the income level that would have occurred if expenditure had been insensitive to the interest rate.

Q 23   Here is another sequence for you to work through:

(a)   A fall in the money supply will shift the *LM* schedule upwards/downwards.

(b)   This will leave the asset market in disequilibrium at the initial levels of *Y* and *r* as, with these unchanged, the demand for money will be greater than/less than the new supply.

(c)   The public will seek to buy/sell bonds, thus raising/lowering the interest rate.

(d)   The change in the interest rate will result in higher/lower investment and the *IS* curve will shift out/remain the same/shift in, while income will rise/fall.

(e)   The rise/fall in the interest rate will not be as great as it would be if income were unchanged, as the rise/fall in income increases/decreases demand for transaction/speculative balances.

(f)   The new equilibrium will be at a higher/lower rate of interest and a higher/lower level of income than existed before the change in the money supply.

Q 24   Suppose the economy is in disequilibrium and at a point such as *A* in Fig. 2.

(a)   At point *A*, the demand for money is greater than/less than the supply, and aggregate desired expenditure is greater/less than income.

(b)   If income is unchanged, what will happen to *r*? _____

(c)   Why is it unlikely that income will not change? _____

       _____

       _____

(d)   For a new equilibrium to be established, income must rise/fall and the rate of interest must rise/fall.

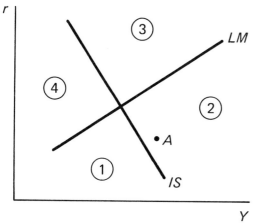

Fig. 2

Q 25   Referring to the numbering of segments in Fig. 2, complete the following:

	Segment number	Y rises/ falls	r rises/ falls
(a) When $M_d > M_s$ and $E > Y$, we are in	_____	_____	_____
(b) When $M_d < M_s$ and $E > Y$, we are in	_____	_____	_____
(c) When $M_d > M_s$ and $E < Y$, we are in	_____	_____	_____
(d) When $M_d < M_s$ and $E < Y$, we are in	_____	_____	_____

Q 26   You are given the following information about an economy:
autonomous consumption is £10m and autonomous investment £125m; the marginal propensity to consume is 0.8; $b = -10$, $d = 0.3$ and $3 = -15$. $M*/P = £90m$.

(a)   Find the equation of the IS curve. _____

(b)   What is the equation of the LM curve? _____

(c)   What is autonomous expenditure, $A*$? _____

(d)   What is the equilibrium level of income and rate of interest? _____
_____

Q 27   Using the information from the previous question:

(a)   Find the interest-constant multiplier. _____

(b)   What is the value of the interest-variable multiplier? _____

(c)   If there is an increase of £10m in the autonomous component of investment, what will be the new equilibrium levels of income and interest rate? _____ _____ What are consumption and investment? _____
_____

(d)   Suppose that the interest rate had been fixed at 3.75 instead of rising. Find consumption, investment and aggregate expenditure. _____
_____

Did you use the multipliers to find the answers to (c) and (d)? Draw (overleaf) an IS–LM diagram to illustrate your answers, showing the crowding-out. Be sure to label the axes.

Q 28   Using the information from Question 26:

(a)   If the money supply were to rise to £112.5m, find the new equilibrium.
_____

(b)   Draw (overleaf) an IS–LM diagram to illustrate your answer.

Q 29 What would be the effect of the following on the equilibrium levels of income and rate of interest?

(a) The marginal propensity to save rises. _____

_____

(b) The demand for transactions balances rises. _____

_____

(c) Businessmen's pessimism about the recession deepens. _____

_____

(d) Demand for speculative balances falls. _____

_____

If you found it difficult to answer these questions by examining the equations for the *IS* and *LM* curves, try deriving the *IS* and *LM* curves by the geometric method explained in the Appendix to Chapter 40. The quadrant diagrams will permit you to examine each of the above changes, but you will need some graph paper to do it properly.

QUESTIONS FOR DISCUSSION

1   If you purchase shares in the stock market, are you investing?

2   What is the importance of interest rates in the theory of investment? What do the theories discussed in this chapter predict about how interest rates behave in response to changes in investment?

3   What will be the effect of changes in interest rates on housing investments and the demand for housing?

4   In his Budget speech on 11 April 1978 the Chancellor of the Exchequer said, 'A major

purpose of this Budget is to adjust taxation so as to help and improve our industrial performance ... I have therefore decided again to make no major changes this year in the rate of Corporation Tax or in the levels of investment incentives.' What theory of investment do you think lies behind this statement?

5   Is a university education a good investment? Is it possible to calculate the rate of return?

6   This is an extract from an article by Roger Elgin printed in *The Observer* (7.3.71). Sadly, many of the points he makes still apply today.

'Squirrels that don't stock up on nuts in the autumn are dead by spring. Nations that don't invest in extra capacity and all the other tools of a modern, competitive industrial society don't actually die, they go into a painful decline.

' "The long, slow sapping of our strength by under-investment" as Sir Fred Catherwood, director-general of Neddy, calls it, is what is happening in Britain at the moment.

'Faced with inflating costs and tight purse strings, three major companies, BP, Shell and Alcoa, have cut back or curtailed major investment projects.

'Over the past few years, another disturbing element has crept into the equation. Until 1965, it was broadly true that the income going to companies represented roughly 15.2 per cent of the gross national product. Since this date, profits as a percentage of GNP have dropped by a quarter to what looks like being 10 per cent last year. The share of GNP going to wages has gone from 67.8 per cent to comfortably over 70 per cent.

'Diverting British industry from this inexorable march to the knacker's yard is not going to be easy. Industry has not only lost the confidence to invest, but has also run out of cash.

'Wage bills and material costs are rocketing. The stock market is so depressed that the chances of raising money through it at anything but penal terms are impossible at the moment. To keep afloat many have resorted to increasing their bank overdrafts. But any industrialist who uses casual bank finance to pay for investment deserves to follow Rolls-Royce.'

What theories of the determination of investment are contained in this article? Why does a 'depressed stock market' mean that to raise money through the stock market would be very expensive?

7   If the government wished to lower interest rates, how could it achieve this?

8   What is 'crowding-out'?

9   If the government wishes to raise the level of income and, at the same time, avoid crowding-out, can you suggest how it might do this?

10   What might be adjustment paths towards equilibrium starting from points *A*, *B* and *C* in the diagram below?

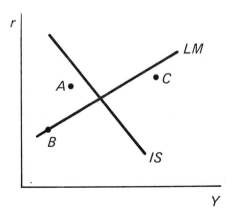

CHAPTER 41

Closure Version 1: Aggregate Demand and Aggregate Supply

THE AGGREGATE DEMAND CURVE

Q 1   The aggregate demand curve shows all combinations of _____ _____ which ensure equilibrium in the _____ and the _____ markets.

Q 2   A fall in the price level

    (a)   means that the real money supply rises/falls and raises/lowers the nominal demand for money;

    (b)   creates excess demand for/excess supply of money, which will cause interest rates to rise/fall and the level of real national income to rise/fall.

    (c)   This change in the rate of interest means that the aggregate expenditure function shifts up/is unchanged/shifts down, the IS curve shifts up/is unchanged/shifts down, the LM curve shifts up/is unchanged/shifts down and the aggregate demand curve shifts to right/is unchanged/shifts to left.

Q 3   The aggregate demand curve slopes downwards.

    (a)   What behavioural parameters determine the slope? _____ _____ _____ _____ _____

    (b)   A low interest responsiveness of demand for money will make the slope of the AD curve steeper/flatter. Why? _____ _____ _____

    (c)   A high interest responsiveness of aggregate expenditure makes the slope of the AD curve steeper/flatter, as _____ _____

    (d)   Given both a low interest responsiveness of demand for money and a high interest responsiveness of expenditure, a small increase in the price level will bring about a small/large _____ in the income level.

    (e)   When parameters b, d and e are constant but the marginal propensity to consume falls, this will make the AD curve steeper/flatter.

Q 4   What variables are held constant

    (a)   for a given IS curve? _____

    (b)   for a given LM curve? _____

    (c)   for a given aggregate demand curve? _____ _____

Q 5 Increasing the nominal money supply means that, at the current price level, the *IS/LM* curve will shift up/down resulting in higher/lower income level and higher/lower rate of interest, and the *AD* curve shifts to right/is unchanged/shifts to left.

Q 6 If the nominal money supply increases by 10% and prices increase by a similar amount, the *AD* curve shifts to right/is unchanged/shifts to left and income rises/remains the same/falls.

Q 7 If the nominal money supply is increased by 5% *but income is held at the same level*, by how much would prices rise? _____

Q 8 If prices and money supply change in the same proportion, real money supply, the rate of interest and income level will be the same. T/F

AGGREGATE DEMAND AND AGGREGATE SUPPLY

The *aggregate supply curve* shows the relationship between the aggregate price level and the amount firms supply, and the interaction of this schedule with the aggregate demand schedule will determine equilibrium levels of real national income and price. As before, we must start by considering what determines the slope and position of the aggregate supply schedule.

Q 9 What are the three main characteristics, cited by Lipsey, which should be captured by any aggregate supply curve if it is to conform to empirical evidence? _____
_____
_____
_____

Q 10 Which of the aggregate supply curves drawn below are consistent with the following statements?

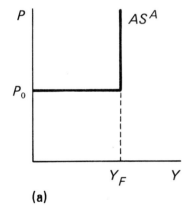 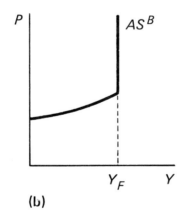 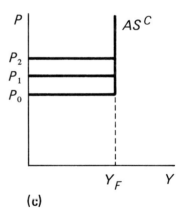

Fig. 1

(a) Supply is perfectly elastic up to potential income. _____

(b) Supply is perfectly inelastic at potential income. _____

(c) There is a ratchet effect. _____

(d) When there is an output gap, an increase in aggregate demand will always result in higher prices. _____

(e) When $Y = Y_F$, an increase in aggregate demand will raise both price and income. _____

(f) When there is an inflationary gap, a decline in aggregate demand will always reduce prices. _____

(g) Excess aggregate demand raises the price level and excess aggregate supply lowers the price level. _____

(h) Falling aggregate demand along the perfectly elastic section of aggregate supply reduces income but not prices. _____

Q 11 What would be the effect of the following on the aggregate supply schedule?

(a) Construction of a new factory in Wales for producing new laser-read compact disc players. _____

(b) The government removes the National Insurance Surcharge on employers.

_____

(c) The pound is devalued. _____

_____

(d) The school-leaving age is lowered by one year. _____

Q 12 Suppose that we have an aggregate supply curve which is perfectly elastic up to Y_F. and perfectly inelastic at Y_F. In the first period aggregate demand is equal to aggregate supply at Y_F. Now analyse the effect of the following events:

(a) An increase in autonomous expenditure shifts the IS curve inwards/outwards and AD shifts to right/left, with the result that the price level rises/is unchanged. At the new equilibrium, the price level is _____ , income is _____ and the interest rate is _____
Draw two diagrams to illustrate your answer.

(b) In the next period, AD returns to its previous level. What will happen to output prices and the rate of interest if there is a ratchet effect? _____

_____.

Draw two diagrams to illustrate your answer.

(c) In the following period the prices of imported raw materials rise significantly. What happens to output, price and the rate of interest? Draw two diagrams to illustrate your answer.

QUESTIONS FOR DISCUSSION

1   Why does the aggregate demand curve slope downwards?

2   What determines the shape and the position of the aggregate supply curve?

3   When aggregate demand exceeds aggregate supply what happens to the price level and to income?

4   What is the effect of a one-period increase in the money supply

   (a)   when there is an output gap?
   (b)   when there is an inflationary gap?

5   In a letter to the *Financial Times* (28.2.83) C. A. Williams argued that 'the trouble with the [Government's] strategy has been that while it set a path for public expenditure no target was set for the composition of that expenditure. It is clear that the consequences of cutting public expenditure will be very different if this is done by slashing the road programme than if the savings are made in the social security programme, or if the borrowing target is met by sale of assets.'
   Do changes in the composition of government expenditure affect the position of the aggregate demand curve?

6   As reported in Hansard, Mr Baker asked the following question on 8 February 1979:

'Does the Prime Minister appreciate that if there is a choice between a policy of high money interest rates and reducing government expenditure, for the government always to choose to increase money interest rates means that they are sacrificing future growth prospects of the economy?'

   (a)   What circumstances might make high interest rates or reduced government expenditure appropriate policy options?
   (b)   What considerations might guide the choice of one option over the other?
   (c)   What link between interest rates and growth do you think Mr Baker had in mind?

7   'The Government is urged to embark on a gradual but sustained reflation of the UK economy to be spread over several years, by the National Institute of Economic and Social Research.
   'The most cost-effective way of increasing output, according to the NI, is to increase public spending on goods and services. Over the past eight years the share of public investment in

national income has been halved, only a minor part of which was an object of government policy. It happened because the public sector, faced with financial constraints, found it easier to cut back capital projects rather than people.

'The Institute also points out that a recovery induced by cuts in indirect taxes could be achieved with very little upward pressure on prices. It says: "Whilst a higher level of output and employment might add to pressure for nominal wage increases, the effect in the other direction of a higher level of real wages (together with the direct consequence of tax cuts for prices) might well be enough to offset it." ' (The *Guardian*, 24.2.83.)

    (a)   How would a cut in indirect taxes help reduce unemployment?

    (b)   Can you draw an aggregate demand and aggregate supply diagram to illustrate the effects of the Institute's recommendations to increase government expenditure and cut indirect taxes?

8   ' "Why can't they just print more money?" a senior official in a public-sector union is reported to have asked during the recent pay talks. "They've always done so before." Perhaps he was joking. Certainly the one thing which the Chancellor has made repeatedly and quite courageously clear is that the Government will not yield to the old temptation to finance big settlements in the public sector by ditching its targets for monetary growth and public sector borrowing.' (Leader in the *Guardian*, 20.2.79.)

What would be the effect on the economy of printing more money?

9   In this chapter we have assumed that the aggregate supply schedule is perfectly inelastic at potential output. Do you think this is realistic? Is it possible to exceed this output level in the short and the long run?

CHAPTER 42
Fluctuations and Growth

On pages 627–8 Lipsey describes four stages in a cycle and he then goes on to examine attempts to explain why national income fluctuates in the short term. In the first part of this chapter of the Workbook we concentrate on changes in investment expenditure: in particular we examine in more detail the accelerator and multiplier-accelerator theories discussed by Lipsey on pages 631–3.

Investment is also important in determining potential output. So far we have considered the level of potential output to be fixed, but in the long run the aggregate supply schedule will shift to the right if the economy grows. Investment in capital together with changes in both the quantity and quality of labour will affect the growth rate, and the second part of this chapter will turn to an examination of the factors determining the level of potential income in the long term.

INVESTMENT AND CHANGES IN INCOME: THE ACCELERATOR THEORY

The rate of change of national income is usually a reasonable approximation to the rate of change of output. So a change in income usually means a change in output, and so long as entrepreneurs have some desired ratio of capital equipment to output (a ratio based on profit maximization, convention, or anything else), they will have sought to change the level of their capital to produce this different output. If they were successful, therefore, investment (positive or negative) will have taken place.

Q 1 Can you represent the accelerator theory symbolically? _____

Q 2 Is the accelerator coefficient likely to be smaller or greater than 1? Greater/Smaller. Explain why in a line. _____

_____

Q 3 Suppose a manufacturer is currently producing £200,000 worth of goods. He has 20 machines, each costing £15,000 and each capable of producing £10,000 worth of goods in a year.

(a) How many £s worth of capital does he need to produce £1 of output p.a.?

_____

(b) If demand increases so that the manufacturer could sell an additional £50,000 of goods next year, how many additional machines would he have to purchase?

_____

Q 4 Complete the following table:

(a) What assumption are we making about delivery times for new capital?

_____

(b) What is happening to the capital stock in period 8?

_____

(c) This example is an instance of capital-deepening rather than capital-widening. T/F

TABLE 1

Year	Sales (£000)	Change in sales (£000)	Required stock of capital assuming capital-output ratio of 4/1 (£000)	Net investment (£000)
1	15	0		0
2	20			
3	24			
4	25			
5	26			
6	27			
7	27			
8	25			

CUMULATIVE MOVEMENTS

Three sorts of cumulative movements are described on pp. 632–3:

(1) the multiplier;
(2) the accelerator;
(3) self-realizing expectations.

Q 5 Which of these do the following exemplify? (They may exemplify more than one, or none.)

(1) A factory's installation of new plant to meet rising demand for its product.

_____

(2) New expenditure of the owners of the factory on holidays in Spain.

_____

(3) Expenditure of the owners on Jaguar cars._____

(4) If speculators expect the rate of interest to fall, they will demand more bonds and less money. This will cause the rate of interest to fall. _____

_____

FLOORS AND CEILINGS

Q 6 There is a ceiling beyond which income cannot rise in the short run. What is it?

_____

Q 7 What sort of investment generally continues, even in the worst slumps?

_____

Q 8 If gross investment did fall to zero, what would still prevent national income from falling to zero?_____

THE MULTIPLIER-ACCELERATOR CYCLE

This offers an explanation why turning points need not necessarily be at the floors and ceilings mentioned above. The multiplier is, of course, straightforward.

Q 9 What is the accelerator assumption? _____

_____

Illustrating the multiplier-accelerator cycle. Consider a very simple economy with no foreign trade in which consumption is a function of the previous year's income. Symbolically we can write this as $C_t = f(Y_{t-1})$ where t means the current year and $t-1$ stands for last year.

232

Q 10   Thus, $t-2$ would mean _____

        We are given the following information:

$$C_t = 100 + 0.5Y_{t-1}$$
$$I_n = 1.2(Y_{t-1} - Y_{t-2}), \text{ where } I_n \text{ represents net investment.}$$

Replacement investment amounts to £20m a year and government expenditure is £80m in period t and rises to £90m in period $t+1$. Now fill in the columns of Table 1 below (all amounts in £ million).

Q 11   Between period $t+1$ and period $t+3$:

        (a)   output increased by approximately _____ %;

        (b)   total investment increased by _____ %.

Q 12   In period $t+7$, output has fallen and replacement investment is _____
        Explain your answer.

_____

Q 13   The increase in government spending starts an upswing which lasts until period
        _____ . Output rises at an increasing rate up to period $t+2$ but then slows down as
        the rate of induced investment declines. Output falls from period _____ until period
        _____ when it begins to rise again. Unless the system receives any further 'shocks',
        it will eventually reach an equilibrium income of £ _____

TABLE 2

Period	C_c	I_r	I_n	Total invest- ment	G	Y	Change in Y
t	300	20	0	20	80	400	0
$t+1$		20			90		
$t+2$							
$t+3$							
$t+4$							
$t+5$							
$t+6$							
$t+7$							
$t+8$							
$t+9$							
$t+10$							
. . . .							

THE INVENTORY CYCLE

The essential point to remember about the inventory cycle is that there comes a stage after a recession when entrepreneurs are not producing as much as they are selling, because they wish to run down their abnormally high stocks. As soon as they have run them down they will have to expand production, and recovery will start. Unlike the multiplier-accelerator theory, this provides a symmetric explanation of both turning points.

Q 14   Circle the correct alternatives in this description of part of a cycle. 'A drop in/a rise in
        demand has led to a depletion of inventories. More labour and plant had been hired in
        order to reduce/replenish the inventories. The increased income will lead to more
        demand for the good/supply of the good and there will be another reduction of the
        inventories below the desired level. More factors however will be employed until the

normal level of inventories is reached since at each stage the *APC/MPC* being less than unity, the increased demand will not absorb *all* the new production. When this happens the extra factors will be laid off, and a recovery/recession may start.'

Q 15   According to the hypotheses of this chapter, net investment would be likely to occur

   (a)   when profits are falling, in order to raise them.
   (b)   in the recovery rather than the recession stage of the cycle.
   (c)   when prices are falling, because capital is cheap then.

ECONOMIC GROWTH

In this section we consider what factors affect or determine the rate of growth of goods and services. Much of the chapter in Lipsey is taken up with discussing the economic and social implications of growth for any society and with weighing the benefits against the costs. This is an area in which opinions are divided and there are no easy, clear-cut answers—you will have to form your own opinion. In this part of the Workbook, we will concentrate on extending our understanding of the concepts and of their usefulness in analysing the process of growth.

   In Fig. 1 the production-possibility curve for a very simple economy is drawn, in which only two goods, vegetables and clothing, are produced.

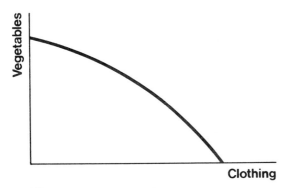

Fig. 1

Q 16   Potential national income is represented by _____

_____

Q 17   If productive capacity is not being fully utilized, this will be represented by

_____

Q 18   What will change in Fig. 1 if

   (a)   new varieties of vegetable seed are discovered which yield larger crops?

   _____

   (b)   the minimum school-leaving age is *lowered* by one year? _____

   _____

   (c)   the country receives some looms under a UN aid programme? _____

   _____

Q 19   Suppose now that the country starts to produce investment goods such as tractors, knitting machines, etc. As we have seen from Q 18, growth is represented by a movement outwards of the production-possibility curve. From Fig. 2, would you expect the rate of growth to be greater if current output is represented by point *A* or point *B*?

Q 20   Summarize the main sources of economic growth: _____

_____

_____

   If we put a larger proportion of our resources into investment goods, we do so in the hope

234

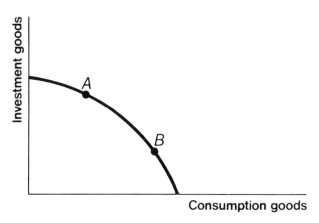

Fig. 2

that the consumption we sacrifice today will be compensated by higher consumption levels, i.e. standards of living, in the future. Problems facing any economy therefore include what proportion of national income to invest and how to ensure that the desired level of investment does occur. To extend our understanding of these and other problems, we will work through a very simple model of growth.

Output depends both on the amount of available resources and on their productivity, and potential output (Y_F) is that output which is achieved when this productive capacity is operating at its fullest extent. We will start by assuming that the relationship between potential output (Y_F) and the capital stock (K) takes the following form:

$$Y_F = \frac{1}{\alpha} K$$

Re-arranging this, we get
$$\frac{K}{Y_F} = \alpha$$

Now K/Y_F is the capital-output ratio, but what is α? Well, α represents the amount of capital which is needed to produce one unit of total output—or, in other words, $1/\alpha$ is the productivity of capital. To take an example, if the marginal efficiency of capital is known to be 0.20, then

$$Y_F = 0.2K$$

and *five* units of capital will be needed to produce *one* unit of output.

Q 21   If the marginal efficiency of capital is constant and equal to 0.25, what is the equilibrium capital-output ratio? _____

Q 22   Assume that in 1975 a country's capital stock is £160,000m, and that the marginal efficiency of capital is the same as in Q 21. What is the value of potential output?

_____

(Note that by assuming the marginal efficiency of capital is constant, the capital-output ratio is also constant. This is of course unrealistic—see Lipsey, pp. 644–5.)

Q 23   Now suppose that in 1975 investment amounted to £8,000m and that it is increasing at a rate of 2% per annum. (To keep matters simple, we will assume that all capital has an infinite life so that we can ignore depreciation.) This means that capital stock amounted to:

(a)   In 1976 _____

(b)   In 1977 _____

You should now be able to complete columns 1, 2 and 3 in Table 3, showing potential income, capital stock and investment.

TABLE 3 (INVESTMENT INCREASING AT 2% P.A.)

	Potential income (Y_F) 1	Capital stock (K) 2	Investment (= savings) 3	Equilibrium income (Y) 4
	(£m)	(£m)	(£m)	(£m)
1975	_____	160,000	8,000	_____
1976	_____	_____	_____	_____
1977	_____	_____	_____	_____
1978	_____	_____	_____	_____

Q 24   What is the annual rate of growth of potential output? _____

We now need to explore whether the actual equilibrium level of output achieved by the economy will be the same as the potential output—in other words, will we be on the production-possibility frontier as it moves outwards, or inside it?

Q 25   For simplicity, we will assume that in this economy there is no government sector and no foreign trade. If consumption (C) = $0.8Y$, the multiplier is _____.

Q 26   Assuming the country is producing at full capacity in 1975, consumption will be _____ and savings will amount to _____ .

Now complete the remaining column in Table 3 showing the equilibrium levels of income.

Q 27   Does the country continue to produce at full capacity? Yes/No
        What is the actual growth rate achieved? _____

Q 28   Why does the economy run at less than full capacity? _____
        _____

Complete Table 4 on the assumption that investment is now increasing *at 5% per annum.*

TABLE 4 (INVESTMENT INCREASING AT 5% P.A.)

	Potential income (Y_F) (£m)	Capital stock (K) (£m)	Investment (= savings) (£m)	Equilibrium income (Y) (£m)
1975	_____	160,000	8,000	_____
1976	_____	_____	_____	_____
1977	_____	_____	_____	_____
1978	_____	_____	_____	_____

Q 29   What is now the actual growth rate? _____

Q 30   What is the rate of growth of potential output? _____

Q 31   If population is 50 million in 1975 and is growing at an annual rate of 3%, find income *per capita* in:

        (a)   1975 _____

        (b)   1978, when income reaches the level shown in Table 3: _____

        (c)   1978, when income reaches the level shown in Table 4: _____

GROWTH AND UNDERDEVELOPED ECONOMIES

The relative rates of growth of population and GNP are important in determining living standards. In richer countries a fall in *per capita* GNP is not likely to be a matter of life and death for members of such societies; for less developed countries it may well be so. In 1798 Malthus published his *Essay on Population* in which he argued that as population increases in a geometrical ratio and the means of subsistence increase in an arithmetical ratio, population can only increase up to the point at which living is at subsistence level. We can examine his argument by using some of the ideas you studied in Chapter 17.[1]

Suppose there is a country which has a simple agricultural economy. The food it produces, we will call it 'rice', is all that is available for domestic consumption. We will assume that this country does virtually no trade with other countries so that its output of rice will determine the standard of living. How much rice will be produced? Here we can use our knowledge of the theory of production; assuming that the stock of land and of capital are fixed, then as labour (population) increases we might expect output to change as shown in the total product curve plotted in Fig. 3.

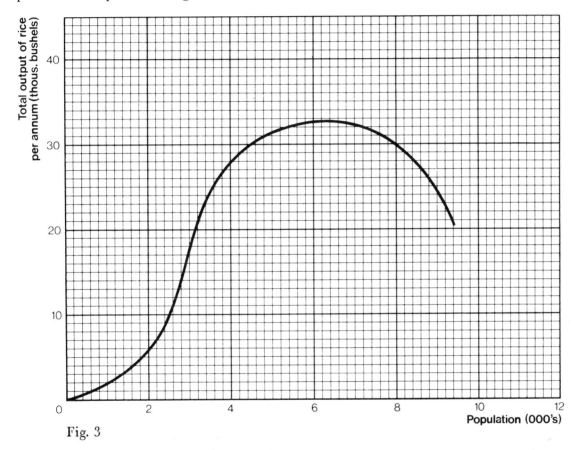

Fig. 3

Q 32   What is the hypothesis underlying this curve and suggesting this shape? _____

_____

Q 33   (a)   Up to what level of output is the marginal product of labour increasing?

_____

(b)   What happens to the marginal product of labour when the population increases beyond 6.3 thousand? _____

(c)   As the population grows from 2.75 thousand to 6.3 thousand, what is happening to the marginal product of labour? _____

[1] The following example and questions are adapted from R. L. Meek, *Figuring Out Society* (Fontana, 1971), Chapter 2. The interested student should follow up this reference.

Q 34   Suppose now that the minimum subsistence level is 3 bushels of rice a year per person. This means that an output of 30 thousand bushels of rice a year could just support a population of _____

Q 35   On Fig. 3, plot population as a function of output.

Q 36   Malthus predicted that population will increase up to the point that living standards will be at the minimum subsistence level; beyond this point he predicted that the population would be checked by famine and plague. From Fig. 3, find the point up to which population will grow. _____

Q 37   What is the optimum level of population if the country's objective is to seek the highest *per capita* standard of living (measured in terms of bushels of rice per person)? _____ (If you have problems in answering this question, remember that a ray from the origin will give you the measure of the average product of labour.) What is output *per capita* at this population? _____

Q 38   When total output is at a maximum, what is output *per capita* (i.e. average product of labour)? _____

Q 39   The total product of labour curve drawn in Fig. 3 assumes that, over time, all inputs other than labour are constant and that the technology of producing rice is constant. This, of course, is unrealistic. What would happen to the total product curve if, say, new and improved varieties of seed rice are introduced? _____

Q 40   Of course labour, capital, quality of land and seed are not the only factors in determining the output of crops in any year. Can you think of another very important factor? _____

You may think that this example is unrealistically abstract and that Malthus's predictions are overly pessimistic. If so, you might be interested to read the following extract from *The Times* (5.11.74):

'BANGLADESH BEARS OUT MALTHUS'S PROPHECY

'. . . with more than 1300 people on average to every square mile, Bangladesh is already the world's most densely populated country. It is . . . an agrarian community, in which agriculture is the livelihood of 75 per cent of the labour force . . .

'The average size of landholding is already very small, and the number of landless peasants, who are dependent on what they can earn as labourers during the sowing and harvesting seasons, is steadily growing.

'Although rice production has just about doubled over the last twenty-five years, keeping somewhat ahead of population growth, output flattened out in the late 1960's and has hardly increased since then, while population has continued its upward progress.

'Even before the slow-down in food output, some 45 per cent of rural families and 75 per cent of urban families were getting below the minimum acceptable calorific intake and about two-thirds of families were deficient in protein and vitamins. Since then the per capita availability of rice has steadily declined. The consequence of these inadequate nutrition levels is a drastic lowering of the physical and mental efficiency, resistance to disease and work capacity of perhaps half the adult population.

'Foreign agriculturalists believe that rice production could be substantially increased by better application of fertilizers, pesticides and high yielding varieties of seeds, particularly in the non-irrigated, rainfed areas, to the point of eliminating the need for imports but this would require heavy foreign assistance, both of capital and personnel.

'The implications are thus clear. Bangladesh must either achieve an unprecedented reduction in birth rates through family planning, or continue to import food at heavy cost, or accept a marked rise in mortality.'

QUESTIONS FOR DISCUSSION

1   'The only thing we have to fear is fear itself—nameless, unreasoning, unjustified terror which paralyses needed efforts to convert retreat into advance . . .' So said Franklin D. Roosevelt in his Inaugural Address in 1933 at the height of the most serious depression ever recorded in American history. Is this statement consistent with the theory of the business cycle we have developed? What theory of the cycle was Roosevelt propounding?

2   A great deal of talk in the Great Depression was of 'priming the pump'. How might a small amount of government expenditure do this? What might happen if business confidence is very, very low?

3   Why do we ever level off, once we get into the downward spiral of a depression?

4   Should the UK Government be encouraged by the headline, 'End of US recession in sight'?

5   'The slump is over. The question now is whether the UK economy will emerge from recession. The distinction is important.' (Victor Keegan, *Guardian*, 7.3.83.)

What is the distinction between 'slump' and 'recession', and why is it important?

6   The following are extracts from a letter to *The Times* (5.2.75) from Professor Nicholson of the London Graduate School of Business Studies:

'Once again, with a reported fall in industrial investment intentions, it is presumed that the United Kingdom economy must decline further. But what do we mean by investment and how much is necessary anyway?

'We tend to think of investment in industry as the purchase and installation of new shiny machinery. In fact, investment consists of any change in the production system which contributes to the better capability of a company to meet market needs.

'. . . why do we want all this investment in machinery? The most detailed surveys of industry so far undertaken (excluding oil and chemicals) have shown that machine utilization averages 40 per cent; that work-in-progress in the United Kingdom is twice the level of the United States; that despite the high stocks we have hopeless shortages; that only 5 per cent of deliveries are made on or before their due date; that what you get is in all probability a part delivery; and that for every hour a job spends being worked on it (there are about 20 hours spent waiting around).'

Is Professor Nicholson arguing that investment is not a prerequisite of growth?

7   What is the basic notion of the accelerator theory? Is investment endogenous or exogenous in this theory? Why, when we assume investment to be determined by an accelerator, can we not illustrate the investment function by drawing a graph showing investment expenditure and the level of income?

8   Lipsey discusses why it might take some time to complete an investment project. Can you give examples of lags in connection with government expenditure? Do you think the time-lags will be the same whether the change in expenditure is an increase or a decrease?

9   Ian Richardson writing in the *Birmingham Post* (23.1.79) said '. . . the four indicators (share prices, short-term interest rates, companies' net acquisition of assets, housing starts) which traditionally give twelve months' warning of changes in the course of an economy were pointing to a recession ahead from October 1977'.

Can you provide an explanation why these indicators might suggest changes in national income?

10   As reported in the *Financial Times* (15.3.79) the *Bank of England Quarterly Bulletin* for March 1979 noted that 'the ratio of stock to sales of finished goods remains historically high, though survey evidence suggests that managements do not regard the present level of stocks as excessive. The apparent change in the relationship between desired stocks and the

level of activity may reflect only partial adjustment by companies to the recession of the last few years. . . Some of the increase in stocks during 1978 probably arose from expectation of continuing buoyancy in demand.' The *Bulletin* then went on to say that it thought the recent rise in interest rates might result in a reduction in stockbuilding, or even some destocking, as a response to future growth of demand.

(a) The *Bulletin* is suggesting that there seems to have been a change in managements' view of the desirable level of stock relative to sales. What factors might be responsible for such a shift?

(b) Why should changes in interest rates affect stock levels?

(c) If stocks only partially adjust in recession, will this strengthen or weaken any relationship between inventory levels and fluctuations in national income?

11   Opponents of growth stress the costs of economic growth, many of which are difficult (if not impossible) to measure. Are there any benefits that go unmeasured by conventional measures of economic growth?

12   On which side would you line up in the growth/anti-growth argument? State your reasons carefully.

13   Up to the time of the oil price crisis many industrialized countries were happy to receive migrant workers but as unemployment rates have risen in recent years, these countries have tried to check this inflow. Nevertheless, in many countries migrant workers are still a significant proportion of the total workforce. 'In 1977 foreign manpower accounted for nearly 10% of West Germany's, and over 7% of France's economically active population. But between 1974 and 1977, the number of foreign workers in West Germany had fallen by 19%, and that in France by 16%' (*Economist*, 24.2.79, p. 33). Some of the migrant labour has moved to the oil rich countries, for example the *Financial Times* estimated that 700,000 Pakistanis are working abroad and about half of these are working in Middle East oil-producing countries (P. Bowring, 23.3.79).

What are the benefits and costs of such labour to (a) labour-importing countries, and (b) labour-exporting countries?

14   In November 1974, at the opening of the UN World Food Conference, Kurt Waldheim, UN Secretary-General, said: 'If enough food is to be produced to keep up with the world population growth, if some improvement in living standards is to be achieved for the most underprivileged, and if adequate security stocks are to be established and maintained, then we must begin immediately to work for an expansion of food production in magnitudes never before undertaken or even achieved.' (Reported in *The Times*, 6.11.74.) At about the same time, the EEC, having disposed of a butter mountain, was facing a beef surplus.

Is there really a food problem? Is the problem to be found not in production but in distribution?

CHAPTER 43

Demand Management 1: Fiscal Policy

Now that we have some understanding of what determines the level of national income and hence employment, we can begin our study of *demand management*. In this chapter we concentrate on fiscal policy, that is, the management of aggregate demand through tax and (government) expenditure changes, and we explore how the government can use the multiplier effect to stabilize the economy. An alternative way of managing aggregate demand is through monetary policy, which we will examine in the next chapter. For the moment we concentrate on shifts in the *IS* curve and assume that the government keeps the nominal money supply constant.

FISCAL POLICY AND THE *IS* CURVE

In Chapter 40 we derived the *IS* curve for a simple two-sector economy. Now that we have a third sector, government, we need to find the new equation for the *IS* curve.

Q 1   What is the equilibrium condition underlying the *IS* curve?_____
_____

Q 2   Given the following functions, derive the *IS* curve. Find the equation first in terms of r and then in terms of Y.

$$C = a_0 + cY_d \qquad\qquad 0 < c < 1, \quad 0 < a_0$$
$$I = a_1 + br \qquad\qquad b < 0 < a_1$$
$$T = tY \qquad\qquad 0 < t < 1$$
$$G = G*$$
$$Q = Q*$$

(a) $r =$ _____

(b) $Y =$_____

(c)   What is the intercept with the r axis?_____

(d)   What is the intercept with the Y axis? _____

(e)   What is the slope of the *IS* curve? _____
_____

(f)   What is the (interest-constant) multiplier?_____
_____

Q 3   You are given the following information: $c = 0.8$, $t = 0.25$, $b = -20$, $a_0 = 0$, $a_1 = £140m$, $G = £200m$, $Q = £50m$.

(a)   When $r = 6\%$, find the level of income at which there is equilibrium in the goods market. _____

(b)   What is the value of the (interest-constant) multiplier? _____

Now suppose that the current level of income means that there is substantial unemployment and the government decides to raise aggregate demand by fiscal policy. We start by examining the effect on the *IS* curve and we *assume that the interest rate is held at 6%*.

Q 4   In order to raise the level of income, the government can increase _____
_____ and/or decrease _____

Q 5   Using the information in Question 3, and taking each option in turn, find the effect on income of the following:

(a) Government expenditure on goods and services is increased by £10m.

_____

(b) Transfers are increased by £54m. _____

(c) The tax rate is cut by 2%. _____

(d) When the government increases spending on transfers or on goods and services, the *IS* curve shifts to the right and its slope is steeper/unchanged/less steep; a cut in the tax rate pivots the *IS* in a clockwise/anti-clockwise direction and the slope becomes more/less steep.

THE PARADOX OF THRIFT

Q 6   What does the paradox of thrift predict will be the effect on the level of income and employment if households save more? _____
_____
_____

Q 7   We can use the information in Question 3 to illustrate this.

(a) Suppose that people wish to save more and the marginal propensity to save becomes 0.3. If *r* remains at 6% and all other figures remain the same, what will happen to the level of income? _____
_____
_____

(b) What is the size of the budget deficit? _____
_____

(c) Suppose that the government decides to increase expenditure on goods and services in order to return income to its previous level of £650m. By how much will it have to increase government expenditure? (Use the multiplier.) _____
_____
_____

(d) As a result of increasing government expenditure, has the budget deficit changed?
_____

(e) Suppose that, instead of changing government expenditure, the government cut the tax rate to 0.13. Would this return income to its previous level? _____
_____ . What would happen to the budget deficit?
_____

Q 8   During the post First World War crisis in Britain in the early 1920s unemployment rose to alarming heights and a large deficit appeared in the government's budget. Why do you think this deficit appeared?

(a) _____

In order to deal with this crisis slashes were made in the programme of building houses for servicemen and in pension payments to widows, orphans and disabled servicemen. What items in the national income of the brave new world for which the servicemen had fought were affected by the cuts?

(b) Building-programme cuts which formed part of injections/withdrawals/transfer payments, and

(c) Pension cuts which formed part of injections/withdrawals/transfer payments.

What does the theory predict would have been the effect on the volume of unemployment of each of these cuts?

(d) Building programmes. _____

(e) Pensions. _____

Q 9   In 1930 Sir Oswald Mosley, then a member of the Labour Government, proposed that the government should step up the road-building programme. Would this have reduced or increased employment? _____

Q 10 'Saving always causes investment.' Is this consistent with the paradox-of-thrift theory, as presented here? Yes/No

Q 11 If there were an autonomous increase in the desire to save, the *loanable funds theory of interest* would predict that the rate of interest would rise/fall. At the new interest rate, the level of saving would have risen/fallen and the level of investment would have risen/fallen.

Q 12 The *classical theory of income* determination predicts that the price level rises when there is excess aggregate demand and falls when there is excess aggregate supply. T/F. With which of the aggregate supply schedules discussed in Chapter 41 is this *inconsistent*? _____

_____

_____

Q 13 What is the Keynesian assumption, discussed in Chapter 41, about wage and price movements when there is excess aggregate demand and excess aggregate supply?

_____

_____

Q 14 If savings are less than investment, the classical theory would expect the rate of interest to rise/fall, while the Keynesian theory would expect savings to be equated with investment as a result of_____

Q 15 Work through the following 'Keynesian sequence':

(a) There is an autonomous increase in the desire to save.
(b) The *IS* curve shifts inwards/outwards.
(c) As a result, the level of income will rise/fall.
(d) When the income level changes, this raises/lowers the demand for transactions balances.
(e) Consequently wealth-holders will purchase/sell bonds and the interest rate will rise/fall.
(f) The asset market will return to equilibrium when an interest rate emerges such that _____

_____

_____

The paradox of thrift appears paradoxical because at the individual level relationships are ignored which are crucial at the aggregate level. At the individual level saving is done for many reasons but most of them can be reduced to the desire to have command over *future* rather than *present* goods. But the only way in which this can be achieved at the aggregate level is by physical investment—otherwise when the goods are demanded in the future there will be no capital equipment to produce them. *But our theory rules out any direct link between saving and investment*, so there is *no* assumption which states that aggregate saving now will enable more goods to be produced in the future.

FISCAL POLICY WHEN PRIVATE EXPENDITURE FUNCTIONS DO NOT SHIFT

Throughout this section we shall assume that the aggregate supply curve is perfectly elastic up to potential output and perfectly inelastic at the full-employment level of income.

Q 16 If aggregate demand is equal to aggregate supply at the full-employment level of income, what would happen if the Chancellor of the Exchequer cuts income taxes? Is there any crowding-out? _____

_____

Draw *IS–LM* and *AD–AS* diagrams to illustrate your answer.

Q 17 Suppose now that there is an output gap and that the government adopts fiscal policy to eliminate this. What is the effect on income, the rate of interest and the price level? Is there any crowding-out? Draw appropriate diagrams to illustrate your answer.

_____

_____

Q 18 You are given the following information about the economy:

$$C = 0.8 Y_d$$
$$I = 140 - 20r$$
$$T = 0.25 Y$$
$$G = £200m$$
$$Q = £50m$$
$$M_d = 0.3 Y - 12r$$
$$\frac{M^*}{P} = £150m.$$

244

(a) Find the equilibrium levels of income and rate of interest. Does the budget balance? _____

(b) The government decides to increase expenditure on goods and services by £54m. What effect will this have? _____

_____

(c) If the interest rate had been held at the original level, by how much would income have risen? _____ What is the crowding-out effect when the interest rate is allowed to vary? _____

(d) From your answer to (b), find the (interest-variable) multiplier. _____

_____

(e) Now suppose that instead of increasing expenditure on goods and services, the government had increased transfers by £54m. What effect will this have?

_____

_____

(f) The remaining option is to cut the tax rate. If G and Q are left at their original levels but the tax rate is cut to 0.15, what will be the effect? _____

_____

(g) Suppose that the government knows that Y_F = £780m, and decides to increase expenditure on goods and services so that the output gap is eliminated. By what amount should the government increase G? _____

_____

(h) When the government increases government expenditure or cuts taxes, the IS curve shifts inwards/outwards and the AD curve shifts to the left/right. At the new equilibrium, the level of income and the rate of interest will be lower/higher.

(i) If we wish to increase national income to a given level, this will require a larger/smaller increase in expenditure on goods and services than on transfers.

(j) In your answers to (b), (e) and (f) you saw that the use of an expansionary fiscal policy raised income but also raised the interest rate so that crowding-out occurred. Suppose that the government increases the money supply by £40.5m at the same time as it raises government expenditure on goods and services by £54m. Find the equilibrium level of income and rate of interest, together with the crowding-out effect. _____

_____. Draw IS–LM and AD–AS diagrams to illustrate your answers to this question and to (b) and (c) above.

Q 19 Using the information given in Question 18, find the effect of a simultaneous increase in government expenditure of £54m and an increase in the tax rate to 0.32. What has happened to income, the rate of interest and the budget deficit? _____

_____

Q 20   Find the balanced-budget multiplier and compare it with your answer to Question 18
        (d) above._____

        _____

        _____

When we inject increased government expenditure into the economy, we saw that, *if the tax rate had been held constant*, income would have risen through the multiplier process by £68m (see Question 18 (b) above). A balanced-budget increase in expenditure means, however, that we do not keep the tax rate constant but we raise it and this reduces consumer spending by $c\Delta t$ (i.e. the marginal propensity to consume multiplied by the change in the tax rate). The injection of £54m raises income in the first round of the multiplier chain by £54m but, at the same time, £54m has been taken out in tax revenue so that increasing the tax rate means that in the first round there was no increase in disposable income. The increase in national income results from the subsequent rounds in the multiplier chain and, of course, the final change in income (once equilibrium has been re-established) must be much less than it would have been when the tax rate was unchanged. If the interest rate were constant, then the balanced-budget multiplier would have had a value of 1. However, when the interest rate varies as the level of income changes, the value of the balanced-budget multiplier will be less than 1.

Any government endeavouring to eliminate an output gap by a balanced-budget increase in expenditure faces a difficult control problem in establishing the appropriate changes in G and t.

Q 21   Why will an increase in the level of government activity in an economy have an
        expansionary effect even when increased tax revenues pay for all the extra government
        expenditure? _____

        _____

        _____

Q 22   When government expenditure is decreased by £10m, income will rise/fall by _____
        _____ times £10m. When taxes are cut by £10m, consumption will rise/
        fall by more/less than this amount because _____

        _____ . If 70% would have been spent on
        domestically produced goods, the remaining 30% would have been _____

        _____ . If the government
        had not cut its expenditure by £10m, _____ % of this sum would have been injected
        into/withdrawn from the circular flow. The government's propensity to spend is
        greater/smaller than that of the private sector. If the government balances its cut in
        expenditure by an equal cut in tax revenue, this will have a contractionary/
        expansionary effect on national income.

Q 23   What is the equation of the budget surplus function? _____

        _____

        (a)   If the government's fiscal policy is unchanged, as income rises the budget
              balance moves from deficit to surplus/surplus to deficit and the high-employment
              surplus rises/is unchanged/falls.
        (b)   An expansionary fiscal policy will shift the budget surplus function up/down and
              raise/lower the high-employment surplus.
        (c)   An increase in the tax rate will pivot the function in a clockwise/anti-clockwise
              direction, and raise/lower the high-employment surplus.

246

FISCAL POLICY WHEN PRIVATE EXPENDITURE FUNCTIONS ARE SHIFTING

Up to this point we have assumed that the government knew the consumption and investment functions and that these functions were constant. All shifts in the IS and AD curves have been the result of fiscal policy. If, however, these curves shift for reasons other than government intervention, then the level of income may rise and fall, and we need to consider whether the government can intervene in order to offset such undesirable fluctuations and thus stabilize income and employment. Before you go on with this chapter you might like to stop and think of reasons why private expenditure functions could shift. This might be a good question to discuss in class.

In his discussion of the tools of fiscal policy, Lipsey discusses built-in stabilizers.

Q 24   Define a built-in stabilizer. _____

_____

_____

_____

Two of the built-in stabilizers mentioned by Lipsey are transfer payments (i.e. National Insurance and welfare services) and government expenditure. So far we have taken transfer payments (Q) as exogenous to our model, but now we shall explore whether it makes a difference if transfer payments are endogenous. In particular, we wish to examine whether such transfers will tend to stabilize income, i.e. reduce fluctuations caused by shifts in consumption and investment functions.

Q 25   Given the following information about an economy, examine firstly the case where transfers are exogenous.

$$C = 0.8Y_d$$
$$t = 0.25$$
$$I = 250 - 20r$$
$$Q = 125$$
$$G = 300$$
$$M_d = 0.3Y - 12r$$
$$\frac{M^*}{P} = 312$$

(a)   Find equilibrium income. _____

(b)   Suppose that the autonomous component of investment falls by £50m, what will be the change in income? _____

(c)   What is the value of the interest-variable multiplier? _____

(d)   What is the value of the interest-constant multiplier? _____

Q 26   Now let $Q = 125 - 0.15Y$.

(a)   Find equilibrium income. _____

(b)   Find the change in income following a fall in autonomous investment of £50m.

_____

(c)   What is the value of the interest-variable multiplier? _____

(d)   What is the value of the interest-constant multiplier? _____

(e)   When transfers are endogenous, do they stabilize or destabilize income?

_____

Q 27   Now examine government expenditure on goods and services (G). Up to now we have taken this to be exogenous, but now assume that $G = 0.2Y$. We will consider transfers to be exogenous at £125m (so that we can concentrate on G) and the rest of the information is as set out in Question 25.

    (a)   Find equilibrium income. _____

    (b)   Find the change in income following a fall in autonomous investment amounting to £50m. _____

    (c)   What is the value of the interest-variable multiplier? _____

    (d)   What is the value of the interest-constant multiplier? _____

    (e)   Compare your answers with those to Question 25. When government expenditure is positively related to income, does this stabilize or destabilize income?

_____

_____

FINANCING BUDGET DEFICITS

Q 28   List the three sources of finance for a budget deficit. _____

_____

_____

Q 29   If the government sells bonds to private households, or banks (this means, of course, that it borrows money from them), the money would otherwise have been _____ or _____ . If it had been saved, it could either have been taken up for private investment, or kept as liquid reserves. In all, therefore, it could have been either

    (a)   consumed, or
    (b)   saved, and taken up for investment, or
    (c)   saved, and not taken up for investment.

In which one of these circumstances will there be no extra net withdrawal?

_____

The cost of government expenditure (remember, to an economist, cost means opportunity cost) is incurred by members of the community at the time of expenditure. The government will strive to make this cost as small as possible by utilizing factors with the lowest opportunity cost.

Q 30   The choice of method of finance will affect the _____ of the burden.

If the government expenditure is financed by taxes, the cost is borne by the taxpayer.

Q 31   If government expenditure is financed by borrowing, the cost is borne *in the first period* by _____ and in subsequent periods by those who finance the interest and redemption payments.

Q 32   If a war is financed by borrowing money from abroad, the current burden on the home population can be completely avoided. T/F

Q 33   'As government borrowing for expenditure fluctuates, national income must fluctuate by a factor of K times the fluctuation in borrowing.' T/F

Q 34   The opportunity cost of a given government expenditure is the same regardless of/ varies according to how it is financed. If government expenditures take resources away from consumer goods production, the opportunity cost is borne in the present/future. If government expenditures take resources from the production of capital goods, the opportunity costs will be borne by the _____ generation, in the form of fewer/ more consumer goods produced than otherwise. If government expenditures use unemployed resources, opportunity cost is _____ .

QUESTIONS FOR DISCUSSION

1   The following letter from Mr Graham Presland was published in *The Times* (13.10.78):

'It is sad to find Lord Keynes misrepresented yet again. Sir Frederick Catherwood writes, "Keynesian economics . . . have shifted resources out of the market sector in the public sector and high and progressive personal taxes have discouraged the investment sources on which industry has been built up." '

'The Keynesian position is surely that action is needed to ensure sufficient spending to buy what can be produced with resources fully employed. Whilst this can indeed be achieved by raising public sector spending, cuts in income tax and in corporation tax are equally effective. The choice is the politicians' and not dictated by Keynesian economics.'

(a)   What do you think Sir Frederick means when he talks about resources being shifted from the market to the public sector? What sort of resources might he be referring to?

(b)   Why might 'high and progressive personal taxes' discourage investment sources?

(c)   Would you agree with Mr Presland that changes in tax rates or in government expenditure are 'equally effective'?

2   Samuel Brittan wrote the following in the *Financial Times* (11.3.71):

'As a former member of the "expansionist" lobby, I find it distressing to see the expansionist case so badly put. It was never the contention of those of us who argued the case in the early and middle 1960s that one could simply put one's foot on the accelerator and could grow by 5 per cent by letting demand rip. The real argument was that if industry could look forward to a steady increase in demand at a rate *slightly* above the previous trend, this would generate an increase in investment which would pull up the growth of capacity itself. An increase in the underlying growth rate from 3 to 4 per cent over a period of several years would have been regarded as a triumph, and a great leap forward compared with anything seen in the past.

'On any plausible view of the relationships such an acceleration would have required an increase in investment which would have absorbed most of the extra growth for some years to come; and indeed it would have required very careful management to prevent an actual decrease in the amount left over for the ordinary consumer. The expansionist hypothesis was never disproved, but there was no chance of trying it so long as we had an over-valued currency. And a period when inflationary expectations are at an all-time high, and when we will be lucky to avoid a 10 per cent increase in retail prices, is not the time for making experiments of this kind with demand management.'

What does Brittan mean by 'put one's foot on the accelerator'? What sort of economic mechanism might cause the phenomenon of which he seemed wary— an increase in consumer demand causing a rise in national income, a rise in investment and a fall in consumption?

3   What is the balanced-budget multiplier? How can national income increase if exactly the same amount is put back into the system through spending as is removed from it through taxes?

4   If there is inflation, tax revenue will increase even though tax rates are constant. How can this be?

5   If a single individual is thrifty, we normally expect him to be better off than if he is a spendthrift. The theory developed in Chapter 43 predicts that the thriftier people are in the aggregate (the more they try to save at each level), the lower total income will be, while the more spendthrift they are (the less they try to save at each level of income), the higher their total income will be! The theory also predicts that the actual amount of savings that they make will be the same in equilibrium whether they are thrifty or spendthrift. Derive these predictions, which are often referred to as the paradox of thrift, graphically.

Now, the following article appeared in the *Guardian* in February 1971: 'Britain's consumers are still holding on to their money, and there is little sign of an upward trend in spending this year, according to Sir Bernard Miller, Chairman of the John Lewis Partnership.

'Preliminary estimates for consumer spending in the first quarter of this year show little change from the plateau of the final quarter of last year.

'At the end of 1970, the consumer went against traditional attitudes and saved rather than spent, and although department stores recorded an increase in the value of their sales at Christmas, most of this was accounted for by price rises and there was only a small rise in the volume.

'Speaking in London yesterday, Sir Bernard gave a warning that prices were likely to rise by about 10 per cent, as a result of inflation, and if there was no marked increase in the volume of trading, prices would have to rise still further "because the retail industry does not have adequate profit margins" and the retail industry is pressing for a need for reflation.

'Wage bills in the retail trade were increasing by about 10 per cent each year, and the social revolution of equal pay for women was likely to add something in the region of 25 per cent to the payroll. This, said Sir Bernard, would have to be passed on to the consumer.'

Assuming that wages in the retail trade are increasing faster than in other sectors of the economy, through such factors as the equal pay for women movement,

    (a)   Criticize (or rephrase), in the light of your knowledge of micro theory, Sir Bernard Miller's assertion that wage increases will be 'passed on'.

    (b)   What do you predict will be the effect on employment in the retail trade?

    (c)   Analyse Sir Bernard Miller's statements in terms of the paradox of thrift.

6   Extract from an article by Sir John Clark, Chairman of Plessey, the giant electronics company:

'. . . Four times in the last 15 years we have had periods of strong economic growth, periods of real optimism. In each case our hopes have been cruelly dashed by a return to stagnation. Nobody would claim that it is easy to avoid these cycles. But why is Government so powerless to prolong the good times and smooth out the dips? Why is it always caught unawares? Why does it never correct its course in good time? Why have so many economists concluded that the main effect of Government's so-called "fine tuning" is to make the swings even worse? Whenever we have a little economic growth in Britain the Government lets it run out of control and then has to stop it overnight. How am I supposed to plan the growth of my business against a background like that?' (*The Observer*, 29.9.74.)

Why is it so difficult for the government to undertake counter-cyclical measures? Write a reply to Sir John explaining the problems.

7   In this country, the government's expenditure plans are published and debated before the Budget is announced. In the USA and many other countries, expenditure and revenue proposals are presented at the same time. What difference do you think it might make if the US system were adopted in the UK?

8   '[The 1982] Budget set PSBR a target of £8½ bn. The chancellor's autumn statement revised this to £8bn . . . . . The trouble is that [the chancellor] may set the PSBR as he likes; it will come out differently. Calculations . . . show that the actual PSBR at the end of the year bears precious little relation to the intended PSBR at the beginning of the year, out by an average of more than £2bn. This is the faulty steering wheel. Try as [the chancellor] may to turn left, he may quite by accident turn right.' (David Lipsey, *Sunday Times*, 6.3.83.)

Can you suggest why it is so difficult to hold the PSBR to its target?

9   This is an extract from the *Financial Times* of (12.3.70): 'The real cost of the national debt, in spite of rising interest rates, has been falling steadily over recent years. This fact emerges from a special analysis of the national debt in the March issue of the Bank of England quarterly bulletin. It shows that, because of the increase in the receipts of income from loans made by the central Government, the net "burden" of servicing the central Government's debt has been on a falling trend for some years.

'. . . for the central Government account "a large and rising proportion of the cost of the national debt has been matched by interest on loans, and correspondingly less from tax revenue".

'The Government's loans, it is pointed out, are mainly to other parts of the public sector . . . In contrast to the traditional view of the debt "burden", "the national debt is becoming to an increasing extent backed by tangible assets, including such income-earning investments as power stations, transport facilities, etc., and housing". "It is conceivable", the Bank points out, "that the cost of debt service may, in due course, come to be fully offset by interest receipts".'

If the government *were*, in fact, borrowing to do other things than acquire power stations — such as financing the development of Concorde — and if at the same time the Bank's prophecy in the last sentence comes true, who would really be 'bearing the burden of the national debt'? (*Hint*: how do power stations make a profit?)

10   What is the difference in the 'burden' of the following government expenditures? Which do you think are capital expenditures?

  (a)   Subsidies for fuel bills of old-age pensioners.
  (b)   Research into silicon chips.
  (c)   Government subsidies for industry amounting to £500 million (1979 White Paper on Public Expenditure), the biggest recipients being BL and Rolls-Royce.
  (d)   The purchase in 1978 of 400 bodyscanners for the NHS.
  (e)   New fighter planes.
  (f)   Grants to householders to insulate lofts.
  (g)   Rent relief for service and office firms locating in assisted areas.

CHAPTER 44

Demand Management 2: Monetary Policy

Monetary policy is an alternative way of managing aggregate demand. In the previous chapter we saw that the government could use fiscal policy to shift the aggregate demand curve, and we now see that changes in the money supply can also change aggregate demand. We start by examining the use of monetary policy when there is either an output or an inflationary gap. Once we understand the effect of changing the money supply, we shall be able to compare monetary and fiscal policy.

MONETARY POLICY WHEN THERE IS AN OUTPUT GAP

As before, we shall assume that the aggregate supply schedule is perfectly elastic when income is less than potential income, and perfectly inelastic at potential income. We will also continue to use the same model of an economy that we analysed in the previous chapter. The relevant information is repeated here.

$$C = 0.8 Y_d$$
$$I = 140 - 20r$$
$$t = 0.25$$
$$G = 200$$
$$Q = 50$$
$$M_d = 0.3Y - 12r$$
$$\frac{M^*}{P} = 150$$

As you will remember, we found the equilibrium level of income to be £700m and the equilibrium rate of interest 5%. Assume that potential income is £780m.

Q1   If the government increases the money supply by £33m, what will be the change in the level of income and the interest rate? _____

_____

Q2   What would be the effect of a cut of £33m in the money supply?_____

_____

Q3   By how much would the money supply have to be increased in order to eliminate the output gap? (This may seem a difficult question but have another look at your answer to Question 1. Can you find the 'money multiplier'?) _____

_____

MONETARY POLICY WHEN THERE IS AN INFLATIONARY GAP

Assume that aggregate demand is equal to aggregate supply at potential output.

Q4   Suppose there is an increase in autonomous investment.

(a) This shifts the *IS* schedule inwards/outwards and the aggregate demand curve to the left/right.

(b) Draw *IS–LM* and *AD–AS* diagrams to show what happens to income, the rate of interest and the price level if the money supply (M^*) is constant.

(c) Draw *IS–LM* and *AD–AS* diagrams to show what happens to Y, r and P if the Central Bank keeps the real money supply constant.

(d) Now suppose, however, that the government anticipated the increase in aggregate demand. Can you think of any policies it could adopt in order to maintain $Y = Y_F$ with rising prices? Explain how such policies would work. _____

_____

_____

_____

_____

_____

_____

_____

Q 5 If nominal money supply is held constant when prices are rising, inflation is validated by monetary policy. T/F

Q 6 What causes the *AD* function to shift but leaves the slope unchanged? _____

_____

MONETARY VERSUS FISCAL POLICY

When we considered the effect of changes in autonomous expenditure and the money supply, resulting in shifts of the *AD*, *IS* and *LM* schedules, we have taken the behavioural parameters (i.e. b, c, d and e) as given. Changes in the exogenously determined variables shifted the *AD*, *IS* and *LM* schedules to right or to left but left the slopes of the curves unchanged. However, when we varied the tax rate (t), this did change the slope of the *IS* and *AD* curves. Now the effect of shifts in the *IS* and *LM* curves on the level of national income and the rate of interest is greater or smaller depending on the *slope* of these curves. In this next section we explore what determines the slopes of the *IS* and *LM* curves, and this will help us evaluate the effectiveness of fiscal and monetary policy.

THE SLOPE OF THE *IS* CURVE

Q 7   Write the equation for the *IS* function. _____

_____

(a)   Which parameters affect the slope? _____

_____

(b)   What is b? _____

_____ . When $b = -20$, what is the effect of a 1% fall in the rate of interest when the investment function is given by $I = a_1 + br$?

_____

(c)   The larger b is, the greater/smaller the increase in investment following a fall in r, and the greater/smaller the upward/downward shift of the aggregate expenditure function. Therefore, the larger b is, the steeper/flatter is the *IS* curve.

You should be able to work out the answer to the next question:

(d)   The larger the *MPC*, the steeper/flatter the *IS* curve.

THE SLOPE OF THE *LM* CURVE

Q 8   Write the equation of the *LM* function. _____

(a)   Which parameters affect the slope? _____

(b)   What is d? _____

_____

_____

(c)   When income rises by £10, what is the effect on the demand for money, assuming that r is unchanged? _____

(d)   The larger d is (r held constant), the steeper/flatter is the *LM* curve.

(e)   What is e? _____

_____

_____

(f)   The larger e is (Y held constant), the steeper/flatter is the *LM* curve.

(g)   We conclude that the *LM* curve will be flatter, the larger/smaller is d and the larger/smaller is e. The flatter the *LM* curve, the greater/smaller is the effect of a change in income on the rate of interest.

We are, of course, particularly interested in the effect of a change in the rate of interest on the level of income.

Q 9   When we use fiscal policy to eliminate an output gap, an injection of G raises/lowers income and raises/lowers the rate of interest. When we use monetary policy, increasing the money supply will raise/lower income and raise/lower the rate of interest. The change in the rate of interest following *the increase in G* means that government expenditure has _____ private expenditure.

Q 10   When the *LM* curve is perfectly elastic, the crowding-out effect will be 100%/positive but less than 100%/zero; and when the *LM* curve is perfectly inelastic, it will be 100%/positive but less than 100%/zero. The less elastic the *LM* curve, the greater/smaller the crowding-out effect of any expansionary fiscal policy.

We will now use the model set out at the beginning of the chapter to evaluate the effects of fiscal and monetary policy by making different assumptions about the values of the parameters b and e. We start by examining the effect of a given expansion through fiscal policy when we *vary the slope of the LM schedule.*

Q 11   We know from earlier exercises that when $c = 0.8$, $t = 0.25$, $b = -20$, $d = 0.3$, autonomous expenditure = 380 and the real money supply = 150, the equilibrium level of income is £700m and the rate of interest is 5%, *when $e = -12$.*

   (a)   Following an increase in G of £45m, find:

      (i) ΔY. _____

      (ii) Δr. _____

      (iii) ΔI. _____

      (iv)   Crowding-out. _____

   (b)   Now suppose that the value of e is -15. Would you expect an injection of G = £45m to result in a larger or smaller increase in income than when e was -12? _____

   (c)   Taking $e = -15$, find the equilibrium levels of Y and r for the initial situation when autonomous expenditure is £380m. _____

   (d)   Now check your prediction in (b) above and find ΔY, Δr, ΔI and crowding-out following an injection of G = £45m.

      (i) ΔY. _____

      (ii) Δr. _____

      (iii) ΔI. _____

      (iv)   Crowding-out. _____

Now take the case of a given increase in the money supply, *varying the slope of the IS curve.*

Q 12   When c, t, d, autonomous expenditure and M^*/P are as in Question 11, and $e = -12$ and $b = -20$, we know equilibrium Y = £700m and equilibrium r = 5%.

   (a)   When we increased the money supply by £33m in Question 1, we found the change in income to be £61m and the change in the rate of interest to be -1.22%. Find the change in the level of investment. _____

   (b)   Now let b equal -10. Would you expect a similar increase in the money supply to result in a larger or smaller change in income than before? _____
   _____

   (c)   With $b = -10$, find the equilibrium levels of Y and r. _____
   _____

   (d)   Now, once again, increase the money supply by £33m and check your prediction.

      (i) ΔY. _____

      (ii) Δr. _____

      (iii) ΔI. _____

Q 13   Assuming the *LM* curve to be neither perfectly interest-inelastic nor perfectly interest-elastic, and the *IS* curve to be perfectly interest-inelastic,

   (a)   Increasing the money supply would raise/lower/leave unchanged income and raise/lower/leave unchanged the rate of interest;

   (b)   Increasing autonomous expenditure would raise/lower income and raise/lower the rate of interest.

Q 14   If the *LM* curve is perfectly interest-elastic and the *IS* curve slopes downwards to the right, increasing autonomous expenditure will raise/lower/leave unchanged income, and raise/lower/leave unchanged the rate of interest. If the *LM* curve were perfectly interest-inelastic, an increase in autonomous expenditure would raise/lower/leave unchanged income and raise/lower/leave unchanged the rate of interest.

Q 15   Fiscal policy is more effective the more/less interest-elastic is the *LM* curve, whereas monetary policy is more effective the more/less elastic is the *IS* curve.

THE TRANSMISSION MECHANISM

The transmission mechanism is the means by which an excess demand for or supply of money affects the aggregate expenditure function. The classical quantity theory postulated a direct effect on the demand for new goods and services from a change in the money supply. Modern theories differ in that they predict that changes in the money stock primarily affect the bond market and not the commodity markets. However, fluctuations in the price of bonds will result in fluctuations in the rate of interest and these in turn will affect interest-sensitive expenditure.

Q 16   Suppose that building societies offer a new bond-share so that many people who normally keep their wealth in the form of cash decide to put some of it in building societies.
        The building societies would find that they were receiving so much money that they could reduce/increase the rate of interest which they offer. This would mean that other financial institutions could reduce/increase the rates of interest which they offer their investors, without running the risk of these investors all transferring their loans to building societies. Institutions would, in general, have more/less money to lend, and they would be able to (and have to) charge a higher/lower rate of interest to people or firms who borrow. This cheaper/dearer rate of interest would raise/lower the amount of physical investment done by firms, and this would (via the_____), increase/decrease aggregate demand.

Q 17   If the demand for money exceeds the supply of money, firms and households will seek to buy/sell bonds. As a result, bond prices will rise/fall and interest rates will rise/fall until _____
        _____

Q 18   Following a decrease in the money supply:
        (a) The demand for transaction balances rises/falls/remains the same.
        (b) Which means that there is more/less/the same money available for speculative purposes.
        (c) The price of bonds will rise/fall as people attempt to sell/buy bonds and this causes a rise/fall in the interest rate.
        (d) As a result, investment and such consumer expenditure as is interest-sensitive rises/falls and, through the action of _____,
             income will rise/fall.

Q 19   If the Bank of England indulges in open-market operations—buying bonds—what effect will this have on the level of income? _____

Q 20   If the price of bonds rises, what is the effect on aggregate demand? Rises/Falls

Q 21   Will there be any negative feedback? Yes/No. Explain in a line.
        _____

Q 22   Suppose, instead of a change in the money stock, there is a fall in the marginal propensity to save.

(a) At the existing level of income, saving will exceed/fall short of investment and income will rise/fall.

(b) As income changes, more/less money will be needed for transaction purposes with the result that more/less will be available for speculative purposes. (Remember, we assumed that the money supply is constant.)

(c) As a result, people will sell/buy bonds and the interest rate will rise/fall.

(d) The change in the interest rate will stimulate/discourage investment and stimulate/discourage saving and, thus, will encourage/check the expansion of output.

REGULATION OF THE MONEY SUPPLY

Q 23   How does the central bank alter the money supply? _____
_____

Q 24   What is the main difference between Treasury Bills and government bonds?
_____
_____

Q 25   'When the government borrows from the central bank, which does not undertake commercial transactions, it is equivalent to printing money.' T/F

Q 26   Assume that the Bank of England wishes to contract the money supply by £10m but the commercial banks do not wish to take up government bonds. How will the Bank achieve its purpose on the open market? (The cash ratio is 10%.)
_____

Q 27   In what circumstances will this not work? _____
_____

Q 28   When the Bank undertakes open-market operations and buys bonds, does it pay for these by creating new notes and coins? _____
_____

Q 29   (a)   If the government wishes short-term interest rates to rise, how might it achieve this by open-market operations? _____
_____

(b)   As a result of these open-market operations, the cash reserves of commercial banks will rise/fall and the money supply will expand/contract.

Q 30   The customer of a commercial bank in a many-bank system draws out £100 in cash and hoards it. By how much will *this* bank contract its lending? _____

Q 31   (a)   Suppose the cash-reserve ratio is 10% and banks currently have cash reserves of £12,500m. Complete the balance sheet below (assuming that all banks expand deposits to the legal limit and that there is no cash drain to the public).

Liabilities £m		Assets £m	
Deposits		Cash	12,500
		Other	

(b)   Now suppose the government raises the cash-reserve ratio to 12.5%. By how much must deposits contract in order to comply with the new ratio?

Liabilities £m		Assets £m	
Deposits		Cash	12,500
		Other	

(c) Suppose that instead of contracting deposit money, banks had been able to increase their reserves (as might be possible if the reserve assets do not comprise cash only). By how much would reserve assets have had to rise in order to comply with a reserve-asset ratio of 12.5%? _____

Q 32 Why did the change from a cash-reserve ratio to a reserve-asset ratio, as was the case in Britain from 1971 to 1981, mean that the Bank had less tight control over the money supply? _____

_____

_____

_____

_____

_____

On pages 697–9 Lipsey discusses current measures, introduced in 1981, for the control of the money supply. Make quite sure you understand the implications of setting a target (band) rate of interest, compared with a target money supply.

Q 33 Suppose that the current level of income is £700m, the money supply is £150m, and the demand-for-money function is given as $M_d = 0.3Y - 12r$.

(a) At what rate of interest will the money market be in equilibrium? _____

(b) Suppose that the Bank's target money supply is £120m. By how much must it increase the rate of interest in order to achieve this? _____

(c) How would it manage this? _____

In the previous chapter we noted that some components of expenditure may fluctuate, causing stabilization problems.

Q 34 What might cause the demand for money function to fluctuate? _____

_____

_____

_____

Q 35 Suppose that the Bank adopts a *target money supply* of £150m. The money market is currently in equilibrium as national income is £700m and the money-demand function is given by $M_d = 0.3Y - 12r$. Given this target money supply, find the effect on the rate of interest of the following:

(a) Income rises by £50m. _____

(b) d changes to 0.35. _____

(c) e changes to -10. _____

Q 36 Now suppose that the Bank adopts a *target rate of interest* of 5%. How would it achieve this target when faced with a fluctuating demand-for-money function as a result of the changes listed in (a), (b) and (c) of the previous question?

(a) _____

(b) _____

(c) _____

Q 37 When the Bank of England sets a target rate of interest, this will mean increasing/decreasing the money supply when income is rising and increasing/decreasing the money supply when income is falling, with the result that income fluctuations will be greater/smaller than would be the case if the money supply were fixed. In these circumstances the money supply is endogenous/exogenous.

Q 38 The theory of an exogenous money supply predicts that the behaviour of the commercial banks is asymmetric in the face of an expansionary and contractionary policy. What is this asymmetry? _____
_____
_____

Q 39 What money-market considerations might make commercial banks unwilling to lend to the maximum possible extent? _____
_____

Q 40 If there are unemployed resources, then an increase in the supply of money will result in output increasing/decreasing/remaining constant. If, however, all resources are fully employed, an increase in the money supply will result in output increasing/decreasing/remaining constant, and national income in current prices will rise/fall/be unchanged while national income in constant prices will rise/fall/be unchanged.

Q 41 Suppose that the economy is in equilibrium at full-employment level.
(a) This means that in the money market, _____ = _____ , and in the commodities market, _____ = _____ . Now suppose that, for some reason, people decide to save less.
(b) As the economy is at full employment, real output cannot meet the higher demand and consequently _____ .
(c) The demand for nominal/real money balances will decrease/increase/remain constant.
(d) The nominal money supply is unchanged, so the real money supply has risen/fallen/remained constant.
(e) The nominal demand for money is greater/less than the nominal supply of money.
(f) The excess demand for/supply of money means that people will buy/sell bonds, with the result that _____
(g) This will encourage/check interest-sensitive expenditure, so that aggregate expenditure will rise/fall and the inflationary gap will be enlarged/removed.
(h) If instead of holding the nominal supply of money constant (as assumed in (d) above), it were increased at the same rate as prices increased, then the real demand for money will exceed/fall short of/equal the real supply of money. As a result, interest rates would rise/fall/be unchanged, so that aggregate demand adjusts/is unchanged and the inflationary gap is eliminated/persists.

If you answered either (or both) of the last two questions wrongly you should re-read Lipsey, pages 684–6, again.

QUESTIONS FOR DISCUSSION

1 What is the object of the following actions of a central bank?
(a) Selling bonds in the open market
(b) Lowering the required reserve ratio
(c) Specifying that down-payments on instalment-plan buying may not be less than one-third of the item bought
(d) Exhorting commercial banks to give preference in lending to exporters.

How is each supposed to work?

2 On 11.11.78, *The Times* leader noted 'The growth in the size of the [building society]

movement, so that collectively it now accounts for more deposits than the clearing banks, has posed the question whether it is right that building societies should continue in effect to be left outside the normal controls exercised by the authorities over the rest of the financial system.'

(a) What were the 'normal controls' referred to in the leader and why might it suggest that building societies should be subject to them?

(b) Do you think there is any relationship between the rates of interest charged by commercial banks and building society rates?

(c) If, instead of using a cheque book, you were to open a building society deposit account, put your income in it and withdraw cash to pay your bills, and if all other bank users were to do likewise, what would be the total effect?

(d) According to Mr Robert G. Alexander, President of the Scottish Building Societies Association, building societies are 'safer than a bank' (quoted in *Glasgow Herald*, 19.3.71). What are building societies' assets? What are banks? How liquid is each? Comment on Mr Alexander's assertion.

3   The following is an extract from a report by Clifford German, published in the *Daily Telegraph*, 23.2.79:

'Pandemonium broke out in the new issue office of the Bank of England yesterday morning as hundreds of messengers struggled to get last minute applications for the two new Government stocks across the counter before the deadline at one minute past ten.

'Between 30 and 40 applicants with orders for up to £1,000 million worth of stock were turned away when bank officials closed the counter.

'The two new stocks—£500 million worth of Exchequer $13\frac{1}{4}$ p.c. 1987 and £800 million worth of Treasury $13\frac{3}{4}$ p.c. 2,000 to 2,003—were oversubscribed almost 10 times.'

On 11.3.79, John Davis in the *Observer* reported that the stocks were selling at premiums of £$10\frac{5}{8}$ and £$13\frac{5}{8}$ respectively and he commented:

'The premiums are unprecedented in the history of gilt-edged issues. It means that the Government, assisted by the Bank of England, has effectively given away £164 million.'

(a) Explain what went wrong and what Davis means when he says that the government has given away £164 million. Who were the beneficiaries of this gift and who pays for it?

(b) Can you suggest how such a situation might be prevented from recurring? (*Hint*: can a seller set both price and quantity?)

4   In April 1965, the Bank of England told the commercial banks that they would have to pay in to their accounts 'special deposits' which have the effect of increasing their reserves by £90 million. The next day, the headline in the *Guardian* read, 'Banks' ability to make loans cut by £90 million'. What do you think of this? Suppose the banks raised all the money for their special deposits by restricting loans? Suppose, on the other hand, all they did was to sell government bonds in their possession, the price of which the Treasury was committed to keep fairly steady?

5   The following is an extract from Peter Riddell's report in the *Financial Times* (30.3.79). The Governor of the Bank of England, giving evidence to the Wilson Committee, said that the 'corset scheme was devised because the Bank thought "rather than restrict lending directly it was better to go for the point where the expansion was taking place fastest. We thought also it would be less constricting in the management of portfolios than would a direct control on lending."

'He admitted that the corset inhibited competition and diverted business into possibly less efficient channels. "It is probably true of this and any other direct control that with time it becomes less effective in achieving its purpose, as ways round it develop—in a fairly sophisticated financial system this is inevitable—and at the same time its costs in terms of distortions of the system increases".'

(a) What do you think the Governor meant by 'direct control on lending'? Why should the corset 'go to the point where the expansion was taking place fastest'?

(b) What sort of competition might be inhibited by the corset and what business might be diverted?

6   '[The Chancellor's] first difficulty is to decide which money supply he is trying to control. Official policy—set out in last March's financial statement, is to consider a "range of indicators". Broad money (M3) and narrow (M1) both convey useful information on the tightness of policy, as does the exchange rate, the financial statement said.

'[The Chancellor's] problem is that all three of these measures are now sending out disrupted signals. M1, notes and coin plus bank sight deposits, is increasingly meaningless as the non-bank sector starts its own sight deposits. (One such is the Abbey National's new interest-bearing current account). New banking techniques will increasingly distort M1, until—as has happened in the US—it is abandoned.

'As for M3, the wider measure which includes bank deposit accounts, the monetarists themselves are now having grave doubts as to whether it should be screwed down. Tim Congden, monetarist high priest of Messel's the stockbrokers, . . . [said] "Money, as measured by M3 may increase by more than the underlying growth of productive capacity without generating inflationary pressures."

'As for the exchange rate . . . no one in the market now believes that the pound's weakness reflects too much laxity in [the Chancellor's] domestic money supply policy.' (David Lipsey, *Sunday Times*, 6.3.83.)

(a) Why do you think that the exchange rate is included as an indicator of the tightness of monetary policy?

(b) Explain why new developments in the bank and non-bank sectors may result in M1 becoming useless as a measure of the money supply.

(c) How would you explain Tim Congden's statement about the M3 measure?

7   Extract from an article by Malcolm Crawford in the *Sunday Times* (15.10.78):

' . . . depending on how the banking figures for this month turn out . . . a continuation of the present M3 targets—8% to 12% growth through the year—could be shown as a tightening. The money supply figures out next week will show an annual rate of increase in the first five months (since April) of about 5%. The figures for October could well show the rise over six months at the bottom end of the target range ($8\frac{1}{2}$% per annum since April), or even a shade below.

'Equally, however, the money supply for the first six months could be about 10% per annum up on April. Despite the small increase in money to last month, this could easily happen, for gilt sales are not going well, so the Government is presumably borrowing from the banking system . . . . In that event I expect the target figures for the year ahead to be lowered.

'A further tightening in the money supply . . . would be bad news for business generally. Profits are already being squeezed . . . . With the wage bill in the private sector rising at about 14% per annum, even a 10% growth of M3 (the middle of the present target range) looks pretty tight.'

(a) If the money supply is growing at 8 to 12%, how can this be a tightening of the supply?

(b) If the government is borrowing from the banking system, as Crawford suggests, what effect would this have on the money supply?

(c) If gilt sales had been going well, would the implications for the money supply have been different?

8   Letter from Professor D. Wood to the *Financial Times* (3.3.83):

' . . . the medium-term economic strategy cash limits, control of public-sector borrowing requirements and money supply control were justified not for their own sake but for their claimed effectiveness in improving the performance of the UK's real economy.

'The evidence for this transmission process was extremely patchy, but the experiment was undertaken.'

What is the 'transmission process' to which Professor Wood refers?

9   Consider the following two extracts concerning the money supply and the velocity of circulation (but read the Appendix to Chapter 44 first):

'. . . an increase of about $10\frac{1}{2}$ per cent [in nominal national income] was anticipated for last year, with real output going up to about $1\frac{1}{2}$ per cent and the remainder being dissipated in inflation. In the event, prices rose less but so, unfortunately, did output which increased by only $\frac{1}{2}$ per cent. Thus the rise in expenditure was not on quite the expected scale, but the money stock, as measured by £M3, did rise by about $10\frac{1}{2}$ per cent which was within its target range. The inference is, of course, that the money supply is being used less actively. This is not a new development. The velocity of circulation of £M3 — that is to say, the ratio of nominal GNP to £M3 — had already fallen from 3.80 in the second quarter of 1980 to 3.17 in the last quarter of 1981 and must now be still closer to 3.0.' (Letter from Professor T. Wilson to the *Financial Times*, 9.3.83.)

'The monetary growth targets of 7 to 11 per cent for three different aggregates accord with the predicted 8 per cent growth in the nominal national income (Money GDP) provided that velocity continues to fall slightly. This would be likely if interest rates and inflation were to fall, but at least a temporary upward surge is officially expected in inflation and the possible effects of the oil market on sterling, together with the effects of the huge US budget deficit on world interest rates, should make one very cautious on the interest-rate front. Velocity is as likely to rise as to fall further.' (S. Brittan, *Financial Times*, 17.3.83.)

(a)   What is 'nominal national income'?
(b)   Why does the velocity of circulation vary?
(c)   If velocity varies, what problems does this pose for the government in its monetary policy?

Appendix to Chapter 44; The Classical Quantity Theory of Money

Q 1   'Whatever my expenditure, I only keep the same amount of cash, and the same level of my current account. I never like to "feel short of money".' This statement is/is not consistent with the transactions-demand assumption used by the quantity theory.

Q 2   If the individual speaking in the previous question were given £100, might he spend it all on goods? Yes/No. Would the relationship between this individual's expenditure and his level of cash and current account be the same in the two time-periods both when he was spending his £100 and when he had spent it, and was back to his old level of expenditure? Yes/No

Q 3   In the quantity theory of money, $M_d =$ _____

Q 4   Is the money supply endogenous or exogenous in the quantity theory? _____

Q 5   What is meant by the velocity of circulation (V)? _____
_____

Q 6   What relation does V bear to k?_____

How do we explain this relationship? Well, consider what would happen if k were half its present level. This would mean, for example, that the amount of money in your wallet would be half what it actually is at the moment. But you are still going to make the same purchases, so the average length of stay in your wallet of the pounds in it would halve. Each pound note (on average) would 'move on' twice as quickly, which means that velocity would be double.

Q 7   Suppose that $V = 4$, $Y_F = £100$m and $P = 1$.

(a)   Find the equilibrium money supply. _____

(b)   If the government buys bonds from the public to the value of £1m and if the banks expand to the limit (assume the cash ratio is 10%), what happens to P?

    _____

(c)   What is the value of GDP in current prices? _____

(d)   What is the value of GDP in real terms? _____

Q 8   The quantity theory predicts that increasing the money supply when there is an inflationary gap raises the real/money value of GDP through changes in _____ _____, and that increasing the money supply when there is an output gap raises the real/money value of GDP through changes in _____

CHAPTER 45

Macro Policy in an Open Economy

Q 1   What was the Bretton Woods system? _____
_____
_____

Q 2   Under Bretton Woods, countries fixed the number of dollars which were equivalent to a unit of their currency. This meant that the USA could/could not independently fix the value of dollars in terms of other currencies.

Q 3   How did the IMF intend to achieve one of its objectives, that of preventing competitive devaluation? _____
_____

Q 4   Two of the three major problems of the Bretton Woods system were:

(1)   Handling speculative crises.

(2)   Providing sufficient reserves to iron out short-term fluctuations in receipts and payments.

What was the third?

(3)   _____
_____

Q 5   Given the cost of production, upon what does the supply of new gold depend?
_____

Q 6   Upon what does the supply of new *monetary* gold depend? _____
_____ and _____

Q 7   What does SDR stand for, and what are they? _____
_____
_____

Q 8   If aggregate world demand is insufficient for world full employment, what will be the effect on other countries if one country manages to increase its exports and employment?_____

Q 9   Assume that the exchange rate is fixed and suppose that the inflation rate in this country is higher than in the United States. This means that there will be pressure to devalue/revalue the pound. In order to maintain the current exchange rate, the Bank must buy/sell pounds and buy/sell dollars, which means that its foreign-exchange reserves are rising/falling and the money supply is increasing/decreasing. If the inflation rate continues to exceed that in the United States, pressure to devalue/revalue will continue and any expectations of a change in the exchange rate will bring about large capital inflows/outflows.

Q 10   If a country found itself in the situation described in the previous question, what short-run strategy could it adopt in an attempt to check capital flows?

_____

_____

Q 11   What other strategies are open to this country? _____

_____

_____

_____

Q 12   When the world went over to flexible exchange rates, it was predicted that this would reduce/increase the need for international liquidity, or reserves. Instead of meeting the problem of long-run disequilibria by delayed and politically difficult _____ revisions, difficult domestic price changes or protectionism, a free market would make gradual _____ adjustments.

Q 13   Objections to flexible rates are that such a system will increase the _____ faced by exporters and importers and will thus _____ trade and lead to _____ speculation. Such speculation in the face of a depreciating exchange rate could lead to a decrease/increase rather than an increase/decrease in the quantity of that currency demanded, and to an increase/decrease rather than a decrease/increase in the quantity supplied. Under such circumstances, the price of this currency would _____ further.

Q 14   Destabilizing speculation occurs under which of the following conditions?

(a)   Lower exchange rates increase the quantity of a currency demanded.
(b)   Higher exchange rates increase the quantity of a currency supplied.
(c)   There is no expectation that fixed exchange rates will be changed.
(d)   A change in exchange rates leads to expectation of further changes in the same direction.

Q 15   Those who claim that a system of flexible exchange rates leads to more uncertainty sometimes ignore the existence of an important institution by means of which this risk can be avoided. This is the _____ market, by means of which it is possible to buy now at a known price currency which will be needed for future settlements.

Q 16   In order to reduce any destabilizing effects, the current system of exchange rates is a _____ system.

INFLATION AND THE PURCHASING-POWER-PARITY EXCHANGE RATE

Q 17   Suppose that the current exchange rate is DM4.00 = £1.00. British cars are priced at £5,000 for export while German cars are sold at DM20,000. Find the relative price ratio in pounds sterling.

Q 18   Now suppose that inflation is running at 5% p.a. in both countries and that this is fully reflected in export prices.

(a)   UK car prices will rise to £ _____ , while German car prices will rise to DM_____

(b)   What is the relative price ratio in pounds sterling? _____

(c)   Has the purchasing-power-parity exchange rate changed? _____

Q 19   What if inflation had been 12% in the UK and 4% in Germany, instead of 5%?

(a)   UK car prices rise to £_____

(b)   German car prices rise to DM_____

(c)   What is the relative price ratio now? _____

(d) By how much must the exchange rate change in order to maintain purchasing-power parity? _____

_____

MACROECONOMIC POLICY AND THE CURRENT ACCOUNT

Q 20 Write out the model, including a foreign sector, which will enable you to derive the *IS* and *LM* curves. Remember to specify the appropriate restrictions on the behavioural parameters and the autonomous variables.

_____
_____
_____
_____
_____
_____
_____
_____
_____
_____
_____
_____
_____

Q 21 What is the equation of the *IS* curve? _____

Q 22 What is the equation of the net export function? _____

Q 23 You are given the following information about an economy:

$c = 0.8$; $t = 0.3$; $b = -10$; $m = 0.06$; $d = 0.3$; $e = -12$.
$a_0 = 0$; $a_1 = 250$; $G = 300$; $X = 50$; $M^* = 180$; $P = 1$.

Assuming that the government wishes to achieve full employment and a balanced current account, what problems (if any) does the government face, knowing that potential output is at £1,036m? _____

_____

Q 24 What would happen to the following if the government were to raise government expenditure by £27m?

(a) Income _____

(b) Rate of interest _____

(c) Current account _____

(d) Budget _____

Q 25 Suppose that instead of increasing expenditure, the government were to increase the money supply by £32.4m?

(a) Income _____

(b) Rate of interest _____

(c) Current account _____

(d) Budget _____

Q 26 Suppose that the government combined fiscal and monetary policy, increasing government expenditure by £18m and the money supply by £10.8m?

(a) Income _____

(b) Rate of interest _____

(c) Current account _____

(d) Budget _____

Q 27 As a final alternative, what would happen if the government introduced import quotas so that imports could not exceed £50m and, at the same time, raised the money supply by £10.8m?

(a) Income _____

(b) Rate of interest _____

(c) Current account _____

(d) Budget _____

Q 28 Which of the above policies were:

(a) Expenditure-changing policies? _____
_____

(b) Expenditure-switching policies? _____

MACROECONOMIC POLICY AND THE CAPITAL ACCOUNT

So far we have considered that trade with the foreign sector has been limited to goods and services, but we must now also consider that there is trade in assets—that is to say there are international, as well as national, financial markets. International capital markets are remarkably closely integrated and capital moves rapidly from one country to another following a change in the rate of interest or the rate of exchange.

Q 29 When exchange rates are fixed and when inflation rates differ between countries, countries with lower inflation rates will eventually have to revalue/devalue their currency. Speculators will perceive the opportunity to make large gains and such countries will find that their balance of payments is in deficit/surplus and their money supply decreasing/increasing. Such destabilizing capital flows were behind the change in 1973 to a system of _____ which has been adopted in preference to a system where exchange rates are fully flexible in order to even out short-run/long-run fluctuations in exchange rates.

If foreign capital is *very* interest-elastic, a small fall in the UK rate of interest, relative to foreign rates, will mean that there will be large outflows of capital. If the UK rate is higher than that of the rest of the world, this will attract large inflows of foreign capital. In other words, a very small change in one country's rate of interest relative to other rates would bring large movements of capital. If capital is *perfectly* interest-elastic, a small change results in unlimited flows of capital.

Q 30 Under a system of dirty floating, suppose that sterling comes under pressure because there is a deficit on the current account. In the short run the Bank can maintain the rate of exchange by buying/selling sterling and buying/selling foreign currency. This would mean that foreign-currency reserves will be increasing/falling and the money supply is rising/falling. Maintenance of a stable money supply would necessitate open-market sales/purchases of domestic bonds—a procedure called _____

_____

Demand management with a fixed exchange rate

Unless otherwise stated, you should assume that we start with the balance of payments in equilibrium and the UK rate of interest in line with world rates.

Q 31 A decrease in government expenditure would shift the *IS* curve outwards/inwards and the higher/lower income would mean that imports rise/fall so that the current account moves into, or towards, deficit/surplus. The contractionary fiscal policy has raised/

lowered the rate of interest, which causes capital to flow in/out and brings the capital account into deficit/surplus. When capital is very interest-elastic, these flows will reinforce/offset the current-account deficit/surplus, so that a balance-of-payments deficit/surplus will result. The exchange rate will come under pressure and in order to maintain the current rate, the Bank will have to sell/buy sterling. This increases/reduces the money supply, shifting the *LM* curve upwards/downwards. When capital is perfectly interest-elastic, a new equilibrium will be established at a higher/the original/a lower interest rate.

Q 32   An expansionary monetary policy raises income, moving the current account into deficit/surplus and lowering the interest rate, with the result that _____ _____ . In order to maintain the existing exchange rate, the Bank must buy/sell foreign currency, thus increasing/decreasing the money supply. This reinforces/reverses the increase brought about by the initial expansion of the money supply. If the Bank does not undertake sterilization operations, the outcome will mean that income _____ and the rate of interest _____

    _____

Q 33   Suppose that following a persistent deficit on the current account the exchange rate is changed, that is to say sterling is revalued/devalued. Exports will be dearer/cheaper and imports will be dearer/cheaper, so that the *IS* curve shifts inwards/outwards and the current account has deteriorated/improved. The interest rate has fallen/risen and the capital account moves into deficit/surplus. The inflow/outflow of foreign currency lowers/raises the money supply and the new equilibrium will be at a higher/lower income and, assuming perfectly interest-elastic capital flows, at a higher/the initial/a lower rate of interest.

Demand management with a flexible exchange rate

We make the same assumptions as before about the balance of payments and the UK rate of interest.

Q 34   An expansionary fiscal policy shifts the *IS* curve inwards/outwards, bringing the current account into deficit/surplus and causing sterling to appreciate/depreciate. However, the capital account is moving into deficit/surplus as the lower/higher rate of interest induces capital inflows/outflows and causing the £ to depreciate/appreciate. If the net outcome is an appreciation of sterling, this will discourage/encourage exports and shift the *IS* curve inwards/outwards. Given an expansionary/contractionary monetary policy, a new equilibrium can be achieved where income is _____ _____ and the rate of interest is _____

    _____

Q 35   A contractionary monetary policy shifts the *LM* curve to the left/right so that interest rates rise/fall, which induces an outflow/inflow of capital. The current-account deficit/surplus—resulting from the changed income level—will be reduced as sterling appreciates/depreciates, shifting the *IS* curve inwards/outwards. With the UK interest rate above world rates, the £ will _____ until foreign investors expect that the new rate will not be sustained. Such capital flows reinforce/offset the government monetary policy and may cause sterling to be overvalued/undervalued.

Q 36   An increase in world demand, as world incomes rise, will cause the *IS* curve to shift inwards/outwards. If the money supply is held constant, interest rates will rise. The balance-of-payments deficit/surplus will cause sterling to depreciate/appreciate, which means that exports will become cheaper/dearer and imports cheaper/dearer, so that the *IS* curve shifts inwards/outwards and the levels of income and the rate of interest are

_____

QUESTIONS FOR DISCUSSION

1   Consider two countries, active in international trade. The economy of the first contains many independent firms, producing a wide range of different exports, from raw materials to complex manufactures. The second contains a few large firms, linked together and with the government, producing a very small range of tradeable products. The first, under a fixed-exchange-rate system, will, *ceteris paribus*, require less foreign exchange than the second. Why?

2   In March 1983, after lengthy discussions, members of the European Monetary System realigned their currencies—some revaluing their currencies and others devaluing. On 24.3.83, S. Brittan wrote in the *Financial Times* as follows:

'Under the latest currency realignments, the European Monetary System becomes in effect a crawling peg. There has been no harmonisation of underlying inflation rates or of economic policy inside the Community. Thus exchange-rate changes are inevitable. The EMS is simply a way by which the parity changes are made in a series of steps by governments, instead of continuously in the market place.

'The pros and cons of making exchange-rate changes this way are much less important than many people think. But if there is to be a European crawling peg, it might be less disruptive to the foreign-exchange market if the changes were smaller and more frequent.'

(a)   Why are there exchange-rate changes if there is 'no harmonisation of inflation rates'?
(b)   Why does Brittan argue that the EMS has become a 'crawling peg'?
(c)   What are the pros and cons of 'crawling peg' versus flexible exchange rates?

3   What is the difference between expenditure-changing and expenditure-switching policies?

4   Speculation in the stock market is not always destabilizing. Why is this speculation different, in respect of risks borne, from currency speculation under a regime of fixed exchange rates? (*Hint*: in the stock market, except in an established bull or bear market, prices of stocks can easily go up or down. In a fixed-exchange-rate regime, how often is there this sort of uncertainty about the likely direction of changes?)

5   'Sweden's Scandinavian neighbours reacted bitterly yesterday to the decision by the new Stockholm Government to devalue the Krona by 16 per cent. Finland was forced to follow suit by devaluing the Markka for the second time in less than a week, this time by 6 per cent.

'Norway said it would not devalue but it expected to decide today on other measures to protect the competitiveness of its industry. Sweden was exporting its problems, Norwegian ministers said.' (Report in the *Financial Times*, 11.10.82.)

(a)   What did the Norwegian ministers mean when they said that 'Sweden was exporting its problems'?
(b)   Why was Finland forced to devalue again in such a short time when Norway did not? Can you suggest any reasons?

6   A British trade union policy paper of February 1975 read:

'A reasonable objective would be to cut our current trade deficit by £1,000m. Some growth in exports is likely and 3% more in real terms (a very modest goal) would provide an extra £500m. So we would need to reduce imports by £500m (at 1974 prices) to reduce the deficit by £1,000m.

'Until North Sea oil comes on stream, fuel imports cannot be affected more than marginally. Nor is there much to be gained in the short-term by cutting back on food, raw materials or semi-manufactured goods. In general these are essential for consumption or industry.

'The burden must fall chiefly on manufactured goods, which provide about one quarter of all imports. This is also the sector in which unemployment is most prone to occur domestically.

'It makes eminent political and industrial sense to protect British jobs in such industries as motors, electrical consumer durables and telecommunications. In 1974, car imports from West Germany, France and Japan alone contributed £240m to our trade deficit, while textiles and yarns from the EEC contributed £256m.'

Retaliation was not expected: 'After all, the alternative to controls is deflation, which hits the rest of the world as much.'

The *Sunday Times* (9.2.75) reported, however, that the 'second permanent secretary at the Department of Industry warned that import controls would be against the rules of GATT, and could lead to trouble with our EEC partners'.

Discuss this; are there no alternatives to protection or deflation?

7   On 20.3.79 Peter Riddell reported in the *Financial Times*:

'[That there appeared to be] concern about a growing conflict between the strength of the pound and other economic policy objectives . . . . [There was] increasing official discomfort about the possible impact of inflows on domestic monetary control and of an appreciation in the rate of the already weak competitive position of British goods.

'At the same time a stable exchange rate has been seen by both Mr Denis Healey, the Chancellor, and by Mr Gordon Richardson, the Governor of the Bank, as an important weapon in the battle against inflation.'

(a)   What are the 'other economic policy objectives' to which Peter Riddell alludes?
(b)   In what ways does a strong pound help or hinder the achievement of such objectives?

8   The following are extracts from Mr P. Fletcher's letter to the *Financial Times* (23.3.79):

'I wonder at what level of minimum lending rate the pound would cease to be so absurdly strong and would fall to a level at which our exports would once again become competitive? If we could determine this we might also discover how much support the pound is really receiving from North Sea oil, which along with high interest rates appears to be the main prop to the pound.

'In a properly managed economy interest rates should be geared to optimize investment at home and export performance abroad. These are the foundations for a genuinely strong currency. It is also what reducing unemployment is about rather than tinkering with job creation schemes and subsidies.'

(a)   What are the goals and the policy instruments outlined in these extracts?
(b)   Do you agree with Mr Fletcher that it would be possible to achieve all goals simultaneously if we could find the appropriate interest rate?

9   '. . if you run an import-prone economy, like Britain's, you simply dare not get out of line on competitiveness. When you have done whatever can be done by increasing efficiency and moderating wage settlements, there is no other option but to allow the exchange rate to decline to absorb any residual loss of competitiveness.' (David Lipsey, *Sunday Times*, 19.12.82.)

'How far devaluation helps to maintain employment and how far it is just frittered away depends crucially on the wage response. A successful devaluation is a way of reducing real wages below what they would otherwise be, just as putting the clock forward is a convenient way of making us all get up a little earlier.' (Sam Brittan, *Financial Times*, 24.3.83.)

Why do both writers stress wage settlements when talking about devaluation? How does devaluation reduce real wages?

10   According to the *Guardian* (29.3.79) Malaysia 'is fast becoming one of the richest [countries] in South-East Asia', '. . . Malaysia is the world's leading producer of rubber, palm oil, hardwood, cocoa, and pepper, with large resources of petroleum and natural gas.', '. . . Malaysia last year registered its third trade surplus in excess of $3 billion [despite] the fact

that for the greater part of the year, surplus showed an alarming downward trend. This situation is a reflection of the vulnerability of Malaysia's open economy, which is heavily dependent on exports. About 75 per cent of the exports are made up of primary raw materials . . . . This means that in times of recession export earnings are drastically trimmed by the sharp drop in demand by Malaysia's main trading partners, particularly Japan, United States, and the EEC countries.'

Trace out the effect on the Malaysian economy of:

(a) recession in the US and EEC economies;
(b) decline of the US dollar;
(c) appreciation of foreign currencies against the ringgit (Malaysian dollar).

What policies would you recommend to the Malaysian Government in order to make the economy less vulnerable to recession in other parts of the world?

CHAPTER 46

Employment and Unemployment

So far we have examined how the government can eliminate unemployment when actual income falls short of potential income, but we have not examined the different kinds of unemployment which can occur.

Q 1   At potential output, Y_F, is there any unemployment? _____

Q 2   If unemployment can be eradicated by expansionary fiscal and monetary policy, what sort of unemployment are we talking about? _____

Q 3   What other categories of unemployment does Lipsey discuss? _____
_____

Q 4   In 1942, while in the Treasury, Keynes wrote a Memorandum in which he classified unemployment as follows:[1]

   (a)   the hard core of the virtually unemployable;
   (b)   seasonal factors;
   (c)   men moving between jobs;
   (d)   misfits of trade or locality due to lack of mobility;
   (e)   a deficiency in the aggregate effective demand for labour.

   Are these categories the same as the ones used by Lipsey?

   _____
   _____
   _____

Q 5   If labour were homogeneous, perfectly informed and mobile, would there be any structural and frictional unemployment? _____
_____

Q 6   Why is the UV curve in Lipsey's Fig. 46.1 hyperbolic and not a straight line?

   _____
   _____
   _____
   _____
   _____
   _____

   If unemployment is made up of demand-deficient unemployment (D), structural unemployment (S) and frictional unemployment (F), total unemployment (U) is given by

$$U = D + S + F$$

Q 7   On page 727 Lipsey suggests that one measure of the number of demand-deficient

---

[1] See R. Kahn, 'Unemployment as seen by the Keynesians' in G.D.N. Worswick (ed.), *The Concept and Measurement of Involuntary Unemployment* (George Allen & Unwin, 1976).

unemployed is 'the difference between the number of persons seeking jobs and the number of unfilled job vacancies'. We could write this as

$$D = U - V$$

$$\text{or } D = U - S - F$$

(a) When the number of unemployed exceed the number of vacancies, using this measure, $S + F =$ _____

(b) If the number of vacancies is equal to or greater than the number of unemployed, $S + F =$ _____

Q 8   Use this measure to find demand-deficient unemployment and structural plus frictional unemployment from Fig. 1 below.

	D	S + F
(i) At point A on UV curve:	_____	_____
(ii) At point B	_____	_____
(iii) At point C	_____	_____
(iv) At point D	_____	_____

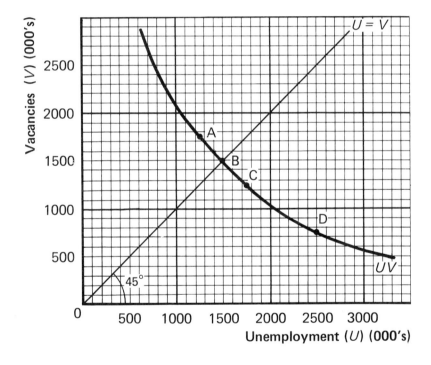

Fig. 1

Q 9   Using this measure, it would seem that structural and frictional unemployment is higher/lower when the economy is in recession and rises/falls as aggregate demand picks up.

It can be seen from this, that the measure we have just used is not satisfactory and Lipsey advances an alternative measure on page 728. The new measure requires that we make an *estimate* of frictional and structural unemployment—we will call this U^*. Demand-deficient unemployment is now measured by subtracting U^* from total unemployment.

Q 10   When vacancies exceed unemployment, structural and frictional unemployment is equal to _____

Q 11   Use the new measure to separate out the different types of unemployment from Fig. 1.

		D	$S + F$
(i)	At point A	_____	_____
(ii)	At point B	_____	_____
(iii)	At point C	_____	_____
(iv)	At point D	_____	_____

Q 12   If structural unemployment increases, how would we show this on Fig. 1.?

_____

Q 13   What effect on the UV curve might an increase in the unemployment benefit have?

_____
_____
_____

The second measure discussed by Lipsey avoids the undesirable property of the first one, but we are faced with the problem of how to estimate the level of structural and frictional unemployment.

Q 14   How can too high an average real wage result in a rise in unemployment in the short run? _____

_____

Q 15   How could this effect be shown on Fig. 1? _____

_____

Q 16   What do we mean when we talk about 'putty-clay' capital? _____

_____
_____

Q 17   What do you think 'putty-putty' capital is? _____

_____
_____

Q 18   Draw a diagram to illustrate what the isoquants look like when we have 'putty-putty' capital.

Q 19   Now draw one for the case of 'putty-clay' capital.

Q 20   With the putty-clay case, what is the marginal product of labour? _____

_____
_____

Q 21   In Chapter 25 you learned that the firm's demand for labour is its _____
_____ of labour and that the demand curve for labour sloped
upward to the right/downward to the right.

Q 22   What will the firm's demand curve for labour look like in the case of putty-clay
capital? _____
_____

Q 23   How do we represent on Fig. 1 a rise in unemployment due to the long-run effect of
too high an average wage? _____
_____

QUESTIONS FOR DISCUSSION

1   The provisional unemployment figures for February 1983 showed considerable
regional variation. The rate of the UK was 13.7% but in the south-east the unemployment rate
was 10%. The highest rate was in Northern Ireland where it was 20.6% but the northern region
and Wales were both over 17%. Within the West Midlands, unemployment rates varied from
16.1% in Coventry to 20.6% in Telford. Why do you think there were such variations? Outline
the main causes of unemployment in the region in which you live.

2   If there are regional differences in unemployment rates, what problems may arise if
demand-management policies are used to reflate the economy?

3   The following extract was taken from 'City Comment' in the *Daily Telegraph*
(21.2.79):

'For the second month running the underlying level of unemployment has risen sharply.
. . . Seasonally adjusted the number of unemployed registered in Great Britain, excluding
school leavers, has risen 21,900 this month to 1,302,000. School leavers continued to find
jobs and before seasonal adjustment total unemployment in Great Britain fell 3,459 to
1,387,761. The 36,723 school leavers still left on the register are nearly 7,000 less than this
time last year.
'The trend nevertheless is not encouraging. Nor, unlike last month, is there any relief in the
figures for vacancies. Vacancies notified to employment offices were 4,800 lower, seasonally
adjusted, though they remain 43,900 higher than a year ago.
'Faced with such disagreeable electoral fear the Government has reacted predictably.
Yesterday it announced new subsidies.'

(a)   Why are seasonal adjustments made to unemployment and vacancies figures?
(b)   The subsidies mentioned were employment subsidies. Trace out the possible effects
       of such subsidies on unemployment figures. (Be sure to start at the level of the firm.)
(c)   Will such subsidies have any effect on the level of national income?

4   The following is an extract from a letter from Mr Robert A. Paterson published in *The Times* (9.9.78):

'The traditional methods (of clearing the problem of unemployment) have all been tried by most modern politicians without any great success. Would it be too naive to put forward a simple solution which would help cure unemployment and at the same time help to solve the other curse of modern society – the no-tax cash payment?

'If one was allowed to employ one person as a first charge out of one's gross income this would help. At the same time if the tax bands were lowered at the lower end, the incentive to work would be given and a new group of future employers would emerge.

'The new executive class would then be able to afford gardeners, chauffeurs, etc. and the relevant "moonlighting" would be left within the tax structure thus giving work and extra net income to those who want to work but who would have been put off by the higher rate bands of taxation.'

What do you think of Mr Paterson's proposal?

5   Blake Leslie wrote to the *Birmingham Post* on 2.3.83 as follows:

'During the water workers' dispute the phrase "the earnings league" was used *ad nauseam*.

'Whoever first coined this expression as a justification for another wage increase has surely done incalculable harm over the years to British industry by encouraging competitive demands for no other reason than to be one up on one's fellows.

'But the field of comparison, football, is indeed ironic, for it is in almost as parlous a condition as is, alas, so much industry.

'Constant rivalry for rises will neither score goals nor achieve promotion only relegation, and in the end put more firms out of business. There will be no point in being top of the league then.'

Is Mr Leslie's letter about relative wages or about the average real wage?

6   In the House of Commons on 18.3.83, Mr Arthur Bottomley said that 'low pay caused great sacrifice and was a nationwide problem. The Government's philosophy was job creation through low pay, but this did not work.

'Low wages, as well as being a cause of poverty, hardship and injustice, were also the cause of gross economic inefficiency. Whole industries had come to rely on low wages as a way of life. As a result there was high staff turn-over, low productivity, and little incentive to invest in training.

'The main cause of unemployment in Britain today, as most people now recognized, was the low level of demand. A minimum wage would raise the living standards and therefore spending power of the poorest workers and provide a stimulus for jobs.' (*The Times*, 19.3.83.)

Evaluate Mr Bottomley's argument.

7   'There are many areas, from gardening to retailing, where the labour to capital ratio changes quickly in response to labour and capital costs. But there is much long-lived equipment that cannot easily shift to new production methods.

'The moral is that the main influences of real wages on employment are long term.' (Sam Brittan, *Financial Times*, 16.9.82.)

Explain why the effects of changes in real wages are experienced in the long, rather than short, term.

8   '. . . this year's Budget [will] raise tax thresholds and child allowances, aiming to disarm the poverty traps which subject people on low incomes to high marginal tax rates (thought to deter them from seeking work).

'But the high and still rising unemployment level shows that encouraging people to enter the labour market should scarcely be the top priority; the main problem of that market just now is a deficiency of demand. In this context it is not surprising that industrial lobbyists have been clamouring for abolition of the National Insurance Surcharge, which is a flat-rate tax on the hiring of additional workers.

'Arguments against the abolition (or even reduction) of the NIS have hinged on the idea that an income-tax cut would be more effective as an instrument of reflation.' (Jeremy Stone, *Financial Times*, 14.3.83.)

Evaluate the argument for abolition of the National Insurance Surcharge against the case for an income-tax cut. Are both tax cuts examples of demand management?

CHAPTER 47

Closure Version 2: a Core-augmented Phillips Curve and Inflation

Q 1   The rate of inflation can be decomposed into three separate components:

(a)   _____

(b)   _____

(c)   _____

Q 2   If the short-run Phillips curve is given by the curve H_1 in Fig. 1 below,

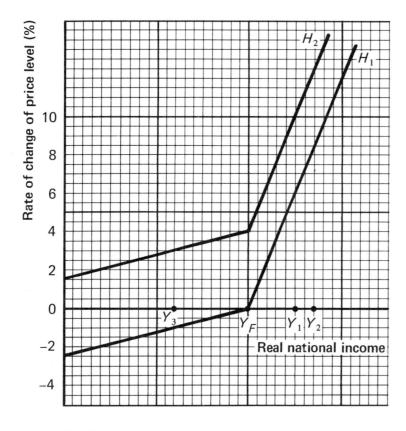

Fig. 1

(a)   when $Y = Y_1$ and the inflation rate is 6%, find

(i)   demand inflation
(ii)   core inflation

(b) when $Y = Y_2$ and the inflation rate is 9%, find

    (i) demand inflation
    (ii) core inflation
    (iii) shock inflation

(c) when $Y = Y_3$ and the inflation rate is 1%, find

    (i) demand inflation
    (ii) core inflation
    (iii) shock inflation

Q 3   If the short-run Phillips curve is given by the curve H_2 in Fig. 1,

(a) when $Y = Y_1$ and the inflation rate is 6%, find

    (i) demand inflation
    (ii) core inflation
    (iii) shock inflation

(b) When $Y = Y_3$ and the inflation rate is 2%, find

    (i) demand inflation
    (ii) core inflation
    (iii) shock inflation

Q 4   In Fig. 2 below, the economy is at potential output of £700m and then an increase in aggregate demand raises income to £750m.

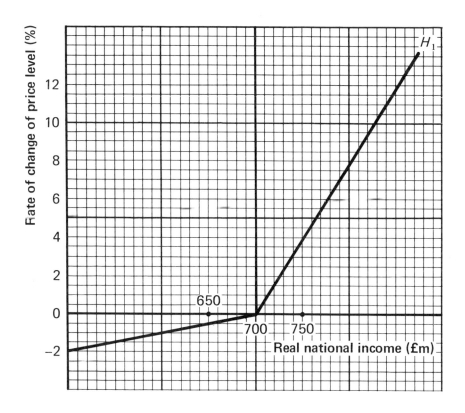

Fig. 2

(a) What will happen to the price level? _____

(b) If the nominal money supply is held constant, the *IS/LM* curve will shift to the left/right.

(c) The equilibrium level of income will be _____ , with the price level lower than/the same as/higher than before.

Q 5 Suppose that the demand inflation arising from the short-run Phillips curve H_1 in Fig. 2 is validated. Assume that, at the end of the first period, firms and workers believe that inflation is likely to continue at a rate equal to 0.75 of the current period's rate.

(a) Draw the new short-run Phillips curve (H_2) on Fig. 2.

What is the core inflation rate? _____

What is the demand inflation rate? _____

What is the actual inflation rate? _____

(b) In the third period the government lowers VAT, with the result that prices are reduced by 1.25%.

What is the core inflation rate? _____

What is the demand inflation rate? _____

What is the actual inflation rate? _____

(c) Find the inflation rate in the fourth period, assuming no shock inflation.

_____

(d) Now suppose that instead of income remaining at £750m in period 4, the government adopted contractionary demand-management policies and lowered income to £650m.

What is the core inflation rate? _____

What is the demand inflation rate? _____

What is the actual inflation rate? _____

(e) Assuming that income remains at £650m, by how much would the inflation rate have fallen in the next period? _____

You might like to experiment with different assumptions about the formation of expectations concerning the inflation rate and see what difference this makes.

Q 6 Which of the following statements are consistent with Lipsey's discussion of the core-augmented Phillips curve?

(a) The short-run Phillips curve shows a positive relationship between income and price levels.

(b) A validated inflation can continue indefinitely when the economy is at full employment.

(c) Fiscal policy expanding at a constant rate will result in a constant rate of inflation.

(d) The short-run Phillips curve shows that the lower the unemployment rate, the more rapid the rate of inflation.

(e) Any validated stable inflation rate is compatible with potential output.

QUESTIONS FOR DISCUSSION

1   Why is the short-run Phillips curve steep above and flat below potential output? What difference would it make if it were linear?

2   Under what circumstances will the Phillips curve shift up or down?

3   Explain carefully the difference between a theory of inflation based on an independent wage push and a theory where wage changes are endogenous.

4   What options are open to a government for financing a budget deficit? Is there any link between budget finance and inflation?

5   Will expansionary monetary policy always lower interest rates?

6   'Inflation is always and everywhere a monetary phenomenon, arising from a more rapid growth in the quantity of money than in output' (Milton Friedman).

Do you agree?

7   Extract from William Keegan's article in the *Observer* (21.1.79):

'For many years, economic policy was conducted on the assumption that there was some sort of "trade off" (or choice) between inflation and unemployment. Governments could reduce unemployment and stimulate economic growth at the cost of some acceleration of inflation. More recently, that concept has been stood on its head. Inflation, especially accelerating inflation, is seen to be inimical to growth, and hence to employment.'

What are the assumptions about the nature of the aggregate supply function which underlie this discussion of inflation and growth?

8   The then Prime Minister, Mr Callaghan, said at the Labour Party Conference in 1976:

'We used to think that you could just spend your way out of a recession and increase employment by cutting taxes and boosting government spending. I tell you in all candour that that option no longer exists . . . .'

What must be the circumstances so that 'that option no longer exists'?

9   The following is an extract from an article by Ronald Butt in *The Times* (18.12.74):

'The rationale of the Government's resistance to doing more starts from its assertion that our domestic problem is one of inflation, but not one of excess demand. It therefore insists that deflationary measures which would damage productivity are ruled out; that the wage increases must be kept within manageable limits by the social contract . . .

'If wage increases enable people to sustain the same standard of living on the basis of rising import prices, the danger is that we shall continue to build external inflation into our own economic structure. On this analysis, it is arguable that wage settlements ought to be marginally *below* what is necessary to sustain the standard of living, with the result that people reduce their consumption, if inflation is to be checked.'

(a) Can inflation occur without excess demand?
(b) Evaluate the argument that wage settlements should not keep up with the cost of living in order to check inflation.

10   The following is part of a leading article in the *Guardian* (11.12.74):

' "No taxation without representation" is an old slogan. Thanks to inflation, it is beginning to acquire a new relevance. "With inflation", as Professor Milton Friedman argued in a *Guardian* article earlier this year, "you are subjected to taxes that no member of Parliament would ever have voted for. You could not have got through Parliament taxes on low and middle incomes as high as the taxes that are now imposed on people because inflation has automatically pushed them up into higher tax brackets."

'In his November Budget, Mr Healey crept a little further towards recognizing the need for some kind of indexing in the taxation system, by giving special relief to companies whose profits have been inflated by the appreciation in the value of their stocks. With inflation apparently here to stay at double-digit rates, there must now be an unarguable case for extending indexing further in the tax system.

'Perhaps the most compelling argument against doing so is that it would remove the built-in deflationary effect of the personal tax system. In a period of too rapid inflation, it is frequently argued, it is safer to have a tax system which helps to stabilize the economy by taking more out of incomes when they are rising too fast. But this argument cuts both ways. It may also be true that the rising tax taken in times of high inflation adds to pressures for higher wages—that workers are well aware of how much of their incomes the tax man takes, and ask for yet higher wages to compensate.'

(a)   Explain how inflation may bring about 'taxation without representation' and what is meant by indexing.
(b)   Evaluate the argument that higher income taxes may increase rather than decrease inflation.

11   Extract from a speech by Sir Keith Joseph (5.9.74):

'Incomes policy alone as a way to abate inflation caused by excessive money supply is like trying to stop water coming out of a leaking hose without turning off the tap; if you stop one hole it will find two others.'

Explain.

12   The following are extracts from an article by Professor Thomas Wilson, published in the *Guardian* (17.2.75):

'. . . Unemployment can be caused by inflation as well as by deflation. Competitive exports are needed in order to keep up employment in the export industries and our competitive advantage has been eaten away. Exports must be on a sufficient scale to pay for our imports both in order to protect the standard of living and in order to provide our factories with raw materials. Presumably no one will still pretend that a declining exchange rate provides an easy way out.

'In an emergency import controls could be used but would not help unless there were corresponding adjustments in the domestic economy. For the big import surplus has kept down the inflationary pressure . . . [However] ever more stringent import controls would not be consistent with growth or even, ultimately, with the maintenance of employment . . .

'Thus we come again to the central problem: the slowing down of the rise in wages and salaries which is causing such an alarming rate of inflation. It is important to record that higher profit margins have not contributed to the rise in prices in recent years. On the contrary, corporate profits (net of stock appreciation but before allowing for the depreciation of fixed capital) have fallen as a percentage of GDP from about 15 per cent in 1964 to something like 7 or 8 per cent in 1974 . . . It is necessary to ask whether the situation has been allowed to get so much out of hand that we now need a freeze . . . '

(a)   Why won't a declining exchange rate provide an easy solution to the problems mentioned in the first paragraph?
(b)   What are the probable implications of the falling profit rates noted in the last paragraph?
(c)   What are the pros and cons of introducing an incomes policy. Is it necessary to control both prices and incomes?

13   Extract from an article by Malcolm Crawford in the *Sunday Times* (13.8.78):

'Money wage settlements minus the expected rate of increase in consumer prices represent the real wage increases the wage negotiators are trying to achieve. If these are higher than the real wage gains actually available, prices rise faster (reducing real wages to what is available via production). But if the Government resists this escalation of inflation by means of its fiscal and monetary policy, the level of unemployment must rise. Although Labour ministers have mainly presented pay policy as a counter-inflation policy, its main function is to mitigate the increase in unemployment which would result from the Government's grip on the monetary aggregates (assuming that the Government is controlling these) when desired wage levels are unrealistic.

'In short, if real wage expectations are unrealistic, the Government can control the rate of inflation, but not the level of unemployment. An incomes policy, if the public complies, may restore its ability to control both.

'None of this analysis depends on a statistically proven Phillips curve—which is widely believed to have collapsed and died around 1970—nor upon any concept of a "natural rate" of unemployment. In a sense it reverses the Phillips proposition, making the unemployment level the result, rather than the cause of, the rate of wage settlements.'

(a) Is an incomes policy effective by itself or only in conjunction with fiscal and monetary policy?

(b) Comment on the view expressed in the last paragraph.

14   Extracts from a letter to the *Financial Times* (5.2.79), from Professor Dudley Johnson:

'. . . if aggregate monetary demand is not increased to sustain cost induced increases in prices, a wage rate growth in excess of productivity improvements creates unemployment and not rising prices. Therefore (it has been) argued that the behaviour of the authorities is not independent of market processes—that is, the Government's commitment to maintain high employment creates a quasi automatic link between wages and prices. Thus, unions, by currently anticipating the response of economic policy makers, can set a wage rate which can uniquely determine the inflation rate but . . . even under these conditions accommodating expansionary growth in the money supply would be a necessary condition for inflation to continue.

'. . . a country with continuous high rates of inflation has only a choice between when it wants the unemployment to come: during the time of the disease (inflation) gets worse, or when it is getting better.'

(a) Does Professor Johnson's analysis of inflation coincide with the theory set out by Lipsey?

(b) Is he arguing that unions hold rational or adaptive expectations?

15   Extracts from an article by David Lipsey, *Sunday Times* (23.1.82):

'. . . the markets are still in the grip of an inflationary psychology. Whatever Mrs Thatcher may think and hope, they do not expect the 5.4% inflation rate announced on Friday to stick.

'This is bad news for Mrs Thatcher . . . But for those concerned with the real world of output and jobs it is very good news indeed. For the plain fact is that if inflationary expectations came down much further, the prospect of economic recovery would be substantially reduced.

'The reason lies in what lower inflationary expectations would do to real interest rates. If you are a businessman thinking of borrowing to invest, you consider first what the funds to do so might cost you—at present, at least 12% from a bank. But you have to consider also what, over the years, you will get for the products that the investment enables you to produce. The faster you expect prices to go up, the more you will expect to get back, and thus, the more attractive the investment becomes.'

(a) What are the real and nominal interest rates faced by businessmen at this time?

(b) For any given nominal interest rate, what is the relationship between the real rate and the inflation rate?

CHAPTER 48

Current Issues in Macroeconomic Theory

QUESTIONS FOR DISCUSSION

1   'Differences between Monetarists and neo-Keynesians over the control of inflation arise because of different views about the aggregate supply function.'

   Do you agree?

2   Analyse carefully the reasons why neo-Keynesians believe that changes in the money supply are caused by fluctuations in business activity, rather than the other way round.

3   Are expectations about the values of economic variables as important in influencing behaviour as actual observations of the values of these variables?

4   Is there agreement amongst economists as to the usefulness of systematic stabilization policy?

5   Extract from a speech by Lord Kaldor in the House of Lords on 16.4.80, published in *The Economic Consequences of Mrs Thatcher*, Fabian Tract 486, Jan. 1983, p. 9:

   'When Lord Cockfield told the House the other day that the "money supply was the critical factor in the level of inflation" he was saying in effect no more than a doctor who says "body temperature is a critical factor in health". You cannot cure disease by bringing down the temperature, even though your temperature will necessarily come down if and when the disease is cured.
   'The true instrumental variables are fiscal policy and interest rate policy. These influence the level of expenditure of consumers and businesses and, through them, the public's demand to hold liquid assets, cash and bank deposits.'

   Is Lord Kaldor arguing that monetary policy is ineffective?

6   Extracts from an article by Alan Budd, *Financial Times* (6.10.82):

   '[The Conservative Government] has, however, shown itself exceptionally determined to concentrate on inflation. That leaves it open to two types of criticism. The first is that the gains in reducing inflation have not been worth the cost in terms of lost output and high unemployment. The second is that the gains could have been achieved at much lower cost.
   'If the government continues to concentrate on reducing inflation, it must believe that the economy will eventually recover of its own accord.'

   (a)   Prepare two brief statements: (i) defending the government's policy against the criticisms made above; (ii) elaborating the criticisms.
   (b)   What is the monetary adjustment path which will cause the economy to recover?

7   '. . . given the constraints of monetary control, the remedy for slump discovered by Keynes will not work in an inflationary environment. On the contrary, governments now think that they can achieve low interest rates by adopting more deflationary rather than more expansionary fiscal policies.' (Anthony Harris, *Financial Times*, 2.9.82.)

   Can we experience both a slump and an inflationary environment?

8   Extracts from an article by Sam Brittan, *Financial Times* (16.9.82):

'One argument . . . which was used by Keynes in the 1930s is that if wages fell product prices would also fall, and labour would be no more profitable to employ than before.

'To price labour into work, product prices will indeed have to fall less than wages; or wages will have to rise less than product prices.

'Keynes himself did not believe in constant profit margins come what may. His point was that in the situation of the early 1930s it would be better to increase monetary demand, allowing prices to rise and the real product wage to fall indirectly, rather than make a direct onslaught on the money wage. But if, as has been the case in most recent cycles, wages rise in response to higher monetary demand, it must mean that workers or other representatives are resisting the real wage reduction required to price them into jobs.'

Is Sam Brittan arguing that unemployment is voluntary?

9   In '*Economic Recovery*: *What Labour Must Do*', Fabian Tract 485, published in December 1982, the following proposals were put forward:

(a)   Increases in government capital expenditure;
(b)   Abolition of the National Insurance Surcharge, and cuts in employees' National Insurance contributions;
(c)   Raise income tax thresholds by 10%;
(d)   Reduce interest rates to 6% (long-term) and 4% (short-term);
(e)   Subsidize food by £3 billion;
(f)   Maintain real value of social security payments.

The authors of the pamphlet argue that 'a package on these lines would boost real income and reduce prices. It would change inflationary expectations and make it worthwhile for all sections of the community to cooperate in helping to achieve price stabilization in conditions of rapid expansion . . . .

'Our problems are entirely due to a combination of an overvalued exchange rate, combined with excessive saving and they will only be solved by giving people the opportunity to spend more and, as a necessary corollary, allowing a more flexible monetary policy to bring down the exchange rate. We must not be afraid of increasing the quantity of money by whatever amount is required to achieve this objective. We must likewise ignore pressure from the City to fund the borrowing requirement, because funding takes out of circulation money which would be better spent on goods and services.' (pages 5–8.)

Evaluate these proposals.

Answers

CHAPTER 1

1.
(1)	P	(8)	N
(2)	P	(9)	P
(3)	N	(10)	P + N
(4)	A	(11)	N
(5)	P + N	(12)	P + N
(6)	P	(13)	P
(7)	P + N	(14)	P + N
		(15)	N

2 Behavioural

3 (1), (4)

CHAPTER 2

1

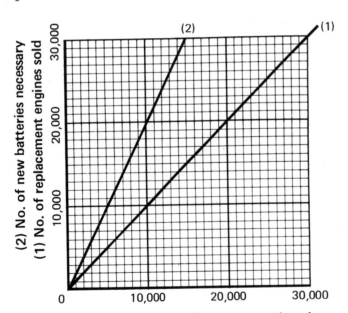

2 6

3 (b)

4 5.30 pm

APPENDIX TO CHAPTER 2

1 (2) $y = 4(x + 5)$
   (3) $y = (x \div 5)^2$
   (4) $y = x + 4\sqrt{x}$

2 (1) Output depends on price two months previously.
   (2) Price in three months' time depends on output now and next month's price.

3 $Q_{t+2} = Q(P_t)$

4 (1) Exogenous   (2) Endogenous

5 (1) and (4)

6 (1) F   (2) T   (3) F

CHAPTER 3

1 Random

2 (a) and (b)

3 No

4 No

5 Because people with telephones will naturally have more communication with other people than those without telephones. Our sample would be *biased*.

6 Observe, for example, individuals 2 and 3 — same size of estate, different number of acquaintances.

7
		47	
—	38.5	37	55
17	28	33.5	—
—	—	17	—

8 People whose gardens join three other gardens know on average less people, the larger the size of the estate they live on.

9 People who live on an estate of between 81 and 120 houses know on average less people, the fewer back gardens their own gardens join.

10 They cannot conduct laboratory experiments.

APPENDIX TO CHAPTER 3

1 (1)   100   (2)   Yes
2 (1) 116   (3) Bacon
   (2) Potatoes   (4) Too high

CHAPTER 4

1 (1) Land, Labour, Capital
   (2) Entrepreneurship
   (3) Labour

2 (1) Land, Labour
   (2) All three
   (3) All three (scissors and shop buildings are capital)
   (4) Labour
   (5) All three

3 No

4 To satisfy demands

5 Opportunity cost

6   (1)   (3)   How is society's output of goods and services divided among its members?
                  (4)   How efficient is the society's production and distribution?
                  (5)   Are the country's resources being fully utilized, or are some of them lying idle?
                  (6)   Is the purchasing power of money and savings constant, or is it being eroded because of inflation?

      (2)   (1)   2   (6)   6
                  (2)   7   (7)   4
                  (3)   4   (8)   5
                  (4)   1   (9)   3
                  (5)   1

7   Price mechanism

8   (1)   What commodities are being produced, and in what quantities?
      (2)   By what methods are they produced?
      (3)   How are they divided?
      (4)   How efficient is production and distribution?

9   (1)   7,200
      (2)   To the South West
      (3)   Yes—by a movement along the existing curve
      (4)   30
      (5)   2,400 kg of butter

10   (1)   3%   (2)   Could be   (3)   No

11   There was much greater unemployment in the USA in 1940 than in Germany in 1939.

CHAPTER 5

1   (a), (c), (d), (e)

2   (a), (c), (e)

3   (b), (d)

4   Rise

5   (1)   An increase in demand is followed by a rise in price.
      (2)   An increase in the cost of cricket bats causes the substitution by some people of tennis for cricket.
      (3)   This is the reverse of (2).
      (4)   This is incorrect reasoning.

6   (b)

CHAPTER 6

1   One

2   Yes (hospital meals, etc.)

3   No

4   Yes (it has to decide upon its method of production)

5   Yes

6   Yes; advertising space

7   Profit maximization

8   Factors of production; firms; maximize their profits; maximize their satisfaction

9   No

10   An area over which buyers and sellers negotiate the exchange of a well-defined commodity

11   Lancashire

12   The world

13   England (and wherever else they are bought and sold)

14   London

15   Competitive

16   Yes

17   Different goods; transport; tariffs

18   Firms; households, firms or central authorities; households; firms or central authorities

19   Controlled

20
(1)	B	(4)	M
(2)	M	(5)	M
(3)	NM	(6)	B

21   An economy

22   Free; controlled

23   Both

CHAPTER 7

1
(1)	5	(4)	2	(7)	5	(10)	4
(2)	7	(5)	1	(8)	2		
(3)	3 and 7	(6)	6	(9)	3		

2
(1)	2, 3	(3)	2
(2)	7	(4)	1

3   You should have written something like 'per year' and 'per cwt'.

4   Stock; flow

5   £2.87½

6   £2

7   3

8   17

9   (No answer)

10   (1) 14,000   (2) 11p   (3) 22½p

11   (1) 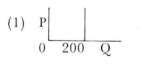   (2)

12   (1) 9,750   (2) 15,500

13
(1)	Left	(5)	Indeterminate
(2)	Right	(6)	Right
(3)	Left	(7)	Left
(4)	Right	(8)	Right

14   (1) A good the demand for which falls as income rises.
            (2) No. If it were it would never be traded at all.

15   (a), (d)

16	(1) right	(3) not at all	(5) left
	(2) right	(4) right	

17 (1) Shift   (2) Movement along   (3) Shift

18 True: Since nothing must be bought when income is zero, the income-demand curve must go through the origin or have a positive intercept on the income axis (what would it mean if it had a positive intercept on the quantity axis?). Thus, with income plotted on the X axis, the income-demand curve cannot have a falling segment before it has a rising one.

19 True

20 False

21 False

22 False

23 False

24 Unsound

25 False

26 True

27	(a) No	(c) Yes	(e) No
	(b) No	(d) No	(f) No

28	(a) No	(c) Yes
	(b) Perhaps	(d) No

29 (a), (d)

30	(1) 5	(3) 4	(5) 3
	(2) 3	(4) 1	

31 Linear

32 Less

33 (1) 16

34 14p

35 The curve itself

36 500 more will be demanded at each price.

37 3,250

38 c. £110

39	(1) right	(3) not at all
	(2) right or not at all	(4) right

40 (1) not at all   (2) left   (3) not at all

41 (1) 3   (2) 4   (4) 5

42 False

43 False

44 True

45 False

46 True

47 True

48 (b), (c)

49 (d)

290

50   (b)

51   (d)

CHAPTER 8

1   The price at which quantity supplied equals quantity demanded.

2   £3.50

3   4 tons per year

4   Yes

5   False

6   False

7   True

8   Upward

9   Downward

10   (1)   5½   (3) $-1½$
           (2)   1½   (4) $-6¼$

11   £4

12   2

13   5

14   right

15   left

16   impossible

17   about 6

18   +1¾

19   Because the rise in price to induce the extra supply has choked off some of the extra demand.

20   Yes

21   No

22   (1)   down; down
           (2)   up; down
           (3)   down; up
           (4)   There are two effects. Less coke will be used in existing central-heating plants, but more coke-fired plants may be installed in place of, say, oil-fired ones. If the first effect predominates, demand falls, as do price and quantity; if the second predominates, demand, price and quantity rise. (This will be dealt with systematically in Chapter 14.)
           (5)   up; down
           (6)   up; up
           (7)   down; indeterminate

23   (1)   demand left, supply no shift
           (2)   supply left, demand no shift
           (3)   supply right, demand no shift
           (4)   demand right or left, supply no shift
           (5)   supply left, demand no shift
           (6)   demand right, supply no shift
           (7)   supply right, demand left

24   (1)   No
           (2)   Because at the minimum price at which producers will supply any, none is demanded.

25	False
26	False
27	True
28	True
29	False
30	True
31	True
32	(c)
33	(a)
34	(b)
35	(a)

CHAPTER 9

1      $\dfrac{\text{the percentage change in quantity demanded}}{\text{the percentage change in income}}$

2      $\dfrac{\text{the percentage change in quantity supplied}}{\text{the percentage change in price}}$

3   (b)   ; 5   (d)   ; 10

4   By always choosing the former

5

−35	0.7
−16	0.8
−9	0.9
+11	1.1
+25	1.2
+85	1.7

6   (1)   No   (2)   1½

7   (1)   ⅔   (2)   4

8      $\dfrac{\Delta Q}{\Delta P} \cdot \dfrac{P}{Q} : \dfrac{\Delta Q}{\Delta P}$

9   That below price x none will be supplied, and at or above price x as many will be supplied as the market will take.

10   No

11   £6

12   £2

13   Rise

14   Rise

15   £0–£5

16   £5–£10

17   Not changed

18   Greater

19   If people spend more on keg beer as their incomes increase up to a point and then switch to more expensive drinks, the curve will look like this:

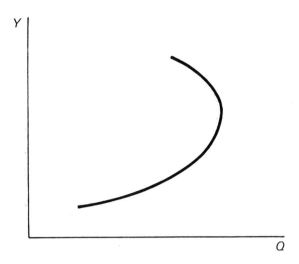

20    $\dfrac{\% \text{ change in quantity demand of good } X}{\% \text{ change in price of good } Y}$

21   > 0

22   False

23   True

24   True

25   True

26   False

27   True

28   False

29   (a)

30   (a)

31   (b)

32   (b)

33   (f)

34   Inferior

CHAPTER 10

1   (d)

2   £20 and over

3   Approximately 35

4   Approximately 25

5   £0–£5

6   Rise

7   Yes: less than 1

8   When the elasticity of demand for labour is greater than 1 over the relevant range.

9   No

10   Approximately 80

11   (2) You should have shifted the D curve to the right.
      (3) Elastic

(4) q_1
(5) Yes
(6) q_3
(7) $q_2 - q_3$

12   (1) £21,000   (2) £3,500   (3) 150

13   No

14   Rectangular hyperbola

APPENDIX TO CHAPTER 10

1   (1) £4   (4) £1.55   (7) 28
     (2) $t + 2$ (5) 20.5   (8) £2.05
     (3) $t + 4$ (6) £2.70   (9) 24

2   Stable

3   Stable

4   2: never

5   Stable

6   True

CHAPTER 11

1   Autarky

2   (a) price   (b) imports   (c) price   (d) exports

3   (a) Consumption-possibility set   (b) 70   (c) Yes
     (d) True   (e) $60x$ and $100y$

4   (a) 900 exported   (b) 700 imported   (c) Decrease of 2
     (d) No change in price, decrease of 400 units

5   (a) Surplus   (b) Deficit   (c) Appreciated

6   (a) 2200   (b) 1200   (c) 400

7   (a) decreases; increases   (b) increases; decreases

8   That it is 1:2.5

9   That it is 30:7

10   (1) right, falls   (2) right, rises   (3) left, falls
      (4) right, rises   (5) right, falls   (6) right, rises

11

	Demand	*Supply*
(1)	pounds	dollars
(2)	dollars	pounds
(3)	another currency	pounds
(4)	pounds	dollars
(5)	dollars + pounds + kronen	marks
(6)	Canadian dollars + francs	dollars
(7)	dollars	Canadian dollars + francs

CHAPTER 13

1   The household

2   (1) One below the line   (6) No
     (2) Both   (7) No
     (3) 2; down by £2.50   (8) Yes
     (4) Free   (9) Yes
     (5) Zero

3   No; it is inconsistent

4   p

5   2½ x

6   (1) (a)   (2) (c)

7   (1) 0   (3) 2
       (2) 2   (4) 2

8   (a)

9   Down ⅜

10   Down ⅙

11   Relative

12   True

13   True

14   True

CHAPTER 14

1   The consumption of all other commodities is held constant.

2   False

3   False

4   Households seek to maximize their total utility.

5   No

6   (1) 0.25   (2) 0.25   (3) Oppose

7   (1) Smaller   (3) (b) and (c)
       (2) (b)   (4) (b)

8

(1)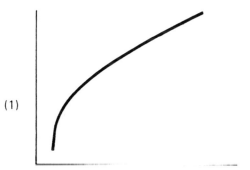

(2)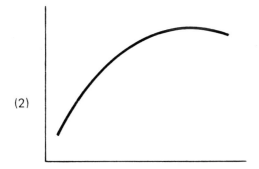

9      $$\frac{MU \text{ of good 1}}{\text{price of good 1}} = \frac{MU \text{ of good 2}}{\text{price of good 2}} \cdots = \frac{MU \text{ of good } n}{\text{price of good } n}$$

10   other commodities; too little

11   (1)   5   (2)   5

12   (1)   50   (2)   8

13   (1)   £48.50   (3)   £29
                (2)   £20   (4)   £9

14   (2)   Yes; 1.6
                (3)   Yes; Yes; Yes; 13

15   (2)   Right
                (3)   2½ times
                (4)   (a)   No
                         (b)   No
                         (c)   Yes
                         (d)   Less than 14 clothes, or more than 26 clothes

16   (1)   750   (2)   775

17   (c)

18   (c)

19   (1)   100 loaves   (4)   +25
                (2)   −30   (5)   −35
                (3)   −10

CHAPTER 16

1   Creditors; before

2   (c)

3   (c)

4   (c)

5   (b)

CHAPTER 17

1   (a)   The cost of any input is what the firm must give up in order to obtain the use of that input.
                (b)   The rate of interest at which the firm can lend money.
                (c)   Bygones.
                (d)   Any excess of revenue over all opportunity costs.
                (e)   Cost is measured by the value obtainable by a different use of the input concerned.

2   False−the firm could lend its money.

3   (1)   £500
                (2)   £500
                (3)   Zero
                (4)   £1,000
                (5)   £500
                (6)   During the first two years car parts wear a lot, but do not usually have to be replaced until after this period. During subsequent years the opportunity cost of using the vehicle is the fall in its resale value *plus* the cost of replacement parts and repairs.
                (7)   Zero, zero
                (8)   It halves
                (9)   True
              (10)   Yes, down by ½

4   True—this means that their present wage is not a measure of their opportunity costs.

5   Because otherwise farmers might have to pay to have it removed.

6   The relation between inputs and outputs

7   Neither

8   1

9   Very long

10   (1) Yes
     (2) Short
     (3) *AP* *MP*
          10   10
          14   17
          16   22
          18   24
          19   23
          18   16
          17   7
          15   2
          14   1
     (5) Yes
     (6) 73
     (7) 96

11   True

12   (1)

1	10	500	20	520	50	2	52	2
2	27	500	40	540	18.5	1.5	20	1.18
3	49	500	60	560	10.2	1.22	11.4	0.9
4	73	500	80	580	6.9	1.10	7.9	0.8
5	96	500	100	600	5.2	1.04	6.3	0.9
6	112	500	120	620	4.5	1.07	5.5	1.2
7	119	500	140	640	4.2	1.18	5.4	2.9
8	121	500	160	660	4.1	1.5	5.5	10
9	122	500	180	680	4.1	1.5	5.6	20

     (3) 73
     (4) 119
     (5) 96
     (6) Never
     (7) Lowest

13   119

14   True

15 and $$\frac{MP_K}{P_K} = \frac{MP_L}{P_L} \quad \text{and} \quad \frac{MP_K}{MP_L} = \frac{P_K}{P_L}$$
16

17   (1) Yes   (4) 1.9
     (2) 3 extra labour   (5) 28.5
          1 extra capital   (6) 1.9
     (3) 1.93   (7) 1.86

18   (a)

19   (1) *LRATC*
     (2) One
     (3) Because the capital usage of the *SRATC* curve is inappropriate to the output of Q^1.

20	(1)	isoquants		(5)	£340
	(2)	right		(6)	20
	(3)	capital		(7)	£380
	(4)	£265		(8)	up 2 down 2½
				(9)	substitution

21	(1)	6		(4)	No
	(2)	75		(5)	£12.75
	(3)	Yes		(6)	Reduce; 2.75; less

22	(1)	1	(3)	3	(5)	5
	(2)	4	(4)	2		

23   Either that it is possible to substitute unskilled labour for other factors indefinitely at present, or that processes which allow such substitution will be invented in response to the stimulus of a very low price for unskilled labour.

24   False

25   False

26   True

27   True

28   (d)

29   (d)

30   (d)

31   (c)

CHAPTER 18

1   Average revenue = Total revenue ÷ output.

2   The change in total revenue resulting from an increase in the rate of sales per time-period by one unit.

3   Divide, total, output: divide, total, output

4	(1)	25	(3)	45p	(5)	£1
	(2)	30p	(4)	£1.70		

5   False

6   False

7   True

8   False

9   (d)

10   (a)

CHAPTER 19

1   Price-taker
Freedom of entry and exit

2   Same horizontal straight line

3   One

4   (1) No   (2) £250

5   Cost; revenue; marginal cost

6   It is not a profit-maximizer.

7	(1)	23	(2)	£15
	(3)	£4.25	(4)	£5.25, 20, £65

8   (1) £1; 6,000   (2) 10 per week   (3) 12.5 per week

9   Yes; 15

10 Any new firm is free to set up production and any existing firm is free to cease
    production. The industry has freedom of entry and exit.

11 (1) neither
    (2) out of
    (3) into
    (4) It should be tangential to the price line at the point where the MC curve cuts it.

12 No

13 (a) no change   (b) number; identical

14 (a) No   (b) higher

15 (e)

16 (f)

17 (e)

18 (b)

19 True

20 False

21 False

22 True

23 False

24 True

25 (1) $-\dfrac{\text{\% change in firm's output}}{\text{\% change in world price}}$

    (2) η_F
    (3) η_m
    (4) 25,000
    (5) 1/25

CHAPTER 20

1   (1) The quantity of a good demanded at each price.
    (2) The change in revenue resulting from a change in sales of one unit.
    (3) 1. The total cost of producing a given output with existing capital, divided by
             that output.
         2. The total cost of producing a given output with the optimal factor propor-
             tions, divided by that output.
    (4) The cost of all the factors variable in the short run used to produce a given
         output, divided by that output.
    (5) The change in cost resulting from a change in the rate of output by one unit
         per period.
    (6) The excess of revenue over total costs.

2   No; $MR \neq (AR = P)$.

3   (1) £136.5   (5) £149.6
    (2) £144   (6) £−0.4
    (3) £7.5   (7) greater than
    (4) £150   (8) less than

4   (1) less than   (4) falls   (7) $\frac{2}{3}$
    (2) increase   (5) halfway down   (8) $1\frac{1}{2}$
    (3) £10   (6) $\dfrac{\Delta Q}{\Delta P} \times \dfrac{P}{Q}$ (9) +£60

5	£3.50		

6   Both

7	(1)	100	(5)	£16
	(2)	£700	(6)	Zero
	(3)	£15	(7)	need not
	(4)	Until the fixed equipment wears out		

8   They can all constitute barriers to entry.

9   Resale

10   £00

11   No

12   Yes

13   Lower

14   Yes

15   Yes

16   (a)   11   (b)   13.75   (c)   5.25   (d)   3.25

17   (b)

18   (b)

19   (b)

20   True

21   True

22   True

23   False

24   False

25   True

26   True

27   True

28   True

29   False

30   True

31   (b)

CHAPTER 21

1   By shifting it

2   (2)   0.7
     (3)   1.475m
     (4)   0.35 per gallon, a total of £516,250

3   They will wish to enter the industry

4   (1)   Left
     (2)   Yes
     (3)   Leave the industry

5   40p

6   Necessary

7   (1)   Are not   (2)   (2)

8	Tangential

9   *SRATC*

10   (1) £5; Q 12   (2) £10; Q 22

11   (1) £16   (2) Zero

12   The *LRAC* curve is tangent to the *D* curve.

13   (1) Downward   (3) Attract   (5) Left
    (2) False   (4) Fall   (6) *LRAC*
    (7) Because the demand curve falls more sharply than the short-run average cost curve, so to sell the extra output price would have to drop more than average cost.

14   (1) Higher, because the firm is not at the minimum point of the *ATC* curve.
    (2) Marginal cost
    (3) Over capacity
    (4) Excess capacity

15   (1) Normal capacity
    (2) Full capacity

16   (2) Because you can't shut down part of a main-frame computer.

17   (1) 130; £27   (2) 12   (3) 90; £27

18   (a)

19   (1) £160,000   (3) £80,000
    (2) £116,667   (4) £50,000

20   Less

21   (d)

22   (g)

23   (d)

24   (c)

25   (d)

26   (d)

27   True

28   False

29   True

30   False

31   True

32   False

CHAPTER 22

1    $p^{\circ} \times q^{\circ}$

2   No (but it will be yes unless $\eta = 1$ at the point of equilibrium).

3   (1) Elasticity of demand > 1 between the old and new equilibrium quantities.
    (2) Shallower
    (3) Less
    (4) Because costs fall more

4   Because the legal restrictions on their output held their *MC* below the price, so they could increase their profits provided that other farmers did not do so.

5   Trade unions

6	(2)	£1 per pig
	(3)	£280 per month
	(4)	about £580
7	(2)	$p = 12$ $Q = 3,000$

7   (3)   (1) $p = 32 - \dfrac{Q}{200}$

(3)   + about £2.10

(5)   about £17

8   The incentive to other firms to enter the industry, thus increasing total production.

9   The assumption that the *LR* supply curve is a horizontal straight line.

10   By the production of the new firms which entered the industry.

11   No change; number of firms

12   False

13   True

14   True

15   True

16   Variable

17   Rise

18   Fall

19   (1) $+ c.£1.20, - c.18$
      (2) $+ c.£0.80, - c.10$
      (3) competition

20   Per unit; Lump sum; Profits

21   False

22   Neither

23   All passed on

24   A lump-sum tax has the same effect of raising the *LRAC* curve as any fixed cost.

25   (a)   130   (b)   85   (c)   £7.25

26   A 'profits' tax is usually levied on items treated by the economist as costs, most importantly on the return to capital.

27   (c)   The monopolist could allow his price to react as suggested in (a) or (b), but this would in neither case be the price which maximized his profits.

28   (c)

29   (d)

30   (f)

31   (b)

32   True

33   False

34   True

35   True

36   True

37   False

38   False

39   True

40   True

CHAPTER 23

1   greater than

2   (1) £1.10, 180   (4) opportunity cost
      (2) £1.70, 105   (5) competitive
      (3) 130

3   (1) $y = 64\frac{2}{3} - \frac{13}{6} x$ (6) £2.05; 21
                                                (7) c.£30
      (2) price = £1.55; quantity = 31   (8) higher
      (3) No   (9) lower
      (4) Yes
      (5) marginal revenue

4   (1) 1,150   (3) 0.50   (5) £1.00
      (2) c.£1.48   (4) £3.00   (6) £1.00, 3

5   £1.90; 24

6   £1.80; 26

7   £2.37; 20

8   (1) No   (3) No
      (2) Yes   (4) Yes

9   (1) False   (2) True

10   (1) less than   (3) less than   (5) greater
      (2) marginal cost   (4) will

11   (1) 3   (2) 2   (3) 1

12   That they should be publicly controlled

13   (b)

14   True

CHAPTER 24

1   No

2   £218.75

3   (1) (1) 175,000
           (2) £52,500
           (3) £32,500
      (2) about £71,000

4   Yes

5   None

6   (1) 900
      (2) Because the firm would make losses, would eventually go out of business, and
           they would lose their jobs.

7   Yes

8   No, if this alibi is used whenever a firm is observed not to be maximizing short-run
      profits.

9   (b)

10   (a)

CHAPTER 25

1	£1,250				
2	left; £850				
3	It will fall.				
4	The demand for the products it helps to produce.				
5	Marginal revenue product				

6   (1) £20   (3) £5   (5) −50p
        (2) £9   (4) £1.5   (6) 24

7   (1) −12   (3) 11
        (2) −9   (4) 20

8   (1) 14   (3) 41
        (2) 21   (4) 7

9   marginal cost; wage rate; all factors

10   diminishing returns

11   not at all

12   Correct

13   150

14   125

15   100

16   £0.10

17   550

18   £0.10

19   550, £0.10

20   75

21   £0.13

22   625

23   625, £0.13

24   675, £0.20

25   700, £0.40

26   £0.10

27   £5

28   £0.15

29   £20, 2.7 (2 full time, one part time)

30   Steeper (remember, the steeper the demand curve, the less the change in quantity demanded for a given change in price)

31   right; fall; left

32   False

33   more

34   (1) minus about £53
        (2) plus about £1.37

35   inelastic

36   increase

37   easily

38   £4

39   £2.5

40   measure

41   Non-monetary advantages change much more slowly than do monetary advantages.

42   (1)   shift to left
      (2)   shift to right
      (3)   shift to right
      (4)   the equilibrium position will move *up* the curve
      (5)   shift to left
      (6)   shift to right

43   (f)

44   (a)

45   (f)

46   True

47   True

CHAPTER 26

1   (a)   Dynamic, or disequilibrium causes.
      (b)   Static, or equilibrium causes.

2   (1)   D   (2)   S   (3)   D

3   Transfer earnings

4   Yes (although this is a personal conjecture it could be tested by cutting her wage).

5   None

6   £250 per year

7   Yes—if you are paid less than your transfer earnings.

8   Transfer earnings £50,000, rent £50,000 (intra-industry); transfer earnings £3,120, rent £96,880 (inter-industry)

9   TE 36, rent 2 if intra industry (the worsted industry)
      TE 34, rent 4 if *inter* industry

10   (1)   £4 per week;   (2)   £8 per week

11   Quasi rent

12   A factor payment which is an economic rent in the short run and a transfer payment in the long run.

13   It does not affect the allocation of resources.

14   No; some would be transfer earnings, because the rooms would be used for some other purpose, such as the ex-landlord's own use.

CHAPTER 27

1   (a)   Yes   (b)   No

2   (1)   No   (3)   2.4m
      (2)   c.£48   (4)   1.75m

3   2.4m

4   equal to

5   Because the extra wages which have to be paid to induce more labour to be offered will also have to be paid to the labour already employed.

6   (a) Yes   (b) Yes

7   (1) 20,000   (2) higher; £2,400,000   (3) £150; 100,000

8   increase; above; below; maximum

9   £195

10   Yes, about £6.40

11   That the D curve should have less than unit elasticity over the range between the old and the new equilibrium positions.

12   (1) £70   (2) 140,000

13   £90; £180

14   *c.* 180,000

15   £3,800,000

16   £190

17   £174

18   (a) If the transfer costs of the capital equipment are higher than present earnings.
        (b) If the transfer costs of the variable factors (remember, labour is not now a variable factor) are higher than present earnings.

19   True; False; (b)

20   (a) profitable   (c) monopolistic   (e) inelastic
        (b) small   (d) increasing

CHAPTER 28

1   Because production is based upon the use of capital, which is publicly owned (like the railways in Britain).

2     $X = £100 \times 1.05$

3     $Y = X \times 1.05$

4     $Z = Y \times 1.05$

5     $Z = (£100 \times 1.05^2) \times 1.05 = £100 \times 1.05^3$

6     $Z = K(1 + i)^t$

7     $K = \dfrac{Z}{(1 + i)^t}$

8   (1) *c.*£91   (2) *c.*£97   (3) *c.*£56   (4) £244

9   £24.40

10   0.469

11   (b)

12   (i) 11.25% (ii) £9,500 (iii) £5,500 (iv) Yes; No

13   False

14   rise

15   raising

16   Minus 3%

17   Yes

18   more

19   A loss of £667

20   £500

21   Higher

22   Because of the greater risk involved.

23   Lower

24   Because you can get your money back quicker if you want to.

25   (d)

26   (b)

27   14%

28   raise; not alter

29   (b)

30   (1)   rate of interest   (2)   fallen

CHAPTER 29

1   Expand its employment of the factor.

2   Yes—horizontal passing through *a*.

3   (b), (c), (d), (f), (g)

4   By preventing wage differentials reflecting changes in demand and supply, in different regions and industries (remember, most British trade unions are not based on merely a single industry).

5   No

6   If the elasticity of demand is less than unity over the relevant range.

7   No. The wage rate per worker must fall, but since the number of workers rises it is impossible to say what will happen to labour's share in total income.

8   No. All that the theory predicts is that the per unit price of land will rise but since total income is rising as well we can say nothing about the proportion going to land.

9   Yes. Since the price per unit is rising, and the number of units is constant, the absolute earning must rise.

CHAPTER 30

1   (1)   coffee beans, Land-Rovers, Land-Rovers, coffee beans.
        (2)   50, Land-Rovers, 250, coffee beans, 5,000, coffee beans, 5, Land-Rovers
        (3)   4,750,   45

2   absolute

3   Reciprocal absolute advantage

4   No

5   False

6   comparative

7   amplifiers, speakers

8   10,000, amplifiers, 5,000, speakers, 4,000, speakers, 3,000, amplifiers

9   1,000 fewer; 7,000 more

10   4,000; 3,000

11   3,000 more; 4,000 more

12   200,000 litres; 20,000 litres

13   (1)   0.2 Land-Rovers
                  1,000 bushels of coffee beans
          (2)   0.75 amplifiers   1.3 speakers
                2 amplifiers   0.5 speakers
          (3)   0.4 litres of olive oil   2.5 litres of wine
                0.2 litres of olive oil   5 litres of wine

14   lower

15   Terms of trade

16   below 1.3

17   (1)   No   (2)   No   (3)   Yes

18   Tariffs, quotas

19   Some retaliatory tariff; Yes

20   No; toy factories should open again

21   Addition to reserves, purchase of goods, acquisition of foreign assets.

22   (1)   acquisition of foreign assets
          (2)   leave some over to buy foreign goods and consume them in Britain

23   unemployment; beneficial; rise

24   the stimulation of home demand

25   might; retaliatory tariffs

26   more; less (or less; more)

CHAPTER 31

1   In developed countries the marginal health problems are those which need high technology. In developing countries the margin is much further back, and the investments in health which have the highest ratio of marginal product to cost are much simpler, like better nutrition.

2   Approx. 90%

3

	Rate of natural increase
1931–5	1.5
1944–8	14.3
1949–53	32.2
1954–8	28.7
1960	28.1
1961	29.6
1962	29.2
1963	30.3
1964	29.5
1965	26.9

4   Approx. 2½

5

	1944 (thousands)	1952 (thousands)	1962 (thousands)
under 15	150	194	314
15–64	266	276	348
65+	13	14	20
Total	429	484	682

6   No complete answer, but you should note that in addition to feeding and clothing the larger number of dependents, it will also be necessary to provide schools, hospitals, etc.

	$\dfrac{P}{A}$	$\dfrac{P}{E}$	$\dfrac{E}{A}$
1928–46	1.95	—	—
1947–51	2.69	7.4	0.363
1952–6	2.90	9.5	0.304
1957–9	2.95	9.9	0.297
1960	—	—	0.281
1961	—	—	0.303
1962	—	—	0.297
1963	3.36	(11.3)	0.296
1964	—	—	(0.306)

CHAPTER 34

1   False

2   (c)

3   True

4   current

5

	GDP Deflator
1975	100
1976	114
1977	128
1978	143
1979	162
1980	192
1981	212

6   1975

7   (a) 8.4%   (b) −2.9%   (c) 5.2%

8   Risen, from approx. £1,685 to approx. £1,765.

9   £94,482m

10   False

11   True

12   cost of materials purchased

13   (1) *Fishermen*

Output		Factor incomes	
Sales of goods	£12,000	Wages	£8,000
less goods purchased from		Rent	100
other firms	−900	Interest	500
		Profits	2,500
Total	£11,100	Total	£11,100

(2) *Factory*

Output		Factor incomes	
Sales of goods	£60,000	Wages	£15,000
less goods purchased from		Rent	7,000
other firms	−11,000	Interest	6,000
		Profits	21,000
Total	£49,000	Total	£49,000

(3) *Fishmonger*

Output		*Factor incomes*	
Sales of goods	£10,000	Wages	£2,000
less goods purchased from other firms	−7,000	Rent	1,000
		Interest	100
		Profit	−100
Total	£3,000	Total	£3,000

    (a)   Value-added: fishermen £11,100, factor £49,000, fishmonger £3,000.
    (b)   Total value-added: £63,100.
    (c)   Profits: fishermen £2,500, factory £21,000, fishmonger−£100.

14    $C + I + G + (X - M)$

15   No—we define investment as the act of *producing* goods that are not for immediate consumption.

16   Inventories, capital goods and residential housing

17   unsold; rising; intentional

18   False

19   True

20   True

21   True

22   less

23   False

24   False

25   any part not paid over to households *minus* income tax *plus* transfers.

26

National Product		*National Expenditure*		*National Income*		
Value-added in:		Consumers' expenditure	450	Wages and salaries		430
Agriculture	100	Government		Self-employed		60
Manufacturing	700	expenditure	130	Company profits:		
Construction	120	Gross fixed invest-		Dividends	500	610
Distribution	180	ment	150	Retained profits	110	
Other sectors	290	Change in stocks	10	Public corporations		20
Less Imports	−220	Exports	210	Rent		50
		less Imports	−220			
Gross national product	1170	Gross national expenditure	1170	Gross national income		1170
less depreciation	−70	less depreciation	−70	less depreciation		−70
Net national product	1100	Net national expenditure	1100	Net national income		1100

27   There is the necessary information to calculate gross national income. As gross national income is, by definition, equal to gross national product at factor prices, and we are given amounts for gross and net fixed investment, we can find net national product.

    (a)

Wages and salaries	1850
Incomes of self-employed	780
Gross trading profits of companies	170
Gross trading surplus of public corporations	40
Rent	60
GNI = GNP at factor prices	2900
less depreciation	−40
NNP at factor prices	2860

(b)	GNP at factor prices		2900
	plus indirect taxes on expenditure		120
	GNP at market prices		3020

(c)	GNP		2900
	less	Retained profits of companies	−130
		Gross trading surplus of public corporations	−40
		Income tax	−600
	plus	Transfers	30
		Disposable Income	2160

CHAPTER 35

1   (c)

2   False

3   decreased

4   (a)   False   (b)   True

5   True

6   True

7    $E = C + I$

8   (a) $Y = C + I$ (b) $S = I$

9   (a)   7.   Unplanned fixed investment:
             Canoes   40
         8.   Unplanned inventory investment:
             Yams   20
     (b)   £410,000
     (c)   £350,000
     (d)   £90,000
     (e)   £60,000
     (f)   less than

10   falling

11   True

12   £410,000

13   $S = Y - C = £150,000$

14   greater than; equal to

15   zero; positive or zero or negative

16

	Saving	Investment
Changes in business inventories		−10
Expenditure on plant and equipment (net)		100
Personal saving	90	
Total volume of transactions on the Stock Exchange	—	—
Expenditure on residential construction (net)		50
Undistributed business profits	60	
Value of individuals' building society deposits	120	
	270	140

17   False

18	National income (Y)	Consumption (C)	Saving (S)
	0	10	−10
	20	22	−2
	40	34	6
	60	46	14
	70	52	18
	100	70	30
	120	82	38
	125	85	40

21   Add consumption and investment

22   investment; the aggregate expenditure function

23    $S = Y - C$, therefore $S = Y - (10 + \frac{3}{5}Y) = \frac{2}{5}Y - 10$

24   £58m

25   £10m

26    $E = 18 + \frac{3}{5}Y$

27   £45m

28    $S = I$, i.e. $\frac{2}{5}Y - 10 = 8$ and $Y = £45m$

29   (a) $Y = 0.75Y + 100$ $Y = 400$
       (b) $0.25Y = 100$ $Y = 400$

30   (a) False   (c) False
       (b) False   (d) True

31   less than

32   (a) Total consumption expenditure divided by total income, or the proportion of income spent on consumption.
       (b) $\dfrac{C}{Y}$

33   (a) The change in consumption divided by the change in income that brought it about.
       (b) $\dfrac{\Delta C}{\Delta Y}$

34   (a) APC 1.3; 1.05; 0.97; 0.93; 0.9
           MPC 0.8
       (b) falls; constant
       (c) £8
       (d) £24

35   (a) Total saving divided by total income, or the proportion of total income devoted to saving.
       (b) $\dfrac{S}{Y}$

36   (a) The change in saving divided by the change in income that brought it about.
       (b) $\dfrac{\Delta S}{\Delta Y}$

37   APS −0.3; 0.05; 0.03; 0.075; 0.11
       MPS 0.2

38   (a) 0.25   (b) 1/3   (c) 0.72

39   (a) OM; SM/OM; OS
       (b) RL/OL; OR; greater

(c) *UP/OP*; *OU* (not drawn); less
(d) *UW/NP* (or *UW/TW*); *AC* (or *TU*)
(e) *SV/LM* (or *SV/VR*); *AC* (or *RS*)
(f) constant; less than; falling
(g) equal to; greater than; less than

40   (a) *OA*   (b) −*OA*   (c) *AC*

41   (a) £10m   (b) 3/5

42   (a) zero   (b) 0.75   (c) 0.75   (d) 0.25   (e) 0.25

43   remains constant

44   (a) C_2 (c) Neither
       (b) Neither   (d) C_1

45   part; 0; 1

46   £100m

47   £116; £4; £24; £24; contract output

48   £72; £18; £20; £92; £2; £18; £18; £2; £20; £20

49   £100

50   Rises to £110m

51   £94; £72; expand output; rise; £22

52   £75m; £60; £15; £25

53   £80; £60

54   changes the slope of; changes the slope of

55   shifts down; shifts down

56   0.9; £20

57   £150; 0.8; £30; shifts down

58   clockwise; decreases

59   anti-clockwise; increases

60   up; down; increases

61   less than; the *MPC* is positive but less than unity

62   the change in national income; change in expenditure

63   £25

64   (a) $S - 0.2Y$ (b) The *MPS*

65     $Y = cY + I*$; *c* is *MPC* and *s* the *MPS*

66   False

67   (a) 4
       (b) Income rises by £4m
       (c) £24m

68   (a) 4
       (b) £44m
       (c) Fall by £4m

APPENDIX TO CHAPTER 35

1   Region A — *MPC*: 0.85, 0.8, 0.75, 0.70
       Region B — *MPC*: 0.8
       (a) (1) £15,600 (2) £15,400 (3) £14,800

(b) (1) £14,800 (2) £14,800 (3) £14,800

2   (a) £12,250
    (b) Increase by £500
    (c) (i) £50; £450   (ii) £50; £400
    (d) £12,750 plus approx. £3,111

CHAPTER 36

1   An addition to the income of domestic firms that does not arise from the expenditure of domestic households, or an addition to the income of domestic households that does not arise from the spending of domestic firms.

2   (a) Withdrawal   (f) Neither
    (b) Withdrawal   (g) Neither
    (c) Injection   (h) Injection
    (d) Both   (i) Injection
    (e) Injection

3   saving; investment

4   contractionary; expansionary

5   fall

6   £1,500

7   less than; government expenditure on goods and services and government transfer payments

8   income received by households after taxes have been deducted and transfers have been added

9   $Y_d = Y(1-t) + Q$

10   (a) $C = c(1-t)\,Y + cQ$
     (b) $S = s(1-t)\,Y + sQ$ or $S = (1-c)\,Y(1-t) + (1-c)\,Q$

11   (a) $C = 0.8(1-0.30)\,Y + 0.8(10) = 0.56Y + 8$
     (b) £36m
     (c) Tax revenue = 0.3(£50m) = £15m and is therefore sufficient to cover transfers
     (d) $S = £9m$
     (e) $Y_d = £45m$

12   $C + I + G$

13   $W + J$, where $W = s(1-t)\,Y + sQ + tY$ and $J = I + G + Q$
    or $s(1-t)\,Y + tY = I + G + cQ$

14

Level of national income (£m)	Consumption (£m)	Investment (£m)	Government expenditure (£m)	Tax revenue (£m)	Aggregate expenditure (£m)
0	32	78	70	0	180
150	122	78	70	37.5	270
250	182	78	70	62.5	330
350	242	78	70	87.5	390
450	312	78	70	112.5	450
550	372	78	70	137.5	510
650	432	78	70	162.5	570

    (a) £450m
    (b) $E = C + I + G = 180 + 0.6Y$
    (c) Slope is 0.6 and intercept is £180m
    (d) $C = £302m$, $S = £72.5m$, $Y_d = £377.5m$
    (e) Surplus of £2.5m
    (f) $W = 0.15Y + 0.25Y = 0.4Y$. $J = 78 + 70 + 32 = 180$. When $W = J$, $Y = £180m$.
    (g) £80m

(h) £60m

15 (a) It will be lowered or, in other words, it will pivot in a clockwise direction.
   (b) The slope will be less steep as the function pivots from the same intercept in a clockwise direction.
   (c) It will fall.

16 (a) 0.56
   (b) 0.56 and £180m
   (c) It will fall to approx. £409m.
   (d) greater than
   (e) £122.7m

17 (a) The slope will be unchanged but the intercept will be lower by the amount of the decrease in G, shifting the function downwards
   (b) It will fall

18 (a) £436.4m approx.
   (b) The surplus will fall to approx. £0.9m.
   (c) The tax increase resulted in income falling by approx. £41m, but the increased government expenditure has offset this to some extent by raising income from £409m (see Question 16(c)) by approx. £27.4m.

19 (a) £430.9m approx.
   (b) Moves to a deficit of approx. £0.7m.
   (c) Both shift the aggregate expenditure function upwards but injection through transfers will shift it by a smaller amount, $c(\Delta Q)$, rather than ΔG. The transfer payments' multiplier is smaller than the government expenditure multiplier as only a proportion ($c = 0.8$) enters the income stream.

20 The new equilibrium would have been the same at approx. £430.9m, however the government budget would have been in surplus.

21 remain unchanged; rise; rise; rise

22 remain unchanged; fall; fall; fall

23 The marginal propensity to withdraw is the proportion of income not passed on through consumption spending, i.e. $s = 1 - c$.

24 $1/s$

25 (a) savings and tax payments
   (b) investment and government expenditure
   (c) $S = s(1 - t)Y$
   (d) $W = s(1 - t)Y + tY$
   (e) $J = I* + G*$
   (f) $Y = \dfrac{I*}{s(1 - t) + t} + \dfrac{G*}{s(1 - t) + t}$
   (g) $\dfrac{1}{s(1 - t) + t}$
   (h) $\dfrac{1}{s(1 - t) + t}$

26 (a) $S = s(1 - t) + sQ$
   (b) $W = s(1 - t)Y + sQ + tY$
   (c) $J = I* + G* + Q*$
   (d) $Y = \dfrac{I*}{s(1 - t) + t} + \dfrac{G*}{s(1 - t) + t} + \dfrac{cQ*}{s(1 - t) + t}$
   (e) $\dfrac{c}{s(1 - t) + t}$

27 (a) 2.5   (b) 2

28 5

29   (a) £10m   (b) £8m   (c) £25m

30   rise

31   fall; fall

32   (a) fallen   (b) fallen

33   Households, firms, government and foreign trade

34   Savings, taxes and imports; none

35   Investment, government expenditure and exports; exogenous

36   Aggregate desired expenditure = national income; withdrawals = injections

37     $E = C + I + G + (X - M) = Y$
       $W = J$

38   True

39   (a) $X; J$ (e) $I; J$
       (b) $F; W$ (f) $N; W$
       (c) $I; J$ (g) $M; W$
       (d) $C; N$ (h) $G; J$

40   (a) The marginal propensity to import.
       (b) $E = 0.5Y + 230$
       (c) £460m
       (d) $X - M = £4m$
       (e) $\dfrac{1}{1 - c(1 - t) + m}$ or $\dfrac{1}{s(1 - t) + t + m} = 2$
       (f) £20m
       (g) (i) Fall to approx. £383m
           (ii) £26.6m approx.

41   reduces; leakage from

42   rise; less than

CHAPTER 37

1     $N = 50 - 0.1Y$

2   £500m

3   (a) £600m   (b) £300m   (c) £667m approx.

4     $A = C + I + G$

5   (a) $E = 230 + 0.5Y$
      (b) $C = 32 + 0.6Y$
      (c) $A = 180 + 0.6Y$
      (d) $Y = E = A + (X - M)$ or $Y = 230 + 0.5Y$

6   (a) 0.6   (f) £6m
      (b) 180   (g) £460m; £456m
      (c) 0.5   (h) £420m; £432m
      (d) 230   (i) greater than; negative
      (e) less than; rise; fall

7   upwards; shift up; rise

8   downwards; remain the same; down; fall

9   downwards; shift down; fall

10   £2,000

		Transactions	
		valued in £	*valued in $*
11	(a)	400,000	800,000
	(b)	400,000	800,000
	(c)	zero	

12   $1

		Transactions	
		valued in £	*valued in $*
13	(a)	400,000	400,000
	(b)	800,000	800,000

13 (c) *If* sales continue at the same rate, UK trade balance will be in deficit while that of the US will be in surplus.
(d) 100
(e) 50
(f) falling; risen

14 the proportional change in quantity demanded divided by the proportional change in price.

		Transactions *valued in £*
15	(a) 75; 275	550,000
(b) 250	500,000
(c) 220	440,000
(d) 50	200,000
(e) 100	400,000
(f) 160	640,000

16 (a) surplus
(b) deficit
(c) upwards; upwards; rises

17 increase; shift up; rise

18 shift down; lower; fallen; risen

19 remain the same; move from surplus to deficit

20 Goods bought and sold on world markets at world prices set in terms of foreign currency.

21 rise; remain the same; out of; rise; towards; relative; exports; imports; up; up; rise

22 £500 more; $1,000 more

23 rise; fall; down

24 $2,500; £4,000; fall; rise; up; up; remain the same; rise

25 It could cut government expenditure and/or raise taxes.

CHAPTER 38

1 In order to repay a claim in gold, if it did happen to be demanded.

2 The fact that they would be required to redeem the paper claims on themselves in gold to the value of one-third of their outstanding debt.

3 The fact that the cowrie shell is generally acceptable is sufficient to give it the attributes of money — so the missionary does not understand the nature of money.

4 False

5 A fiat currency ('fiat' is Latin for 'let it become').

6 Commercial banks, discount houses and the central bank (i.e. Bank of England).

7 Banker to commercial banks; banker to the government; controller and regulator of the money supply; manager of the public debt; lender of last resort and supporter of money markets.

8 Borrow from the central bank (in Britain the commercial banks would call in their loans to the discount houses which in turn borrow from the central bank).

9 £450

10 (1) 50 cash; 50 deposits
        450 loans; 450 extra deposits
    (2) expand its loans immediately to the maximum.

11

	A		B		C		D		E	
	A	L	A	L	A	L	A	L	A	L
	100	100	90	90	81	81	72.9	72.9	65.61	65.61
cash:	10	100	9	90	8.1	81	7.29	72.9	6.561	65.61
loans:	90		81		72.9		65.61		59.049	

12 (a) (1)

I

L	A
+300	+300
(deposit)	(cash)

(2)

I

L	A
+329.66	+32.94 cash
(deposits)	+296.73 loans

(3) True

(b) (1)

I			II-X		
L	A		L	A	
+300	+30 cash		+2700	+ 270 cash	
deposits	+270 loans		deposits	+2430 loans	

(2) True

13 (a) Zero   (b) £50m

14 Reduce it by £2,000.

15 That the public does not wish to hold any of its money in cash.

16 (a) £2,000   (b) £1,148.94   (c) £918.92

17 smaller

18 Near money

19 Near money is an asset which fulfils the store-of-value function but, while transferable, cannot be transformed into a medium of exchange at a moment's notice and thus has not achieved the monetary status of notes and coins. Money substitutes fulfil the medium-of-exchange function but are not themselves money.

	Store of value	Medium of exchange
Building society deposits	√	X
Company securities:		
– ordinary shares	√	X
– debenture & preference shares	√	X
Local authority bonds held by the private sector	√	X
Notes and coins	√	√
New domestic share issues	√	X
Deposits in current accounts at commercial banks	√	√
UK government bonds	√	X
Money held in deposit accounts at commercial banks	√	X

21   (a) £13,440m   (b) £32,339m

CHAPTER 39

1   That the size of the money supply is determined by forces outside the model of the economy, i.e. by the central bank.

2   Because that money could have earned interest if it had been held in, say, a deposit account at a bank.

3   Transactions, precautionary and speculative.

4   The level of income.

5   transactions and precautionary; rise; precautionary and speculative; rise

6   Wealth held in money form rather than in interest-earning assets.

7   fall

8   buy. If they can buy bonds at one price and subsequently sell them at a higher price, they will make a capital gain.

9   directly; directly; inversely

10   (a) Transactions   (c) None
       (b) Precautionary   (d) Precautionary

11   (a) Raise precautionary   (e) Raise precautionary
       (b) Raise transactions   (f) Lower transactions
       (c) Raise speculative   (g) Raise precautionary
       (d) Raise all

12   False

13    $M_d = L(Y, r, W)$

14   Real demand is measured in purchasing-power units. In order to obtain the nominal demand we have to multiply the real demand by the price level, P.

15   rises by 10%; is unchanged

16   (a) rising   (b) rising

17   (a) £50m   (c) £80m
       (b) £70m   (d) £40m

18   (a) rises; transactions and precautionary; risen
       (b) (iii)

19   (a) Curve shifts to right.
       (b) Curve shifts to left.

(c)   This is already represented by the curve.

20   the demand for bonds is equal to the supply of bonds.

21   (a) $M_d = £40\text{m} < M^*/P$
        (b) $M_d = £80\text{m} = M^*/P$
        (c) $M_d = £100\text{m} > M^*/P$

22   buy; fall; rise; the demand for money is equal to the supply

23   (a)   remains the same
        (b)   more
        (c)   fall; buy; fall

24   (a)   rise   (c)   rise
        (b)   greater than   (d)   raising

25   (a)   £90m   (b)   8½%   (c)   £10m

26   income and interest-rate

27   Set $M_d = M^*/P$ and solve for r.

28      $r = \dfrac{M^*}{P}\dfrac{1}{e} - \dfrac{d}{e}Y = 0.02Y - 4$

29   Slope is 0.02 and intercept is -4.

30   (a)   Shifts LM curve upwards.
        (b)   No change—this reflects movement along the LM curve.
        (c)   The LM curve shifts upwards in an anti-clockwise direction.
        (d)   Pivots LM in clockwise direction, only the slope changing.

31   10%

32   rise to 10.5%; fall to £675m

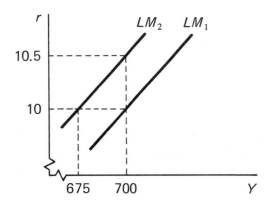

33   rise to 20%; fall to £450m

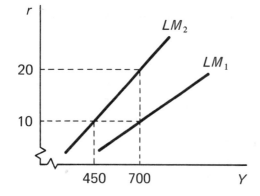

34   8.25%; rise to £800m

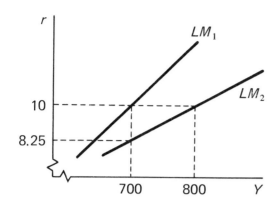

35   (a) greater than; rise
      (b) less than; fall

CHAPTER 40

1   False

2   smaller

3   False

4   (a) Increase; raise revenue
      (b) Decrease; raise costs
      (c) Increase; raise revenue
      (d) Decrease; raise costs
      (e) Increase; raise revenue
      (f) Decrease; raise costs
      (g) Decrease; lower revenue

5   False

6   True

7   (a) 12%
      (b) K_2
      (c) $K_3 - K_2$
      (d) less than
      (e) By not replacing plant and machinery as it wears out.

8   The capacity of capital-goods producing industry may be unable to meet all orders immediately and subsequent variation in the interest rate may cause firms to revise their orders.

9   Current savings of firms; current savings of households; newly created money.

10   The sale of bonds to the public.

11   (a) The lending of money by the public to financial institutions;
      (b) The sale of bonds by firms to financial institutions.

12   (a) $E = 184 + 0.8Y - 10r$
      (b) £420m

13   income and interest rates

14   (a) Set desired aggregate expenditure equal to national income and solve for r.
      (b) $r = 18.4 - 0.02Y$
      (c) -0.02
      (d) The marginal propensity to save divided by the behavioural parameter b which denotes the change in investment brought about by a 1% change in the rate of interest.

15   (a) $C = £360m$, $I = £80m$ and $E = £440m$
            (b)   less than
            (c)   fall; increase
            (d)   9½%
            (e)   £85m

16   As income rises, consumption also increases but by an amount less than the change in income (as the *MPC* is less than one). If aggregate expenditure is to equal the higher level of income, the interest rate must fall so that the other component of expenditure (i.e. investment) rises and raises aggregate expenditure to match income.

17   (a)   £8m
            (b)   9.8%
            (c)   £470m
            (d)

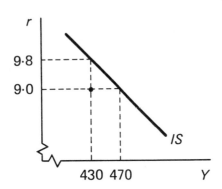

18   (a) $0 < a_0, c$ and $c < 1$; $b < 0 < a_1$
            (b) $r = \dfrac{(1-c)}{b} Y - \dfrac{A^*}{b}$, where $A^* = a_0 + a_1$

            (c)   Aggregate expenditure function shifts down and *IS* curve shifts inwards.
            (d)   Aggregate expenditure pivots anti-clockwise and *IS* shifts outwards and is flatter.
            (e)   Aggregate expenditure shifts down, *IS* shifts inwards and is steeper.

19   goods; asset

20   (a)   Desired aggregate expenditure = real national income
            (b)   The demand for money = the supply
            (c)   An income level and an interest rate that satisfy the equilibrium conditions for both markets. Put another way, that Y and r at which the *IS* and *LM* schedules intersect.

21   (a) $r = \dfrac{(1-c)}{b} Y - \dfrac{A^*}{b}$

            (b) $r = \dfrac{M^*}{P} \dfrac{1}{e} - \dfrac{d}{e} Y$

            (c) $Y = \dfrac{1}{(1-c)+bd/e} A^* + \dfrac{1}{e(1-c)/b+d} \cdot \dfrac{M^*}{P}$
               If you looked this up in Lipsey, you ought not to have done! You must be sure you can work this out for yourself – what would you do if you didn't have Lipsey handy?

            (d) $\dfrac{1}{(1-c)}$

            (e) $\dfrac{1}{(1-c)+bd/e}$

22   (a)   greater than   (d)   exceed   (f)   curb
            (b)   raises; outwards   (e)   fall; rise   (g)   higher; high
            (c)   rises

23   (a) upwards
      (b) greater than
      (c) sell; raising
      (d) lower; shift in; fall
      (e) fall; fall; decreases; transaction
      (f) higher; lower

24   (a) greater than; less than
      (b) It will rise.
      (c) As E is less than Y, unplanned inventory investment is rising; this will lead
           producers to cut back on output and income will begin to fall.
      (d) fall; rise

25   *Segment number*   *Y rises/falls*   *r rises/falls*
      (a) 1   rises   rises
      (b) 4   rises   falls
      (c) 2   falls   rises
      (d) 3   falls   falls

26   (a) $r = 13.5 - 0.02Y$ (or $Y = 675 - 50r$)
      (b) $r = 0.02Y - 6$ (or $Y = 300 + 50r$)
      (c) £135m
      (d) $Y = £487.5m$ and $r = £3.75\%$

27   (a) $1/(1 - c) = 5$
      (b) $1/0.4 = 2.5$
      (c) $Y = £512.5m$ and $r = 4.25\%$; $C = £420m$, $I = £92.5m$
      (d) $C = £440m$, $I = £97.5m$ and $E = £537.5m$

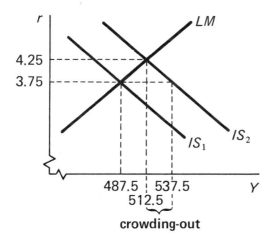

28   (a) $Y = £525m$ and $r = 3\%$
      (b)

29   (a)   Shifts *IS* downwards, lowering income and rate of interest.
        (b)   Shifts *LM* upwards, raising *r* and lowering *Y*.
        (c)   Shifts *IS* inwards, lowering *Y* and *r*.
        (d)   Shifts *LM* downwards, increasing *Y* and reducing *r*.

CHAPTER 41

1   the aggregate price level and national income level; goods; asset

2   (a)   rises; lowers
        (b)   excess supply of; fall; rise
        (c)   shifts up; is unchanged; is unchanged; is unchanged

3   (a)   *c*, the marginal propensity to consume; *b* and *e*, measuring the interest responsive-
              ness of investment expenditure and demand for money, respectively; *d*, measuring
              the responsiveness of demand for money to changes in the level of national
              income.
        (b)   flatter. A low responsiveness means that for any given change in real (speculative)
              balances, there will be a larger change in the rate of interest.
        (c)   flatter; a fall in the interest rate results in a large increase in investment
              expenditure.
        (d)   large fall
        (e)   steeper

4   (a)   Autonomous expenditure
        (b)   Nominal money supply, the price level
        (c)   Autonomous expenditure and nominal money supply

5   *LM*; down; higher; lower; shifts to right

6   is unchanged; remains the same

7   5%

8   True

9   The Keynesian asymmetry of response to variations in demand above and below
        potential income; irreversibility of price-level increases; and instability when output
        is held above potential output.

10   (a)   (a) and (c)   (e)   None
        (b)   All   (f)   (b)
        (c)   (c)   (g)   (b)
        (d)   (b)   (h)   (a) and (c)

11   (a)   Shifts *AS* to right, raising Y_F.
        (b)   Shifts *AS* downwards.
        (c)   Shifts *AS* upwards, as cost of imported raw materials rises.
        (d)   Shifts *AS* to right.

12   (a)   outwards; right; rises; higher; unchanged; higher as the rise in the price level
              shifted the *LM* curve upwards.

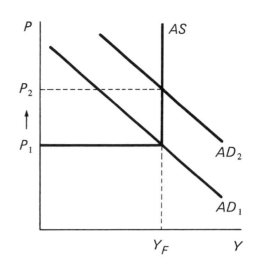

(b) Prices will remain at the higher level, income will fall and the rate of interest falls.

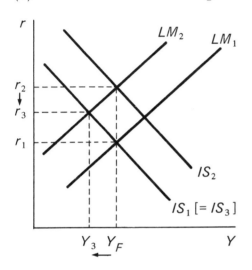

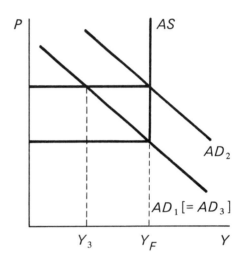

(c) Output falls, prices rise and the rate of interest rises.

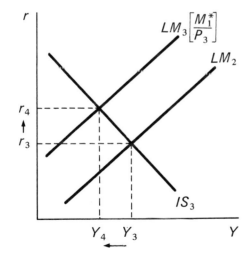

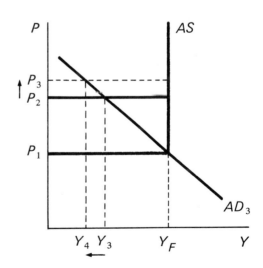

CHAPTER 42

1    $I = I(\Delta y)$

2   Greater. The value of a machine is usually more than its annual production.

3 (a) 1.5   (b) 5 machines

4

Year	Change in sales (£000)	Required stock of capital assuming capital-output ratio of 4/1 (£000)	Net investment (£000)
1	0	60	0
2	5	80	20
3	4	96	16
4	1	100	4
5	1	104	4
6	1	108	4
7	0	108	0
8	−2	100	0

(a) That immediate delivery is possible.
(b) £8,000 of capital stock is idle as it is now surplus to requirements.
(c) False

5 (1) Accelerator   (3) Multiplier
   (2) None   (4) Self-realizing expectations

6 The income produced when there is full employment.

7 Replacement investment.

8 The 'subsistence' level of income, where consumption equals income.

9 The desired level of new investment depends on the rate of change in income.

10 the year before last.

Period	C_c	I_r	I_n	Total invest-ment	G	Y	Change in Y
t	300	20	0	20	80	400	0
$t+1$	300	20	0	20	90	410	10
$t+2$	305	20	12	32	90	427	17
$t+3$	313.5	20	20.4	40.4	90	443.9	16.9
$t+4$	322	20	20.3	40.3	90	452.3	8.4
$t+5$	326.2	20	10.1	30.1	90	446.3	−6
$t+6$	323.2	12.8	(−7.2)	12.8	90	426	−20.3
$t+7$	313	0	(−24.4)	0	90	403	−23
$t+8$	301.5	0	(−27.6)	0	90	391.5	−11.5
$t+9$	295.8	6.2	(−13.8)	6.2	90	392	0.5
$t+10$	296	20	0.6	20.6	90	406.6	14.6

11 (a) 8%   (b) 100%

12 zero. There would be no point in replacing a machine when there is already more capacity than is needed to meet demand.

13 $t+4; t+5, t+9$; £420m

14 rise; replenish; demand; MPC; recession

15 (b)

16 points on the production-possibility frontier.

17 points inside the frontier.

18 (a) The production-possibility curve will move out along the vegetable axis but the intercept with the clothing axis will remain the same.

326

(b) To the extent that the loss of one year's education lowers the quality of human capital and labour productivity, the frontier will move inwards. Offsetting this, however, will be the increase in the labour supply if people choose to leave school as soon as it is legal. If growing vegetables and making clothing requires relatively unskilled labour, it is probable the curve will shift outwards.

(c) The curve will move out along the clothing axis but the intercept on the vegetable axis will be unchanged.

19   Point A, as this represents a greater proportion of resources being used for investment good production than does point B.

20   (a) Increases in the availability of resources, (b) changes in the productivity of these resources as a result of changes in technology, increased efficiency in the use of existing resources, changes in the composition of the output of consumption and investment goods.

21   4

22   £40,000m

23   (a) £168,000m   (b) £176,160m

TABLE 3

	Potential income	Capital stock	Investment (= savings)	Equilibrium income
	£m	£m	£m	£m
1975	40,000	160,000	8,000	40,000
1976	42,000	168,000	8,160	40,800
1977	44,040	176,160	8,323.2	41,616
1978	46,120.8	184,483.2	8,489.7	42,448

24   Approx. 5%

25   5

26    $C = £32,000m$ and $S = £8,000m$

27   No; 2%

28   Aggregate demand is not increasing fast enough to keep up with the increase in productive capacity.

TABLE 4

	Potential income	Capital stock	Investment (= savings)	Equilibrium income
	£m	£m	£m	£m
1975	40,000	160,000	8,000	40,000
1976	42,000	168,000	8,400	42,000
1977	44,100	176,400	8,820	44,100
1978	46,304	185,220	9,261	46,305

29   5%

30   5%

31   (a) £800   (b) approx. £777   (c) approx. £848

32   The hypothesis of diminishing returns

33   (a) 13,000 bushels   (b) Negative   (c) Declining

34   10,000

35    $P = \frac{1}{3} Q$

36   Approx. 8.75 thousand

37   3.7 thousand; approx. 7.8 bushels

38   Approx. 5.2 bushels

39   It would move up and out. See diagram below.

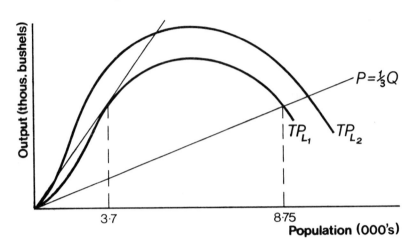

40   Weather

CHAPTER 43

1   Desired aggregate expenditure equals real national income.

2
(a) $r = \dfrac{1 - c(1 - t)Y}{b} - \dfrac{(A^* + G^* + cQ^*)}{b}$

(b) $Y = \dfrac{(A^* + G^* + cQ^*)}{1 - c(1 - t)} + \dfrac{br}{1 - c(1 - t)}$

(c) $(A^* + G^* + cQ)/b$
(d) $(A^* + G^* + cQ^*)/[1 - c(1 - t)]$
(e) $[1 - c(1 - t)]/b$ or $b/[1 - c(1 - t)]$
(f) $1/[1 - c(1 - t)]$ for A^* and G^*; $c/[1 - c(1 - t)]$ for Q^*

3   (a) £650m   (b) 2.5

4   expenditure on goods and services and/or transfers; taxes

5   (a) Income rises by £25m to £675m.
(b) Income rises by £20m.
(c) Income rises by £27.1m.
(d) unchanged; anti-clockwise; less

6   The more thrifty households are, the lower will be the level of national income and the lower will be employment.

7   (a) The marginal propensity to consume is now 0.7, the *IS* curve pivots in a clockwise direction and income falls to approx. £536.8m.
(b) $G + Q = £250$, $T = 0.25(536.8) = £134.2$m. Deficit = £115.8m.
(c) Increase G by £53.6m. (Did you remember that the value of the multiplier changed?)
(d) Increased to £141.5m.
(e) Income would rise to £652.2m. approx. Deficit rises to £165.2m.

8   (a) Because taxes are a function of income.
(b) injections
(c) transfer payments

(d)   Raise unemployment
(e)   Raise unemployment

9   Increased

10   No

11   fall; risen; risen

12   True. Any aggregate supply schedule which is perfectly elastic over the range where output is less than potential output.

13   Prices will rise when there is excess aggregate demand but will not fall significantly when there is excess aggregate supply.

14   rise; rising income

15   (b)   inwards
      (c)   fall
      (d)   lowers
      (e)   purchase; fall
      (f)   the demand for bonds is equal to the supply of bonds, and the demand for money is equal to the supply of money.

16   AD shifts to right raising prices, but output and employment would be unchanged. Crowding-out is 100%.

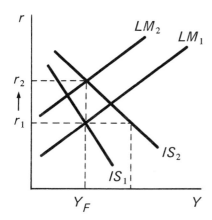 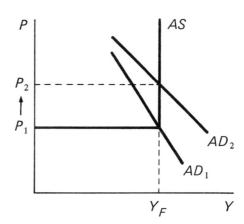

(I hope you did not forget that the higher price level shifts the LM curve upwards— the nominal money supply being unchanged.)

17   Income rises to Y_F, the rate of interest rises and the price level is unchanged. There is crowding-out equal to $Y_2 - Y_F$

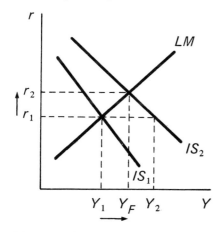 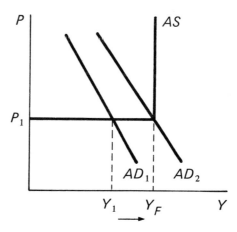

18   (a) $Y = £700m$, $r = 5\%$. Deficit of £75m.
      (b) Y rises by £60m, $r = 6\frac{1}{2}\%$ and budget deficit increases to £114m.
      (c)   £135m. Crowding-out £75m.

(d) $\dfrac{\Delta Y}{\Delta G} = \dfrac{60}{54} = 1.1$

(e)   Income rises by £48m, $r = 6.2\%$ and deficit is £117m.

(f) $Y = £768.3m$, $r = 6.7\%$ and deficit is £135m.

(g)   £72.7m. Did you remember to make use of your answer to (d)?

(h)   outwards; right; higher

(i)   smaller

(j) $Y = £835m$, $r = 5\%$ and crowding-out is zero.

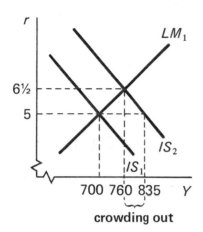
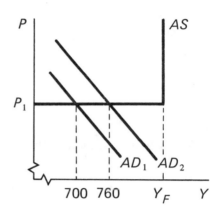

(b) and (c)

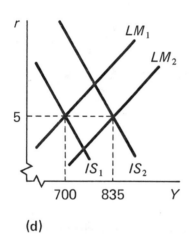
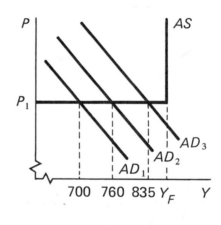

(d)

19   Income rises by £15.5m, r rises by 0.4% and deficit remains at £75m.

20   The balanced-budget multiplier is 0.29 and is therefore lower than the multiplier when the change in income is brought about by an increase in G with *tax rates constant*.

21   Because the government spends all its income, whereas some of it would have been saved if left in private hands.

22   fall; the multiplier; rise; less; only some of the money would have been injected into the circular flow; saved (or—if there is a foreign sector—spent on imported goods; 100; injected into; greater; contractionary

23   Budget surplus $= tY - (G + Q)$

(a)   deficit to surplus; is unchanged

(b)   down; lower

(c)   anti-clockwise; raise

24   Anything that causes government expenditure to be positively related, and government tax receipts to be negatively related, to national income, without the government's having to make policy decisions to bring about these changes.

25   (a) $Y = £1,300m$ (c)   1.1
             (b)   Falls by £55.6m   (d)   2.5

26   (a) $Y = £1,147m$
             (b)   Falls by £49m
             (c)   0.98
             (d)   1.923
             (e)   Stabilize, as they reduce the value of the multiplier.

27   (a) $Y = £1,175.7m$
             (b)   Falls by £67.7m
             (c)   1.354
             (d)   4.16
             (e)   Destabilize, as this increases the value of the multiplier. Only when G is stable will it act as a built-in stabilizer.

28   Borrowing from the central bank, from the commercial banks and from the public.

29   spent or saved; (c)

30   distribution

31   purchasers of government bonds

32   True

33   False. (If you were wrong, look at Question 29 again.)

34   varies according to; present; future; fewer; zero

CHAPTER 44

1   Income rises to £761m, rate of interest falls to 3.78%.

2      $Y = £639m$, $r = 6.22\%$ (I hope you saw this straightaway!)

3      $\dfrac{\Delta Y}{\Delta M_s}$ is the money multiplier. You know ΔY and ΔM_s from Question 1, so you can now find the value of the money multiplier which enables you to work out that the money supply would have to increase by £43.2m.

4   (a)   outwards; right

         (b)

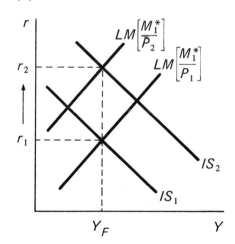
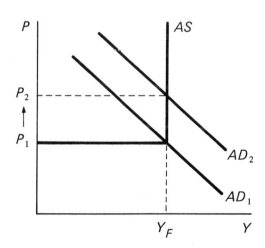

(c)

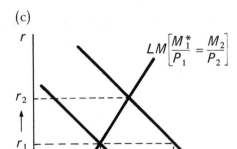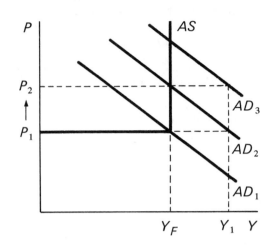

(d) Contractionary fiscal policy, which offsets the injection to the circular flow (from the additional autonomous investment). This would shift the *IS* curve back to its original position. Alternatively, contractionary monetary policy, i.e. lowering the money supply, which would shift the *LM* to the left and would leave the economy at a higher rate of interest than before.

5   False

6   Changes in autonomous expenditure and changes in money supply.

7   $r = \dfrac{[1 - c(1 - t)]\,Y}{b} - \dfrac{(A^* + G^* + cQ^*)}{b}$

   (a)   *b* and *c*. *t* is an instrumental variable.
   (b)   *b* measures the responsiveness of investment to a one-point change in the rate of interest. *I* rises by £20m.
   (c)   greater; greater; upward; flatter
   (d)   flatter

8   $r = \dfrac{M^*}{P} \cdot \dfrac{1}{e} + \dfrac{d}{e}\,Y$

   (a)   *d* and *e*
   (b)   *d* measures how the demand for money (for transactions and precautionary balances) responds to a one-point change in the level of income.
   (c)   Rises by £3m.
   (d)   steeper
   (e)   *e* measures the responsiveness of the demand for money (for speculative balances) to a one-point change in the rate of interest.
   (f)   flatter
   (g)   smaller; larger; smaller

9   raises; raises; raise; lower; crowded out

10   zero; 100%; greater

11   (a)   (i) + £50m; (ii) + 1.25%; (iii) − £25m; (iv) £62.5m
   (b)   Larger, as *LM* now more interest-elastic.
   (c)   *Y* = £725m, *r* = 4.5%
   (d)   (i) + £56.25m; (ii) + 1.126%; (iii) − £22.5m; (iv) £56.25m

12   (a)   + £24.4m
   (b)   Smaller, the *IS* curve is steeper.
   (c)   *Y* = £777m, *r* = 6.9%
   (d)   (i) + £42m; (ii) − 1.7%; (iii) + £17.2m

13   (a)   leave unchanged; lower
   (b)   raise; raise

14   raise; leave unchanged; leave unchanged; raise

15	more; more

15   more; more

16   reduce; reduce; more; lower; cheaper; raise; multiplier; increase

17   sell; fall; rise; the demand for money is equal to the supply.

18   (a)   remains the same   (c)   fall; sell; rise
      (b)   less   (d)   falls; multiplier; fall

19   Raise it

20   Rises

21   Yes, as AD rises the transactions demand for money will rise so that the interest rate will also rise.

22   (a)   fall short of; rise   (c)   sell; rise
      (b)   more; less   (d)   discourage; stimulate; check

23   By open-market operations or by varying the reserve-asset ratio.

24   Treasury bills are instruments for *short-term* borrowing, whereas government bonds are *long-term*, fixed-interest securities.

25   True

26   By selling £1m in bonds to the public.

27   If the public buy bonds with funds not within the money-creating system—e.g. cash, or deposits held in foreign countries—instead of from bank accounts.

28   Only to the extent that credit expansion results in some cash drain to the public.

29   (a)   By sale of bills. This will drive down the price of bills with the result that short-term interest rates will rise.
      (b)   fall; contract

30   £90

31   (a)

	Liabilities £m		Assets £m
Deposits	125,000	Cash	12,500
		Other	112,500
	125,000		125,000

(b)

	Liabilities £m		Assets £m
Deposits	100,000	Cash	12,500
		Other	87,500
	100,000		100,000

Therefore deposits contract by £25,000m.

(c)   £3,125m.

32   Because it is less easy for the Bank to control the quantity of such reserve assets—as compared with cash—since changes in the relative prices of these assets and other assets which are close substitutes (but not included in the reserve base) can enable the commercial banks to purchase appropriate assets and thus adjust their reserves.

33   (a)   5%   (c)   By open-market operations.
      (b)   1.5%

34   Changes in the level of income, changes in the parameters d and e. For example, the demand for transactions balances may vary at different times of the year.

35   (a) r rises by 1.25%   (c) r rises by 1%
      (b) r rises by 2.9%

36   (a)   Raise money supply by £15m
      (b)   Raise money supply by £35m
      (c)   Raise money supply by £10m

37   increasing; decreasing; greater; endogenous

38   A contractionary policy forces banks to reduce loans. An expansionary policy *permits* them to increase loans. This asymmetry is a consequence of the legal reserve requirement being only a minimum and not also a maximum ratio.

39   They expect the rate of interest to rise.

40   increasing; remaining constant; rise; be unchanged

41   (a) Demand for money equal to money supply; aggregate demand equal to aggregate supply
        (b) prices will rise.
        (c) nominal; increase
        (d) fallen
        (e) greater
        (f) demand for; sell; the rate of interest rises
        (g) check; fall; removed
        (h) equal; be unchanged; is unchanged; persists

APPENDIX TO CHAPTER 44

1   is not

2   Yes; no

3   *kPY*

4   Exogenous

5   The average number of times a unit of money turns over in transactions.

6   *V* is the reciprocal of *k*

7   (a) £25m   (c) £140m
        (b) Price rises to 1.4   (d) £100m

8   money; the price level; real; the level of income

CHAPTER 45

1   An adjustable-peg, gold exchange standard with countries holding their exchange reserves either in US dollars or pounds sterling.

2   could not

3   By consultations with countries wishing to alter their exchange rates.

4   Making adjustments to long-term trends in the balance of receipts and payments.

5   Its price.

6   Its price and its demand for non-monetary uses.

7   Special Drawing Rights; credits which are an addition to the capacity of the IMF to supply foreign exchange to members.

8   Their unemployment will increase.

9   devalue; buy; sell; falling; decreasing; devalue; outflows

10   It could raise the short-term rate of interest in the hope that this would attract capital; speculators, however, would be reluctant to transfer capital to this country unless the interest differential, *after taking into account any expected devaluation,* is sufficiently attractive.

11   It can devalue; it can attempt to restrict the demand for dollars, and it can attempt to raise the supply of dollars. In the longer run, it will try to reduce the rate of inflation.

12   reduce; exchange-rate; exchange-rate

13   uncertainty; reduce; destabilizing; decrease; increase; increase; decrease; decline

14 (d)

15 forward exchange

16 managed or dirty float

17 One

18 (a) £5,250; DM21,000   (b) One   (c) No

19 (a) £5,600
   (b) DM20,800
   (c) 1.0769
   (d) Fall to DM3.7143 = £1, i.e. a fall of just over 7%.

20 *Definitions* $E \equiv C + I + G + (X - M)$
                $Y_d \equiv Y - T + Q$

   Behaviour $C = a_0 + cY_d$ $0 < c < 1; \quad 0 < a_0$
                $T = tY$ $0 < t < 1$
                $I = a_1 + br$ $b < 0; \quad 0 < a_1$
                $G = G^*$
                $Q = Q^*$
                $X = X^*$
                $M = mY$ $0 < m < 1$
                $M_d = dY + er$ $0 < d < 1; \quad e < 0$
                $M_s = \dfrac{M^*}{P}$

   Equilibrium conditions
                $E = Y$
              $M_d = \dfrac{M^*}{P}$

21 $r = \dfrac{(1 - c(1 - t) + m)Y}{b} - \dfrac{(A^* + G^* + cQ^* + X)}{b}$

22 $N = X - mY$

23 There is an output gap of £36m and a deficit on the current account of £10m.

24 (a) would rise to £1,036m, i.e. to Y_F
   (b) rises to 10.9%
   (c) deficit increases by £2.16m
   (d) deficit of £16.2m

25 (a) rises to £1,036m
   (b) falls to 8.2%
   (c) deficit increases by £2.16m
   (d) surplus of £10.8m

26 (a) rises to £1,036m
   (b) remains at 10%
   (c) deficit increases by £2.16m
   (d) deficit of £7.2m

27 (a) rises to £1,027.5m leaving an output gap of £8.5m
   (b) falls to 9.79%
   (c) in balance—providing exports remain at £50m
   (d) surplus of £8.25m

28 (a) Changing government expenditure and money supply
   (b) Import quotas

29 revalue; surplus; increasing; dirty floating; short-run

30 buying; selling; falling; falling; purchases; sterilization.

31 inwards; lower; fall; surplus; lowered; out; deficit; offset; surplus; deficit; buy; reduces; upwards; the original

32   deficit; capital flows out; sell; decreasing; reverses; returns to its original level; is also at its initial level.

33   devalued; cheaper; dearer; outwards; improved; risen; surplus; inflow; raises; higher; the initial

34   outwards; deficit; depreciate; surplus; higher; inflows; depreciate; discourage; inwards; expansionary; at a higher level than before; the initial rate.

35   left; rise; inflow; surplus; appreciates; inwards; continue to appreciate; reinforce; overvalued.

36   outwards; surplus; appreciate; dearer; cheaper; inwards; unchanged.

CHAPTER 46

1   Yes—frictional

2   Demand-deficient

3   Structural and real wage

4   (a) and (d) structural; (b) and (e) demand-deficient; (c) frictional. Some of the unemployment within categories, except (c), may be real wage unemployment

5   No locational structural unemployment; lower level of frictional unemployment.

6   When demand is low there are few vacancies and it is easy for employers to fill jobs without having to notify or advertise vacancies. As aggregate demand rises, more jobs are available and the number of people seeking work declines; firms compete with each other for labour and have to search further afield. They find it more difficult to fill jobs without advertising vacancies and the number of vacancies notified or advertised will rise sharply.

7   (a) V
      (b) U

8   (i) D = zero; $S + F$ = 1,250,000
      (ii) D = zero; $S + F$ = 1,500,000
      (iii) D = 500,000; $S + F$ = 1,250,000
      (iv) D = 1,750,000; $S + F$ = 750,000

9   lower; rises

10    $U*$

11   (i) D = zero; $S + F$ = 1,500,000
      (ii) D = zero; $S + F$ = 1,500,000
      (iii) D = 250,000; $S + F$ = 1,500,000
      (iv) D = 1,000,000; $S + F$ = 1,500,000

12   UV curve shifts outwards.

13   People might take longer to search for the sort of job they want and, in this case, frictional unemployment would rise and the UV curve would shift outwards.

14   Marginal plants will no longer be able to cover their variable costs and would close down.

15   By a movement along the UV curve, e.g. from B to C.

16   At the design stage capital can be substituted for labour and vice versa; once the plant is built, capital and labour are not substitutable.

17   Substitution between capital and labour is possible both at the design stage and after the plant has been built.

18

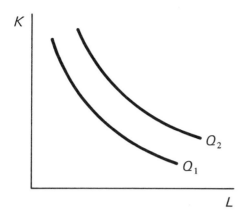

19

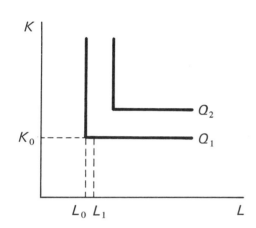

20   Zero—in the diagram above, if you increase labour by one unit, output does not rise (when capital held constant at K_0).

21   marginal revenue product curve; downward to the right

22   It will be independent of the real wage and will be determined by the level of planned output. The diagrams below illustrate this.

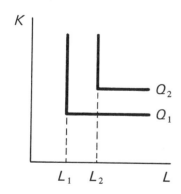 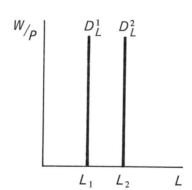

23   A shift of the UV curve outwards.

CHAPTER 47

1   (a)   demand
      (b)   core
      (c)   shock

2   (a) (i) 6%; (ii) zero
        (b) (i) 8.5%; (ii) zero; (iii) 0.5%
        (c) (i) −1%; (ii) zero; (iii) 2%

3   (a) (i) 6%; (ii) 4%; (iii) −4%
        (b) (i) −1%; (ii) 4%; (iii) −1%

4   (a) rise—demand inflation of 4%
        (b) LM; left
        (c) £700m; higher

5   (a) Core = 3%, demand = 4%; actual inflation = 7%
        (b) Core = 5.25%, demand = 4%, shock = −1.25%, actual inflation = 8%
        (c) Core = 6%, demand = 4%, actual inflation = 10%
        (d) Core = 6%, demand = $-\frac{1}{2}$%, actual inflation = $5\frac{1}{2}$%
        (e) Actual inflation = 3.625, therefore inflation rate has fallen by 1.9% approx.

6   (b), assuming no shock inflation, and (d) and (e)